Globe Law
and Business

Trust Laws in the Czech Republic and Hungary

Consulting Editors
Paolo Panico, István Sándor and **James Turnbull**

Consulting editors
Paolo Panico, István Sándor and James Turnbull

Managing director
Sian O'Neill

Trust Laws in the Czech Republic and Hungary
is published by

Globe Law and Business Ltd
3 Mylor Close
Horsell
Woking
Surrey GU21 4DD
United Kingdom
Tel: +44 20 3745 4770
www.globelawandbusiness.com

Printed and bound by CPI Group (UK) Ltd, Croydon CR0 4YY, United Kingdom

Trust Laws in the Czech Republic and Hungary

ISBN 9781837230068
EPUB ISBN 9781837230075
Adobe PDF ISBN 9781837230082

Table of contents

Part II: Trust laws in Hungary

The excursions of the trust

Paolo Panico
STEP Europe

1. Introduction

The Excursions of Mr Brouček (*Výlety pana Broučka*) is a 19th century literary masterpiece by the Czech author Svatopluk Čech. It describes the voyages of a Prague middle-class gentleman to the moon, and a journey back in time to the 15th century.

The title of this introductory chapter is inspired by the novel and alludes to the great distances covered by the trust in its excursions to legal systems that are apparently remote and distinct from their English roots. As this book will demonstrate, the trust – unlike the fictional Mr Brouček – has found a convivial environment in jurisdictions as far away as the Czech Republic and Hungary, and it is definitely there to stay.

2. Why are trusts useful?

An example will serve to illustrate why a number of civil law systems have found it necessary to avail themselves of some form of legal arrangement corresponding to the English trust, and have passed legislation to this effect.

A Dutch brokerage firm maintained an 'omnibus account' with a Dutch custodian. The broker's clients had transferred funds to that account with a view to having investments made on their behalf. Those funds were therefore beneficially owned, not by the broker, but by its clients. At the same time the broker had taken a loan from the same custodian. When the broker became insolvent, the custodian satisfied its claim against the omnibus account. In practice, the loan was repaid with the money of the broker's clients. Litigation followed and the matter ended up before the Dutch Supreme Court, which found for the custodian.[1] To the extent that the trust as an institution was unknown to Dutch law at the time, no segregation of movable assets was enforceable and the broker's clients lost their money.

It has to be said that this result, which is now 30 years old, would be less likely if a similar case were heard by the Dutch courts today. The trust has made its way into the Dutch legal system by virtue of the Hague Trusts Convention –

1 *Kas-Asociatie*, 23 September 1994, NJ 1996 461.

on which more in section 3.2 below – and modern anti-money laundering legislation would prevent a Dutch custodian bank from ignoring the fact that certain funds were held on behalf of beneficial owners who were different from the account holder.

A striking contrast to this early Dutch example is provided by a case from the Supreme Court of Bermuda. *Kingate Global Fund Limited v Knightsbridge (USD) Fund Limited* concerned a 'feeder fund' to the Madoff funds in the United States.[2] The investors sent their money to this feeder fund at the same time as their subscription forms. In the event the subscription applications were accepted, the corresponding number of units would be issued and the money would be forwarded to the Madoff funds in the United States. The very last subscriptions made before the Madoff business went bankrupt had not yet been processed, and the court held that the funds should be returned to the investors and not forwarded to the receivers in bankruptcy. The reason was that such funds were deemed to be held on trust for the investors with a view to performing the required investment, and should be returned if the transaction was no longer possible. This particular type of trust is called a 'Quistclose trust' after an English precedent of 1970.[3] Critically, no express trust instrument was ever executed between the investors and the feeder fund administrator – the case is an example of a constructive trust held by the court to exist on the basis of established facts.

It might be thought that a trust of this nature could hardly be imported by a legal system that does not include equity and legal precedent among its sources of law – that is, a system outside the common law tradition; however, express trusts have found their way into civil law systems by a variety of mechanisms. The rest of this chapter will illustrate some of the legal developments in this regard and put recent Czech and Hungarian experience of trusts in context.

3. Trusts without equity: an introduction

Examples like the early Dutch case above clearly show that trusts are an important factor in the development of a sound and reliable financial system. Many examples could be found to demonstrate the desirability of trusts in other social and economic areas, ranging from philanthropy to the making of adequate provision for pets after their owner's demise.

Three main methods have been followed by various jurisdictions in order to import trusts into their legal systems:

- a natural development in jurisdictions such as Scotland, the state of Louisiana and the Canadian province of Quebec that bordered the leading common law jurisdictions;

---

2 [2010] WTLR 1201.
3 *Barclays Bank v Quistclose Investments Ltd* [1970] AC 567.

- the recognition of trusts governed by foreign law under *ad hoc* private international law provisions, notably the Hague Trusts Convention; and
- special legislation on trusts or trust-like arrangements.

Each of these methods is reviewed in some detail in the following sections. We shall concentrate on legislation facilitating any legal arrangement that can go under the name of 'trust' or – regardless of its denomination – that has the main features of what is referred to as a trust under English law. Alternative legal arrangements – private foundations in particular – are disregarded even though they have an important role in some Continental European systems such as, of late, the Czech Republic and Hungary.

3.1 Natural development of trusts: Scotland and Quebec

The legal systems of Scotland and Quebec are quite different from one another and the histories of the two jurisdictions have little in common. Nonetheless, two notable and distinct developments in trust practice and the establishment of trust legislation are worth mentioning, particularly in how they compare with the more recent Hungarian and Czech legislative experiments.

(a) Scotland

Until 1603, Scotland and England were separate kingdoms, and in contrast to the common law system of England, much of Scottish jurisprudence had evolved since the Middle Ages according to the principles of Roman law. Even after the Union of the Crowns in 1603, when James VI of Scotland became James I of England, and the Treaty of Union a little over a century later, when the two kingdoms became constituent parts of the same political entity, the Kingdom of Great Britain (later the United Kingdom of Great Britain and Ireland and finally, in 1927, the United Kingdom of Great Britain and Northern Ireland), Scots law survived as a separate legal system.

For our purposes, two key differences between the systems are worth noting.

First, the Scottish legal system does not include the principle of equity – in the technical sense understood under English common law – as a source of law. A residual power may be exercised by the Inner House of the Court of Session, Scotland's highest civil court, when no statutory provision, binding precedent or authoritative comment can be found on a particular matter, and indeed some instances of this power – known as '*nobile officium*' – were reported in the 19th century in relation to trusts or, more precisely, certain trustee powers; but the extent and reach of this case law is incomparably smaller than the body of equity in England.

Second, the system of property rights in Scotland is crafted after Roman law.

This may seem surprising given that the Roman Empire extended only as far north as Hadrian's Wall, which divides Scotland from England. But paradoxically, while Roman property rights disappeared in the southern part of Great Britain that had been exposed to Roman rule, they resurfaced in the northern part, where the Romans had hardly set foot. This was a gradual development, mainly resulting from the leading Scottish legal scholars of the 16th and 17th centuries studying in the civil law jurisdictions of Continental Europe rather than in London. These so-called 'institutional writers' came back from universities in Paris, Leyden or Utrecht, where they had been trained in Roman law, and transposed the same principles into their treatises, often referred to as 'the institutions of the law of Scotland'.[4] In the context of property rights, for example, Scots law has the notion of 'usufruct' or 'liferent' – the right to use (Latin *usus*) and enjoy for life the fruits (*fructus*) of somebody else's property – which is a concept unknown to English law. The holder of this right is known in civil law jurisdictions as a 'liferenter' and the owner, who has no right to economically enjoy his or her property, as a 'naked owner' or 'bare owner' – in Scots law, a 'fiar'.

Despite a legal environment that does not include equity and relies on a system of property rights of Roman origin, trusts have been known in Scotland at least since the 16th century:

> *In 1542 Sir Alexander Mortoun is going off to fight the invading English. He expects to be killed in action. He conveys his land to his son, Alexander the younger. If he does return alive, his son is to reconvey. Otherwise, his son is to hold for the heirs and assignees of his father, though the lands are to be burdened by provisions for the daughters (ie, sisters of Alexander the younger), Isabella, Janet, Margaret and Elizabeth.*[5]

This is probably the earliest reported case of a Scottish trust and it closely resembles the types of trust created at the same time in England. To put it in Professor George Gretton's terms:

> *The Scottish express trust is similar in its practical effect to the English express trust, though the underlying software is different, a difference inevitable given the absence of equity.*[6]

This Scottish trust 'software' developed through a range of local precedential authorities, from 17th century decisions that confirmed asset segregation – that is, the inability of the trustee's personal creditors to seize the

---

4 The main institutional writers and their works are: John Darlymple, Viscount Stair (1619–1695), *Institutions of the Law of Scotland*, 1681; John Erskine (1695–1768), *An Institute of the Law of Scotland*, 1771; Baron David Hume (1757–1838), *Commentaries on the Law of Scotland respecting Crimes*, 1797; and George Joseph Bell (1770–1843), *Commentaries on the Law of Scotland and on the Principles of Mercantile Jurisprudence*, 1810, and *Principles of the Law of Scotland*, 1829.

5 *Protocol Book of Sir Alexander Gaw*, at note 43, p3, in George Gretton, "Scotland: The Evolution of the Trust", in Richard Helmholz and Reinhard Zimmermann, *Itinera Fiduciae*, 1998.

6 George Gretton, "Scotland", in William Swadling (ed), *The Quistclose Trust: Critical Essays*, Hart Publishing, Oxford and Portland, 2004.

trust assets towards satisfaction of their claims[7] – to a 20th-century tax case that defined the legal position of a trust beneficiary.[8] The legal nature of the beneficial interests under a trust has been a source of misunderstandings and misconceptions between English and Continental European legal scholars since the 19th century. The Scottish approach reconciles the trust with the Roman system of property rights. The trustees are the absolute owners of the trust property,[9] while the beneficiary has a right *in personam* to sue them in order to compel them to administer the trust as prescribed in the trust instrument.

Legislation has also played an important role in the development of Scottish trusts. The Trusts (Scotland) Act 1921 provided fairly comprehensive regulation of the law of trusts in Scotland – more so than the corresponding legislation in England. The Trusts and Succession (Scotland) Act 2024, which repeals all previous legislation, is on par with or ahead of the equivalent statutes of any of the leading international trust jurisdictions.

Among the innovative features introduced by the Trusts and Succession (Scotland) Act 2024 are the following:

- the non-charitable purpose trust;[10]
- express regulation of the role of protectors;[11]
- the ability of the beneficiaries to remove a trustee;[12]
- the limitation of a trustee's liability to third parties for contractual obligations properly incurred in the performance of the trustee's functions;[13] and
- the express inclusion of ESG considerations in the formulation of an investment strategy for a trust.[14]

On the basis of the foregoing, Scotland can be expected to be considered as a jurisdiction option by increasing numbers of practitioners in civil law jurisdictions where trusts are recognised under the Hague Trusts Convention (see section 3.2, below) or other instruments of private international law.

(b) Quebec

Quebec, the only French-speaking province in Canada, has a civil law system, albeit it is quite different to that of France.[15] The French crown established a

---

7 *Livingston v Forrester* (1664) Mor 191 and 10200, 1 Stair 232; *Mackenzie v Watson* (1678) Mor 10188, 2 Stair 607.

8 *Inland Revenue v Clark's Trs*, 1939 SC 11.

9 "The property of the thing intrusted, be it land or moveables, is in the person of the intrusted, else it is not proper trust." (John Darlymple, Viscount of Stair, *The Institutions of the Law of Scotland*, 1681).

10 Trusts and Succession (Scotland) Act 2024, Sections 46–52.

11 *Ibid*, Sections 53–57.

12 *Ibid*, Section 10.

13 *Ibid*, Section 38.

14 *Ibid*, Section 20(2)(b).

15 Maurizio Lupoi, "Trusts in mixed jurisdictions", *Pravovedenie*, Vol 67 No 1, 2023, p35 *et seq.*

Sovereign Council in Canada in 1663. At that time, French private law consisted of various regional rules (*coutumes*), and the Coutume de Paris in particular was introduced to apply throughout Canada in 1664. Under the Treaty of Paris of 1763 Canada passed to the British crown, but attempts to impose English common law were unsuccessful and led to the reintroduction of the previous laws under the Quebec Act 1774. As a result, the Code Napoléon of 1804 did not apply to Quebec, nor did it influence legislation in the province, which continued to be based on the Coutume de Paris.

The Civil Code of Lower Canada (as Quebec was then known) of 1866 was not crafted after the French Civil Code then in force, the Code Napoléon, but was rather a codification of existing rules, mainly dating back to the pre-revolutionary Ancien Régime.

As a result, the Civil Code of Quebec included some institutions that had roots in Roman law and the Continental European *ius commune* but had disappeared under the Code Napoléon, such as the *fideicommissum* and the *heres fiduciarius*.[16] The notion of *fiducie* (trust) was introduced in 1879 with a view to regulating an English-style trust.

The new Civil Code of Quebec, which came into force in 1994, contains very different and somewhat ingenious regulatory provisions relating to trust, at Articles 1260–1298. The new notion of trust in Quebec drew extensively on the legal writings of Pierre Lepaulle, a French scholar who spent time at Yale and developed a strong interest in trusts which manifested in his *Theoretical and Practical Treatise on Trusts* (*Traité Théorique et Pratique des Trusts*) from 1933, in which he defined the trust as "a legal institution consisting of a fund, independent of any legal subject, and whose unity is constituted by an affectation, which is free within the limits of the actual law and public policy".

Articles 1260 and 1261 of the Quebec Civil Code are the direct enactment of Lepaulle's doctrine:

> ***Article 1260:*** *A trust results from an act whereby a person, the settlor, transfers property from his patrimony to another patrimony constituted by him which he appropriates to a particular purpose and which a trustee undertakes, by his acceptance, to hold and administer.*
>
> ***Article 1261:*** *The trust patrimony, consisting of the property transferred in trust, constitutes a patrimony by appropriation, autonomous and distinct from that of the settlor, trustee or beneficiary and in which none of them has any real right.*

The main feature of the Quebec trust is that it comprises an ownerless patrimony (*patrimoine sans maître*), or in this context an ownerless fund, where

16 In Roman law a *fideicommissum* was a legal institution where a testator could request that a beneficiary transfer property to another person after the beneficiary's death. The *heres fiduciarius*, or fiduciary heir, was the initial beneficiary designated in the *fideicommissum*.

the trustee acts solely as the administrator and not the owner. Pierre Lepaulle considered this the only route by which the trust could find its way into a civil legal system – an ownerless fund appeared to be the only way to reconcile the trust with the then prevailing theory of the unicity of patrimony. This notion was introduced by the two 19th century French scholars Chares Aubry and Charles Rau[17] and basically links the notion of patrimony to that of person. Patrimony is the economic status of a person, encompassing their assets and liabilities. Accordingly, each person has one and only one patrimony that is available to satisfy the claims of their creditors.[18] This is in direct contrast with asset segregation, one of the main features of trusts, which prevents the personal creditors of a trustee from attaching trust assets. If the trustee, as in the Quebec notion of trust, is simply the administrator of the trust fund without having title to it, the trust is compatible with asset segregation and can perform the same functions as under English common law. A trustee continues to have his or her own patrimony, which is available to personal creditors, while the patrimonies of the trusts they administer are not so available, because they do not belong to the trustee.

The Quebec model had a powerful influence on trust legislation passed in the Czech Republic, as we shall see in section 3.2 below (and indeed as will be explored in detail in this part of the book).

3.2 Private international law and the Hague Trusts Convention

In a number of jurisdictions trusts could not develop organically because of their geographical location and the absence of a relationship with the English common law system. In some of these cases, however, recognition of trusts governed by a foreign law could rely on an instrument of private international law.

The Hague Convention of 1 July 1985 on the Law Applicable to Trusts and on their Recognition ('the Hague Trusts Convention') provides a statutory basis for the recognition of trusts in the jurisdictions that have ratified it. It came into force in 1992 after ratification by the first three signatory countries: the United Kingdom, Italy and Australia. The Hague Trusts Convention was then ratified (or acceded to) by the English-speaking provinces of Canada as well as by Malta (1996), the Netherlands (1996), Luxembourg (2004), Liechtenstein (2006), San Marino (2006), Switzerland (2007), Monaco (2008), Cyprus (2017) and Panama (2018). Ratification by the United Kingdom implied its extension to the Crown dependencies and British Overseas Territories of Bermuda, British Antarctic Territories, British Virgin Islands, Falkland Islands, Gibraltar, Guernsey, Isle of

---

17 Charles Aubry and Charles Rau, *Cours de droit français d'après la méthode de Zachariae*, Book 2, Section 573, Imprimerie et librairie générale de jurisprudence Marchal, Billard et C, 1873.

18 French Civil Code, Article 2284: "Whoever has undertaken personal obligations shall discharge his commitments on all his movable and immovable assets, present and future."

Man, Jersey, Montserrat, Saint Helena, South Georgia and the South Sandwich Islands, and Turks and Caicos; and to the sovereign base areas of Akrotiri and Dhekelia in Cyprus.

The Hague Trusts Convention essentially covers two areas:

- the law applicable to trusts; and
- the recognition of trusts.

(a) Law applying to trusts

As far as the law applicable to trusts is concerned, the Hague Trusts Convention covers conflicts of law matters and specifies which law governs a trust. In essence, the governing law of a trust is the law freely chosen by the settlor,[19] which may be any law in the world and need not be the law of a jurisdiction where the Hague Trusts Convention has been ratified. There are rules for when a settlor fails to identify the governing law or indicates a jurisdiction that does not exist or does not regulate that particular type of trust.[20] A settlor may even choose more than one governing law to regulate different aspects of the trust, a practice known as '*dépeçage*' ('dismemberment').[21]

The governing law or laws chosen by the settlor will exclusively govern the validity of a trust, its construction, its effects, and its administration;[22] as such, the Hague Trusts Convention provides clarity in respect of any potential conflicts of law, and for this reason it has been adopted by federal states such as Canada and Australia, where trust law is not a federal, but a provincial or state, matter.

(b) Recognition of trusts

The other function of the Hague Trusts Convention is to enable a jurisdiction unfamiliar with the concept of trusts to recognise legal arrangements that exhibit certain basic features. For such cases, the Convention provides a definition of trusts at Article 2:

> ***Article 2:*** *For the purposes of this Convention, the term 'trust' refers to the legal relationships created –* inter vivos *or on death – by a person, the settlor, when assets have been placed under the control of a trustee for the benefit of a beneficiary or for a specified purpose.*
>
> *A trust has the following characteristics:*
>
> *a) the assets constitute a separate fund and are not a part of the trustee's own estate;*
>
> *b) title to the trust assets stands in the name of the trustee or in the name of another person on behalf of the trustee;*
>
> *c) the trustee has the power and the duty, in respect of which he is*

19 Hague Trusts Convention, Article 6.
20 *Ibid*, Article 7.
21 *Ibid*, Article 9.
22 *Ibid*, Article 8.

accountable, to manage, employ or dispose of the assets in accordance with the terms of the trust and the special duties imposed upon him by law.

The reservation by the settlor of certain rights and powers, and the fact that the trustee may himself have rights as a beneficiary, are not necessarily inconsistent with the existence of a trust.

A detailed analysis of this provision is beyond the scope of this chapter.[23] For present purposes it is sufficient to note that the definition of a trust under the Hague Trusts Convention does not require that title to the trust property vests in the trustee – simply that "assets have been placed under the control of a trustee". A trust defined in these terms is much broader than a trust under English law, which has rightly led Professor Maurizio Lupoi to call it a "shapeless trust".[24]

Under the Hague Trusts Convention, a number of legal arrangements where title to the trust property does not vest in the trustee can be recognised as trusts provided that the other requirements are met. This is the case for the Quebec trust which, as we have seen, is an ownerless patrimony, as well as the Dutch *bewind*, where title to trust assets remains with their original owner. The delegates of some civil law jurisdictions at the Hague Conference on Private International Law insisted that the definition should be broad enough to encompass similar trust-like arrangements in order to secure their use internationally and their recognition as trusts.

The Hague Trusts Convention provides a basic toolkit for the courts of the civil law jurisdictions that have ratified it, enabling them to recognise a legal arrangement that qualifies as a trust and to enforce its effects.

The civil law jurisdiction that has made the most of this opportunity was the first to ratify the Hague Trusts Convention – Italy.[25] The experience of Italy is unique inasmuch as trusts have become an ordinary estate planning and asset management tool for many families to an extent unparalleled in other civil law jurisdictions with no domestic trust law of their own. This practice is often referred to as '*trust interni*' ('domestic trusts') where all relevant elements are Italian except for the governing foreign law. In an Italian domestic trust, a resident settlor settles property with an Italian *situs* on trust with an Italian resident trustee for the benefit of Italian resident beneficiaries. The only non-Italian element in this relationship is the governing law – an existing trust law enforced in Italy by virtue of the Hague Trusts Convention.

A large number of judgments have been issued by the Italian courts, in some cases the Supreme Court, as to the application of a foreign governing law in

23 For an in-depth analysis of the Hague Trusts Convention, see Jonathan Harris, *The Hague Trusts Convention. Scope, Application and Preliminary Issues*, Hart, 2002.

24 Maurizio Lupoi, "The Shapeless Trust", *Trusts & Trustees*, Vol 1, No 3, 1995, p15.

25 Italy, Law of 16 October 1989 n 364, ratifying of the Hague Trusts Convention, in force from 1 January 1992.

Italian *trust interni*. These judgments extend beyond the basic aspects of the validity of trusts that are usually considered by the courts of civil law jurisdictions in which trusts are only occasionally encountered. Many Italian judgments on trusts exhibit a level of sophistication comparable to that of the leading trust jurisdictions. One example is from 2010, when two Italian courts had to deal almost at the same time with the case of a retiring trustee where the trust instrument did not contain adequate provision for the appointment of a successor. Both trusts were governed by Jersey law. The court of Genoa agreed to provide directions to the trustee under Article 51 of the Trusts (Jersey) Law 1984, as amended.[26] The court of Reggio Emilia took a different approach, applying the recently enacted Article 17(1A) of the same statute, which provides that where the terms of the trust for the appointment of a successor trustee have lapsed or failed, the outgoing trustee has the power to appoint its successor.[27] In a more recent example, from January 2023, the Italian Supreme Court issued an extensive and insightful judgment about the interaction of a discretionary trust with Italian forced heirship rules.[28]

One reason for the strength of the Italian trusts environment, which in the absence of domestic legislation relies extensively on local case law applying foreign laws, is its capillary diffusion all over the jurisdiction. Judgments on trust matters have not only been handed down by the courts of major Italian cities such as Rome or Milan, but also by of a number of provincial towns, where local families have found the trust to be the only legal arrangement to effectively solve some existential problem.

It is telling to compare the Italian experience with that of Switzerland, where trusts are also recognised by virtue of the Hague Trusts Convention in the absence of domestic legislation.[29] There is no domestic trust in Switzerland comparable to the Italian one. Switzerland as a financial centre can rely on a number of regulated professional trustees, whose services are mainly devoted to foreign settlors and not the domestic market. The result is a smaller number of judgments and a perception that the trust is another type of financial service essentially available to the affluent foreign clients of the Swiss financial services industry.

In conclusion, the Hague Trusts Convention is not the only instrument of private international law relevant to the recognition of trusts governed by a foreign law. Some countries that have not ratified the Hague Trusts Convention have enacted their own private international laws to achieve the same purpose:

- Chapter XII of the 2004 Belgian Code of Private International Law deals with trusts in a very similar way to the corresponding provisions of the Hague Trusts Convention.

---

26 Trib Genova, 29 March 2010.
27 Trib Reggio Emilia, 6 March 2010.
28 Italian Supreme Court (Corte di Cassazione), Ric 2017 n 23060, 18 January 2023.
29 Switzerland, Federal Decree of 20 December 2006, Hague Convention, in force as of 1 July 2007.

- The new Civil Code of Romania, which came into force in 2011, contains some provisions that allow the recognition of foreign trusts on terms similar to those of the Hague Trusts Convention.[30]
- Section 73 of Czech statute 91/2012 on Private International Law, which came into force in 2014 at the same time as the new Civil Code, deals expressly with the recognition of foreign law trusts.

3.3 Legislation enacting 'trusts': some examples

A number of countries, in particular the Czech Republic and Hungary, have enacted special legislation to provide domestic legal arrangements with equivalent features to trusts of common law jurisdictions.

Various approaches have been adopted in this regard, including:

- attempting to recreate the English common law trust in the form of a new legal arrangement transplanted into the domestic legal system;
- attempting to recreate the common law trust by relying on existing domestic legal arrangements or institutions that may have had similar functions; and
- establishing a legal arrangement that is functionally equivalent to the trust but possesses marked structural differences.

(a) New legal arrangements

An example of the first approach is that of Liechtenstein, where the first case of codification of trusts in a civil law environment was attempted. With the end of World War I and the demise of the Austro-Hungarian Empire, Liechtenstein lost its main geopolitical ally and needed to find a new international strategy. It is perhaps no exaggeration to say that this is how offshore finance came into being. Liechtenstein adopted the Swiss franc as legal tender, entered into a customs union with Switzerland and in 1926 enacted the Personen und Gesellschaftsrecht (PGR) – Law of Persons and Companies – that has since then coexisted with the Austrian Civil Code, or ABGB. The PGR introduced a number of legal innovations that are relevant to estate planning today, such as comprehensive regulation of family foundations (*Stiftungen*), a new legal arrangement known in German as an '*Anstalt*' (often translated as an 'establishment'), and comprehensive regulation of trusts following the English and American approaches of the time.[31] The definition of trustee under Article 897 of the PGR makes it immediately clear that the legal arrangement represents the trust of a common law jurisdiction transplanted into the civil law system of Liechtenstein:

---

30 Civil Code of Romania, Articles 2659–2662.

31 The fact that not only the English model but also that known as the 'Massachusetts trust' was followed is expressly reported in a short commentary to the PGR by its two draftsmen. See Wilhelm and Emil Bech, *Kurzer Bericht zum Personen- und Gesellschaftsrecht*, 1926, pp49–51.

*A trustee (*Treuhänder, *Salman) for the purposes of this Law is an individual, a partnership or a corporation, to whom another person (*Treugeber, *settlor) transfers movable or immovable property or a right of any kind (trust property) with the obligation to administer and to dispose of the trust property in his own name as an owner in his own right for the benefit of one or more third parties (Beneficiaries) with effect against all other persons.*

In addition to this notion of trust, an innovative arrangement called a *Treuunternehmen* (trust enterprise, also known as a 'Trust reg') was introduced under a special law in 1928, eventually finding its way into the PGR as Article 932a. This type of trust may be used to carry on a commercial enterprise and can have legal personality like a company or a foundation. In this respect it is very close to the arrangement known in the United States as a statutory entity trust, which has legal personality and comes into existence as a result of its registration with the competent state authority.

(b) ***Existing legal arrangements***

The second approach attempted to build on existing legal arrangements or institutions to recreate the mechanisms and functions of the English common law trust. A notable example is the approach of Malta, where a new Article 1124A was inserted into the Civil Code to describe the notion of fiduciary obligations. This was not the enactment of a new legal concept but simply a provision stating the position believed to have always existed under Maltese law:

Fiduciary obligations arise in virtue of law, contract, quasi-contract, trusts, assumption of office or behaviour whenever a person (the 'fiduciary') –

(a) owes a duty to protect the interests of another person; or

(b) holds, exercises control or powers of disposition over property for the benefit of other persons, including when he is vested with ownership of such property for such purpose; or

(c) receives information from another person subject to a duty of confidentiality and such person is aware or ought, in the circumstances, reasonably to have been aware, that the use of such information is intended to be restricted.

Accordingly, the trust that is regulated under Malta's Trusts and Trustees Act 2004[32] is but a special case of the general notion of a fiduciary obligation.

A comparable approach was followed in San Marino, a civil law jurisdiction that never enacted a civil code. The trust resulting from the Law of 1 March 2010, 'The institution of the trust', is an accurate recreation of the legal relationships typical of an English trust, but draws extensively on the European *ius commune* that is at the heart of the San Marino legal system.

The Hungarian *bizalmi vagyonkezelés* (fiduciary property management

---

32 Available at: https://legislation.mt/eli/cap/331/eng/pdf.

contract) under Sections 6:310–330 of the new Civil Code of 2014 also falls within this second category. The Hungarian 'trust' is in fact a special contract regulated by Book VI of the Civil Code which deals with the law of obligations, specifically Title XVI dealing with 'engagement contacts', immediately following the provisions on agency.

The contractual nature of the Hungarian trust is self-evident from the definition at Section 6:310(1):

> *Under a fiduciary asset management contract, the trustee shall manage on his own behalf and for the benefit of the beneficiary the things transferred to his ownership, as well as the rights and obligations transferred to him by the settlor (hereinafter 'trust property'), and the settlor shall pay the fee.*

Trusts are not, in fact, contracts under English law because they lack the fundamental requirement, in a common law context, of consideration. The traditional English view of a trust is a unilateral disposition of property to a trustee for no consideration. This outcome is largely accidental, stemming from the underdeveloped state English contract law in the Middle Ages, when trusts began to develop in practice.[33] In a different context trusts could, and can, very well be contracts – or 'fiduciary contracts' – as demonstrated by the position in Hungary.

(c) Functionally equivalent arrangements

The third approach, of a legal arrangement that performs the functions of a trust but has an entirely different structure, is exemplified by the Czech *svěřenský fond* (fiduciary fund) established under Sections 1448–1474 of the 2014 Czech Civil Code.[34] Czech trust legislation was heavily influenced by the *fiducie*, or trust, of the Quebec Civil Code of 1994. Most Czech provisions are a near word-for-word translation of the corresponding provisions of the Quebec Civil Code, though some incorporate improvements given the 20-year gap between the two statutes.[35]

This approach does not aim to transplant the English trust into a civil law environment or create a special type of contract based on pre-existing legal arrangements with comparable functions. Instead, the trust is conceived as something different. It might be seen as an ownerless patrimony under Quebec legislation and the theories of Pierre Lepaulle, as it is in the Czech Republic. Alternatively it could be a private foundation, building on legal arrangements familiar to Continental Europe for centuries, initially for charitable purposes and gradually to support the members of a family.[36]

---

33 The notion of a contract for the benefit of a third party (*stipulation pour autrui*) entered the English legal system in the form of an express exception to the principle of the privity of contracts under the Contracts (Rights of Third Parties) Act 1999.

34 See Appendix I.

35 Paolo Panico, "Il trust nella Repubblica Ceca", *Trusts e attività fiduciarie*, Vol 23, 2022.

36 Paolo Panico, "Private foundations and trusts: just the same but different?", *Trusts & Trustees*, Vol 22, No 1, 2016, p132.

Both Hungary and the Czech Republic have incorporated various forms of private foundations in their new Civil Codes, alongside institutions that more closely resemble trusts.

4. Conclusion

The chapters that follow offer an in-depth analysis of these legal arrangements and their potential for domestic and international estate planning, asset protection and wealth management. This chapter aimed to place these new legal developments in context and demonstrate that they are not isolated experiments, but rather build upon a well-established tradition in civil law, where trusts *per se* were not originally present but are now being imported using a variety of techniques to address gaps in local legal institutions.

Part I: Trust laws in the Czech Republic

Introduction

James Turnbull
Uplift

1. A brief history of *svěřenské fondy*

A *svěřenský fond* is the Czech version of a common law trust (for simplicity, we shall use the term 'Czech trust').

It shares most of the features of the trusts typically found in common law jurisdictions. However, the Czech Republic is a civil law jurisdiction, and as a consequence, while the practical results are the often the same, the underlying legal basis is quite different.

1.1 History

Many people think that trusts are new to the Czech Republic, having only been introduced as part of a new Civil Code in 2014. This is true, but not true. In fact, trusts have a much longer history which, at the risk of oversimplifying a complex story, we attempt to present here.

In the 17th century, Czech lands became part of the Hapsburg monarchy. This change brought with it the importation of concepts similar to a trust from the Austrian lands. These trust-like structures flourished, especially during the reign of Ferdinand II, who sought to destroy the economic power of noble estates and non-Catholic religions through confiscations following the Battle of White Mountain in 1620. As a result, relatively large property portfolios were created, and these trust structures were an ideal tool to consolidate such holdings.

These structures flourished for many years, with attempts to limit or even cancel them coming only in the second half of the 18th century during the reigns of Maria Theresa and Joseph II. However, the trust was not completely abolished until 1924 after the formation of an independent Czechoslovak State.[1]

There followed a period of 90 years in which we saw many fundamental changes to the Czech state and Czech society including, most significantly, World War II, the rise and subsequent fall of the Communist regime, and the peaceful divorce of the Czech Republic and Slovakia. During this period, trusts

1 Act No 179/1924 Coll.

were neither part of the Czech legal system nor recognised under Czech law. Not surprisingly, the Czech Republic did not sign the Hague Trust Convention.

This state of 'trust limbo' existed until the early 2000s, when more than 10 years of discussion culminated in a new Czech Civil Code, which came into force in 2014.[2] The objective of the drafters of the new code was to align Czech private law with European traditions and to bring to an end the socialist legal regime that had dominated the pre-1989 era. An important part of this change was also focused on enabling individual freedom – as specifically expressed in Section 3(1) of the new law:

Private law protects the dignity and freedom of the individual and his natural right to pursue his own happiness and the happiness of his family or people close to him in a way that does not unreasonably harm others.[3]

The reintroduction of trusts fitted perfectly into this narrative. Prior to 2014, testamentary freedom was very limited and family business succession planning was difficult, verging on impossible.

Trusts, along with a number of other new planning possibilities introduced by the new code, gave families and family businesses a modern set of tools to plan and implement succession strategies. These tools collectively prevented the kind of injustices seen under the old law and, perhaps most importantly, made a 'family business culture' possible.

1.2 Canadian inspiration

The drafters of the new law were heavily inspired by the Civil Code of Quebec (CCQ), and indeed Quebec provided an excellent model. First, like the Czech Republic it is a civil law jurisdiction. Secondly, Quebec law had a track record of success in this area – trusts had existed without problems since 1991.

There are some differences between the Quebec and the Czech implementations, but the two models are very close. Compare, for example, Section 1294 of the CCQ[4] with Section 1469 (1) of the Czech Civil Code.[5] Here is an English translation:

On the application of a person with a legal interest therein, a court may decide

---

2 Act No 89/2012 Coll, the Civil Code. Available (Czech language only) at: www.zakonyprolidi.cz/cs/2012-89#cast5. An English translation is available at: http://obcanskyzakonik.justice.cz/images/pdf/Civil-Code.pdf.

3 Section 3(1) of the Czech Civil Code.

4 Section 1294 of the Quebec Civil Code:
Lorsqu'une fiducie a cessé de répondre à la volonté première du constituant, notamment par suite de circonstances inconnues de lui ou imprévisibles qui rendent impossible ou trop onéreuse la poursuite du but de la fiducie, le tribunal peut, à la demande d'un intéressé, mettre fin à la fiducie; il peut aussi, dans le cas d'une fiducie d'utilité sociale, lui substituer un but qui se rapproche le plus possible du but original.

5 Section 1469 (1) of the Czech Civil Code:
Soud může na návrh osoby, která na tom má právní zájem, rozhodnout, že svěřenský fond zruší, pokud je dosažení účelu svěřenského fondu nemožné nebo obtížně dosažitelné, zejména následkem okolností zakladateli neznámých nebo pro zakladatele nepředvídatelných. Jedná-li se o svěřenský fond zřízený za veřejně prospěšným účelem, může soud rozhodnout, že jeho původní účel nahradí podobným účelem.

> *that a trust be cancelled if it is impossible or difficult to achieve its purpose, primarily due to circumstances unknown or unforeseeable to the founder. Where a trust has been established for a publicly beneficial purpose, a court may decide to replace its original purpose with a similar one.*

Just for clarity, this is a translation into English of both those sections. They are exactly the same – that is very close inspiration indeed!

Of course, not all sections are identical; indeed, there are some important differences. For example, a Czech trust must be established by way of a notarial deed, and a private trust in Quebec must have a determined or determinable beneficiary,[6] which a Czech trust does not require, as we shall see below.

However, at their heart, Czech trusts and Quebec trusts are substantially the same. This is a very positive thing for the Czech model because it means that it is not really 'new' at all. The Quebec trust has a history dating back to 1995, since when it has functioned without problems.

Despite the fact that the new law offered a proven model and delivered excellent solutions to previously insoluble problems, it was greeted initially with a mix of bewilderment, scepticism and even fear. In the first month of the new law, just one Czech trust was established, and by the end of 2014, the cumulative total was just 49. The following year was not much better, with just 75 trusts established.

The reasons for this underwhelming initial response are to some extent understandable. They include the following:

- There was no recent history or tradition of trusts in the Czech Republic and no 'core knowledge' of this new institution and its potential.
- Czech people and the Czech legal profession are conservative by nature.
- Many Czech lawyers were overwhelmed at this time by a complete revision of the entire Civil Code. They tended to be focused on coming to grips with the changes that affected their core areas of practice and did not have the time or inclination to look into new and, from their perspective, irrelevant, parts of the code. This resulted in low levels of basic knowledge of trusts amongst the legal profession – a problem that, even after 10 years, sadly persists.

There were other, less understandable factors behind the initially poor take-up:

- The response from normally professional and well-respected transparency and anti-corruption NGOs was very disappointing. Again, this was mostly driven by misunderstanding and lack of knowledge. The core of the response was the rather simplistic argument that trusts were primarily tools for international tax evasion and money laundering. We

6 Section 1267 of the Quebec Civil Code.

do not, so the argument went, want to encourage such things and therefore trusts should be removed from Czech law. These arguments were made quite forcefully,[7] without any evidence that Czech trusts would (or could) be used in this this way and without recognition or understanding of the substantial benefits the new institution offered ordinary families.

- The media, and especially the tabloid media, picked up on these ill-informed arguments and press releases and ran articles focusing on the perceived potential for misuse. Headlines such as, "How to launder money after the New Year? The Civil Code will introduce trusts"[8] meant that although the general public did not know much about trusts, what they did know was that they were not good – that they were tools for criminals, not for ordinary families.
- This frenzy was in turn picked up by politicians, in some cases for populist reasons and in others from a genuine belief that trusts were not needed. Examples included the then deputy ministers of justice, JUDr Hana Marvanová and JUDr Robert Pelikán (later minister of justice). There were various discussions and pronouncements at top levels about the need to amend or revoke the new trust law.

All of this had a chilling effect and essentially prevented the use of trusts for any serious purpose due to the likelihood that they would be abolished.

Some of this uncertainty was removed as a result of the conclusions of an expert working group of the Ministry of Justice that took place in May 2014. From that point on, the future of trusts in the Czech legal system became more certain. However, it was hardly an auspicious start.

2. Lex Babiš

In January 2017 there were a total of 226 trusts in existence in the Czech Republic. Then an amendment[9] to the Conflict of Interest Act,[10] also known as Lex Babiš, was approved. The new law prohibited government officials from owning media and receiving state subsidies through their companies. As a result, controversial Czech prime minister Ondrej Babiš transferred shares in his businesses to two Czech trusts that he had established for the purpose.

---

7 See, for example: https://nfpk.cz/aktuality/o---hrozba-jmenem-sverensky-fond.

8 See Jiří Táborský, "*Jak vyprat peníze po Novém roce? Občanský zákoník zavede trusty*" ("How to launder money after the New Year? The Civil Code will introduce trusts"), *Lidové noviny*, 22 December 2013. Available at: www.lidovky.cz/byznys/jak-vyprat-penize-po-novem-roce-obcansky-zakonik-zavede-trusty.A131220_173815_firmy-trhy_mev. See also Jan Januš and Jan Klesla, "*Robert Pelikán: Svěřenské fondy v Česku k ničemu nepotřebujeme*" ("Robert Pelikán: We don't need trust funds for anything in the Czech Republic"), *Hospodářské noviny*, 28 February 2014. Available at: https://archiv.hn.cz/c1-61775870-robert-pelikan-sverenske-fondy-v-cesku-k-nicemu-nepotrebujeme.

9 14/2017 Coll.

10 159/2006 Coll.

These trusts were not effective as 'blind trusts' as there was no effective separation of control from the founder. However, they were sufficient to satisfy the requirements of the new law. This development was significant only in that it generated a huge amount of media coverage for trusts. Public awareness jumped as a result, as did the number of new trusts established.

3. Trust registration

The next major development occurred in January 2018, by which time there were around 522 trusts in existence. This was the introduction of a register. From this point forward (July 2018 for pre-existing trusts) all trusts had to be registered on the Czech Register of Trusts. This new legal requirement created some additional paperwork and compliance obligations for trustees, but was almost universally welcomed for two reasons. First, it put to rest any lingering concerns regarding the potential criminal misuse of trusts. Secondly, it meant that each trust was issued with an identification number, equivalent to those issued to companies and other legal entities. This in turn made it far easier for trustees to deal with state organs, banks and other similar organisations – for whom the existence of that number was vital.

Since then, the number of trusts and their usage and acceptance has continued to grow. As of August 2023, there were around 4,500 Czech trusts in existence.

The future looks assured. However, many issues remain, including:

- a lack of proper expertise by much of the professional community;
- a resulting large number of very poorly constructed trusts, which will create significant issues in the years ahead;
- strong residual resistance from many parts of the legal community; and
- a continued lack of widespread public knowledge of the benefits and uses of trusts.

With time, we can only hope that the situation will continue to improve.

The law: peculiarities and adaptations

James Turnbull
Uplift

1. Introduction

The core of Czech trust law is set out in Sections 1448–1474 of the Civil Code. An English translation can be found in Appendix I.

In practice, a Czech trust looks and feels very similar to a common law trust. Practitioners who have experience working with trusts in the United Kingdom, for example, can very easily incorporate Czech trusts into their client strategies because the same big picture logic applies.

2. Peculiarities/adaptations of Czech trusts

There are two interesting peculiarities worth mentioning (as well as some adaptations in practice – see sections 2.3 and 2.4 below) that differentiate the Czech concept of trust:

- ownerless property; and
- purpose.

2.1 Ownerless property

The first is the nature of ownership of trust property. Common law practitioners will be familiar with the concepts of legal ownership and beneficial interest (sometimes, 'equitable ownership'). This ownership model is at the core of common law trust principles. If an asset – let's say a house – is in a trust, common law sees two kinds of title:

- *Legal title:* This is ownership based on the law. For example, if I look at the land register entry for a house, I will see the names of the trustee (or trustees): for example, 'Fred Smith as Trustee for the XYZ Trust'. Fred has legal ownership of the house.
- *Beneficial ownership:* The house is not actually Fred's. He 'owns' it only in his capacity as trustee of the trust. He has the legal power to deal with the asset – for example, to sell it – but it does not really belong to him. Instead, it belongs to the trust ... except that the trust doesn't have legal personality and so cannot own things. So in fact it really 'belongs' to the beneficiaries of the trust, because they are the people who, one day, will

assume full ownership of the house. They have what is referred to as a 'beneficial interest'.[1]

To summarise, assets in common law trusts are owned. The trust operates to create a dual system of ownership: legal ownership and beneficial interest. This means that if we (theoretically) add these two interests together, for example, if a trust has one trustee and that person is also the sole possible beneficiary of the trust, then that person would have full ownership:

Legal ownership + beneficial interest = full ownership[2]

In other words, there would no longer be a trust at all – despite what any pieces of paper might say to the contrary.

As someone with a common law background, I find this system eminently clear and logical and consider it a foundational aspect of the trust concept.

However, various French academics and jurists take a different view. This is reflected in the Civil Code of Quebec (CCQ)[3] and even more clearly in the Czech Civil Code which, at Section 1448(3), says as follows:

The rights arising from the right of ownership in the assets of the trust are exercised by the trustee in his or her own name and on behalf of the trust; however, the property in a trust is not owned by the trustee or the founder, or the person entitled to receive performance from the trust.[4]

Thus, in Quebec and Czech law, there is no concept of equitable or legal ownership. Instead, the property in the trust is not owned at all. This is a difficult concept for common law practitioners to swallow, but in fact it is rather helpful from a practical perspective. There is no impact on the key aspects of trust establishment or management, but the concept undoubtedly strengthens the arguments of a trustee as they attempt to defend their trust from external attack – especially by the creditors of the founder.

2.2 Purpose

The second peculiarity is also, for the most part, theoretical. In common law most trusts are established for the benefit of a person or, more often, a group of people (the beneficiaries). It is not always possible to establish trusts that give effect to a purpose other than to provide benefit to specified people. In the

---

1 Some writers stop short of classifying this beneficial interest as 'ownership' – see F Maitland, *Equity: A Course of Lectures*, Cambridge University Press, 1936, p112. However, notwithstanding this, the courts have generally continued with a dual system of property rights. See J Tarrant, "Equitable ownership after the Judicature Act", *Australian Property Law Journal*, December 2007, p29.

2 *DKLR Holding Co (No 2) Pty Ltd v Commissioner of Stamp Duties (NSW)* (1982) 149 CLR 431, p163 per Aikin J: "If one person has both the legal estate and the entire beneficial interest in the land he holds an entire and unqualified legal interest and not two separate interests, one legal and the other equitable."

3 Section 2641.

4 See Appendix I.

United Kingdom, for example, such trusts (known as 'purpose trusts') are possible only in very restrictive circumstances – mostly for charities.

In contrast, look at Section 1448 of the Czech Civil Code (the emphasis is mine):

> *A trust is created by setting aside part of the property owned by the founder in such a way that the owner entrusts the trustee with the assets* **for a specific purpose** *through a contract or disposition* mortis causa, *and the trustee undertakes to keep and administer those assets.*[5]

This means that every Czech trust is a purpose trust.

In most cases, this difference is theoretical only – the purpose specified is to provide benefits to some particular person or people. However, that need not be the case. We have seen a number of examples of private (non-charitable) Czech trusts being created to achieve a range of purposes – something that is not possible in many other jurisdictions.

In addition to these two peculiarities, a couple of features or adaptations of Czech trusts have evolved from practice, concerning:

- beneficiaries vs eligible people; and
- supervisors/vacant supervisors.

2.3 Beneficiaries vs eligible people

The first adaptation is revealed by an understanding of notarial practice and a close reading of Section 1457(1) and (2) of the Czech Civil Code:

> *(1) A founder has the right to appoint a beneficiary and determine the performance to be provided to him or her from the trust, unless the statute of the trust provides otherwise.*
>
> *(2) If the founder fails to exercise his or her rights under Subsection (1), the trustee appoints the beneficiary and determines the performance to be provided to that beneficiary from the trust. In the case of a trust established for private purposes, a trustee may exercise that right if the statute determines the group of persons from which the beneficiary may be appointed.*[6]

The relevant practice notes are as follows:

- Notarial opinion is that if the founder does not exercise his or her right in Section 1457(1) at the time the statute is issued, he or she cannot do so later.
- There is considerable uncertainty as to how, or even if, it is possible to amend a trust statute.
- A beneficiary becomes a beneficiary only with effect from his or her registration (by name) in the Register of Trusts.[7]

---

5 See Appendix I.
6 See Appendix I.
7 Czech Civil Code Section 1457(3). See Appendix I.

As a result, it is not typical for Czech trust statutes to specify a complete list of beneficiaries or even groups of beneficiaries. This is mainly because those components would become 'locked' and impossible to subsequently change. Normal practice now is that only one or two core beneficiaries are actually named in the statute. This includes, in particular, anyone who is expected to receive any benefit in the near future.

In contrast, most of the real beneficiaries are specified by inclusion in (usually very widely defined) groups of 'possible beneficiaries' or 'eligible persons'. They are only actually appointed at the time in the future that it is necessary to do so in order to make a distribution.

In some cases, you will find trusts with only groups of these eligible persons but no actual beneficiaries at all – although this can sometimes be problematic for banks etc. This, in turn, means that the true purpose and intended recipients of the assets of a Czech trust can sometimes be quite opaque. However, everything ultimately becomes transparent due to the fact that every beneficiary must ultimately be named on the register before they can receive any benefit.

2.4 Supervisors/vacant supervisors

The Czech Civil Code is silent on the role of supervisors or protectors. However, there is nothing to prevent them being appointed, and such positions are very common in practice in Czech trusts; most commonly as what are known as 'vacant supervisors'.

This is done in the Czech Republic mainly (but not only) for asset protection purposes. Most professionally drafted Czech trust instruments contain comprehensive rules for the (irrevocable) appointment of a supervisor.

Most such positions are specified, but never actually filled. The founder has the power to appoint the supervisor, but normally never does so. Instead, he or she keeps this possibility in reserve for use only in the case of some concrete threat to the trust. Until the supervisor is appointed, the founder retains the power of appointment of the trustees. From the moment a supervisor is appointed, the power of appointment of the trustees is removed from the founder and is vested instead in the supervisor.

This is seen as a way for the founder to more clearly demonstrate to the court and creditors that he or she has no influence or control over the trust assets.

How effective such a strategy might be is yet to be tested in the courts.

These are two examples of local adaptations. There are others, and we expect this localisation of the trust concept to continue as our sector grows and the industry develops.

Formalities and documentation: statute, contract, changes

Bohumil Havel
Charles University; PRK Partners
Vlastimil Pihera
Kocián Šolc Balaštík

1. Nature and origins of the Czech trust

The Czech trust is best understood as an entity,[1] an object with rights and obligations but lacking legal personality.[2] Developing this notion, the Czech trust is not a legal person, but a setting aside of property (object) which is managed by the trustee on behalf of and for the account of the trust. Although the law requires the existence of a contract for its creation, evoking the historical concept of fiduciary contracts, the Czech trust does not have the characteristics of a contractual relationship. The Czech legislator has emphasised this by requiring that the main conditions of trust administration be contained in the 'statute', in contrast to the position for its inspirational source, the Quebec Civil Code. A statute in the context of Czech trust law is a unilateral legal act of the founder, similar in nature to a foundation deed. Thus, while the statute constitutes the central organisational document of the trust, the contract in respect of the establishment of a trust, concluded between founder and trustee, is exhausted when the trust is created. If the trust is a rocket, the contract on its establishment is a rocket booster.

After the adoption of the new Czech Civil Code, passionate and often emotional discussions were sparked as to whether trusts might be used for money laundering or other corrupt purposes. The first amendment to the Civil Code in 2016[3] responded to these fears by introducing the mandatory registration of Czech trusts by linking (with the exception of *mortis causa* trusts) the creation of a trust to the constitutive registration. This brought the concept of a Czech trust even closer, functionally, to a foundation. As a result, Czech law requires three legal conditions to be met for the creation of an *inter vivos* trust:

---

1 Decision of the Supreme Court Case No 27 Cdo 3033/2019 of 15 December 2020.

2 Cf the same conclusion for Quebec law formulated by M Cantin Cumyn: "La fiducie, un nouveau sujet de droit?" ("The trust, a new subject of law?"), in Jacques Beaulne (ed) and Ernest Caparros, *Mélanges Ernest Caparros*, Wilson & Lafleur, 2002; cited by A Popovici, "Trust in Quebec and Czech Law: Autonomous Patrimonies?", *European Review of Private Law*, 6-2016, p945.

- a statute drawn up by the founder;
- a contract between the founder and the trustee; and
- registration in the Register of Trusts.

As scary as it may sound, all these formalities are usually handled by the notary before whom the statute is drawn up in a single meeting. The actual registration of the Czech trust in the register is then a technical operation, also managed by a notary.

Regulation of the creation of a *mortis causa* trust is specific. Under Czech law, such a trust is established by a testamentary instrument (ie, a will, an inheritance agreement or a codicil) and comes into existence at the time of the founder's death. A flaw in the elegance of a *mortis causa* trust is the interpretative uncertainty of how such a trust behaves in the context of Czech inheritance law. There are ongoing discussions in the professional community as to whether or not the property allocated to such a trust is subject to succession proceedings (and thus the trustee of the trust acts as an heir). This question is still awaiting an authoritative opinion by the Czech higher courts.

2. Documents

2.1 Statute

The statute is the central document of the Czech trust. The statute does not preclude the existence of other contractual arrangements between the founder and the trustee, but such contractual arrangements remain just that – not the rules for the trust's administration. The statute must therefore be given careful consideration.

Czech law provides that the statute is issued by the founder. This does not preclude the possibility that statutes may be issued jointly by more than one founder. Here, the specific regulation of the adoption of the foundation charter by several founders, who are regarded by the law as a single founder, is clearly applicable by analogy.[4] This has the technical effect that if the founders retain any founding rights, they can only exercise them unanimously.

The statute must be drawn up in the form of a notarial deed before a Czech notary. The founder is represented by a notary on the basis of a power of attorney.[5] The signature on the power of attorney should be officially certified; if it is certified abroad, it should be apostilled (unless certification is by one of the few countries with which the Czech Republic has a treaty on recognition of

3 Amendment No 460/2016 Coll.

4 Cf Section 309(3) of the Czech Civil Code. Available (Czech language only) at: www.zakonyprolidi.cz/cs/2012-89#cast5.

5 Decision of the High Court in Prague in case No 14 Cmo 188/2018.

certification). The notary is an obliged person within the meaning of anti-money laundering legislation (AML),[6] which means that he or she is obliged, among other things, to identify the founder and verify the sources of the assets contributed to the trust. In practice, however, Czech trusts are established with minimal contributions. Substantial assets are transferred to them after their establishment (ie, without the involvement of a notary).

The statute must contain at least the following information (Section 1452(2) of the Civil Code):

- the designation of the trust;
- the description of the assets constituting the trust at its establishment;
- a statement of the purpose of the trust;
- the conditions for the provision of benefits from the trust;
- an indication of the duration of the trust – if no indication is given, the trust is deemed to have been established for an indefinite period;
- (if it is not a purpose trust) the names of beneficiaries or the manner in which the beneficiaries are to be selected; and
- the number of trustees and the manner in which they must act.

The statute, of course, usually regulates a number of other matters, such as processes for appointing trustees, protectors and beneficiaries, and the status of protectors, family councils or other bodies of the trust. As the central legal document of the trust, the statute regulates many issues only in general terms and require the trustee or other bodies of the trust to lay down more detailed rules in implementing directives.

Section 1469(2) of the Civil Code provides that "if, in accordance with the original intention of the founder, the purpose of the trust can be achieved or better served by amending the statute of the trust, the court shall amend the statute". It is disputed whether the founders of trusts can reserve in their statutes the power to amend their statutes for themselves or for another (trustee, protector, etc) without having to seek authority from the court. According to some authorities, the law does not restrict the founder from providing for other procedures for amending the statute, on the following bases:

- Czech foundation law allows founders of foundations to do so (Article 317 of the Civil Code);
- the Supreme Court so concluded in 2018 on the basis of the analogy to foundations in relation to endowment funds;[7] and

6 Act No 253/2008 Coll, on Certain Measures against the Legitimisation of Proceeds of Crime and Financing of Terrorism.

7 Supreme Court Case No 29 Cdo 3225/2016 of 27 March 2018.

- it is possible to do so in the majority of jurisdictions regulating trusts or 'trust-like' structures.[8]

Some have held that the statute must be immutable for the duration of the trust and can only be changed by court order. They justify this conclusion by reference to Article 978 of the Civil Code, according to which the provisions of the section of the Civil Code on absolute rights, which includes the regulation of trusts, "may be derogated from by an arrangement having effect against third parties only if the law so permits".[9] Although some lower courts have come to the conclusion that the founder may not change the statute, their decisions are not generally binding,[10] and the market is eagerly awaiting precedent-setting decisions by the higher courts. In any event, it is worth pointing out that there is a consensus that, unless the statute expressly allows for other changes, it can only really be changed through the courts.

2.2 Agreement on establishment of a trust

In the agreement on the establishment of a trust, the founder transfers certain assets from his or her property into the trust and the trustee undertakes to administer them in accordance with the rules of the trust set out in the statute. The contract should, therefore, be concluded only after the statute is drawn up.

Under the agreement there is a transfer of ownership – a change in ownership of the property to be allocated – and the agreement is therefore of a translational nature, and must contain the elements required of a contract for the transfer of ownership of the relevant property. The agreement itself may also create the property to be appropriated if the founder creates a right in favour of the trust, whether it is an obligational claim for performance or a right *in rem* (such as a building right or an easement). Logically, even in such a case, the agreement must meet the formal requirements for the creation of such a right. The contract constitutes a change in the ownership regime of the property to be transferred and is therefore, *inter alia*, the basis for the registration of such a change in the relevant registers, such as the Land Registry or the Public Register (of Legal and Natural Persons). However, the translative effects of the contract cannot take effect before the trust is created; that is, before the trust is entered in the Register of Trusts. For the avoidance of doubt, it may therefore be

---

8 V Pihera and K Ronovská, "Foundation principles and the limits of their flexibility. On the question of the possibility of additional changes in the conditions of functioning of trusts and foundations", *Právník*, No 9, 2018, pp705–722; K Ronovská and V Pihera, "On the possibility of amending the constitutive charter (including changes to the purpose) of a foundation fund", *Právní rozhledy*, 2018, no 15–16, pp556–559; V Pihera and K Ronovská, "On some myths and misconceptions about trust funds", *Bulletin of Advocacy*, 2020, no 7–8, pp44–47.

9 J Svejkovský, "Trust Funds – Statute, Institute of Property Law", *Bulletin of Advocacy*, no 5/2020, pp36–39.

10 See decision of District Court for Prague 1, file 33 Nc 1601/2020 of 16 November 2020.

advisable to expressly link the effectiveness of such contracts to the moment of registration of the trust in the Register of Trusts.

2.3 Deeds in *mortis causa*

A trust may also be created by a will or a contract of inheritance; and its terms may also be moderated by an endowment. A trust *mortis causa* is created at the time of the death of the founder (testator).

A deed in *mortis causa* creates a right to the estate (ie, a right of succession) or a right of bequest. Thus, we consider that when such an instrument creates a trust, the founder sets aside property for the benefit of the trust by reserving a right of inheritance or ordering a bequest.[11] According to other views, by means of a deed in *mortis causa* the founder sets aside his or her property directly, which is then not subject to succession proceedings.

Because of these uncertainties, it is currently probably the least legally risky course to set up a trust *inter vivos* and either to assign assets into it by gift on death (where the assets will be transferred to the trust outside inheritance proceedings) or to establish a right of inheritance in favour of an (already existing) trust (where the trustee of the trust will act as an heir in inheritance proceedings). In practice, there are also cases where the establishment of a *mortis causa* trust is effected differently and linked to testamentary succession. It must be said that notarial practice varies and all approaches have been employed; the issue, therefore, awaits a precedent-setting judicial decision.

2.4 Agreement on contribution to the trust

The assets in the trust may be increased by an additional contribution after its creation. Such a contribution may be made by the founder or by anyone else. This practice is widespread because (as noted above) when trusts are set up only minimal assets are usually contributed to them. The reason for this may be a desire to save on notary fees (the amount of which depends on the value of the assets in the trust), a desire for greater secrecy, or simply the founder's intention to 'test' the trust first before putting significant assets into it. The agreement is concluded between the person who contributes the property – that is, its owner or a person otherwise entitled to dispose of it – and the trustee. As in the case of agreement on establishment of a trust, the agreement on contribution to the trust has a translational nature, and must therefore possess the characteristics required for a contract for the transfer of ownership of the relevant property. If more than one such agreement is concluded in succession, it is good practice to number them in ascending order. The agreements on contribution to the trust should then be filed with the collection of deeds in the Register of Trusts.

---

11 V Pihera, "§ 1451 (Creation of a trust fund)", in Jiří Spáčil, Michal Králík *et al*, *Civil Code III. Property Rights* (§ 976–1474), 2nd edition, CH Beck, 2021, p1554.

2.5 Other documents

Along with the above documents, other optional agreements are often concluded. The founder and the future trustee frequently enter into an agreement whereby the founder provides the trustee with some form of indemnity. Such arrangements may include an undertaking by the founder to provide for the funding of the trust should it fail to be sufficiently funded or otherwise to support the trust. In some cases, the founder undertakes to pay the trustee's remuneration out of their own funds (ie, not out of the assets in the trust). All such arrangements are merely bilateral contractual obligations and cannot be construed as rules of the trust itself. They are governed by the general rules of contract law. It may be noted that this type of agreement often raises doubts as to its compatibility with the trustee's duties, and in particular with the requirement of his or her independence. Trust structures often arise within the broader structure of family wealth management, and family philanthropic foundations or family offices may be set up alongside them. The range of documents relating to these structures is very wide, and it is beyond the scope of this chapter to describe them, but they include family charters, founder's principles of conduct and founder's wishlist.[12]

3. Registering the trust

3.1 Register of Trusts

An *inter vivos* trust is created only by registration in the Register of Trusts. The registration of trusts is based on the same principles as the registration of legal persons (which is regulated by the same statute);[13] however, registration of trusts has limited public exposure and therefore much less information about trusts is available to the public than about legal persons.[14] Only the date of registration, the name of the trust, the definition of its purpose, the date of its creation (and termination), its identification number and the identification of its trustee are publicly available.[15] Information about the founder, beneficiaries and protectors (or other persons entrusted with overseeing the administration of the trust), although recorded in the Register of Trusts, is not publicly available (unless the persons concerned specifically request it). It can only be inspected by public authorities and persons conducting client reviews in accordance with AML regulations.

---

12 See also M Gruna and K Ronovská, "Governance around family wealth: How to preserve a long-term value for families?", *Trusts & Trustees*, Oxford University Press, 2023, Vol 30, Issue 1, pp1–8.

13 Act No 304/2013 Coll, on Public Registers of Legal and Natural Persons and on Registration of Trusts.

14 The public part of the Register of Trusts is available at: https://esf.justice.cz/ias/isesf/rejstrik. It is noted that the method of searching the Register of Trusts is limited compared to the Register of Legal Persons, as it can only be searched by the name of the trust or its identification number, but no longer by the name of the trustee.

15 In addition, information on any transfer or pledge of the trust's enterprise or information on trust's insolvency is publicly available.

The Register of Trusts includes a collection of deeds. In particular, it is compulsory to file the trust's statute, proof of the appointment or removal of a trustee, a decision on the dissolution of the trust, financial statements and (somewhat surprisingly) all contracts by which any property is contributed to the trust. If any document filed in a document collection contains information about persons that is not publicly available (see above), then that document is not publicly available either. In practice, the only documents available are usually the financial statements, but sometimes not even these. Failure to file any of the required documents other than the statute, which is required in order to register the trust, has no immediate consequences.[16] This means that these obligations are probably not regularly fulfilled.

A strange provision in the Civil Code, according to which the appointment or other designation of a beneficiary of a trust established for a private purpose is effective only on the date on which the beneficiary is entered in the Register of Trusts (Section 1457(3) of the Civil Code),[17] causes problems in practice. It means that it is a condition of the payment of any benefit from the trust that the beneficiary be registered in the Register of Trusts, which in turn raises a number of difficulties, particularly in the case of discretionary trusts, where beneficiaries are appointed even for the payment of a one-off benefit (and it is not clear whether they should be removed from the register again once the benefit has been provided). One may even encounter notaries who make the entry of the beneficiary in the register conditional on their written consent, which is usually not practical, especially for minors. Banks also often require beneficiaries to be entered in the Register of Trusts when they set up bank accounts for the benefit of the trust. We consider such a requirement to be unjustified.[18]

An application for registration of a trust in the Register of Trusts is made by the trustee. He or she may submit an application to the registry court or use the option of direct registration through a notary. In practice, all trusts are probably registered through a notary, to whom it is necessary to go to draw up the statutes anyway. The notary will usually enter the trust into the Register of Trusts on the same day that the statute is drawn up (and the trust deed is executed).

3.2 Register of Beneficial Owners

Like other EU member states, the Czech Republic introduced, in the course of the implementation of the 4th Anti-Money Laundering Directive ('the AML

16 Only failure to comply with the court's request that the missing documents be added to the document collection is sanctioned.

17 See Appendix I.

18 It is an incorrect application of Section 12 of Act No 304/2013 Coll which applies only to entries in the publicly accessible register (data on beneficiaries is not publicly accessible).

Directive'),[19] a Register of Beneficial Owners (of corporate and other legal entities) which is regulated by a special statute of 2021.[20] The law, in accordance with the AML Directive, declares the founder and the trustee to be beneficial owners. It treats the protector (or persons entitled to supervise the administration of the trust) as the beneficial owner only if they can appoint or remove a trustee or beneficiary. Any beneficiary is also one of a trust's beneficial owners.

A natural person who has been entered in the Register of Trusts as a founder, trustee or nominee is automatically entered in the Register of Beneficial Owners as the beneficial owner of the trust. If the founder of the trust is a legal person, the beneficial owner of such legal person is automatically entered as the beneficial owner of the trust. However, if the trustee of the trust has its seat or registered office abroad, there is no such automatic transcription (on the status of trusts with a foreign aspect, see below). The beneficial owners of trusts whose trustees are domiciled in the Czech Republic are therefore automatically entered into the Register of Beneficial Owners upon the trust's creation or entry into the Register of Trusts, and any subsequent change to the relevant entry in the Register of Trusts is automatically reflected in the Register of Beneficial Owners.

The trustee of the trust is obliged to ensure that the Register of Beneficial Owners includes the other beneficial owners of the trust whose details are not automatically copied from the Register of Trusts. Protectors are considered by Czech law to be the ultimate owners of the trust only if they can decide on the appointment of the trustee or appoint beneficiaries. As the rules of trusts can be relatively complex, doubts sometimes arise in practice as to what specific aspects of these rights already qualify the protector as the beneficial owner (for example, whether a right of veto is sufficient). Given that the AML Directive considers protectors to be beneficial owners without further qualification, it is probably appropriate to interpret Czech law broadly in this respect.

Some doubt arises in practice whether persons who are part of the group from which a beneficiary may be appointed – usually an issue with discretionary trusts – should be registered in the Register of Beneficial Owners. In fact, the law is worded in such a way that the ultimate owner is each one of the group of persons in whose main interest the trust was established.[21] However, we consider (*inter alia*, with reference to the AML Directive)[22] that only those beneficiaries to whom the right to receive the benefit has already

19 Directive (EU) 2015/849 of the European Parliament and of the Council of 20 May 2015 on the prevention of the use of the financial system for the purposes of money laundering or terrorist financing. Available at: https://eur-lex.europa.eu/legal-content/EN/TXT/?uri=celex%3A32015L0849.

20 Act No 37/2021 Coll, on the Register of Beneficial Owners.

21 See Section 6(3)(e) of the Act on the Register of Beneficial Owners.

22 See the Article 31(1) of the AML Directive where only "the beneficiaries or class of beneficiaries" are mentioned.

accrued (and therefore to whom the benefit has been or is to be unconditionally paid) should be registered.

Unlike information on beneficial owners of legal entities, information on beneficial owners of trusts is available to the public only to the extent that it is publicly available in the Register of Trusts. Other information about the beneficial owners of a trust will be made available by the registry court only to those who demonstrate an interest related to AML measures.

3.3 Registration for corporate income tax

Although in terms of private law a Czech trust does not have legal personality, public law often views it as a (tax) subject. The trust is thus a separate accounting entity and a payer of corporate income or other taxes. The trust is obliged to apply for registration for corporate income tax within 15 days of its establishment. All Czech trusts are registered with the Tax Office for the City of Prague. (For more on the tax regime, see the chapter "Taxation of trusts", by Ivan Kovář.)

4. Trust in legal relations

Ownership rights to property in a Czech trust are exercised by the trustee in his own name on behalf of the trust (Section 1448(3) of the Civil Code).[23] It follows that the trustee is not an agent, but acts alone on behalf of the trust. This power is connected with the exercise of their office and if they cease to exercise it, they also lose this power. Although not expressly provided for in law, the trustee also performs in their own name on behalf of the trust the debtor's obligations in respect of debts incurred in connection with the administration of the trust. The concept of a Czech trust as an autonomous patrimony implies that, in addition to the property, it also includes debts, and just as the property is not the trustee's personal property, neither are the debts the trustee's personal debts.

All contracts and other legal acts on behalf of the trust must be carried out by the trustee or a person authorised by the trustee. It should then be clear from the act that the person acting is doing so on behalf of the trust; if this is not clear, creditors may also seek satisfaction against the trustee personally (ie, from his or her personal assets). The trustee shall be entered in the public register or other records as the owner of the property in the trust with the notation 'trustee'. If the trust has more than one trustee, they should all be entered.

In everyday life, it is often the case that a trust is referred to as if it were a legal entity. Some legal acts are then incorrectly referred to as acts of the trust (eg, the trust is referred to as a party to a contract or as a principal on a power of attorney). Such situations should be resolvable by a standard interpretation of

23 See Appendix I.

the content of the act in question. Moreover, the Czech Civil Code has a rule according to which "if a person creates a right or imposes an obligation on what is not a person, the right or obligation is attributed to the person to whom it belongs according to the legal nature of the case" (Section 17(2) of the Civil Code).[24] This should at least be applicable to trusts.[25]

5. Foreign trusts in the Czech Republic

Certain requirements are imposed by Czech legislation on foreign trusts or trusts with a foreign element. The Act on Private International Law simply states that a trust or some similar instrument governed by foreign law shall be recognised under Czech law as long as it manifests the essential elements required for such an instrument under Czech law.[26] The prevailing view is that those essential elements could be the characteristics of trusts set out in The Hague Convention on the Law Applicable to Trusts and on their Recognition of 1985, to which the Czech Republic is not a party, but to which the explanatory memorandum to the Act on Private International Law nevertheless refers.[27] If a foreign trust structure meets these criteria, Czech law will consider it a valid foreign trust.

Czech law requires that recognised foreign trusts operating within the territory of the Czech Republic are registered in the Register of Trusts. This qualification is met by any trust that satisfies one (or more) of the following material conditions:[28]

- it is administered from the Czech Republic;
- it is constituted by assets located primarily within the territory of the Czech Republic;
- it administers some real estate entered in the Land Registry;
- its trustee or a person in a similar position has their permanent residence or registered office in the Czech Republic;
- its trustee or a person in a similar position with respect to the property administered has established a business relationship in the Czech Republic; or
- the purposes for which the trust has been set up are to be achieved within the territory of the Czech Republic.

If the trustee of a foreign trust is based outside the European Union, the

---

24 Available (Czech language only) at: www.zakonyprolidi.cz/cs/2012-89#cast5.

25 However, the Supreme Court, in its decision of 31 August 2023, Case No 33 Cdo 456/2022, essentially confirmed that a power of attorney "granted by a trust" is an apparent legal act, as the power of attorney for representation is granted by a non-entity. However, we consider this statement to be somewhat in error, and this has been confirmed in discussions with other Supreme Court judges.

26 Section 73(4) of the Act No 91/2012 Coll, on Private International Law.

27 K Ronovská and V Pihera, "Foreign trusts in the Czech Republic: mostly recognised and (sometimes) registered", *Trusts & Trustees*, Oxford University Press, 2020, Vol 26, No 6, pp527–533.

28 Section 65a(2) of the Act No 304/2013 Coll, *supra* note 13.

information about the foreign trust from the Register of Trusts is automatically entered into the Register of Beneficial Owners.[29] Beneficial owners of foreign trusts whose trustees are established in another EU member state should be recorded in the Register of Beneficial Owners in that member state. It may be noted that if a trust established under Czech law has a trustee who is not domiciled in the Czech Republic, the data on its beneficial owners are entered into the Czech Register of Beneficial Owners only if it meets the above-mentioned conditions for registration of foreign trusts.

29 Section 12(2) of the Act No 37/2021 Coll, *supra* note 20.

How trusts are used in the Czech Republic

Helena Svárovská
J&T Family Office

1. Introduction

To our knowledge there has been no comprehensive study or formal research conducted on how trusts are being used in the Czech Republic. For this reason, some of the information in this chapter is based on our observations with our own clients and on the shared experiences of other practitioners.

Trusts have a relatively short history in the Czech Republic, the first being established around 2014, and we are still far from reaching saturation point in terms of both public and professional awareness of this legal tool and how it can be used. However, even over this relatively short 10-year period, it is possible to identify some evolutionary trends in the way trusts are used.

Trusts were almost not used at all. In the first three years, just 214 were established.[1] There was considerable mistrust of this new legal tool. Many believed, and some still believe, that trusts primarily serve as tools to hide assets from the state or spouses, or as mechanisms for receiving bribes. There was a degree of uncertainty as to whether trusts would be retained. So perhaps we can say that these very early adopters were brave adventurers with a pioneering spirit, and that many of those 214 trusts operated as test cases, established by lawyers and others with the objective of exploring how well the new tool operated in practice before recommending its use to clients. And indeed, at that time trusts did not operate very well at a practical level. There were significant challenges when presenting this new and largely unknown legal instrument to banks, to state registries and to counterparties. These challenges were compounded by a trust's lack of legal personality and the fact that at first, trusts did not even have state-issued identification numbers.

In the next period, from 2017 to 2020, the predominant use of trusts was for asset protection, especially by the owners of smaller, but perhaps higher-risk, businesses in areas such as tourism and property development. The main asset held in these trusts was owner-occupied residential real estate.

However, since 2020 there has been a clear shift towards the use of trusts for

1 M Šindelář and T Čudová, "Trust funds in the Czech Republic", *Czech Financial and Accounting Journal*, 2020, Vol 15, Issue 3–4, p46.

more traditional purposes. Businesses, families and their advisers have become increasingly comfortable with trusts. As a result, the previously dominant asset protection focus has faded slightly, replaced by a recognition that trusts can be an excellent tool for solving inheritance, as well as family and business succession, challenges.

In this chapter we focus on the primary uses of trusts and explain client motivations and objectives. However, the possible uses of trusts are limited only by the imagination and creativity of the professionals who design them, and there are plenty of examples of trusts being used to achieve a wide range of less standard objectives, so we will also look at some examples of these less common uses. We conclude by looking at things that Czech trusts cannot – or should not – be used to do.

2. Primary uses of trusts in the Czech Republic

2.1 Asset protection

This, as mentioned above, is where the Czech trust started, and although other objectives such as inheritance are now the primary drivers, asset protection remains important to many clients as an 'add-on extra'.

Practitioners from other jurisdictions will already be familiar with asset protection trusts, so here we concentrate on the unique features of Czech implementation of the concept.

An asset protection trust is designed to safeguard an individual's assets from potential risks such as creditors, lawsuits and financial instability. Assets placed in the trust are no longer the property of the client and therefore, at least in theory, they should be ringfenced and protected in situations such as bankruptcy, lawsuits and divorce.

In the Czech Republic this model is reinforced by the wording of the Civil Code which says, at Section 1448(3), that "the property in a trust is not owned by the trustee or the founder, or the person entitled to receive performance from the trust".[2]

If property is not owned by anyone, then how can it be contested? However, in the Czech Republic, as elsewhere in the world, it is not quite that simple.

The courts can claw back dispositions of property in some cases. Subject to time limits, these powers can be applied especially in cases where the court believes a transaction prefers one party over another, is completed at below market value or is intended to disadvantage creditors. This is compounded by the fact that transfers into trusts are typically gratuitous. The courts can also look through or even set aside the trust itself in some circumstances, including where they consider the trust to be an artificial construct.

2 See Appendix I.

So far there have been only a limited number of court decisions in this area,[3] and not from the highest courts. There is nothing we have yet seen that would enable us to specify a set of criteria for how such powers might be exercised in the case of trusts; however, what is clear is that the courts are prepared to exercise these powers in principle.

Because of this, we believe that Czech asset protection trusts should be designed with caution, noting especially the following:

- The longer the trust is established before the problems arise the better. Like good wine, asset protection trusts improve with age.
- There should be good apparent motivation for establishing the trust, such as inheritance planning. Asset protection should not be identifiable as the primary or only purpose.
- There must be clear alienation of control. This means that the founder most certainly should not be a trustee, and that ideally the power of appointment of trustees in the trust documents should not be vested in the founder.
- The trust documents must not attempt to create a revocable structure or otherwise provide the founder with an easy way to reclaim trust assets.
- The trust needs to be properly administered so that the record keeping reinforces that the trust is being administered by the trustees (and not the founder).
- Ideally, the founder should not be a beneficiary of the trust.

If these rules are followed it would be our expectation that a well-designed asset protection trust is likely to be effective in the long term – subject to the caveat that there are still many unknowns, especially in relation to the approach of the courts. Sadly, our experience is that the majority of so-called asset protection trusts so far established in the Czech Republic fail to observe these rules and may therefore also fail to protect client assets.

This is an evolving area which will be developed further in the years ahead as we receive guidance from the courts.

2.2 Inheritance

(a) Forced heirship

Trusts are now widely used to solve inheritance problems. In sections 2.2(b) and (c) below, we focus on two examples:

---

3 Some examples (this is not an exhaustive list) include: Resolution of the Municipal Court in Prague No 253 Icm 2268/2022-17 of 31 August 2022; Resolution of the High Court in Prague No 101 VSPH 925/2022-37 of 5 January 2023; Resolution of the Municipal Court in Prague No 205 Icm 2629/2021-10 of 24 September 2021; and Resolution of the High Court in Prague No 103 VSPH 904/2021-53 of 9 December 2021.

- mixed families; and
- generation skipping.

There are other ways that trusts can be used in the area of inheritance, but by analogy these two examples will illustrate more general usage.

First, however, we should establish what is meant by forced inheritance or, sometimes, forced heirship. These terms describe rules that govern the distribution of an individual's estate upon their death and specify, in particular, that certain close relatives, typically children or spouses, are entitled to inherit a certain portion of the deceased person's estate, regardless of the deceased person's wishes as expressed in a will or other testamentary document.

The purpose of forced inheritance is to protect the interests of close family members, particularly minor children or surviving spouses, by ensuring that they receive a minimum share of the estate.

The specific rules governing Czech forced inheritance are set out in the Civil Code and especially at Section 1643(2), which states:

> *If a forced heir is a minor, he must inherit at least three-quarters of his statutory inheritance share. If the forced heir is an adult, he must inherit at least a quarter of his statutory inheritance share.*[4]

The legal inheritance share is defined based on the structure of the deceased's family and is set out in more detail in Sections 1633–1641.[5]

What this means in practice is that even if the client makes a will, he or she cannot completely cut out certain people – and most especially not children or spouse. On paper, that sounds like a reasonable and sensible rule, and indeed it works well for the average family. However, particularly in the case of mixed families and generation skipping, it can lead to problematic outcomes, and that is where trusts come into play. It is important to point out that it is not written anywhere that a settlement of funds on a trust takes precedence over forced inheritance, and there is no legal clarity on this point one way or the other. Thus, a disposition to a trust *mortis causa* may not be any more effective a tool for solving forced inheritance problems than a will.

On the other hand, there is every reason to hope that a transfer of assets to a trust which occurs *inter vivos*, and ideally many years in advance of death, and which involves the valid transfer of legal title, will be effective except in the most egregious of cases.

(b) *Mixed families*

Mixed families are very common in the Czech Republic and are one example of

---

4 See Appendix I.

5 Sections 1633–1641 of the Czech Civil Code. Available (Czech language only) at: www.zakonyprolidi.cz/cs/2012-89#cast5.

where forced heirship goes wrong. By mixed families we refer to families that include children from previous relationships.

Let's take an imaginary client, David.

David was married to Anna and had three children with her. Some years ago, he and Anna went through a bitter divorce. Since then, David has remarried. Anna has custody of the three minor children, but David and his new wife Klara spend every second weekend and some holidays with them.

David and Klara both contribute financially to their new family. They live in a nice house which David already owned before they got married.

Unfortunately, David unexpectedly dies.

If David has no will, then standard intestacy rules will apply, and Klara and the three children will each inherit their 'statutory inheritance share', in this case one-quarter of David's assets.[6] Because David brought the house into the marriage, it is not matrimonial property. That means that the entire house will also be subject to this quarter/quarter/quarter/quarter split.

That means that in effect Anna, as the surviving legal guardian of the three children, will indirectly have 75% control over David and Klara's house, leaving Klara with a 25% minority interest only. This compounds an already tragic situation for Klara. Anna may be cooperative, but she might also force the sale of the house. What then happens if Klara remarries?

David could have made a will, but this would do little to solve the problem as the minor children must still receive three-quarters of their quarter share, or 18.7% each.

A trust is one tool that can be used to address the dilemma.[7] A trust can be used to provide Klara with a life interest in the house (and perhaps some other assets), with the residue then passing to the children on her death.

Dealing with this and similar problems is now a significant use of trusts in the Czech Republic.

(c) Generation skipping

Another, similar, use of trusts is by parents who consider their adult children to be unsuitable heirs due, for example, to problems with poor relationships, substance abuse, financial irresponsibility or otherwise.

In this scenario, the parents typically prefer their wealth to be redirected and used to ensure a good education for their grandchildren and to give them every opportunity for a good start in life, with the main assets of the trust being passed to them when they become responsible adults (for example, at age 25).

---

6 Section 1635(1) of the Czech Civil Code. Available (Czech language only) at: www.zakonyprolidi.cz/cs/2012-89#cast5.

7 Another is fiduciary succession. See Czech Civil Code, Sections 1512–1524. Available (Czech language only) at: www.zakonyprolidi.cz/cs/2012-89#cast5.

This desire to skip the generation and pass wealth directly on to grandchildren would normally be frustrated by the forced heirship rules, but a trust can make it possible.

There are numerous other situations where the forced inheritance rules can lead to problematic outcomes – for example, for LGBT couples. Trusts can, and do, provide one of the sets of tools that can be used to address the problems.

2.3 Family wealth and business succession

In recent years, trusts have started to gain in popularity with wealthy families who are seeking to move inheritance strategies to the next level, solve the transfer of assets or secure the needs of relatives, children and future generations. The most common transferors are individuals, founders who began building their wealth in the 1990s.

Currently, given their own age and the age of their children, they are starting to give serious thought to how best to pass their businesses and their wealth on to the next generation. The COVID-19 pandemic and the death of billionaire Petr Kellner also made business owners and other asset holders realise their mortality, and this has led to the development of comprehensive family succession solutions, typically involving a family constitution and the establishment of family councils, assemblies, or other governance as a platform for open communication, collaboration and decision making. This has also involved the formulation of detailed business succession plans, and often the creation of family financial dynasties. These models are not dramatically different to those used in other jurisdictions. Trusts are just one of a suite of tools that can form a part of these solutions.

While such trusts are relatively small in number, the amount of money held in them is substantial.

These trusts also deliver a key societal benefit to the Czech Republic. We know from international evidence that without trust-based succession plans many businesses do not survive the transition from the first generation to the second – let alone the third. Without trusts and associated tools there would be an enormous loss, not just of accumulated family wealth, but also of the business enterprises themselves upon which that wealth was built. That, in turn, would have significant negative impacts on the Czech economy.

Despite the increased interest in the process of transferring wealth to the next generations, there remain barriers that deter transferors. The most commonly cited is that business and entrepreneurship are an important part of founders' lives, and they do not want to part with either. Furthermore, it is often mentioned that the transfer is not urgent and can easily be postponed, and that founders do not want to lose their influence on the management of the company and their social status. Last but not least, many fear the conflicts that the transfer process might bring.

As time passes and as we benefit from more court rulings, more knowledge and experience, we expect this use of trusts to become even more important.

2.4 Family business holding structures

Holding structures play a crucial role in modern business structures, facilitating the ownership and control of multiple subsidiary companies.

Trusts are becoming more popular as holding structures, especially for family enterprises. They enable businesses to become truly family owned and offer efficient control, decision making and protection of assets, as well as full integration with family governance structures.

3. Other (less common) uses

3.1 Art collections

Preserving the integrity of an art collection using a trust is a strategic approach that can address various concerns including conservation, succession planning and public access. Depending on the size and nature of the collection, a standalone trust can be created to deal specifically with the collection. Alternatively, special provisions related to the collection can be included in a family's core trust structure.

In either case, the trust can allocate funds for regular maintenance, restoration and conservation efforts to ensure the longevity and quality of the art. A professional art curator can be appointed to oversee the trust's activities, ensuring that best practice is followed in caring for the art. The trust can also include specific provisions to ensure that the collection is treated with care, preventing actions that could damage or devalue the artworks.

If the collection is a family asset, the trust can be structured to maintain ownership within the family across generations. This helps avoid potential disputes over ownership and ensures that the collection remains a family legacy. Fractional ownership through a trust can allow multiple family members to enjoy and share responsibility for the collection, avoiding the need for a single heir to manage the entire collection. The trust can ensure that the collection contributes to the cultural enrichment of the community by providing money for educational programmes and exhibitions.

The trust documents of such a trust will outline conditions under which the art may be sold, loaned or transferred, ensuring that all decisions align with founders' wishes.

3.2 Cottages

Many Czech families own 'cottages'. This term seems to cover a very wide range of buildings ranging in size from small sheds on tiny plots of land through to palatial buildings on large country estates.

Whatever their size, what these cottages have in common is a very close and often emotional connection to families. Memories of past holidays and hopes that children and grandchildren will share similar memories are common.

Perhaps more than any other asset, these cottages are seen as truly 'family' property. At the same time, the prime location of some of this real estate means that values can be substantial. Children and subsequent generations have different needs and priorities. Some will want to keep the story going and enjoy the cottage themselves, together with their children. Others will move too far away, or simply decide that the countryside is not for them. Others still may simply focus on the money, and demand that the cottage be sold, and the proceeds distributed.

These conflicting feelings and objectives can seem almost inevitable. A trust is used in such cases not just to keep the cottage in the family but, as with the art collection, to set rules for its ongoing management and maintenance. In most cases the trust is established by the parents as they age in order to anticipate and prevent future conflict; however, we have also seen cases where subsequent generations have collectively established such trusts.

3.3 Religious communities

Religious communities around the world use trusts to own some of their core assets. Since 2014 we have seen some evidence that the same thing is happening the Czech Republic. The capacity of Czech trusts to be directed towards achieving a specific purpose is key. This makes it possible to do things in a Czech context that are not always so easily done elsewhere.

By placing core assets – land, farms, forests and buildings – into trusts, the communities are able to dedicate them fully to their believers and to the purposes espoused by the particular religion. While the religious organisation typically retains some level of control over the governance of such trusts, it is also common to see ordinary members of the church playing an active role, whether as members of supervisory boards, boards of trustees, or otherwise.

The end result is that the assets cease to be controlled by people or even by organisations. Instead, they are now controlled by communities, by principles and by ideas.

3.4 Charity

In a Czech context, the structures that are most commonly used for charitable giving and philanthropy are foundations rather than trusts.

Czech foundations have a longer history than trusts. Their current iteration is governed by the Civil Code[8] but their existence dates back to before the new Civil Code was enacted in 2014.[9]

---

8 At Sections 306–393. Available (Czech language only) at: www.zakonyprolidi.cz/cs/2012-89#cast5.

9 Foundations established pursuant to Act No 227/1997 Coll on Foundations and Endowment Funds, which was in effect until the end of 2013, continue to exist and are considered foundations under the Czech Civil Code.

These institutions, rooted in philanthropy and benevolence, are fundamental to addressing social issues, promoting education and healthcare, and alleviating poverty. However, creating a foundation is expensive and cumbersome, in terms of both initial set-up and ongoing maintenance and administration. As a result, for those seeking to achieve a philanthropic purpose, foundations are within the reach only of wealthy families willing to dedicate substantial assets and resources.

Trusts are not as well suited to philanthropic purposes as foundations. Foundations are designed specifically with social good in mind and the tax treatment of trusts established for charitable purposes is not quite as attractive as it is for foundations. Having said that, the Civil Code specifically provides that trusts can be established for publicly beneficial purposes.[10] Trusts are less complex and cheaper to establish and manage than foundations. One illustration of this is the requirement for a foundation with assets in excess of CZK 5 million to have not just a foundation council with at least three members, but also a three-member supervisory board.[11] In contrast, it would be possible (although perhaps not a good idea) to establish a publicly beneficial trust with just one trustee and no supervisory body at all.

As well as standalone trusts designed to achieve charitable aims, it is not uncommon for families to include a philanthropic aspect in their private family trust structures. This is typically seen in two variants:

- *Power to make charitable donations:* This is a specific power for the trustees of a private family trust to make charitable donations or to contribute towards a charitable purpose. Such powers need to be specifically included in the trust statute and are also typically subject to further regulation in the family constitution and/or the founder's letter of wishes. These powers are also normally expressed as secondary. That means that the trustees can dedicate money to the charitable aspects only if and to the extent that doing so does not obstruct the private family goals. In other words, the family comes first.
- *'Beneficiary of last resort':* Section 1472 of the Civil Code[12] provides that if, on termination of a trust, there are no beneficiaries and no founder, then the assets of the trust belong to the state. In order to prevent this happening, many families include charitable organisations or charitable purposes in their trust instruments.

3.5 Disabled children

Creating a trust to protect and provide for a disabled child after the death of

10 Civil Code Section 1449(1). See Appendix I.
11 Civil Code Section 368(2). Available (Czech language only) at: www.zakonyprolidi.cz/cs/2012-89#cast5.
12 See Appendix I.

parents is a common strategy internationally which is also now being used in the Czech Republic. In this context, the word 'child' is a little misleading since many of the subjects of these trusts are in fact legally adult, but nevertheless not able to independently manage their own financial affairs.

These trusts are designed to provide dedicated funds to cover the disabled child's ongoing and future needs, including medical care, housing, education and other essential expenses, especially in periods when parents are no longer able to do so.

The Czech Republic has an excellent guardianship system to protect and care for these children once parents have passed on. The trust is not designed to replace, but rather to supplement that system. The trustees of the trust become instead 'financial guardians' who are tasked with ensuring that the assets in the trust are used appropriately and that the child's best interests are always considered. The trust documents can specify the conditions under which distributions are made. This allows the parents to maintain control over how the funds are used and ensures that they are used in ways that enhance the disabled child's quality of life. If there are other siblings or family members, the trust can be a tool to equalise inheritances while still providing for the unique needs of the disabled child.

The trustees of such trusts often work closely with relevant social organisations who are best able to understand the child's needs. Following the child's death, these organisations can sometimes be the beneficiary of any remaining assets in the trust, while in other cases money is redistributed amongst other family members.

3.6 Business trusts

Trusts are also used in the Czech Republic for business purposes.

Internationally, trusts are widely used as a tool to achieve business objectives. Prior to 2014 trusts were not available in the Czech Republic, yet Czech businesses faced a similar set of challenges to businesses in other jurisdictions. As a result, the Czech business community and its professional advisers found alternative ways of achieving those objectives.

However, in 2014, trusts were added to the Czech business toolbox, and they are starting to be used in a number of situations.

As with the business families we mentioned above, this transition is taking a little time, and is reliant on increased awareness, familiarity and confidence in trusts. Sometimes (but not always) trusts offer a better way of doing things than traditional models.

Four of the most interesting such alternative models are set out here. There are others.

(a) *Share option schemes*

Using trusts provides business owners with a great way of recognising and rewarding the contribution of key employees. In the past, contractual arrangements were used to achieve this, but there is an increasing realisation that trusts provide a better and more flexible solution. Most importantly, using a trust obviates the need for frequent and complex changes to the commercial register and prevents the loss of owner access to voting rights attached to shares. The use of trusts in this way is gradually increasing as business owners become aware of the relative advantages.

(b) *Voting share trusts*

Trusts can be used to hold a single share but with 100% of the voting rights. This is an interesting way of separating the control and ownership of a company.

(c) *Employee welfare schemes*

In this model, trusts are used as a vehicle to provide employees with off-balance sheet and non-standard benefits. These usually supplement and sit alongside more traditional employee benefit structures and are designed to provide staff members and their families with crisis support and salary continuance in the event of serious illness, such as cancer or long-term disability. This is a relatively low-cost benefit, but one that is highly valued by employees.

(d) *Consumer protection*

The last, but perhaps most important, use of trusts in business in the Czech Republic is for consumer protection – especially in the situation where a consumer is paying a large amount in advance for products or services that will not be delivered until later. Examples include music festivals, real estate development and package holidays. The objective of such a trust is to hold the money in a protected account until such time as the product or service is delivered. If, in the meantime, the provider goes bankrupt or delivery of the services is cancelled for whatever reason, the money is returned to the consumer.

Before trusts were introduced there was no robust mechanism at all in the Czech legal system for delivering this protection other than relatively expensive insurance. Some lawyers recommended escrow accounts, but in the event of the bankruptcy of the provider, the money in escrow was not protected since there was no valid transfer of legal title.

So far, only a very small number of trusts have been created for this purpose (we estimate less than 10), but the money they hold counts in the billions of Czech crowns.

3.7 Qualified investor funds

Finally, trusts can be used as qualified investor funds under the Act on Collective Investments. However, we are not aware of widespread usage of trusts in this way.[13]

4. Things trusts are not used for

4.1 Anonymity

Trusts in other justifications can sometimes be used with the objective of providing the founder and his or her family with an increased level of anonymity. While Czech trusts do offer some reasonable protection of personal and family privacy, it seems unlikely that a client whose primary goal was anonymity would select a Czech trust.

In particular, all details of the trust are fully available to the state and state organs through the Register of Trusts, the Register of Beneficial Owners and the records held by the tax office.

The wider public, and especially those with a legitimate interest (including potentially journalists) can also access a more limited set of information. For more on this see the chapter, "UBO Register and Register of Trusts".

4.2 Tax planning

Unlike in some other jurisdictions, trusts in the Czech Republic do not offer significant opportunities for tax planning.

The tax treatment of trusts is covered in Ivan Kovář's chapter, "Taxation of trusts", but in a nutshell, trusts are taxed much like companies, and some of the tools (eg, income allocation) that make trusts more attractive in other jurisdictions are not available in the Czech Republic.

It is true that in a number of very specific situations, trusts can offer some limited tax and tax deferral benefits, but these are marginal, and we do not believe they would be sufficient on their own to justify establishing a trust.

For some clients, trusts can in fact be disadvantageous from a tax perspective with respect to personal ownership of assets. This applies especially in cases where the trust is intended to hold investment assets. This is discussed in the next section.

4.3 Investment holding

Because trusts are subject to the corporate tax regime, holding investment portfolios is rarely the primary purpose of a trust.

---

13 For details, see Sections 148–153 of the Act on Collective Investments. Available to download as a Word file from: www.mfcr.cz/assets/attachments/2023-04-13_Act-on-Investment-Companies-and-Investment-Funds.docx.

The reason is simple. An investment owned directly by a client is subject to personal income tax at his or her personal tax rate. Such a personal holding also benefits from exemption from tax on realisation of profits, provided they are held for a sufficient period and certain other conditions are met.

In contrast, trusts are subject to corporate income tax on their income. Then, when distributions are made to beneficiaries, there is another layer of taxation (withholding tax). In very simplistic terms this means that there is a kind of double tax on such investment profits. The holding period exemption mentioned above is also not available to trusts.

Having said that, we have seen clients who are prepared to place investment assets on trust. This typically happens when the primary purpose and the resulting benefits are sufficient in the client's mind to offset a more unfavourable tax outcome.

Individual vs corporate trustees in the Czech Republic

Michaela Dražková
Petr Laštovka
EMUN

1. Introduction

In this chapter, we discuss trustees in the Czech context, comparing the requirements for individual and corporate trustees. Within our practice, the focus is primarily on the use of trusts for the purpose of family arrangement of property, including succession, and although a trust can theoretically have any purpose, we do not examine philanthropic structures or investment schemes (such as pension or investment trusts).

2. Who can be a trustee?

The Czech Civil Code stipulates that any person with legal capacity may be a trustee, and Czech law separately provides for corporate trustees, but only if the law specifically permits it.

2.1 Natural person – individual trustee

The Civil Code stipulates only one condition for an individual trustee to exercise his or her role, which is the capacity to act. In contrast to the position for a statutory corporation (whose function in the context of trusts is very similar to that of an individual trustee), the Civil Code does not require the trustee to meet the good character and other requirements necessary for carrying on a trade. No qualifications or experience are required, even if the trustee performs his or her function in an entrepreneurial manner.

Potentially, with the growing number of trusts, this situation may give rise to problems in resolving disputes between the founders or beneficiaries and the trustee.

2.2 Legal entity – corporate trustee

The only law that currently permits a legal entity to act as a trustee of a trust in the Czech Republic is the Management Companies and Investment Funds Act ('the MCIF Act'),[1] which provides that a management company may be a

1 Act No 240/2013 Coll, on Management Companies and Investment Funds, as amended. A draft English translation is available at: www.mfcr.cz/assets/attachments/2023-04-13_Act-on-Investment-Companies-and-Investment-Funds.pdf. (Note: the translation refers to '*Investment* Companies and Investment Funds' – the correct translation is 'Management Companies'.)

corporate trustee if it is authorised to manage the assets of a client on a discretionary basis under a contractual arrangement (portfolio management). Very strict criteria are set out for corporate trustees, as management companies are financial institutions subject to regulation and supervision by the Czech National Bank. We discuss the specific requirements for obtaining the relevant licence in section 4.2, below.

The idea of the legislators was to ensure that the trustee would be personally liable for the performance of his or her duties, qualifying the limited liability otherwise attaching to a corporate entity. We believe that more complex trusts with a larger volume of assets under management should require high standards and qualifications for their administration, including integrity and fungibility criteria and robust internal regulations and controls, as well as requirements for risk management, compliance and internal audit. Increased security and professionalisation of trust administration will mean higher costs, but this should not necessarily be a negative for founders and beneficiaries – it is just a matter of choosing the right type of trustee for the particular situation.

2.3 Comparison with foreign jurisdictions

While in some jurisdictions the use of specialised legal entities is the predominant form of trust administration, in the Czech Republic individual trustees are dominant for the time being, with only one entity – management company EMUN – holding a corporate trustee licence as of the date of writing. EMUN has around 10 trusts under administration out of a total of approximately 6,000 created in the Czech Republic.

There is no official body in the Czech Republic with the authority to determine the professional prerequisites, or the minimum knowledge and experience, of a natural person to perform the function of a trustee.[2]

2.4 Future development of trust services in the Czech Republic

In our opinion, Czech legislation is highly contradictory in terms of the requirements for trustees, as it does not set any prerequisites for an individual trustee, whereas it sets the same conditions for corporate trustees as for financial institutions, which are among the most regulated entities given the importance of protecting the stability of financial markets.

We believe that setting minimum professional qualifications for individual trustees is a necessary prerequisite for limiting the abuse of trusts by fraudsters. Greater professionalisation of the sector could be facilitated, for example, by the international Society of Trust and Estate Practitioners (STEP), which could

---

2 A number of self-regulatory associations have been established in the Czech Republic aiming to support and develop trust administration – for example, by communicating with the public or organising educational courses – but their rules, including ethical ones, affect only their members.

provide an appropriate benchmark. For example, in the long term, we would consider that obtaining Trust and Estate Practitioner (TEP) certification is the right way to assemble a high level of professional advisers to provide trust services on a business basis. Alternatively, the Czech Republic could take the route of limiting the maximum volume of assets under administration for non-professional trustees, or trustees without minimum qualifications who do not carry out trust administration on a professional basis.

3. The founder as trustee: is this a problem?

Trust structures, like foundation structures, can be used for a variety of purposes. However, as they can play a role in succession planning, it is important to be vigilant as to the proper governance of the trust in the following areas, to ensure that the trust operates in accordance with its purpose and the law:

- the processes, procedures and rules that determine how and by whom the trust will be administered;
- how key decisions will be made;
- who will have oversight of the trust assets and with what authority; and
- the fulfilment of obligations to the beneficiaries.

The Civil Code provides that the founder or beneficiary of the trust may also be the trustee (although in the latter case the trust must have another, third-party trustee and the trustees must act together). Such a set-up can be somewhat unfortunate, as we shall see below.

In this section, we discuss the absence of ownership and asset protection, the approaches to trust governance, the risks of sham or *alter ego* structures, and how to set a reasonable level of control for the founder.

3.1 The absence of ownership and the principle of property protection

The basic characteristic of trust structures in the Czech Republic, as in some other jurisdictions,[3] is the absence of an owner, where the separation of assets from their owner creates independent ownership of the assets.[4] The ownership rights of a founder are exercised by the trustee by virtue of the performance of his or her function. Earmarked property without an owner is to be used for the benefit of clearly defined persons, present and future (for example, as yet unborn) – the beneficiaries.

Why is the idea that there is no owner important? Simply put, if the founder does not own the trust (the founder is not a shareholder), the property in the trust cannot be subject to inheritance (claims of non-passing heirs, etc), nor can

---

3 For example, Quebec.
4 Section 1448(2) of Act No 89/2012, Civil Code, as amended. See Appendix I.

it be used to satisfy claims of the founder's creditors (business creditors, governmental authorities, etc), which provides a relatively high degree of protection to the property in the trust. This is a fundamental difference from the situation where the founder contributes assets to some other structure, for example, a family holding company, as the share in the holding company or the equivalent value of the assets contributed to the holding company is still subject to the claims of any creditors.

The asset protection function focuses on the use of the trust to protect the founder's or beneficiaries' assets from various risks and includes strategies and clauses in the trust structure to minimise the risk of loss of assets due to external threats. The protection of assets greatly enhances the attractiveness of this arrangement for family succession resolution purposes. In general, therefore, as part of succession planning, we recommend that what the founders do not wish to disperse among the heirs should be placed in a trust.

However, asset protection only functions when the trust is properly set up – there must not be a 'disguised' state of affairs or an abuse of law that would cause a violation of creditors' rights, otherwise legal action, relative nullity or *proti dobrým mravům* (conflict with good morals) may apply. In the case of creditors and their claims, there is a grace period in the Czech Republic in insolvency proceedings for examining whether there has been an intentional diversion of the debtor's assets. For example, mistakes resulting from the passing of rights by a spouse are common, where assets that are part of the community of property are allocated to the trust by one spouse without the consent of the other. Less discussed, so far, in the Czech Republic is the 'disguised' situation where, although the property is formally separated from the founder, the founder still retains not only control but also dispositive rights to the property within the trust, for example, by having a formal or *de facto* veto right under the governance structure of the trust (see section 3.3 on the risk of a sham trust or *alter ego* trust).

3.2 Comparing approaches to trust governance

An individual is free to manage and dispose of his or her private property without restrictions; there are no limitations other than the obvious obligation to comply with applicable laws. That's to say, what is not forbidden is permitted.

By contrast, the assets of a corporation (for example, a joint stock company) are managed by the corporation's governing body and are intended to work primarily to generate profits benefitting the owners (shareholders). The law provides that members of governing bodies must be of good character and they are presumed to understand the business. The larger the number of shareholders – the less private the company – the greater the requirement for control mechanisms (for example, audits and audit committees, supervisory board and so on). A publicly traded company listed on a stock exchange has the highest such requirements. The duty of the governing body is to act with due care, not to favour the interests of one group of shareholders over another and to focus on asset value growth.

So how is a family trust administered, and are there parallels with a private estate and a corporation's business assets?

The handling of family property is often not strictly subject to professional management standards.[5] Emotions, the preference for good family relations over efficiency, family traditions and the authority of the head of the family all play a role. Where, in order to deal with succession issues, assets that the family is accustomed to using and administering in a certain way are set aside in a trust, there is often a tendency for the same form of administration to be exercised to some extent by the trustee. It is common to request that the gardener for the family residence should always be the gardener, regardless of cost, because the family is used to his or her presence; or that the furnishings of the house should not be insured because the family is not prepared to bear the cost; or that the administrative support of the trust should be provided by a retired family retainer or similar figure.

These wishes should be taken into account when structuring the trust, as described below. Reconciling the founder's requirements for 'usual' governance with a trustee's requirements for due care is an important element in the proper governance of the trust.

Although trusts do not have their own owners (shareholders) they are established for the benefit of a clearly defined group of individuals, the beneficiaries, who, according to the Civil Code, have the right to supervise the trust.[6] The breadth of the right of supervision and the closely related right to information can be laid out in the trust's statute. Should the beneficiaries form the view that the trustee is violating the purpose of the trust or violating the trustee's duties (eg, by acting contrary to due diligence or in violation of the rule of equal treatment, or by misusing information), they may pursue their interests in court.[7]

In practice, we often see the concept of so-called 'discretionary beneficiaries', where in order to be designated as a beneficiary, a specific person must first be named as a beneficiary based on the discretionary power of the trustee (often this happens only in relation to a specific benefit). In contrast, 'direct beneficiaries' are considered *a priori* beneficiaries (no further action by

---

5 This would be different if the administrator declared him or herself a professional within the meaning of Section 5 of the Civil Code, as amended. Available at: http://obcanskyzakonik.justice.cz/images/pdf/Civil-Code.pdf.

6 Section 1463(1) of the Civil Code, as amended. See Appendix I.

7 This right is granted under the Civil Code to the beneficiaries of a trust, but similar protection is lacking for Czech endowment funds – a consequence of the initial intention to use foundations and endowment funds in the Czech environment for philanthropic purposes, where the recipient of donations does not have and should not have the rights of a beneficiary.

the trustee is required) and their rights (including rights of supervision and information) may be more extensive. In this concept there is a parallel with corporations, where different classes of shares can be distinguished and assigned different rights, but all shareholders must be equal within a given class.

A trustee must not favour or disadvantage, without good reason, one beneficiary of the same class over another, even where the founder and his or her descendants are in the same class of beneficiaries. If the founder is to have specific rights over the other beneficiaries (reserved powers), those rights must be assigned to him or her at the level of the statute. However, it should be noted that as the number of beneficiaries or categories of beneficiaries increases, the requirements for proper governance, communication and reporting also increase.

3.3 Risk of sham trust or *alter ego* trust

One of the most complex issues in structuring a trust is the elimination of the risk of creating a sham trust, which will be declared by the court to be void *ex ante*, with all the consequences for creditors, heirs, divorcing spouses, financial authorities and so on that flow from that. Trusts may be considered to be sham trusts where the founder and the trustee together deliberately created the appearance of a trust to mislead third parties.

Trusts are considered to be *alter ego* trusts where:

- the founder has retained the same degree of control over the trust property after the trust has been created as if it were his or her personal property, such that the trust was clearly not established with the intention of separation of the property for the benefit of a wider group of beneficiaries; or
- the founder has retained too much control over the separated assets.

Alter ego trusts will be treated as though there is no material separation of the assets from the founder, and the trust structure is simply a tool to disadvantage creditors or to circumvent conflicts of interest – always a complex matter.

We believe that when establishing and structuring trusts it is necessary to balance the reserved powers of the founder very carefully, and not to recommend that the founder be one of the trustees (which is paradoxically encouraged by Czech law), let alone have a right of veto; or to combine the position of founder and sole protector (who would have the ability to remove the trustee for no reason or to veto any significant decision of the trustee).

We draw attention to the above because the principle of 'dishonest disguise' applies in the Czech Republic, where the creation of a trust to circumvent or mitigate tax or legal obligations will be assessed as circumvention of the law;

and because the Czech Republic, like most legal systems, has mechanisms to protect against abuse of law or trust structures.

The above risks in structuring trusts have their origins in a number of factors:

- The tradition of fiduciary administration in the Czech Republic is relatively recent.
- There are no minimum professional requirements for an individual trustee who carries out the activity by way of business, despite the fact that trust administration is a sophisticated activity.
- There exists no widely observed good practice in terms of administration.
- The Civil Code expressly allows the founder to be the trustee (although there must then be at least one other trustee and they must make decisions jointly), giving the founder a *de facto* veto right. The founder's veto right is one of the most significant elements present in a sham/*alter ego* trust, albeit the entire context must always be assessed.

Colleagues from Liechtenstein often wonder why Czech founders can be distrustful, perhaps expecting to be cheated instead of receiving professional services. Our experience confirms that the Czech environment is unlike that of more advanced trust jurisdictions. If Czechs are more sceptical and distrustful, this may have historical origins both in the communist past and in the 'wild 1990s', when the world of business and capital markets was rather chaotic. We therefore consider it necessary to professionalise trust services. It would be optimal to set minimum requirements for individual trustees, especially if the function is to be practised as a profession.

3.4 How to leave the founders with a reasonable degree of control

So how should founders proceed if they wish to retain a reasonable level of control over family assets, and how should trustees proceed in managing those assets and receiving contributions?

There is a simple procedure that we apply in our practice, which takes into account both the asset protection function and the risk of a sham or *alter ego* trust. The trustee makes a fair assessment with each individual asset contribution as to its ability to perform 'active' or 'passive' management. By 'active management', we mean exercising direct management of the property by keeping it on the balance sheet of the trust, the trustee thus being the direct executor of the property rights (holding the separated property, portfolio, business separately). By 'passive management' we mean having control of such an asset through an underlying entity (special purpose vehicle (SPV) or holding company), where management of the asset is exercised by the governing body of the underlying entity. The trustee should always assess whether this body has sufficient technical and professional capacity and, if it does not and cannot provide it, the trustee must refuse the contribution.

Figure 1: Active asset management

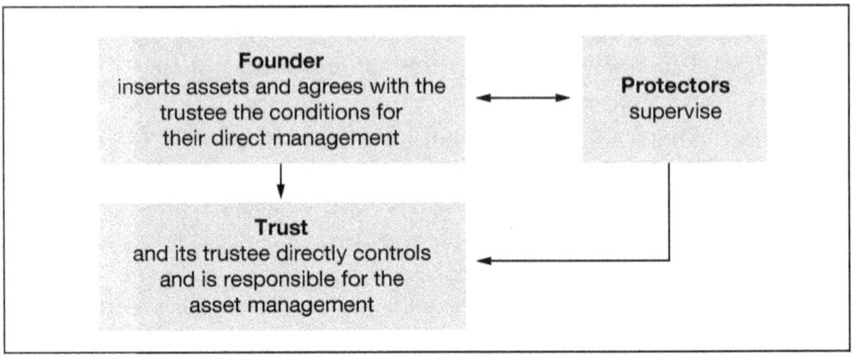

Figure 2: Passive asset management

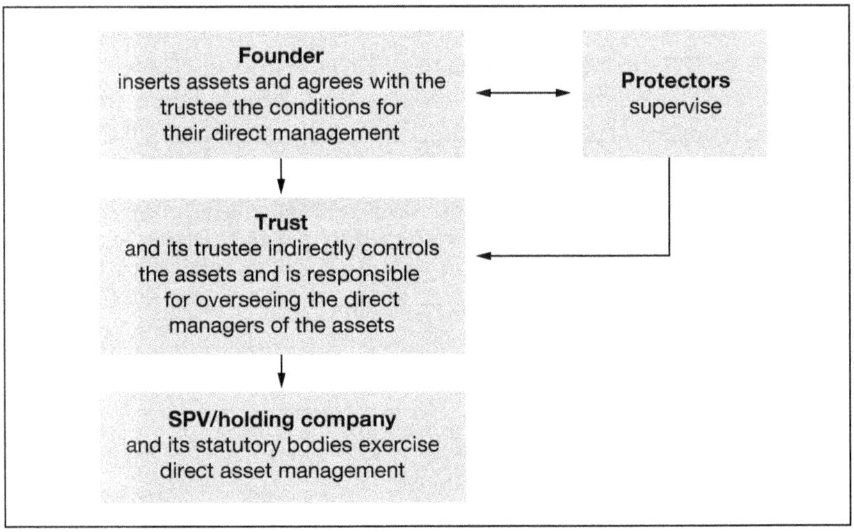

It is open to the founders, as the most frequent contributors of assets to the trust, to insert persons with the desired characteristics into the underlying entity (under the trust). A practical example might be where the founder intends to put a family business with a specific scope of business into the trust, but the trustee has no specific experience in managing such a business, or lacks the necessary qualifications. The solution may be to insert such a business not directly into the trust but into an underlying holding company, such that the governing entity will be appointed by the founders, in accordance with the 'letter of wishes' and the relevant rules created when the assets are contributed. We consider that the trustee is free to take such a wish into account if they agree with the founder's view that the person in question has the necessary professional qualifications. In our experience, it may be advisable to agree benchmarks or KPIs which the trustee must monitor in the exercise of passive administration – failure to do so may lead to difficulties and trigger an agreed 'rescue' scenario (eg, a personnel change or a decision to sell the asset).

4. Corporate trustees in the Czech Republic

As mentioned above, only a financial institution, specifically a management company, can be a corporate trustee of a trust in the Czech Republic. Management companies, of which there are fewer than 50 in the Czech Republic at the time of writing, are normally authorised to provide investment fund management and/or administration services. Only some investment companies, of which there are fewer than 15 in the Czech Republic, are authorised to offer investment services,[8] the provision of which is otherwise reserved mainly for securities brokers.[9] Permitted activities include:

- management of customer assets, including investment instruments, on a discretionary basis under contractual arrangements (ie, portfolio management);
- having custody and administration of investment instruments, including related services;[10]
- receiving and transmitting instructions relating to investment instruments; and
- providing investment advice relating to investment instruments.

4.1 The difference between a trust and an investment trust

Investment funds, in respect of which a management company has basic authority to carry out management and administration, may include investment trusts. However, these are not trusts established under the Civil Code but special trusts established under the MCIF Act.[11]

It is characteristic of an investment trust that its statute designates multiple qualified investors as beneficiaries – the founder, or individuals who have increased the assets of the trust by contract. The corollary is that beneficiaries can only be those who have contributed assets. The purpose of an investment trust is to invest on the basis of a defined investment strategy, generally based on the principle of risk spreading, for the benefit of the beneficiaries.

Paradoxically, obtaining permission to be trustee as a legal entity is far more difficult than obtaining permission to administer investment trusts. In addition

---

8 Section 11(1)(c) to (f) of the MCIF Act (*supra*, note 1).

9 For more information, see Section 4 of Act No 256/2004 Coll, on Capital Market Business, as amended. A draft translation is available at: www.mfcr.cz/assets/cs/media/Konzultace_2017_ZPKT-translation-081117.pdf.

10 However, only in relation to securities and book-entry securities issued by an investment fund or a foreign investment fund.

11 See Sections 95, 100 and 148 of the MCIF Act (*supra*, note 1).

to being authorised to carry out the management and administration of investment funds, a trustee must be authorised to exceed the 'basic relevant limit'[12] and to manage the client's assets, of which the investment vehicle is a part, on a discretionary basis under a contractual arrangement (portfolio management). In addition, authorisation can only be for an alternative fund manager under Directive 2011/61/EU on Alternative Investment Fund Managers,[13] authorised under UCTIS IV;[14] therefore, it does not apply to management companies managing standard investment funds (funds primarily intended for ordinary retail investors).[15]

In relation to this issue, we consider the terminology to be very unfortunate. The MCIF Act does not use the word 'investment' in relation to trusts created under the act, instead referring to a "trust that is not an investment fund" in relation to trusts created under the Civil Code. In view of the novelty of the legal institution of trust in the Czech Republic, and the generally low financial literacy that pertains, especially in the field of investments, we believe that the difference between a trust created under the Civil Code and an investment trust created under the MCIF Act may be obvious only to experts, and therefore it would be appropriate to make a change at the terminological level. The reason, among other things, is that in practice trusts created under the Civil Code are sometimes abused for collective investment. There are cases in which the legal institution of a trust, which should primarily serve to protect assets and resolve succession issues, has been exploited for collective investment, trusts being offered to the public as investments in the normal course of business – so-called 'Ponzi schemes'.

For the sake of completeness, we would highlight the fact that there is currently no investment trust in the Czech Republic.

4.2 Basic regulatory requirements for management companies

The management company must carry out all activities with professional care[16] and in an orderly and prudent manner, which is ensured by a management and control system that must meet the robust requirements set out in the MCIF Act and other legislation, including:

- strategic and operational management;
- an organisational structure and internal regulations;

---

12 Under Section 15 of the MCIF Act (*supra*, note 1), an amount corresponding to €100,000,000 in volume of assets under management.

13 Directive 2011/61/EU of the European Parliament and of the Council of 8 June 2011 on Alternative Investment Fund Managers and amending Directives 2003/41/EC and 2009/65/EC and Regulations (EC) No 1060/2009 and (EU) No 1095/2010 (AIFMD).

14 Directive 2009/65/EC of the European Parliament and of the Council of 13 July 2009 on the coordination of laws, regulations and administrative provisions relating to undertakings for collective investment in transferable securities (UCITS).

15 Section 11 (4) of the ICIF Act, *supra* note 1.

16 Which is a qualitatively higher requirement than the due care standard.

- a risk management system; and
- an internal control system (control of subordinates, ongoing monitoring of compliance with legal obligations and internal audit).

In general, the management and control system must be effective and comprehensive, and proportionate to the nature, scope and complexity of the activities carried out, in its entirety and in its parts; and these characteristics must be verified and regularly evaluated.

A management company must have staff and technical facilities appropriate to the nature, scale and complexity of the range of activities it carries out and shall ensure that the persons through whom it carries out its activities are trustworthy and have sufficient knowledge and experience of the procedures and regulations necessary for the proper performance of the tasks assigned to them.

A management company must have at least two senior persons on its governing body (typically the board of directors) who have sufficient experience in the performance of the activities necessary for each of the activities that the management company will undertake. These facts shall be documented in regulatory filings with the Czech National Bank or in the application for a licence. The following are the key requirements in respect of the applicant, and the documents and annexes attending the licence application:

- The applicant must be a joint stock company with its registered office in the Czech Republic, which proves the transparent and reliable origin of the capital or funds of the founders of the management company, constituting the equity capital of the management company in an amount that allows the proper performance of the activity. (The requirements for initial capital vary according to the type of licence – the minimum is €125,000.)
- There are requirements to maintain a minimum amount of capital in relation to the management company's activities, administrative expenses and depreciation and to increase capital in the context of risk management with regard to the amount of assets under management. Applications for a licence include applications for authorisation to acquire a qualifying holding for all persons who are to acquire a direct or indirect interest in the share capital or voting rights of a legal entity, or the aggregate of these representing at least 10% that makes it possible to exercise significant influence over its management.
- The applicant must demonstrate that it does not have close links with another person or that the applicant's close links with another person do not prevent the effective exercise of supervision.
- The applicant must submit an organigram that graphically shows the workforce allocation of the management company, including its managers, with regard to its internal structure, including:

- the delineation of responsibilities;
- the representation of relationships; and
- the description of functions (eg, independence, subordination, substitutability, performance, control and regulation).

The organigram is an annex to the organisational regulations, is materially based on them and is crucial for the correct setting of other internal regulations and the formulation of the business plan. This must in turn show the overall business plan of the management company, supported by realistic financial calculations including:

- a breakdown of the revenues from the individual planned services relating to the various components of the authorisation;
- the estimated number of clients of the management company and the costs of providing them (eg, labour, IT and other costs);
- analyses;
- a financial plan for at least three years; and
- a business development strategy.

The application must also include a draft of the internal regulations governing the prudential rules for the provision of any activities or services that the management company intends to carry out. This will include 30–60 documents depending on the robustness of the management company.

The duration of licensing proceedings before the Czech National Bank depends on the total number of applications currently being processed and the quality of the particular application (fewer calls to supplement the application = faster procedure). For this reason, it is highly recommended that the documents for the licensing application are prepared by persons experienced in the procedure.

4.3 Technical and personnel requirements

As a financial institution, a management company must comply with the requirements for IT systems to support all key activities, for example, records of investment instruments, bookkeeping, portfolio record-keeping trading and project management. Although the technical prerequisites are important, they mainly concern the provision of appropriate infrastructure.

However, the human resources of the management company must be considered a key component. The persons through whom the investment firm carries out its activities must be trustworthy and have sufficient knowledge and experience of the procedures and regulations necessary to perform their duties.

Credibility of personnel also takes into account compliance with legal and ethical rules, moral profile and integrity. A person's trustworthiness resides both in his or her personal integrity and his or her professional, business integrity. In assessing trustworthiness, the Czech National Bank takes into account, in particular:

- whether the person concerned has been convicted of a criminal offence in the past;
- whether they have been sanctioned for an administrative offence or ordered to pay compensation for damages in connection with the exercise of their profession, employment, function or business activity;
- whether they have always complied with their obligations towards the supervisory authority or the state supervisory authority in the performance of their duties; and
- whether they have observed the principles of fair business dealings, and not distorted competition.

Professional competence is assessed by the Czech National Bank taking into account the specific function in question, the scope of competence of the person being assessed and the number of persons under his or her management, as well as the nature, scope and complexity of the financial services provider's activities and its overall staffing, and the time that has elapsed since the individual's most recent relevant managerial or professional experience. In general, it is considered that the longer the period of time since the person being assessed last practised, the greater the requirement for the length of earlier experience.

In particular, the Czech National Bank considers a master's graduate to have sufficient knowledge to perform the function of a manager of a financial services provider. When assessing knowledge, account shall also be taken of whether a senior person has passed a professional examination or has attended a professional course appropriate to his or her function. The Bank considers at least three years of professional experience in the financial market to be sufficient for the head of a financial services provider.

Management experience is assessed on a case-by-case basis, always taking into account other indicators of professional competence. When assessing managerial experience, the Czech National Bank takes into account, in particular, the extent of the powers, and the scope of management activities, of the person being assessed in his or her previous experience, and their relevance to the specific function that the person will be expected to perform. The Bank considers sufficient managerial experience to be two years' experience in a managerial function in a legal entity, where it has been possible to gain experience appropriate to the management of the entity in which the person concerned intends to work (taking into account the size, organisational structure and business activities of the legal entity).

4.4 Our experience to date as corporate trustee

It should be clear from the foregoing that there is a vast difference between the prerequisites for an individual trustee and a corporate trustee. We take the view that some of the requirements imposed on management companies in terms of personnel prerequisites (trustworthiness, education, completion of specialised courses, management experience) could be transferable to individual trustees when the vast majority of professional individual trustees have long met these prerequisites in any case. In our opinion, setting requirements for personnel qualifications would help to professionalise the trust administration industry.

Experience has shown that the weighty infrastructure and robust internal management and control system of a management company can also be used without major adaptation to perform trust administration, which is in some respects similar to the management and administration of qualified investor investment funds. However, most of the MCIF Act rules do not apply to the administration of trusts as long as trusts are not regulated entities, and corporate trust administration is not a regulated service. However, this would be different in the context of the administration of an investment trust, where all the rules of the MCIF Act would apply.

We consider that using the services of a Czech corporate trustee offers several significant advantages. A corporate trustee provides highly qualified services in accordance with the latest legal and financial standards, and as an entity they fall under the supervision of the Czech National Bank, which monitors whether the prerequisites based on which the entity was granted a licence are met. The corporate trustee is a separate entity, which can reduce the risk of conflicts of interest and ensure that the administration of the trust is carried out in the best interests of the beneficiaries, providing continuity and stability in the administration of the trust. Staff are permanently available and the company will have developed business continuity strategies that ensure the welfare of the trust even in the event of unforeseen circumstances.

In addition, management companies add further value by having in place by default, as regulated entities, robust lines of defence consisting of three components:

- operational risk management at the level of the governing body;
- compliance and risk management functions that aim to ensure the oversight and effective performance of the regulated entity's activities (*ex post* and *ex ante*); and
- an internal audit function (*ex post).*

5. Conclusion

The correct structuring of a trust tailored to a particular founder is the alpha and omega of whether the trust will provide a workable solution in the long term and whether it will fulfil its purpose according to the founder's wishes. It is primarily up to the founder to decide on the appropriate structure and to engage advisers with sufficient experience and expertise to carry out his or her wishes.

Settlors' rationales differ. For some, asset protection may be crucial because they reasonably fear attack from potential creditors or family members, particularly if family or business relationships are complicated. For others, asset protection is peripheral, and the risk of the trust being declared a sham or *alter ego* trust is downplayed. It should be the duty of trust-structuring advisers and trustees to be open with the founders about any risks, and to avoid creating potentially dysfunctional structures, as a dysfunctional or risky trust primarily benefits the business advisers, not the founders. Failure to lay out the risks is unprofessional and shortsighted.

One of the factors in selecting the right solution is the assessment of onshore/offshore options. In the Czech Republic, foreign solutions are still very popular, especially Liechtenstein foundations or Jersey/Guernsey trusts. Their indisputable advantage is a more stable legal environment and the high professionalisation of the industry; disadvantages may be a different culture and language, risk of change of legal and tax environment, or taxation when transferring assets to a trust.

EMUN's trust-structuring clients choose whether they prefer the greater operability and proximity of a trust in the Czech Republic to arrange their assets, or would rather opt for a foreign solution – particularly popular with multicultural or cosmopolitan families. For cross-border structures, the tax assessment of the whole transaction is always crucial, especially regarding the existence or absence of double taxation treaties and the increasingly real risk of the application of a so-called 'exit tax'. Based on our experience to date, we can summarise that one-third of our clients prefer the Czech solution, one-third opt for a foreign solution and the remaining third apply a different asset arrangement from a trust or foundation.

In the Czech legal environment, where the tradition of trusts is more or less absent – unlike in common law countries – it is necessary to proceed cautiously and adopt good practices that have developed in other jurisdictions over many years. It would be a pity if the promising legislative environment, which provides the Czech Republic with a competitive advantage over other CEE countries, were to be destroyed by the creation of sham or *alter ego* trusts which, given increasing litigation, would be swept away by negative judgments that would obscure the potential of their creation in the first place. We are currently seeing cases where some advisers favour endowment funds and dismiss trust solutions out of hand.

Trusts are not for everyone. The main purpose of life, not just for wealthy families, is to seek and create positive emotions and happiness. For founders who see only stress in a trust mechanism or in setting aside assets without the ability subsequently to directly control those assets, the trust solution cannot be recommended. For some, delegating administration of assets to a professional third party is an assault on their mental health. When trust solutions are forced on such founders, trust principles are distorted and sham or *alter ego* structures are created. For these founders, a better solution is often to create family holdings combined with a complex will and family constitution.

We must not forget the origin of the word 'trust'. It derives from the Old Norse word '*traust*', meaning confidence. Without the confidence of the founder in the trustee, and *vice versa*, the arrangement of the property at hand is unstable.

Duties and responsibilities of trustees

Petr Jakubec
ROSE Legal s.r.o., advokátní kancelář

1. Introduction

The duties of a trustee depend largely on the type of trust and the competencies entrusted to the trustee by the founder (settlor). While Czech law does not explicitly define terms such as 'discretionary trust', 'family trust', 'asset protection trust' and 'blind trust', due to the broad scope of Czech law it is possible to structure trusts under any of these headings, and the scope of duties and, if applicable, responsibilities of the trustee will vary accordingly.

The other significant factor influencing the duties and responsibilities of a trustee in Czech law is that any natural person can be a trustee provided they have full legal capacity (Section 1453 of the Civil Code).[1] Unfortunately, Czech law does not currently recognise the concept of a 'corporate trustee', since a trustee can only be a legal person as provided by law. The legal person in this context can only be an investment company,[2] based in the Czech Republic and with authorisation from the central bank (the Czech National Bank) to operate, a process that is involved and expensive. The process is discussed in more detail in the preceding chapter, "Individual vs corporate trustees in the Czech Republic". It is not currently possible for standard legal persons (companies) to act as corporate trustees in the Czech Republic.

1.1 Due managerial care

The foundation for all duties and responsibilities of a trustee in Czech law is the concept of 'due managerial care'.[3] When administering a trust, trustees carry out 'full administration' of the assets in the trust (Section 1456 of the Civil Code).[4] However, since the trustees are managing assets in the trust that belong to someone else and not the trustees themselves, they are obliged to manage the

1 See Appendix I.

2 As defined by Act No 240/2013 Coll, on Investment Companies and Investment Funds, as amended ('the ICIF Act'). Available at: www.mfcr.cz/assets/attachments/2023-04-13_Act-on-Investment-Companies-and-Investment-Funds.pdf.

3 Vlastimil Pihera, "Section 1411 (Due managerial care)", in Jiří Spáčil, Michal Králík *et al*, *Civil Code III. Property Rights (Sections 976–1474)*, 2nd edition, CH Beck, 2021, pp1518–1519. And see Czech Civil Code, Section 1411. Available at: http://obcanskyzakonik.justice.cz/images/pdf/Civil-Code.pdf.

4 See Appendix I.

assets with due managerial care. Trustees must care for the entrusted assets with the same diligence as they would for their own, exercising appropriate caution and foresight. They must always consider and be able to recognise what is in the interest of the beneficiaries, what is beneficial for the preservation, and usually the augmentation, of the managed assets, or what actions (including their own inaction) might cause harm.

While the trustee may not need to possess specific expertise, they must be capable of determining what they can handle adequately on their own and when they need professional advisers or assistants. They should be able to make informed and competent choices in this respect because the trustee bears personal responsibility for the appropriateness of the selections. Therefore, the trustee should have access to the information and documentation necessary to make decisions, including the selection of experts, and be able to justify their choices and decisions. There will inevitably come a day when the trustee will be required to submit accounts of their administration. For decisions that lead to loss or damage the trustees are, in principle, subject to unlimited financial liability unless they can demonstrate that the damage occurred despite their acting with due managerial care.

Exercising due managerial care involves performing the role of trustee with proper loyalty, necessary knowledge and diligence.[5] The trustee must be loyal both in relation to the purpose of the trust established by its founder as outlined in its statute (trust deed) and in relation to the beneficiaries and their legitimate interests arising from the purpose and goals for which the trust was created. The required knowledge does not necessarily need to be expert in all areas of the trustee's activities but must be at a level that enables the trustee to fulfil all duties and tasks independently or to secure another qualified individual as an adviser or representative.

Prudent conduct requires the trustee to act thoroughly and conscientiously, with the same caution as if managing their own property. In general, the trustee is obliged to personally carry out all the administration of the trust. Delegation can only occur to a limited extent, and the trustee cannot fully delegate the entire administration. The trustee must choose his or her assistants or representatives carefully and provide them with adequate instructions (Section 1401(1) of the Civil Code).[6]

It is not about the trustees always acting alone and flawlessly. However, they must not act negligently, recklessly or imprudently. At the same time, the trustee must always bear in mind that for every decision, action (whether legal or factual), or even inaction or omission, including the actions and inactions of

---

5 Jaroslav Svejkovský, Radan Marek *et al*, *Administration of property of others in the new Civil Code*, CH Beck, 2015, pp121–125.

6 Available at: http://obcanskyzakonik.justice.cz/images/pdf/Civil-Code.pdf.

their assistants and representatives, the trustee bears their own non-transferable responsibility and can be asked by the beneficiary (or any supervising person or body) to explain and justify them. It is, therefore, highly advisable for the trustee to keep thorough records and retain documentation or evidence to demonstrate that they have exercised due care and have not failed in their role.

The level of demands imposed will depend on the specific type of trust and the rules for asset administration established by the founder. The more specific the rules or conditions for certain decisions, actions, or distribution of assets, the less opportunity for error there will be for the trustee. Conversely, in the case of structures close to the concept of a discretionary trust, demands on the trustee will be very high since the rules for asset administration will be set out in more general terms. It will be up to the trustee to shape the rules responsibly according to his or her knowledge of the founder's will and the interests of the beneficiaries, ensuring that the purpose of the trust is upheld and risks that could lead to damage to the trust assets or to the beneficiaries are eliminated.

An integral part of due managerial care in relation to someone else's assets is the question of potential conflict of interest. For example, if a trustee owns a company specialising in property maintenance and repairs, can the trustee, as the director of that company, enter into a contract for property maintenance and repairs with the trust where he or she acts as a trustee? The conflict of interest is obvious in this case, albeit it need not necessarily be harmful to the trust – services might be delivered on more favourable terms, to a higher standard and more efficiently. However, the challenge lies in the fact that one person will have to exercise due managerial care as the trustee on the one hand, and the director of the service company on the other, and what may be advantageous to the trust may not be beneficial for the services company, and *vice versa*. Questions can always arise, and it is better to avoid such situations and relationships rather than permit unnecessary doubts, albeit there may be circumstances where such a contract is the appropriate or even the only option available. In that case, it becomes crucial for the trustee to document the relevant facts, his or her method of assessment, and the reasons for a particular decision. From another perspective, however, a similar situation illustrates the potential advantage of a trust managed by multiple trustees. If there are multiple trustees, the vote of other trustees can justify the decision and exclude potential conflict, or the conflicted trustee may abstain from the sensitive decision, thereby preventing any doubts about impartiality and the outcome of the decision.

1.2 Plurality of trustees and joint administration

Czech law does not specifically prescribe how many trustees a trust can have. It is clear from the legal definition that there must be at least one trustee, since the trust involves the administration of someone else's property. While there is no upper limit on the number of trustees, it will depend in practice on the need for flexible administration, the required level of expertise and experience, and the trustees' responsibilities. If multiple trustees are entrusted with joint administration, decisions are made and actions taken by majority vote, unless the founder has set a different ratio or method in the statute (perhaps a qualified majority or unanimous decision). Unless expressly stated otherwise, each trustee has one vote (Section 1428 of the Civil Code).[7]

In practice, solutions are often devised where one of the trustees, typically the chairperson, has a decisive vote or even a veto in the case of a tie. It is also a common requirement for certain decisions to be made by a qualified majority of trustees. If any one of the joint administrators does not promptly inform the others of their disagreement with a decision and does not notify the beneficiary accordingly without undue delay, the decision is deemed approved (Section 1431(1) of the Civil Code).[8]

Given that trustees are jointly and severally liable in case of joint administration (Section 1430 of the Civil Code),[9] then where there are, say, three trustees and two of them jointly make a decision or take an action, in principle the third trustee will be responsible for such decision or action, even if not directly involved. If joint trustees make a decision in the absence of one of them, the absent trustee is deemed to have approved the decision unless he or she expresses disagreement to the other trustees and the beneficiary without undue delay after learning about the decision (Section 1431(2) of the Civil Code).[10]

Personal participation in administration and the avoidance of unwelcome responsibility in the case of joint trustees can be achieved through a system of unanimous decision making. However, this system may not always be sufficiently flexible and efficient considering the operational needs of individual trusts and the interests of the beneficiaries.

If joint trustees, due to an external obstacle or sustained inactivity or resistance from one of the trustees, cannot act, the other trustees may independently make decisions and take actions necessary to maintain the *status quo*, under Section 1429(1) of the Civil Code.[11] Because this rule is aimed at preventing harm, trustees must act in such a case to prevent negative consequences, and not passively wait, citing their inability to act together.

1.3 Obligation to have an additional trustee

This obligation reflects another aspect of Czech trust law, according to which,

---

7 *Ibid.*
8 *Ibid.*
9 *Ibid.*
10 *Ibid.*
11 *Ibid.*

although the founder or a beneficiary can be a trustee, they cannot be the sole trustee (Section 1454(1) of the Civil Code).[12] In the case of a founder, this would involve the administration of his or her originally owned property, and in the case of a beneficiary, his or her future property. Thus, if a trust is formed with only a single trustee, neither the founder nor a beneficiary can take the role.

If the founder or a beneficiary is a trustee, the trust must have at least one additional third-party trustee, and the trustees must act jointly – decisions and actions concerning administration of the trust must always involve an external, independent element. It is the duty and responsibility of each trustee to ensure that at least one unbiased third-party trustee is involved in the trust administration.

1.4 Separation of ownership

Property placed in the trust ceases to be owned by the founder or the person contributing the property, but it does not yet belong to the beneficiary either. Neither is it the property of the trustee, who is not the owner but merely the custodian. Thus, such property formally belongs to no one (Section 1448(3) of the Civil Code).[13] Since Czech law does not include concepts like legal ownership and equitable ownership, trusts find themselves in a situation where the trust represents something like a property cloud – assets that currently have no owner.

According to Czech law, a trust does not have its own independent legal personality. The entrusted property becomes that of the beneficiary only after the given conditions are met, the trustee has approved and the property is handed over to the beneficiary. Only through a relevant decision of the trustee that the conditions have been met does the beneficiary acquire a legal right to claim specific performance.

It is, therefore, the trustee's duty to act in accordance with the rules of asset administration provided for by the founder, including verification of the fulfilment of conditions for the distribution of trust assets and/or the provision of other performance, confirmation of the fulfilment of conditions and decisions on payments, etc. If the conditions for payment are met, and the trustee has not yet given approval or decided against approval, the beneficiary will need to file a lawsuit to compel the trustee to provide the relevant performance. This would be a clear indication that the trustee has violated his or her obligations relating to the administration or purpose of the trust and/or towards the beneficiary.

12 See Appendix I.
13 *Ibid.*

1.5 Trustee's duties

While the duties of a trustee may appear overwhelming and complex, this perception holds only partially true. Despite the requirement for trustees to personally fulfil their responsibilities, they possess the right and in some cases – in line with the principle of due managerial care – the responsibility to enlist assistance or appoint representatives for specific areas or tasks, such as general administration, bookkeeping and tax advice. This collaborative approach is not only permissible but desirable.

Trustees' duties and tasks can be categorised as follows:

- administrative duties;
- accounting and tax duties;
- organisational and operational duties; and
- legal duties.

However, such categorisation is more academically interesting than practically relevant. From a legal perspective and in the context of due managerial care, trustees must fulfil all their obligations and tasks as stipulated by law and the rules of the individual trust, regardless of how we may want to classify these obligations under various headings. Distinguishing between them in terms of the severity of a particular violation is not fundamentally important, because what matters in the end is whether the trustee has violated any of their obligations regarding the fundamental requirement of due managerial care and whether, as a result, any damage has occurred that they might be obliged to compensate.

2. Upon assuming the role of a trustee

2.1 Taking over the administration and the assets

If the trust is established during the lifetime of the founder – typically the case in the Czech Republic – based on an administration agreement between the founder and the trustee, the trustee is obliged to take over the administration of the assets contributed to the trust (Section 1448(2) of the Civil Code).[14] From a formal perspective, this means that there must be a document (as part of the administration agreement or as a separate declaration by the trustee) in which the trustee expressly declares and confirms that he or she is taking over the administration of the initial trust assets. It is his or her duty to physically take over the assets, whether it is money, real estate, or any other form of asset. If there are multiple trustees, it is sufficient for at least one of them to do so, but it should not be the founder or a beneficiary alone, in accordance with the rule that an unbiased third-party trustee should always be involved in the process.

---

14 *Ibid.*

Only based on such an action and the transfer of the assets into administration by the trustee is the trust established, and it can formally come into existence upon registration in the Register of Trusts.

2.2 Duty to inform

The trustee shall, without undue delay after taking on his or her role *vis-à-vis* the administration of the trust property, deliver a notice to the beneficiaries and to anyone who else has the right to supervise the administration of the trust according to Czech law. The notice shall include at least the identification, purpose and duration of the trust, as well as the trustee's name and address. Notification is not required if these facts are already known to the person authorised to supervise (Section 1465(1) of the Civil Code).[15] The purpose is to inform legitimately empowered persons or bodies that the trust exists and who represents it (ie, the trustee).

2.3 Register updates

The application for registration of the trust in the Register of Trusts, including all subsequent changes, is submitted by the trustee. It is the trustee's obligation to maintain the accuracy of the records, particularly regarding the trustee and beneficiaries. In line with the 4th AML Directive,[16] a register of beneficial owners (the UBO Register) was also introduced in the Czech Republic, containing information about the beneficial owners of trusts. Upon the establishment of a trust and its registration in the Register of Trusts, the data is automatically transferred to the UBO Register. However, due to potential errors in computer data processing (which, unfortunately, occur in practice quite frequently), it is the trustee's responsibility to periodically review the entries in the UBO Register and ensure their accuracy. Any deficiencies or errors in the records could have significant, potentially devastating effects, especially if the trust's assets include companies or even entire holding structures that could be adversely affected by these formal shortcomings. It is a crucial duty of the trustee to check regularly that the entries in all relevant registers are up to date.

As for the trust assets that are recorded in public registers (such as the land registry, securities register and vehicle register), the trustee must be registered rather than the owner, with the addition 'as the trustee of' followed by the designation of the respective trust. These entries must also be ensured by the trustees, as they act on behalf of the trust externally (like the statutory representative of a business entity or other legal person).

---

15 *Ibid.*

16 Directive (EU) 2015/849 of the European Parliament and of the Council of 20 May 2015 on the prevention of the use of the financial system for the purposes of money laundering or terrorist financing. Available at: https://eur-lex.europa.eu/legal-content/EN/TXT/PDF/?uri=CELEX:32015L0849.

2.4 **Tax registration**

In the Czech Republic a trust is considered a taxable entity, and the trustee is therefore required, within 15 days of the trust's creation (ie, its registration in the Register of Trusts), to register the trust as a corporate income taxpayer and subsequently fulfil other tax obligations similarly to legal persons such as companies. This obligation is linked to another requirement reflecting the separation of the trust assets from the assets of the trustee or other individuals: the establishment of a separate bank account for the trust, which needs to be notified to the tax authority for tax payment purposes. Depending on the circumstances and the potential economic activities of the trust, an individual trust may also be required to register for other taxes, such as real estate tax, VAT and income tax from dependent activities (eg, in the case of employees). If the trust has employees, which is not very common in the Czech Republic, the trustee will have an obligation to register the trust as an employer with the relevant authorities (eg, the Czech Social Security Administration, health insurance companies and issuers of employer liability insurance), and to perform necessary registrations and updates concerning individual employees (eg, with regard to social security and health insurance).

2.5 **Acquaintance with the trust documents**

If trustees are to administer the trust with due managerial care, they must first be familiar with all the provisions and rules related to the administration of the individual trust. In addition to all relevant laws and other regulations, it is necessary for the trustees to acquaint themselves, in particular, with the founding documents of the trust and any rules that are to be applied to the trust administration. Most significant among these is the statute, as it outlines the purpose of the trust, the beneficiaries (or the circle of individuals from whom beneficiaries are to be determined and the manner in which this will occur), rules for the distribution of assets to beneficiaries, and the overall management of the trust.

The second document is typically the trust administration agreement between the founder and the trustee, according to which the trustee is obligated to take on the management of the trust and its assets. Subsequent trustees enter into the administration agreement with the founder or the person to whom the founder's rights passed on his or her death. If there is no such person, the trustee is obligated to adhere to the previous administration agreement or to declare that he or she will comply with the conditions and rules set out therein. Equally important are the founder's wish list, and legal titles to the managed assets.

If a new trustee assumes the role from his or her predecessor, he or she is naturally obliged to take over all additional documents and books relating to the administration of the trust assets. This includes asset books, accounting records, tax records, records on decisions taken, contracts and many others. The situation is, of course, facilitated if all records and documents were meticulously and responsibly maintained by the previous trustee, especially if there is a well-organised archive. It can be envisaged that the new trustee may be entitled to assert claims on behalf of the trust against the previous trustee if the latter failed in their duties, particularly if this resulted in harm to the beneficiaries or damage to the trust assets (such as incorrectly or not filed tax returns leading to missed tax obligations or imposed penalties).

3. Duties during the administration

3.1 Personal performance and representation

As mentioned above, the law imposes on the trustee the personal performance of trust administration, which generally cannot be transferred to another person, thereby legally relieving the trustee of his or her duties. Delegating responsibilities is only permissible within the standard of due managerial care and always in respect of a specific action or area (Section 1401 of the Civil Code).[17] Delegating the entire trust administration and thus the personal responsibility and liability of the trustee is not permitted – it would be a legally ineffective act and a violation of the trustee's duty.

3.2 Ongoing compliance with due managerial care

This rule has already been discussed. It can be considered the fundamental and most important rule affecting the trust, as it will serve as the benchmark for assessing proper management or any mistakes and possible liability of the trustee. The obligation of the trustee to always act with due managerial care permeates trust management throughout the entire term of the trustee's function.

Proper execution of the trustee's function primarily involves compliance with all relevant provisions of law (including the Civil Code, rules relating to public registers, tax and accounting laws, and other regulations) and further adherence to the specified rules and parameters of administration outlined in the founding documents of the individual trust (the statute, administration agreement, founder's wish list and possibly others). Ignorance of the law is not an excuse and, for any violation, especially of legal obligations, direct sanctions may be imposed on the trust, and personal liability for the trustee may apply.

With regard to the trustee's potential liability and for the purposes of regular (annual) as well as final accounts for the administration, it is advisable to keep all records, especially decisions related to the acquisition, sale or distribution of assets to beneficiaries, in written form, even though it may not be generally

---

17 Available at: http://obcanskyzakonik.justice.cz/images/pdf/Civil-Code.pdf.

stipulated or legally required in specific cases. Without such documentation, the trustee could struggle to meet the burden of proof.

3.3 Full administration and proactive approach

Performance of the trustee's duties includes the obligation:

- to carry out the so-called 'full administration' of the entrusted assets, that is, with due managerial care (Section 1411 of the Civil Code);[18]
- to do anything necessary and useful (Section 1410 of the Civil Code) for the preservation, protection and multiplication of the assets;[19] and
- to use the assets in the interests of the beneficiaries (Section 1409 of the Civil Code).[20]

Since due managerial care also includes an element of diligence, the trustee is required to reasonably anticipate the development of circumstances and risks and take necessary measures in a timely manner. This requires a proactive approach. A trustee cannot passively administer the assets. In case of any need, the trustee is obliged to take action. The duty to properly manage entrusted assets can be violated by failing to act if the trustee could and should have acted, for example:

- to prevent harm (prevention of damage);
- to avoid the loss of legal title to the assets (statute of limitations);
- to ensure that rights requiring active measures do not expire (intellectual property); or
- to use the entrusted assets in the interests of the beneficiary in any other way.

3.4 Exercise of ownership rights

From the moment the assets are taken into trusteeship, the trustee is obligated to exercise ownership rights over the entrusted assets as if he or she was their owner. The trustee does so in his or her own name but on the account of the trust (Section 1448(3) of the Civil Code).[21] This includes not only the actual possession of the assets but also maintenance, repairs, use and appreciation thereof, including prudent investments and, particularly, the protection of the assets against loss, destruction, damage, or depreciation – both practically and legally.

3.5 Taking over contributed assets

A similar procedure for the formal and actual takeover of assets to that during the establishment of the trust will apply to any additional assets that are later

---

18 See note 3, *supra*.
19 Available at: http://obcanskyzakonik.justice.cz/images/pdf/Civil-Code.pdf.
20 *Ibid.*
21 *Ibid.*

contributed by any person to an already registered trust. Whether it is included in the agreement to increase the assets by such contribution, if the contribution is the unilateral act of a third party (eg, by a bequest), there must be a transfer protocol or at least a declaration or record that the trustee has accepted certain new assets into the trust. All assets acquired into the trust after registration, whether by contract from a living contributor or *mortis causa*, are subject to administration according to the statute, contract, and the law (Section 1468 of the Civil Code).[22]

3.6 Separation of assets, avoidance of conflicts of interest

The trustee is obliged to manage the entrusted assets (with due managerial care) separately from his or her own and all other persons' property. This requires appropriate administrative and organisational measures, particularly to:

- ensure that money is deposited in bank accounts opened by the trustee in the name of the trust (not in the name of the trustee);
- maintain separate books and reliable records for the trust assets; and
- separately manage the bookkeeping and fulfilment of tax obligations for the trust.

The trustee must not commingle his or her own property with the assets of the trust (Section 1414 of the Civil Code).[23]

Any contracts relating to trust assets that benefit the trustee may only be entered into with the consent of the beneficiaries. Similarly, using the trust assets or utilising information obtained by the trustee during the administration of the trust for his or her personal benefit requires the consent of the beneficiaries (Section 1415 of the Civil Code).[24]

To prevent conflicts of interest, the trustee must promptly inform the beneficiary and the person supervising administration of trust assets or the beneficiary's interests about any personal interest the trustee may have in his or her own business or in otherwise pursuing financial gain, which could potentially conflict with beneficiaries' interests. Likewise, the trustee is required to promptly notify these parties of any rights he or she may exercise against the beneficiary or the entrusted assets (Section 1413 of the Civil Code).[25]

3.7 Acting in the interest of beneficiaries

From the logic of the trustee's role as the manager of someone else's property, it follows that the trustee cannot and must not act in their own interest (conflict by nature). The trustee must act in the interest of the beneficiaries. However,

22 See Appendix I.
23 Available at: http://obcanskyzakonik.justice.cz/images/pdf/Civil-Code.pdf.
24 *Ibid.*
25 *Ibid.*

this does not mean that the trustee is obligated to do whatever the beneficiaries want. Responsibility for the property, fulfilling the purpose of the trust, achieving its goals and, thereby, the interests of the beneficiaries, lies in the hands of the trustee. The trustee's extensive authority is shaped by legal regulations and rules established by the founder for managing a specific trust. Nonetheless, the role entails significant personal responsibility on the part of the trustee, along with potential liability.

3.8 Impartial approach

In cases of multiple beneficiaries, whether concurrently or subsequently, the trustee must act impartially towards all (both now and in the future) and consider their respective rights (Section 1412(1) of the Civil Code).[26] Therefore, the trustee must responsibly consider that any measure taken or decision made from time to time in the interests or to the benefit of one beneficiary or group of beneficiaries does not negatively impact the interest or benefit of another beneficiary or group of beneficiaries, either currently or potentially in the future.

The obligation of an impartial approach and the challenging situations that may arise for the trustee are most pronounced in the context of discretionary trusts. The less binding and specific the rules for managing the trust (founder's wishes) are, and the greater the discretion the trustee has in decision making, the more the aspect of impartiality and the potential impacts of each decision on all beneficiaries must be responsibly considered. In such cases, a cautious and individual approach to each beneficiary is required, while simultaneously maintaining a balanced approach to all beneficiaries. This does not necessarily mean treating all beneficiaries equally. Beneficiaries' interests, and distributions for their benefit, may vary based on the founder's wishes. However, no beneficiary in a comparable position should be unduly favoured or disadvantaged in comparison to others.

Impartiality also applies in relation to the trustee him or herself. The trustee must not mix his or her own property with the assets under management in the trust. Trust assets must be strictly separated. Similarly, the trustee must not prioritise his or her own interests and assets over the trust assets or the interests of the beneficiaries. The trustee is also prohibited from benefitting from the trust assets outside the rules for compensation for due performance of the trust management.

3.9 Prudent investments

If, as part of the full administration, the trustee is obliged to ensure the increase of the entrusted assets in the interests of the beneficiary (Section 1409 of the

---

26 *Ibid.*

Civil Code),[27] the trustee must, unless relieved of such duty in the statute, strive for the appreciation of deposits in bank and similar accounts, as well as other investments. The trustee is required to make investment decisions with due managerial care and to consider the return and expected profit. If possible, the trustee must allocate investment risk in such a way as to achieve a reasonable ratio between fixed income and variable returns, which reasonably corresponds to economic conditions (Section 1432 of the Civil Code).[28] The trustee must adhere to a cautious, not overly risky investment strategy. If the trustee lacks the necessary knowledge and skills, he or she will be required to use the services of a qualified broker, whom they must carefully select, and agree on an investment strategy within the bounds of due managerial care.

Investments may not always succeed (that is their nature), but they must be reasonable and appropriate, not unreasonably risky and disproportionate. The law explicitly prohibits trustees from acquiring more than 5% of the shares of the same issuer. Trustees are also prohibited from acquiring shares, bonds or other debt securities of a person who breached the duty to pay yield from the securities (Section 1433 of the Civil Code).[29]

Furthermore, the trustee must keep necessary records of investments or obtain them from an authorised broker. It is worth noting that for any losses or failures in the investment strategy (including by the fault of the investment broker), the trustee shall be liable to the founder and the beneficiaries, except when the trustee can demonstrate that the failure or loss occurred despite exercising due managerial care and due to external causes.

3.10 Insurance

The trustee is authorised by law to insure the managed assets, at the expense of the beneficiaries, against common risks. However, it can be assumed that if a certain level of insurance, such as in the case of real estate (given its value), is customary, it is the trustee's obligation to arrange such customary insurance. Otherwise, the trustee could be liable for a breach of due managerial care. If the trustee is managing the trust without receiving compensation, he or she has the legal right to insure their liability at the expense of the beneficiaries (or trust assets if so stipulated in the statute).

3.11 Appointment of a beneficiary

The appointment of a beneficiary is both a right and an obligation of the trustee if the founder did not specify the beneficiaries in the statute. The trustee must appoint a beneficiary from the group of individuals designated by the founder,

27 *Ibid.*
28 *Ibid.*
29 *Ibid.*

thereby determining the distribution from the trust for that beneficiary. Failure to do so would be considered a violation of a specific duty imposed on the trustee by the statute or a duty directly imposed by law (Section 1457(2) of the Civil Code).[30] At the very least, in such a case the trustee would typically be acting contrary to the purpose of the trust which, in the case of a private trust, typically aims to provide benefits to specific individuals. In any case no one, including the trustee, is authorised to appoint a beneficiary or determine performance for his or her own profit (Section 1458(2) of the Civil Code).[31] In other words, the trustee must not derive any benefit from appointing a specific person as a beneficiary or from determining distributions for any such person. This is another reflection of the principle of preventing conflicts of interest. Similarly, if someone other than the trustee is authorised to appoint a beneficiary (if so provided in the statute), it is the trustee's responsibility to ensure that the appointing person does not receive any benefit from the appointment.

3.12 Provision of benefits

The provision of benefits and/or distribution of the trust assets to beneficiaries is another obligation of the trustee. The right to performance from the trust flows to the beneficiary under conditions specified in the statute (Section 1459 of the Civil Code).[32] The fulfilment of conditions and the handling of assets are carried out by the trustee. Therefore, when the beneficiary's right to performance arises, there is a corresponding obligation for the trustee to provide such performance. Throughout the existence of the trust, the beneficiary has the right to demand the relevant performance in accordance with the statute (Section 1461(1) of the Civil Code).[33] If the trustee fails to provide the performance, the beneficiary can take legal action. Related to the provision of performance, the obligation of impartiality and independence of the trustee also applies. The trustee must separate his or her own potential interests or financial motives from such decision-making processes.

3.13 Proper management and compliance with the rules

The trustee is generally obligated throughout the term of his or her office to comply with the established rules of administration and the purpose of the trust and founder's wishes, as well as all applicable regulations. In that sense, the trustee not only has the option and the right to take certain actions, but essentially also has a duty to act. Failing to act could lead to a violation of the rules of management, the trust's purpose, or the interests of the beneficiaries. If

---

30 See Appendix I.
31 *Ibid.*
32 *Ibid.*
33 *Ibid.*

the trustee performs such an action incorrectly or fails to perform it at all, the founder, beneficiary or any other person with a relevant legal interest may petition the court to instruct the trustee to take specific actions or refrain from them (in extreme cases, to remove the trustee or appoint a new one) (Section 1466(1) of the Civil Code).[34] If the trustee does not act despite having the obligation to act, the court may also authorise a person with a relevant legal interest to initiate or pursue proceedings in the interest of the trust instead of the trustee (eg, asserting the trust's property rights, such as in the case of seeking damages, etc) (Section 1466(2) of the Civil Code).[35]

3.14 Annual accounts

The trustee is required to provide beneficiaries with an annual account of the administration (management report) at least once a year. If there are multiple trustees, the report is submitted jointly, unless specified otherwise in the administration contract or by law (Section 1436(1) of the Civil Code).[36] This obligation is typically fulfilled in conjunction with financial statements, tax returns and the annual management report. In the Czech system, a trust is treated as an accounting and taxable entity and must fulfil accounting and tax obligations like companies with legal personality.

Given that the business structures of the founders, namely, companies conducting business activities, are typically part of the trust assets, actions related to the obligation to provide annual accounts of the administration are typically linked to regular annual general meetings of business companies within the trust assets and their financial statements. They are also often coordinated with family council meetings that occur in connection with such general meetings, where financial statements are being discussed and approved.

3.15 Bookkeeping and tax

We have already mentioned that a trust in the Czech Republic is constituted as an accounting entity and a taxpayer, meaning it is subject to taxation. Therefore, the trustee is obliged to maintain or ensure proper accounting records, prepare financial statements, keep tax records, file tax returns and reports, pay relevant taxes and fulfil other obligations prescribed by applicable laws. This is a typical area of activity for accountants and tax advisers, to whom the trustee may (and typically will) outsource these activities in line with the obligation to exercise due managerial care. However, the trustee remains both responsible and liable (to the founder, beneficiaries and relevant state authorities) for the proper fulfilment of such requirements.

---

34 *Ibid.*

35 *Ibid.*

36 Available at: http://obcanskyzakonik.justice.cz/images/pdf/Civil-Code.pdf.

For completeness, it can be added that the trustee would be required to fulfil employer obligations to relevant institutions and public bodies (such as social security, health insurance and tax authorities) if the trust has its own employees rather than just contractual service providers. These obligations may include ongoing employee registrations and deregistrations, reporting of changes, submission of reports and filings, fulfilment of tax and contribution duties, and so on.

Under certain conditions, similarly to a joint stock company, a trust may be obligated to have its financial statements audited. However, a trust is so far not a consolidating accounting entity because, by definition, it is not a business company (even though it may engage in its own economic activities to some extent).

3.16 Cooperation with supervising bodies

Supervision over the administration of a trust is carried out by the founder and each person designated as a beneficiary or, if specified by the founder in the statute, by additional persons (Section 1463(1) of the Civil Code).[37] Upon the request of any of these persons who have the right to supervise the trust administration, the trustee is obligated to allow an examination of documents related to the trust (especially accounting and related records) and to provide them with accounts, reports or other information requested as part of the supervision (Sections 1465(2) and 1437 of the Civil Code).[38]

To such individuals or bodies exercising the right to oversee the administration of the trust under Czech law (eg, the Czech National Bank in case of an investment fund established in the form of a trust under the ICIF Act) the trustee is obliged to promptly deliver a notice, specifying at least the identification, purpose and duration of the trust, as well as the trustee's name and address. This notice (in writing) must be delivered by the trustee without undue delay after assuming the role of trustee (notifying their own function and contact details), or whenever the trustee learns that such person or authority is authorised by law to exercise supervision over the administration of the trust (for instance, if the investment activities of the trust reach a level requiring notification to the Czech National Bank or obtaining the relevant permit for certain regulated activities). However, such notice is not required if the notified facts are already known to the person or body authorised to supervise (Section 1465(1) of the Civil Code).[39]

---

37 See Appendix I and: http://obcanskyzakonik.justice.cz/images/pdf/Civil-Code.pdf.
38 See Appendix I.
39 *Ibid.*

3.17 Cooperation with the court

In addition to cases where, following a lawsuit, the court orders or prohibits certain actions or tasks that the trustee would otherwise be obligated to avoid or adhere to, respectively, the trustee may, under certain circumstances, be required to cooperate with the court – for example, in the event of the termination of the trust. Before deciding on the cancellation of the trust, where achieving its purpose has become impossible or difficult (especially due to circumstances unknown to or unforeseeable by the founder), the court shall seek the trustee's opinion on the matter. The trustee is naturally obliged to comply with such requests and to submit the requested opinion to the court in due course (Section 1470 of the Civil Code).[40]

3.18 Maintaining trustee's capacity; resignation from the office

Considering that the execution of the trustee's function requires due managerial care, encompassing loyalty, knowledge and diligence – qualities that a trustee may no longer possess over the course of a long-term trusteeship due, for example, to health conditions or advanced age – timely resignation from the position if they no longer meet the necessary prerequisites can also be seen as an obligation of the trustee.

Given that nobody can be compelled to continue performing a function he or she no longer wishes to fulfil (or objectively cannot perform anymore), it is the right of the trustee to resign from his or her position. In such event, the trustee is obligated to deliver the notice of resignation not only to the person authorised to appoint a new trustee but also to any co-trustees, all beneficiaries and any other individuals supervising the trust administration (Section 1440(1) of the Civil Code).[41] This stems from the fact that the trustee effectively and legally embodies the trust as an entity without a legal personality. Therefore, it is crucial for the need for the appointment of a new trustee to be widely known within the circle of affected individuals and competent bodies related to the trust.

As protection for the trust and the interests of the beneficiaries, Czech law dictates that trustees may not resign from their position at an inappropriate time or otherwise resign in a way that would violate their obligations to proper management. The trustee is obliged to compensate for any damage that may occur to the trust or the beneficiaries from the breach of this protective measure (Section 1440(2) of the Civil Code).[42]

---

40 *Ibid.*
41 Available at: http://obcanskyzakonik.justice.cz/images/pdf/Civil-Code.pdf.
42 *Ibid.*

4. Duties at the conclusion of trustee's term

4.1 Final accounts and management report

If the trustee's term comes to an end but the trust continues, the trustee's primary obligation is to hand over his or her role and the whole trust (including both assets and all relevant documentation) to his or her successor. The trustee hands over the managed assets to the beneficiary or the incoming trustee at the location of the trust assets unless otherwise agreed (Section 1446(1) of the Civil Code).[43] This encompasses surrendering everything acquired for the beneficiaries during the trusteeship (Section 1446(2) of the Civil Code).[44] In order to prevent damage, the trustee, at the end of the trusteeship, is obligated to take all necessary measures to avoid possible loss (Section 1443 of the Civil Code).[45]

The law requires the trustee, upon extinction of the trusteeship, to submit detailed accounts to the beneficiaries and the incoming trustee (Section 1445 of the Civil Code),[46] ensuring they are comprehensive enough to verify their accuracy (Section 1436(2) of the Civil Code).[47]

4.2 Asset distribution on termination of the trust

Upon the extinction of the administration of the trust (eg, due to the expiry of the trust's term, the fulfilment of its purpose and all beneficiaries waiving their right to performance), the trustee is obliged to surrender the assets to the person entitled thereto. This may not necessarily be the beneficiary; it could be anyone designated in the statute for this purpose. Such individuals are not formally considered beneficiaries of the trust (ie, not in the narrower or primary sense), as the trust administration has already been completed. The distribution of the remaining assets reflects a sort of liquidation and 'substitute' asset distribution rather than necessarily fulfilling the trust's purpose. The law presumes that, upon termination of the trust, the beneficiary shall have the right to the assets, and if there is no beneficiary, then the founder – who may no longer be alive at the time of the trust's end. If neither the founder nor any of the beneficiaries are alive, by virtue of law all remaining assets of the trust will pass into the ownership of the state unless expressly stated otherwise in the statute (Section 1472 of the Civil Code).[48] On the other hand, it is the trustee's obligation to respect the founder's designation of the recipient of last resort and transfer the assets according to the founder's wishes.

---

43 *Ibid.*
44 *Ibid.*
45 *Ibid.*
46 *Ibid.*
47 *Ibid.*
48 See Appendix I.

4.3 Accounting, tax and other obligations on termination

Given that, in the Czech context, a trust is not considered a legal person, its termination does not involve a formal liquidation process, as is typical for business entities. However, though such a procedure is not formally prescribed, a similar approach is followed. On the day of the last asset distribution following the trust termination, it is necessary to close the trust's accounting, prepare a final extraordinary financial statement and submit final tax returns. The trustee must also deregister the trust from all taxes (potentially also from other state institutions where it was registered, such as social insurance, health insurance, etc) and request the tax authority's consent to erase the trust from the Register of Trusts.

4.4 Deregistration from the Register of Trusts

Once, upon the extinction of trusteeship, the trustee has disposed of the remaining trust assets in accordance with the statute – meaning he or she has surrendered the assets to the designated person or entity or placed them into another trust as stipulated by the statute – the trust effectively ceases to exist. Consequently, the trustee is required to file a petition for the deletion of the trust from the Register of Trusts (Section 1474 of the Civil Code).[49]

49 *Ibid.*

Beneficiaries – rights to performance, information and supervision

David Neveselý
Jiří Pokorný
Havel & Partners

1. Introduction

A beneficiary is a person or entity for whose benefit a trust is established by the founder and for whose benefit the trustee administers the trust. This benefit consists primarily of the right to claim certain performance from the trust. Another key right is, in general, supervision over the administration of the trust, a right exercised jointly with the founder (and possibly with other specified persons). Nevertheless, there is no *numerus clausus* of a beneficiary's rights and powers – they depend on the statute and the founder who issues the statute.[1]

The beneficiary is a key figure in the trust, along with the founder and the trustee, as performance to the beneficiary is normally the main purpose of the establishment of the trust.

1.1 Definition of the term 'trust beneficiary'

There is no legal definition of the term '*obmyšlený*' (in the context of Czech trust law, 'trust beneficiary') in the Czech Civil Code. However, a definition can be derived from Section 1400(1)[2] in conjunction with Sections 1452(2)(f), 1457(4), 1461(1) and 1472.

The term 'beneficient' is used in Section 1400(1) of the Civil Code (general provisions for the administration of the property of others), legally defined as a person for whose benefit the administrator (the law does not use the term 'trustee' in this context) administers property that does not belong to him or her. The term 'beneficient' cannot be used as an *en bloc* definition for the trust beneficiary, as it is a broader and more general concept applicable to other cases

1 Kateřina Ronovská, Vlastimil Pihera and Eva Dobrovolná, "Rights of beneficiaries: building foundations and trusts, a Czech perspective", *Trusts & Trustees*, Vol 29, No 6, July 2023, pp509–515.

2 Section 1400(1) of the Civil Code states as follows: "Any person who is entrusted with the administration of property which does not belong to him for the benefit of another (hereinafter a 'beneficiary'), is an administrator of the property of another." The 2013 Ministry of Justice translation of the Czech Civil Code is available at: http://obcanskyzakonik.justice.cz/images/pdf/Civil-Code.pdf. The full text of the current iteration of the Civil Code is available in Czech at: www.zakonyprolidi.cz/cs/2012-89. An official English language version of the full text is not yet available.

of administration of the property of others, not just to trusts (for example, administration of a decedent's estate under Section 1678 of the Civil Code; a security transfer of right under Section 2042 of the Civil Code; or administration of an affiliated fund of a foundation under Section 351 of the Civil Code).[3] The term 'trust beneficiary' is inherently more specific and relates purely to the beneficiary's position *vis-à-vis* the trust. However, it cannot logically conflict with the legal definition of a beneficiary under general provisions on the administration of the property of others, where it is a concept superior to that of trust beneficiary.

The trust beneficiary is granted, under Sections 1452(2)(f), 1457(4), 1461(1) and 1472 of the Civil Code, the right to claim a certain performance from the trust, as determined by the person who appoints the trust beneficiary (typically the founder or trustee) and as set out in the trust statute. Performance is in the form of the fruits and revenues[4] of the trust or trust property, or a share thereof and, where applicable, trust property or a share thereof upon termination of the trust administration and dissolution of the trust (there is a rebuttable legal presumption that the trust beneficiaries have a right to the property of the trust on termination).[5]

Trust beneficiaries can be divided into three groups depending on when and how their right to performance from the trust arises:

- *actual* beneficiaries, who have an unconditional right to performance from the trust;
- *expectant* beneficiaries, who have a right to performance from the trust if certain predefined conditions are met (without the discretion of the trustee); and
- *discretionary* beneficiaries, who earn the status of beneficiaries, and the right to certain performance from the trust, at the discretion of the trustee, to whom this power is given by the statute issued by the founder.[6]

Based on the above, a trust beneficiary is in principle:

- a person for whose benefit the trustee keeps and administers property which the founder has set aside from his or her ownership for a specific purpose in order to establish the trust; and simultaneously

---

3 Jaroslav Svejkovský, Radan Marek *et al*, *Správa cizího majetku v novém občanském zákoníku (Administration of foreign property in the new Civil Code)*, CH Beck, 2015, pp29–73.

4 Typically, it will be a share of the profits/dividends from shares or rent from the lease of movable or immovable property.

5 Explanatory memorandum to Sections 1457–1462 of the Civil Code:

> *The beneficiary of a trust is the person to whom the performance from the trust is to be provided. Performance from the trust may be provided in the form of fruits and revenues, proceeds of the trust or a share thereof, or the relinquishment of the property or a share of the trust property upon its termination.*

6 Ronovská *et al*, "Rights of beneficiaries", *supra* note 1.

- a person who is entitled to claim certain performance from the trust in accordance with the statute issued by the founder and the determination of the person who appoints the beneficiary (typically the founder or trustee).

Expectant as well as actual beneficiaries may have beneficiary status under Czech law, according to Ronovská and Pihera.[7] In contrast, discretionary beneficiaries are unlikely to have the status of beneficiaries under Czech law, but this does not mean that the law does not grant them at least some supervisory powers in the context of a trust.[8]

1.2 Position of the beneficiary in the trust

The definition of trust beneficiary implies its essential role in the trust, alongside that of the founder and the trustee. The position of the founder and the trustee is decisive for the establishment of the trust itself, since the trust is established by setting aside assets owned by the founder in such a way that the owner entrusts the trustee with the assets for a specific purpose through a contract or disposition *mortis causa*, and the trustee undertakes to keep and administer those assets.

The existence of a trust beneficiary is not necessary for the establishment of the trust itself. It is sufficient that if performance is to be provided to a specific person as a trust beneficiary, the designation of that person or the manner of their designation is stated directly in the statute. This points to the possibility of the existence of discretionary beneficiaries.

The role of the trust beneficiary is crucial for the subsequent existence of the trust, which is established for the benefit of certain persons, where:

- the beneficiary acts as the target person for whom the trust is administered (entitled to performance from the trust); or
- the beneficiary acts as the person supervising the administration of the trust.[9]

The position of these three persons (founder, trustee and trust beneficiary) is often rendered as a triangle with the founder, trustee and beneficiary at the vertices. Of course, there could also be a trust established for itself (ie, not for the benefit of certain persons). This is likely to be the case for public benefit trusts, which will not need to have a beneficiary at all.

---

7 *Ibid.*

8 See section 4.4, below, on judicial remedies.

9 If there is no trust beneficiary or if no beneficiary can be determined on the date the trust is established and the trust has been established for the benefit of a certain person(s), the founder is obliged under the law to designate a person who will supervise the administration of the trust for such person (trust beneficiary); if the founder is inactive, the court will appoint such person upon the proposal of the trustee or a person with a legal interest in the trust (Section 1464 of the Civil Code).

The role of the trust beneficiary can therefore be split as follows:

- the person entitled to (claim) certain performance from the trust according to the statute issued by the founder and the determination of the person who appoints the beneficiary (typically the founder or trustee); and
- the person vested with supervision over the administration of the trust.

The first of these roles may include the following statutory rights:

- the right to the fruits and revenues from the trust or a share thereof;
- the right to trust property or a share thereof; and
- the right to trust property or a share thereof on termination of the trust administration and dissolution of the trust (with the rebuttable legal presumption that the beneficiaries have a right to the property of the trust on termination if there is no one else who has right to it).

The second role includes the following statutory rights, which can be extended by the statute:

- the right to information, including:
  - document checks;
  - submission of an account;
  - asset management report; and
  - other information;
- the right to inventory, security and insurance;
- rights in relation to conflict of interest in respect of the trustee, including:
  - the right to impartiality of the trustee;
  - the right to be notified of any conflict of interest; and
  - the right to give consent to acts carried out by the trustee in the event of a conflict of interest with the trust beneficiary; and
- rights in relation to judicial proceedings, to submit a petition:
  - for the removal of a trustee and the appointment of a new trustee;
  - to invalidate the legal acts of the trustee; and
  - in the interests of the trust.

The position of the trust beneficiary is thus critical to the administration of the trust (where the trust is established for benefit of a particular person). The wording of Section 1471 of the Civil Code[10] may imply that in the absence of any trust beneficiary where a trust has been established for the benefit of a particular person – especially but not exclusively in the event existing beneficiaries die or cease to exist and there is no pending future beneficiary (who has yet to be born or established or to have gained capacity) – the

10 See Appendix I.

administration of the trust will be terminated because the purpose of the trust cannot be achieved.[11]

It is also important to mention the personal nature of the right to be a trust beneficiary. In particular, the position of trust beneficiary cannot, in principle, be subject to the law of succession – that is to say, the position of trust beneficiary cannot be inherited. This does not preclude laying down rules in the statute to provide for some form of succession in respect of trust beneficiaries.[12]

2. Designation, appointment, registration and eligibility of a trust beneficiary

This section looks at the process of becoming a beneficiary in a trust and the requirements that a beneficiary must meet. Self-evidently, the founder has a key role in this process, as they are the person on whose initiative the trust is established in the first place. The founder makes the decision on the appointment of the trust beneficiary, or the manner of his or her designation (eg, by specifying a group of individuals).

In general, the trustee has a subsidiary role in the process and:

- implements the founder's instructions according to the statute or the agreement establishing the trust;
- administers the trust; and
- is in closest contact with the beneficiaries.

However, in the case of a discretionary trust the trustee has a bigger role to play, exercising his or her discretion in relation to the appointment of discretionary beneficiaries and the determining of performance from the trust in favour of the beneficiaries.

2.1 Designation, appointment, and registration

We consider that Czech law recognises two separate statutory powers relating to the creation of the position of trust beneficiary:

---

11 Jaroslav Svejkovský, Ivan Kovář *et al, Svěřenské fondy. Příležitosti a rizika (Trust Funds. Opportunities and risks)*, CH Beck, 2018, pp33–36:

If there were no beneficiaries, eg, the individuals named as beneficiaries died, or if the legal entity ceased to exist, the trust would also cease to exist. This can be inferred from Section 1471 of the Civil Code, as the purpose for which the trust was established has been achieved, ie, it is no longer possible to fulfil the purpose, as there are no beneficiaries. This also shows that the conceptual characteristic of a trust is the fulfilment of its purpose, i.e. providing performance to the beneficiaries. We could even draw this conclusion from Section 1439 of the Civil Code, according to which the administration ceases with the termination of the beneficiary's right to the administered assets.

12 Svejkovský, Kovář *et al, Svěřenské fondy, ibid*, pp33–36:

The position of a beneficiary is not inheritable. An heir of a named beneficiary may be designated as a beneficiary, eg, to take over after the death of the beneficiary. The heir of the beneficiary, however, does not become the beneficiary merely based on the law of succession. Claims of the deceased that arose during their lifetime but were not satisfied could be inherited. The position of the beneficiary itself, however, is not inheritable. The entry of the heirs to the position of a beneficiary after the beneficiaries laid down in the statute must also be laid down directly in the statute.

- the right to designate a person as a trust beneficiary (or to determine the manner of designation of that person as a trust beneficiary) in the statute, which by its nature belongs to the founder; and
- the right to appoint a designated person as a trust beneficiary after establishing the trust, which may belong to the founder or the trustee according to the rules stipulated in the statute.

If performance is to be provided to a person as a trust beneficiary, the designation of that person – or the manner of designation – must be specified in the statute (in the case of a trust established for a private purpose, a circle of potential persons must be identified).[13] The statute must therefore contain some guidance (whether more or less specific) as to who may subsequently be named as a trust beneficiary. The statute also sets out the conditions under which the right to performance from the trust may arise. Since the founder is solely vested with the power to issue the statute (it is inconceivable that the statute should be issued by a person other than the founder), the power to designate the trust beneficiary and the conditions for provision of performance belong exclusively to him or her. We consider that the right to designate a person as a trust beneficiary (which belongs to the founder) can be understood to extend to giving full discretion in the matter to the trustee.

In terms of appointment, in principle the founder or the trustee appoints the beneficiary pursuant to Section 1457 of the Civil Code, unless the statute provides otherwise.[14] A trustee may appoint a trust beneficiary only if:

- the founder does not exercise his or her right to appoint a trust beneficiary; and
- the trust is established for a private purpose (in which case the trustee may appoint a trust beneficiary only if the founder designates in the statute the circle of persons from which the trustee may appoint trust beneficiaries – this is a limitation on the trustee's discretion in the case of discretionary trusts and one of the main reasons why we distinguish between designation and appointment of the trust beneficiary – albeit the circle can be wide).

Along with the appointment, the performance from the trust to the beneficiary should be specified (regardless of the fact that the beneficiary's right to performance from the trust arises from the conditions set out in the statute).[15] From the wording of Section 1457(1) in conjunction with Section

13 See Section 1452(1) and (2)(f) of the Civil Code, Appendix I.
14 See Appendix I.
15 Compare Sections 1457(1) and (2) with Section 1459 of the Civil Code. The legislator expressly distinguishes between "the determination of the performance from the trust" and "the creation of a right to the performance from the trust". The former can probably be understood as the scope and manner of the performance belonging to the individual beneficiary (or classes of beneficiaries), the latter as the conditions for making the performance available to the given beneficiary.

1458(1) of the Civil Code, the provision regarding the appointment of a trust beneficiary under Section 1457 (ie, that the founder or the trustee appoints the trust beneficiary) can be assumed to be a non-mandatory provision, and thus the founder may determine in the statute a different method of appointment of the trust beneficiary. The decision to appoint a trust beneficiary and the determination of the performance to be provided to the trust beneficiary (as well as any modification or revocation thereof) must, regardless of who appoints the trust beneficiary and determines the performance to be provided thereto, be in accordance with the statute. The person who appoints the trust beneficiary or determines the performance for the trust beneficiary must not do so for their own profit.[16]

It is important to note that in the case of a private trust, the appointment is effective neither upon the adoption of the constitutive act appointing the trust beneficiary, nor by the beneficiary's consent to the appointment, but only upon registration of the beneficiary in the trust register. However, the registrar shall not proceed with the registration of the trust beneficiary without either his or her prior appointment or his or her consent. The registration of the trust beneficiary in the trust register therefore has constitutive effects; that is, only after registration of the trust beneficiary in the trust register can the trust beneficiary exercise his or her rights arising from their position, noting that this does not mean that the law does not grant him or her at least some supervisory powers.[17]

In view of the above, there are up to three stages in the creation of the status of beneficiary for certain types of trusts, especially trusts established for the purpose of benefitting a particular person or persons, or private trusts:

1. *Designation* of a specific person as a trust beneficiary, or the manner of their designation; or, if it is a trust established for a private purpose, designation of a circle of persons.[18]
2. *Appointment* of the trust beneficiary by the founder, the trustee or another person (if stated in the statute).
3. *Registration* (in the case of private trusts) of the trust beneficiary, with his or her consent, in the trust register, rendering the appointment of the trust beneficiary effective.[19]

---

16 See Appendix I for Section 1458(1) of the Civil Code.

17 See section 4.4, below, on judicial remedies.

18 Jan Petrov, Michal Výtisk, Vladimír Beran *et al*, *Občanský zákoník. Komentář* (Civil Code. Commentary) (2nd ed), CH Beck, 2023:

> *The ability to designate implies the identification of a group of persons from which the founder or another authorised person will be able to select the beneficiary after the establishment of a trust, ie, it is only possible to specify the criteria to be met by the beneficiary (certain age, membership in a certain family or social group, profession or field of activity, type of disability, etc) ...*

19 In Petrov *et al*, *Občanský zákoník. Komentář*, *ibid*, Petrov also distinguishes between the designation and appointment of beneficiaries.

2.2 Eligibility

Only individuals or entities with legal personality, that is, with the capacity to have rights and obligations within the limits of the legal system, and with sufficient legal capacity (ie, with the capacity to acquire rights and assume duties for oneself by making juridical acts, at least through legal representatives/guardians) may be appointed a trust beneficiary.[20] Without legal personality and capacity, appointment is impossible, as is registration in the case of private trusts.[21]

However, when designating a person as a trust beneficiary, the founder need not limit him or herself in the statute to persons who already have legal personality, but may also designate those who have yet to acquire legal personality, for example those yet to be born.[22]

Legal professionals are not yet unanimous as to whether a trust can be a beneficiary of another trust. Svejkovský, for example, is rather sceptical about the status of another trust as a beneficiary:

> *The beneficiary must be a certain person (individual or legal entity). Within the meaning of Section 17 of the Civil Code, only a person can have and exercise rights. Another trust cannot be a beneficiary because a trust is not a person.*[23]

On the other hand, Petrov argues to the contrary in his commentary on the Civil Code:

> *Another trust, fiducié beneficiaire, may also become a beneficiary (Beaulne 2005 227.2); however, given the lack of clarity in the taxation of performance for the beneficiary, this is an impractical solution in our circumstances.*[24]

Use of the word 'person' in Section 1452(2)(f) of the Civil Code is perhaps unfortunate, suggesting – incorrectly – that the law does not allow trusts to be the beneficiaries of other trusts. But given the nature of Czech trusts, where the trustee bestows on the trust, through his or her person, the ability to acquire rights and obligations (ie, legal personality and legal capacity), we believe that a trustee acting on behalf of the trust can be appointed as a beneficiary of his or her trust. It follows that one trust is eligible to be a beneficiary of another trust.

---

20 Section 15 of the Civil Code: "Legal personality is the capacity to have rights and duties within the legal order."

21 Svejkovský *et al, Svěřenské fondy. Příležitosti a rizika, supra* note 11, pp33–36:
> *The beneficiary must be a certain person (individual or legal entity). Within the meaning of Section 17 of the Civil Code,* only a person can have and exercise rights. Another trust cannot become a beneficiary *because a trust is not a person.*

22 Petrov *et al, Občanský zákoník. Komentář, supra* note 18:
> *A child not yet born at the time of the creation of the trust or a legal entity that has not yet been created may become a beneficiary (see Beck III 1457 1). A beneficiary must have the capacity to receive performance from the trust at the time when the performance is to be provided to them; the moment the entitlement is created should be clearly defined.*

23 Svejkovský *et al, Svěřenské fondy. Příležitosti a rizika, supra* note 11, pp33–36.

24 Petrov *et al, Občanský zákoník. Komentář, supra* note 18.

3. Performance from the trust to the beneficiary

3.1 Creation and termination of the right to performance and determination of the performance

The Civil Code distinguishes two concepts that are similar in wording but different in substance, in connection with the provision of performance to the beneficiary from the trust:

- the creation of the right to performance from the trust to the beneficiary; and
- the determination of performance from the trust to the beneficiary.

The former is in principle within the exclusive competence of the founder, who lays down the conditions and requirements for the creation of the right to performance in the statute.[25] If these are met, the trust beneficiary has the right to claim the relevant performance from the trust.

The latter is in principle within the competence of the person who appointed the beneficiary, that is, typically the founder or the trustee (we may assume that, given the non-mandatory nature of the provisions of Sections 1457(1) and (2) of the Civil Code, another person may also be named to determine the performance from the trust to the beneficiary).[26] The idea is to determine the extent and form of the performance (what and how much will be provided) to a particular trust beneficiary or class of trust beneficiaries, and the relevant provisions of the statute must be followed in this regard.

If a trust has been established for a private purpose, a trust beneficiary's right to performance can arise not later than one hundred years from the establishment of the trust, even where the statute stipulates a later time. However, even after one hundred years, a trust beneficiary may acquire the right to performance if he or she is entitled under the statute to a share of the property not later than upon the extinction of the last right to the fruits or revenues, as well as if he or she was a contemporary of the founder or a child of the founder or of his or her contemporary; provided that, according to the statute, he or she is to succeed not later than upon the death of the trust beneficiary who, given his or her order, precedes him or her, in order to be the following ultimate trust beneficiary to acquire the fruits or revenues. Throughout his or her lifetime, other persons may acquire fruits or revenues along with him or her. If a trust has been established for private purposes, a beneficiary's right to fruits or revenues is extinguished not later than one hundred years from the creation of the trust; however, in the case of individuals, such a right may subsist until death.[27]

---

25 For Section 1452(2)(d) of the Civil Code, see Appendix I.
26 See Appendix I.
27 For Section 1460(1) and (2) of the Civil Code, see Appendix I.

3.2 Extent of the beneficiary's right to performance

The beneficiary's right to performance from the trust may include, in particular, the following rights contained in law, which could also be granted under the statute (ie, by the founder):

- the right to the fruits and revenues from the trust or a share thereof;
- the right to the property from the trust or a share thereof; and
- the right to the trust property or a share thereof on termination of the trust administration and dissolution of the trust (there is a rebuttable legal presumption that the trust beneficiaries have a right to the property of the trust on termination of the trust, if there is no one else who has right to it).

The fruits are what the assets of the trust regularly provide by virtue of their inherent nature.[28] The revenues are what the assets of the trust regularly provide by virtue of their legal nature.[29] If there is no trust beneficiary who has a right to the fruits and revenues from the trust, such right passes to the trust beneficiaries who have a right to the property from the trust.[30]

As for the form of performance from the trust, Petrov states as follows:

The performance from the trust may take different forms and vary in scope for different beneficiaries or for various categories of trust beneficiaries. Sometimes it takes the form of a monetary performance, other times it is the ability to use a particular item in the trust's assets in a particular way. The scope of performance must be specified as precisely as possible in the incorporation statute so as not to give rise to disputes, for example, as to what is included in the cost of training of the trust beneficiaries, etc. [see, eg, Trust Général du Canada v Fleury, *1999 CanLII 11604 (QC CS) sub. 48-52].*[31]

3.3 Waiver of the beneficiary's right to performance

In the case of a trust established for private purposes, the trust beneficiary may waive their right to claim performance in accordance with the statute by a declaration made in the form of a public instrument (typically a notarial deed).[32]

There is a question whether or not the waiver of the beneficiary's right to claim performance from the trust in accordance with the statute also means the

28 Section 491(1) of the Civil Code: "A fruit is what a thing regularly provides by its inherent nature, as follows from and is appropriate to its usual intended purpose, whether or not as a result of the endeavour of man."
29 Section 491(2) of the Civil Code: "Revenues are what a thing regularly provides by its legal nature."
30 Section 1462 of the Civil Code: "In the case of a right to fruits or revenues and in the absence of any other beneficiary to whom such a right could pass, it passes to the beneficiaries who are entitled to the right to property from the trust." See Appendix I.
31 Petrov *et al, Občanský zákoník. Komentář, supra* note 18.
32 Section 1461(2) of the Civil Code: "A beneficiary of a trust established for private purposes may waive his or her right under Subsection (1) by means of a declaration made in the form of a public instrument." See Appendix I.

termination of the status of trust beneficiary. This would have an impact on other beneficiaries' rights *vis-à-vis* the trustee, especially in relation to supervision over the administration of the trust. Given that in this context the Civil Code does not specify whether the position of the trust beneficiary is thereby terminated, we are inclined to assume that the legislator intended to mean that the position of the beneficiary should continue and that the trust beneficiary should continue to supervise the administration of the trust (as a residual right not explicitly waived), but without the right to claim performance from the trust. If the intention of the legislator was that the trust beneficiary should *de facto* no longer be the trust beneficiary, and hence waive all his or her rights (not only the rights to performance from the trust), the wording of the law would surely reflect it. A contrary interpretation would create the absurd situation that the trust beneficiary would implicitly waive rights, or more rights than those that were explicitly stated in the waiver.[33]

It is also important to mention the possible consequence of the waiver of the right of the beneficiary to claim performance from a private trust. If all the beneficiaries waive their right to claim performance from the trust in this manner, the administration of the trust terminates.[34]

4. Beneficiary's supervision over the administration of the trust

Supervision over the administration of the trust, although not explicitly defined in law, is a fundamental concept, as it is one of the control mechanisms in respect of the trustee,[35] who otherwise exercises full administration of the property of others and any increase in the value of the assets used in the interests of the beneficiaries of the trust, in which context the trustee may do whatever is necessary and prudent.[36] Supervision of the administration of the trust is exercised in particular by the founder and the trust beneficiaries. If the trust is established for the benefit of a beneficiary who is not present or cannot be identified at the date of the trust, a third person must be appointed to supervise the trust for the benefit of that beneficiary (a so-called 'curator').[37]

---

33 However, a different view is taken by Svejkovský in his commentary to the Civil Code (see Svejkovský, Marek *et al*, *Správa cizího majetku v novém občanském zákoníku*, *supra* note 3, pp482–486):

> *If the beneficiary waives the right to the relevant performance under Section 1461(2), this will undoubtedly include a waiver of the right to supervise the administration of the trust. The purpose of the beneficiary's supervision is to determine whether legitimate claims are being satisfied. If one gives them up, one loses the means (but also the reason) for control.*

34 Section 1471 of the Civil Code: "If a trust has been established for private purposes, its administration shall also end if all the beneficiaries waive their right to receive performance from the trust." See Appendix I.

35 Other control mechanisms are the obligation to perform the office with due care; the limitation of the trustee's acts by the statute; and other obligations imposed by law on the performance of the trustee's office (keeping reliable records, prohibition against commingling assets, obligations in case of conflict of interest, etc).

36 Sections 1409 and 1410 of the Civil Code: "Whoever is entrusted with the full administration of another person's assets shall do its best to multiply it and use it in the interest of the beneficiary" and "The trustee may treat the assets administered in whatever manner is necessary and useful."

37 Ronovská *et al*, *supra* note 1, pp509–515.

The founder may, of course, also stipulate in the statute that a third party, in addition to him or herself and the trust beneficiaries, shall exercise supervision. Such person will typically be called a 'supervisor' or 'protector' (more common in foreign jurisdictions). The law even allows for certain supervisory rights regarding the judicial means of supervision referred to in Section 1466 of the Civil Code[38] to be exercised by a third party (in addition to the founder and the trust beneficiary) who can show a legal interest therein (more about this in section 4.4 below, on judicial remedies). Supervision may also be exercised by public authorities in situations provided for by law, typically by the Czech National Bank in the case of trusts under the Act on Investment Companies and Investment Funds.

4.1 Right to information

One of the beneficiary's rights in respect of supervision over the trustee's administration of the trust is the right to information under Section 1465(2) of the Civil Code,[39] including the right to request from the trustee:

- document checks;
- submission of an account;
- the asset administration report; or
- other information.

This provision reflects the general provisions on the administration of the property of others set out in Section 1437 of the Civil Code, which provide for the obligation of the trustee to allow the trust beneficiary to examine the accounting books and documents relating to the administration at any time and to provide him or her with the necessary information upon request.[40]

Implementation of the document check is linked to the trustee's obligation to keep reliable records of the administered property (trust) in accordance with Section 1414 of the Civil Code (general provisions on the administration of the property of others).[41]

The submission of the account is then linked to the obligation of the trustee to draw up and submit to the trust beneficiary an annual account of the trust administration in accordance with Section 1436 of the Civil Code (general provisions on the administration of the property of others).[42]

---

38 See Appendix I.

39 *Ibid.*

40 Section 1437 of the Civil Code: "An administrator shall allow the beneficiary to examine at any time the accounting books and documents relating to the administration and provide him on his request with the necessary information on the manner in which the administration is exercised."

41 Section 1414 of the Civil Code: "An administrator shall keep reliable records of the administered property and may not combine his own property with the administered property."

42 Section 1436 of the Civil Code:
(1) An administrator shall submit to the beneficiary an account of the administration at least once a year. Where there are several administrators, they shall present joint accounts, unless otherwise provided under a contract or statute with regard to the division of their competence.
(2) The accounts must be prepared in such detail so as to allow the verification of their accuracy.

All of these rights are linked to the actions of the trust beneficiary as the person supervising the administration of the trust; that is, the trust beneficiary must exercise his or her right to information and must ask the trustee to provide the necessary information for proper, and above all informed, supervision over the administration of the trust (except for the submission of the account by the trustee as mentioned above).

A trust beneficiary unaware of the existence of the trust does not have to take any action at all – the trustee is in principle obliged on his or her own initiative to deliver to the beneficiary, as the person supervising the administration of the trust, a notice stating at least the name, purpose and duration of the trust and his or her name and address.[43]

4.2 Right to inventory, security and insurance

Other rights of the trust beneficiary related to supervision arise from the general provisions on the administration of the property of others under Section 1423(1) of the Civil Code, which include:

- the right to ask the trustee to make an inventory;
- the right to ask the trustee to provide security for the proper administration of the trust; and
- the right to ask the trustee to insure the administered property (property of the trust).[44]

The above may be required from the trustee whether the obligation arises from the statute, the agreement with the trustee establishing the trust, or the law. Even if it is not stipulated in the statute or agreement, the trust beneficiary may file a petition with the court to order the trustee to make an inventory, provide security or insure the administered property, taking into account the value of the property of the trust, the position of the parties and the specific nature of the case and at the same time ensuring that the order does not contradict the contract establishing the trust.[45]

---

43 Section 1465(1) of the Civil Code:
The trustee shall, without undue delay, deliver to a person with a statutory right to supervise the administration of the trust a notification which shall state at least the designation, purpose and duration of the trust and the trustee's name and address. The notification is not necessary if the person authorised to supervise is already aware of these facts.

44 Section 1423(1) of the Civil Code:
An administrator shall make an inventory, provide security for the proper administration or insure the administered property, where provided by articles of association, another contract or a statute.

45 Section 1423(2) of the Civil Code:
On the application of a beneficiary or another person with a legal interest therein, a court may impose the duty under Subsection (1) on the administrator, taking into consideration the value of the administered property, the position of the parties and other circumstances of the case. An application may not be granted if it is contrary to the contract establishing the administration concluded between the administrator and beneficiary.

4.3 Rights in relation to conflict of interest

The rights of a trust beneficiary in relation to a conflict of interest within the trust are threefold:

- the right to impartiality of the trustee;[46]
- the right to be notified of the trustee's conflict of interest; and
- the right to give consent to the acts carried out by the trustee (in the event of a conflict of interest with the trust beneficiary).

The right to impartiality of the trustee is set out in Section 1412 of the Civil Code, which specifies as follows:

- the trustee should act equally towards all the trust beneficiaries, if there are more than one; and[47]
- where the trustee is one of the trust beneficiaries, the trustee must take into account the interests of the other trust beneficiaries as well as his or her own and must exercise his or her powers in the common interest.[48]

The right of the trust beneficiary to be notified by the trustee about his or her conflict of interest is mentioned in Section 1413 of the Civil Code, which sets out two instances where the trustee must immediately inform the trust beneficiary (and any other person exercising supervision) of his or her conflict of interest:

- where he or she has an interest in a business or activity pursuing financial gain that may be in conflict with the interests of the trust beneficiary; or
- where there is a right that he or she could enforce against the trust beneficiary or the administered property (trust).[49]

Consent of the trust beneficiary to the trustee's actions is required in the following situations listed in Section 1415 of the Civil Code:

---

46 See: *Pirani v Pirani*, 2022 BCCA 65 (Court of Appeal for British Columbia). The court found that fiduciary duties included a duty of loyalty. Specifically, the judge recognised that fiduciaries were obliged not to place themselves in a position where their duties and interests were or might be in conflict with, or might benefit from, their actions. These rules are often expressed as the no-conflict rule and the no-profit rule. The judge repeatedly defined the relevant fiduciary duty as the duty to act only in the best interests of all beneficiaries.

47 Section 1412(1) of the Civil Code: "Where there are more beneficiaries, either simultaneously or subsequently, an administrator must act against all impartially, taking into account their respective rights."

48 Section 1412(2) of the Civil Code: "If the trustee is a beneficiary, he/she must take his/her own interests into account as well as those of the other beneficiaries and exercise his/her powers in the common interest."

49 Section 1413 of the Civil Code:

> *Where there is no interest or right following from a juridical act establishing the administration, an administrator must, without undue delay, inform the beneficiary and the person who supervises the administration of property or the interest of the beneficiary of: (a) any interest he may have in the course of business or activities seeking property benefit which could conflict with the interests of the beneficiary, and (b) any right he may have which he could assert with regard to the beneficiary or in respect of the administered property.*

- the trustee must be a party to the contract relating to the administered property;
- the trustee is contractually entitled to acquire the right to the administered property, ergo the property of the trust;
- the trustee is to acquire a right against the trust beneficiary;
- the trustee is to use the administered property (property of the trust); or
- the trustee is to obtain information for his or her own benefit in the administration of property of the trust.[50]

In the case of the latter two, however, the consent of the trust beneficiary is not required if the possibility of such action by the trustee arises from the statute or the agreement with the trustee establishing the trust, or by law.

4.4 Judicial remedies

The Civil Code distinguishes three different judicial remedies in respect of a beneficiary's supervision over the trust administration by the trustee:[51]

- application to commence proceedings for measures against the trustee and their removal, and appointment of a new trustee;
- application to commence proceedings for the invalidity of the legal acts of the trustee; and
- application to commence proceedings in the interest of the trust.

(a) Proceedings for measures against the trustee and removal of the trustee

Proceedings for measures against and removal of the trustee and the appointment of a new trustee are conducted on the principle of formality, with the court conducting the evidentiary proceedings *ex officio*. It is for the applicants to state the reasons supporting their claims; the court will take evidence of its own motion, without being obliged to consider the applications of the parties. The applicants therefore do not bear the burden of proof. The following persons have standing in the proceedings:

- the founder;
- the trust beneficiary; and
- any third party that proves a legal interest.

---

50 Section 1415 of the Civil Code:
(1) A trustee may become a party to a contract relating to the administered assets, contractually acquire a right in the assets or acquire a right vis-à-vis the beneficiary only with the consent of the beneficiary.
(2) The trustee may use the administered assets or the information obtained in the course of administration for his/her own benefit only with the consent of the beneficiary unless the possibility of such use is provided for in the trust deed or another agreement or if the law so provides.

51 Decision of the Supreme Court of 21 March 2024, Case No 24 Cdo 1754/2022. According to Supreme Court precedent, it is also possible to bring an action for declaration of invalidity of the founding legal statute pursuant to Section 80 of the Code of Civil Procedure, as such a declaration could create a solid legal basis for the relationships of the parties *inter se*. Such an action should be brought against the trustee. The Supreme Court has generally concluded that the regulation of legal persons cannot be used by analogy to declare the invalidity of a trust.

Examples of third parties that might prove a legal interest are provided by Svejkovský in his commentary to the Civil Code:

> *It will be the person appointed to supervise the administration of the trust, or it may be the legal successor of the founder, or a person demonstrating a certain relationship to the future beneficiary of the trust, etc. These latter persons must first demonstrate to the court their legal interest in such decision which they propose the court should issue imposing an obligation upon the trustee to act or refrain from acting.*[52]

The term 'future beneficiaries' is likely to refer to discretionary beneficiaries and to beneficiaries who should have been appointed and/or registered but the trustee unreasonably failed to do so. The question is the scope of the beneficiary's supervisory rights. Certainly, he or she should at least be able to apply to the court for the appointment of a curator, if no one has been appointed, to exercise supervisory rights on his or her behalf.[53]

Applicants (beneficiaries) may even seek an injunction if certain conditions are met.

The evidence in proceedings to impose duties on a trustee is to be found in the conduct of the trustee, whether in respect of legal or factual acts or omissions, which are or threaten to be harmful to the trust or to the rights of the trust beneficiaries; or in other conduct contrary to the purpose of the trust. The remedy sought is the imposition of an obligation to provide information or ensure particular performance, or a prohibition from carrying out certain actions.

Proceedings for the removal of a trustee and the appointment of a new trustee represent an even more serious interference with the autonomy of the will of the founder of the trust. The court's decision presupposes a long-term neglect or gross breach of the trustee's duties which harms or threatens to harm the trust or the rights of the trust beneficiaries.[54] Proceedings will ordinarily be initiated by the beneficiary or a third party (the founder is likely to have the right to remove and appoint trustees without interference from the court).

Despite the fact that, because the founder's rights are potentially restricted by the court, measures to remove are the exception, we believe that the will of the founder, at whose initiative the trust was established and who determined who should be the trustee in the first place, should stand as a limitation on the

---

52 Svejkovský, Marek *et al*, *Správa cizího majetku v novém občanském zákoníku*, *supra* note 3, pp493–500.

53 Ronovská *et al*, "Rights of beneficiaries", *supra* note 1, pp509–515.

54 *Brassard v Brassard*, 2009 QCCA 898 (Court of Appeal for Quebec). The court concluded that the beneficiaries' subjective reasons alone, consisting of their doubts about the trustee's loyalty, were not sufficient to remove the trustee. Although the court did not absolutely rule out the removal of the trustee and his or her replacement by a person contrary to the testator's wishes, it stressed that this measure should only be used in exceptional circumstances. If the beneficiaries wish to remove the trustee, they cannot merely base their arguments on their concern about the trustee's disloyalty, but must prove a breach of duty.

55 See: Vlastimil Pihera, *Komentář Beck, Občanský zákoník III. Věcná práva* (Sections 976–1474) (2nd ed), Wolters Kluwer, 2021, pp1574–1576.

court in proceedings.[55] We acknowledge the exceptional nature of the provision, but it does allow for considerable judicial interference.

Given the legal fees set, the trust beneficiaries are unlikely to sue the trustee for performance from the trust, which would likely be a costly and one-off solution; instead, they will sue for information about the trust administration, so as to create an evidentiary basis for commencing proceedings to remove a current trustee who is in breach of his or her duties under the law, the statute, or the agreement with the founder establishing the trust, and appoint a new trustee, which can be seen as a more comprehensive and longer-term solution to the situation.[56]

Another legal protection that applicants may seek is an injunction, provided certain conditions are met. Where there is an imminent threat of harm to the protected interests of the trust or its beneficiaries, or other danger due to a default, they can ask the court to impose a duty on the trustee before his or her removal.

(b) Proceedings concerning the invalidity of legal acts of a trustee

Claims for the invalidity of legal acts of a trustee cover a specific category of acts which involve not breach of the law, good morals or public order,[57] but causing harm to legal assets crucial for the trust. The sanction of invalidity penalises legal acts in order to protect specific interests.

The founder, the trust beneficiary or any person with a legal interest may request that the court declare the legal acts of the trustee invalid. It is a case of relative invalidity of a particular act or acts carried out by the trustee.

The term 'harm' may mean not only an act that has caused damage, but also an act connected to an imminent risk of damage. The threat must be immediate. Damage includes both material and immaterial damage. Of course, insignificant damage or consequential damage cannot be attributed to the trustee.

The only benchmark is the negative effect of the conduct, regardless of its object. The basis for a conclusion of invalidity is harm to the trust or the rights of the injured party; acts causing such harm are invalid *ab initio* and have no effect.

An essential for the imposition of the sanction of invalidity is a causal nexus between the conduct and the harm or threat of imminent harm. Harmful or threatening conduct must be attributable to the trustee. However, there is no consensus on whether culpability is required.[58]

---

56 For an action for a remedy other than monetary payment the fee is only CZK 2,000: Item 4(1)(c) of the Schedule to the Court Fees Act.

57 See Sections 580 and 588 of the Civil Code.

58 While Pihera (see note 55) contends that fault of the trustee is a precondition, Luboš Tichý (*Občanský zákoník: Komentář*, Volume III (Sections 976–1474)) argues it is not.

(c) *Proceedings in the interest of the trust*

While the first two proceedings above address breaches of any duty of a trustee, proceedings in the interest of the trust are aimed at misconduct in the performance of 'procedural' duties. If the founder, a trust beneficiary or a third party proves a legal interest, they may request that the court authorise them to bring the action and to continue to conduct the proceedings on behalf of the trust if the trustee has not done so.

However, the court cannot dismiss an application to open proceedings in the interest of the trust simply by referring to the possibility of bringing an action for measures against the trustee or for the invalidity of the legal acts of the trustee.

In his commentary on the Civil Code, Svejkovský gives examples of possible proceedings in the interest of the trust:

> *It could be any proceeding for any performance to the trust, or any proceeding for the defence of the trust, etc. Such proceedings may either have already been commenced (and possibly by the trustee or against the trustee by a person seeking satisfaction of his or her claims from the trust against the trustee, and the trustee may continue to be inactive in those proceedings), or an application may have to be filed, and the trustee may be reluctant, which may lead to a risk of default or preclusion, etc., or there may be procedural consequences due to running of the period of time for an appeal, etc.*[59]

While a decision by the court to take action against the trustee or to invalidate the legal acts of the trustee is an interference with the founder's powers, a decision to take action in the interest of the trust is quite an exceptional restriction on the autonomy of the trustee's will in its activities.

---

59 Svejkovský *et al*, *Správa cizího majetku v novém občanském zákoníku*, *supra* note 3, pp493–500.

UBO Register and Register of Trusts

Daniela Gadasová
CEEtax

1. Introduction

The 4th Anti-Money Laundering Directive (AMLD4)[1] required EU member states to enact, by 26 June 2017, laws to make available beneficial ownership information on trusts. In the Czech Republic this requirement had already been met in 2014: a Czech trust (*svěřensky fond*) can only be established by registration of the trust, including the ultimate beneficial owner (UBO), in the Register of Trusts – a procedure similar to the incorporation of a company. Section 118a *et seq* of the Public Registers Act of 2013 first established the Register of Trusts,[2] to be handled by the regional courts. A reminder here that the Czech trust is a *sui generis* legal arrangement that finds no similarities in other EU member states, since neither the founder nor the trustee holds title to the assets. The European Union recognises the Czech trust to be a legal arrangement similar to the common law trust, and treated as such for registration purposes.[3] The Public Registers Act was supplemented by the UBO Registration Act of 2021,[4] which transposed AMLD5 (the 5th Anti-Money Laundering Directive)[5] into Czech law.

2. Registration of trusts

The Register of Trusts is a public administration information system in which legally defined data on Czech and certain foreign trusts is entered. The record is largely non-public and is kept in electronic form by the relevant regional court.

1 Directive (EU) 2015/849 of the European Parliament and of the Council of 20 May 2015 on the prevention of the use of the financial system for the purposes of money laundering or terrorist financing. Available at: https://eur-lex.europa.eu/legal-content/EN/TXT/PDF/?uri=CELEX:32015L0849.

2 Act No 304/2013 Coll of 12 September 2013 on Public Registers of Legal and Natural Persons. Available at: www.zakonyprolidi.cz/translation/cs/2013-304?langid=1033 (access requires registration).

3 Report of 16 September 2020 from the Commission to the European Parliament and the Council, assessing whether Member States have duly identified and made subject to the obligations of Directive (EU) 2015/849 all trusts and similar legal arrangements governed under their laws. Available at: https://eur-lex.europa.eu/legal-content/EN/TXT/PDF/?uri=CELEX:52020DC0560.

4 Act No 37/2021 Coll of 19 January 2021 on the Registration of Beneficial Owners. Available at: www.zakonyprolidi.cz/translation/cs/2021-37?langid=1033 (access requires registration).

5 Directive (EU) 2018/843 of the European Parliament and of the Council of 30 May 2018 amending Directive (EU) 2015/849 on the prevention of the use of the financial system for the purposes of money laundering or terrorist financing. Available at: https://eur-lex.europa.eu/legal-content/EN/TXT/?uri=celex%3A32018L0843.

It is administered centrally by the Czech Ministry of Justice. The records also include a collection of documents. An entry into the register may be carried out by the competent regional court and/or a notary public. The registration process is initiated on the basis of an application that is submitted using a prescribed electronic form, which must include documents substantiating the facts that are to be entered into the register.

According to Section 1451 of the Civil Code,[6] an *inter vivos* trust is created by a trustee (or at least one of the trustees in the event there are more than one) accepting the authorisation to administer it and entering the trust in the register. Only in case of a disposition *mortis causa*, where a trust is created upon the death of the decedent, is an entry in the register not an essential constituent element of the creation of the trust; the trustee is still required, however, to apply for its registration subsequently.

The UBO Register is to some extent separate from the Register of Trusts. It stems from the concern that criminals might otherwise be able to hide their identity behind a corporate or trust structure for the purpose of money laundering or terrorist financing. Anti-money laundering (AML) and 'know your client' (KYC) obligations ensure that the information in the UBO Register is correct and up to date. In addition to the Register of Trusts and the UBO Register, Czech trusts have other registration obligations. Even though trusts are not legal entities (they have no legal personality or domicile) a Czech trust is a taxable entity and is treated as a legal entity in tax proceedings. Furthermore, since a trust is a taxable entity it has a registration obligation for taxes under Section 125 *et seq* of the Tax Code[7] and the relevant provisions of individual tax laws.

3. Registration in the registers

AMLD4 requires that trustees of any express trust – and of any legal arrangement similar to a common law trust – obtain and hold adequate, accurate and up-to-date information on beneficial ownership regarding the trust. That information must include the identity of the following:

- the founder(s);
- the trustee(s);
- the protector(s) (if any);
- the beneficiaries or class of beneficiaries; and
- any other natural person exercising effective control over the trust.

Breaches of this obligation are subject to proportionate measures and sanctions. AMLD5 requires that certain aspects of the data are made public.

6 Act No 89/2012 Coll of 3 February 2012, the Civil Code. See Appendix I.
7 Act No 280/2009 Coll of 22 July 2009, the Tax Code. Available at: www.zakonyprolidi.cz/translation/cs/2009-280?langid=1033.

The Czech Register of Trusts and UBO Register are separate but interlinked, accessible through the Public Register and Collection of Documents of the Ministry of Justice.[8] Although access to the registers is not very user friendly and only available in the Czech language, since the start of the COVID-19 pandemic there has been a push towards digitalisation of the Czech administration, and much of the filings and other communication with courts and registers is now digitalised. The Czech UBO Register is part of the EU Beneficial Ownership Registers Interconnection System (BORIS), set up in line with the EU AML directives and connecting the national registers of EU members as well as Iceland, Liechtenstein and Norway.

4. Register of Trusts

The following basic information is recorded in the Register of Trusts:

- identification of the trust and the date of its settlement;
- the purpose of the trust and details about its business activities (if any);
- the names and residential addresses of the founder and the beneficiary/beneficiaries (or if no specific beneficiary has been designated, the way in which they will be determined);
- the trustee and protector and their dates of birth, nationalities and ID numbers; and
- any other important fact that the trustee wishes to register.

Important information about the functioning of the trust is also included, such as information about any insolvency or bankruptcy proceedings, reasons for the cancellation or deletion of the trust, and decisions about transfer of a business of the trust. Following entry of a trust in the Register of Trusts, and any other registrations, the court informs the tax authorities, the state statistical office and the trade licensing office.

Certain data needs to be supported by documents, copies of which in electronic form are included in the Register of Trusts. These documents include:

- the statute of the trust fund;
- documents regarding the appointment or dismissal of a trustee;
- decisions regarding the termination of a trust, or that the fund's assets are transferred to another fund or entity;
- decisions regarding insolvency or bankruptcy of the trust or the trustee;
- a decision on changing the original purpose of a public benefit trust; and
- documents relating to the increase of assets in a private purpose trust.

Personal data on the founder, the beneficiary and the protector is publicly

8 See: https://or.justice.cz/ias/ui/rejstrik.

accessible only if consent for disclosure has been given. Of the trustee, only their name, year and month of birth, country of residence, nationality and contact details are published. Only the trustee and a person with a legitimate interest have access to the full record.

The proposal for registration in the Register of Trusts of the settlement of a trust, or any changes to it, is submitted by the trustee without undue delay. If they do not comply with this obligation to submit a proposal for registration within 15 days, then the proposal can be submitted by any interested party. Any proposal for registration must be accompanied by supporting documentation. Proceedings to correct the record in the registers can be initiated by the registering court – this may occur when a court or other public authority detects an inaccuracy in the Register of Trusts, in which event they are obliged to notify the appropriate court of the discrepancy. The court makes a decision on a proposal for registering data in the registers within five working days, and it notifies the relevant parties by sending an updated extract from the register.

The Public Registers Act includes the principle of 'material publicity'. One purpose of the registers is for third parties to be able to rely on certain legal facts in their dealings with organisations, including trusts, that are not natural persons. Therefore, if someone takes legal action on the basis of information publicly available in the register, then the entity to whom the information refers cannot object that the data in the register is incorrect (Section 8 of the Public Registers Act).[9] If a decision by a trustee is invalid, the trust register records can be corrected within a period of three years only if this does not interfere with the rights of a third party acting in good faith (Section 79 of the Public Registers Act).[10] Also, third parties acting in good faith are not affected by the court's refusal to register a trustee or protector (Section 10 of the Public Registers Act).[11] A trustee can apply for correction of facts in the register for up to three years unless it affects the rights of good-faith third parties. Finally, in order to protect third parties, the court may, even without a proposal, decide to terminate the trust, unless the trustee corrects the relevant deficiencies (Section 65a(4) of the Public Registers Act).[12] The court will notify the founder, the beneficiaries and the protector of the trust before cancelling the trust.

5. UBO Register

The UBO Register applies to the beneficial owners of companies as well as trusts. As regards trusts a UBO includes the founder, trustee and protector, as well as the beneficiaries or class of beneficiaries. It further includes any natural person who, directly or indirectly, exercises decisive influence over the

9 *Supra* note 2.
10 *Ibid.*
11 *Ibid.*
12 *Ibid.*

administration of the trust's assets, regardless of its legal basis. The definition of 'protector' in the UBO Register Act seems somewhat limited, since apart from exercising supervision the protector should also be able to nominate or recall a trustee or a beneficiary. The UBO of a regulated investment company or investment fund that acts as trustee of a trust is also considered a UBO of that trust.

The trustee is responsible for obtaining up-to-date information about the UBO, and for recording all actions undertaken in the KYC process to check the completeness and accuracy of the information. The data to be registered includes the UBO's name, residential address, date of birth, nationality and ID number, as well as information about the character of the beneficial ownership and the name of any other individual related to the trust.

Irregularities in the UBO Register consisting of incorrect, incomplete or missing data (current or historical) are rectified through a 'discrepancy procedure' conducted by the relevant court. In this procedure the court also deals with any specific consequences arising under private law from non-compliance with the registration requirement. Along with the discrepancy procedure, a 'discrepancy note' about the potential incorrectness is prepared, which is included in the non-public part of the UBO Register.

A discrepancy procedure requires no proposal and may be initiated by a court on the basis of a notification from a responsible party, and also at its own initiative. A notifier should reasonably believe that they have detected a mistake in the UBO Register, which they should support with facts and/or documents, typically showing that the entered data is out of date or incomplete. Before proceeding on the discrepancy, the court will provide the registering person with a chance to rectify or explain the discrepancy without the need for further steps.

Discrepancies are generally reported to the court by service providers, since they are required to do so under the Czech AML Act.[13] Service providers are most often able to detect a discrepancy when identifying clients or carrying out their due diligence on them. Before reporting a discrepancy, service providers should bring their findings to the attention of the client and give them an opportunity to explain or rectify. Apart from obliged persons in the sense of the AML Act, public authorities also have a notification obligation to the court. If a public authority or a UBO reasonably assumes that it has identified a mismatch between current information in the UBO Register and reality, or when no information is registered, they should report the discrepancy, substantiated by facts or documents, to the responsible court.

The discrepancy procedure is initiated by the court with a resolution

---

13 Act No 253/2008 Coll of 5 June 2008 on selected measures against legitimisation of proceeds of crime and financing of terrorism. Available at: www.mfcr.cz/assets/attachments/Zak_2013-253.pdf.

delivered only to the participants in the proceedings. The court generally decides on a discrepancy based on presented documents and its own investigation, but usually without any hearing. The court finally decides whether the data in the register is incorrect within the framework of the discrepancy procedure and sends a copy of the decision to the administrative authority competent to handle offences.

The UBO Registration Act places the responsibility for the accuracy of the information in the UBO Register in first instance with the trustee. A fine of up to CZK 500,000 (approximately €20,000) may be imposed for violating the obligation to register accurate data, or the obligation to provide the necessary cooperation to the trustee, and this violation is confirmed by the court in a 'discrepancy proceeding'. The court decides whether the data in the UBO Register is incorrect during an irregularity procedure. But it is the administration – the local municipality with extended powers in the place where the offender resides – that decides whether and to what amount a fine is levied. There is a limitation period of one year for the violation of failing to ensure the entry of new data within 15 days from a court decision. Furthermore, no sanctions will be applied if a period of two years has passed before the court-initiated proceedings on a discrepancy.

Under their respective rules of professional conduct, auditors, lawyers, notaries and tax advisers are prohibited from dealing with clients if they are not sufficiently able to establish the client's real identity. Also, the AML Act obliges service providers, banks, notaries, lawyers, auditors etc to identify their client before establishing a business relationship. If these providers do not fulfil their KYC obligations due to irregularities in the UBO Register, they may be penalised with fines of between CZK 100,000 and CZK 1,000,000.

An indirect consequence may also be where the trust holds shares in a business corporation. If the data of the trust in the UBO Register is incorrect or incomplete, it cannot exercise voting rights, the subsidiary company will not be able to make profit distributions, and certain other actions by members of the governing body of the company may be invalid. This would severely restrict the activities of the subsidiary company.

Finally, under the Czech Public Procurement Act,[14] failure to comply with the requirement to register a UBO will result in exclusion from any public contract. Under the State Budget Rules,[15] UBOs are also required to be registered if they wish to receive grants or subsidies.

---

14 Act No 134/2016 Coll of 19 April 2016, the Public Procurement Act. Available at: https://s-ic.cz/wp-content/uploads/2018/08/Annex_2_procurement_law_Czech_Rep_Serbia.pdf.

15 Act No 218/2000 Coll of 27 June 2000 on Budget Rules and Amendments to certain Relating Acts (Budget Rules), available at: www.zakonyprolidi.cz/translation/cs/2000-218?langid=1033 (access requires registration); and Act No 250/2000 Coll of 7 July 2000 on Budgetary Rules for Territorial Budgets, available at: www.zakonyprolidi.cz/translation/cs/2000-250?langid=1033 (access requires registration).

6. UBO registration process

Registration of the UBO can be done either by a court in court proceedings or through a notary. The notary and the court are essentially equal authorities from the point of view of entering data in the UBO Register. The court, however, reserves the power to resolve discrepancies in the register. Notarial entries are not subject to direct control or review by the court. The registration proceedings are highly standardised, and electronic communication is preferred. Registrations are executed by the relevant regional courts (except in the capital, Prague, where the Municipal Court is empowered). The applicable court is determined by default according to the address of the trustee and, in the case of a legal arrangement, the location of the relevant general court.

Proceedings are initiated based on a proposal, which is usually submitted by the notary or the trustee. However, the proposal can also be submitted by any person with a legitimate interest, including the UBO. The proposal must be submitted in electronic form, which means through the proposer's digital data box or with a recognised electronic signature. Only in the case of a legal arrangement is it possible to submit a proposal in paper form. In such case the registering person's signature must be notarised. If a legal representative submits the proposal on behalf of the registering person, a power of attorney in the same format (electronically or in notarised paper form) must be attached. The proposal can only be submitted using a template form, which is filled out on the website of the Ministry of Justice. The completed form is downloaded in PDF format and sent to the relevant court. Alongside the proposal, documents proving the identity of the UBO need to be presented, as well as documentation proving the UBO relationship. There also exists a mechanism of automatic registration, which in some cases occurs without action by a registering person. This happened, for example, when the registers established under the Public Registers Act of 2013 were transformed into the central register under the UBO Registration Act of 2021.

7. Transparency vs privacy

AMLD5 required the general public to have access to data on the beneficial owner, at least to the extent of name, date of birth, country of residence, nationality and the nature and extent of participation. Member states can also decide to make other data available. However, there is a right to privacy, protected by the Czech Charter of Fundamental Rights and Basic Freedoms,[16] which forms a part of the constitutional order of the Czech Republic. Its Articles 7 and 10 provide for the inviolability of a person's privacy, protection from

16 Constitutional Act No 2/1993 Col Resolution of the Presidium of the Czech National Council of 16 December 1992 on the declaration of the Charter of Fundamental Rights and Basic Freedoms as a part of the constitutional order of the Czech Republic. Available at: www.psp.cz/en/docs/laws/1993/2.html.

unauthorised intrusion into their private life, and protection from the unauthorised misuse of their personal data. This is similar to the right to respect for private life as defined in Article 8 of the 1950 European Convention on Human Rights,[17] and the United Nation's Universal Declaration of Human Rights,[18] which states at Article 12 that "no one shall be subjected to arbitrary interference with his privacy".

On 22 November 2022 the Court of Justice of the European Union (ECJ), published its decision in two cases[19] and determined that provisions under AMLD4, amended by AMLD5, regarding the general public's access to the register were invalid, since they were incompatible with the right to private life and the protection of personal data of the registered beneficial owners. According to the ECJ, the principle of transparency is indeed essential for a democratic system, but only in relation to public administration bodies, not in relation to private individuals. The ECJ did not question the importance of the fight against money laundering and the financing of terrorism, but emphasised that this is primarily the job of the state. It is therefore entirely legitimate for such records to be accessible to the state and its authorities, and persons obliged to identify and check a client according to special AML regulations. However, according to the ECJ, making records available to other persons without further distinction is neither appropriate, nor necessary to achieve the intended purpose. It would make it possible for members of the public to compile a profile of properties and investments of the individual concerned, which would mean a loss of control over the scope and use of the information, particularly on the internet. The ECJ further stated that a public UBO register constitutes processing of personal data within the meaning of Article 8 of the EU Charter[20] and therefore violates EU GDPR (General Data Protection Regulations).[21]

EU member states were thus obliged to make their registers of beneficial owners unavailable to the public and to allow access only to persons with a legitimate interest. The ECJ decision led to the immediate suspension of access to several EU national registers. In the Czech Republic, the trustee and UBO themselves have, of course, full access to all data (including historical data) that is recorded in the UBO Register. The Czech UBO Register is only searchable by

17 Convention for the Protection of Human Rights and Fundamental Freedoms of 4 November 1950. Available at: www.echr.coe.int/documents/d/echr/convention_ENG.

18 The United Nations Universal Declaration of Human Rights of 10 December 1948. Available at: www.un.org/en/about-us/universal-declaration-of-human-rights.

19 *WM and Sovim SA v Luxembourg Business Registers*, joint ECJ Cases C-37/20 and C-601/20 of 22 November 2022.

20 Charter of Fundamental Rights of the European Union 2012/C 326/02. Available at: https://eur-lex.europa.eu/legal-content/EN/TXT/PDF/?uri=CELEX:C2012/326/02.

21 Regulation (EU) 2016/679 of the European Parliament and of the Council of 27 April 2016 on the protection of natural persons with regard to the processing of personal data and on the free movement of such data. Available at: https://eur-lex.europa.eu/eli/reg/2016/679/oj.

the public, free of charge and without the need for any registration, in respect of the name of the trust, its registration number and file number. And the only other public items of information in the register are the date of settling the trust, the identity of the trustees and an indication of the purpose of the trust.

Full electronic access to the Register of Trusts and the UBO Register is in the first instance given only to competent authorities, including courts, law enforcement and tax authorities, banking authorities and providers of grants and subsidies. The Ministry of Justice will also allow access to identifying information about a trust and an individual UBO of a trust – that is, the name, state of residence, year and month of birth and nationality of a UBO – as well as names of other persons related to it, to anyone with a 'legitimate interest'. This includes any person who has a proven interest in the prevention of money laundering and terrorist financing, or requests access in relation to a trust through which a non-EU legal entity is owned or controlled (Section 15 of the UBO Registration Act).[22] Discussion continues about widening the access, and the position of the EU Parliament and EU Commission seems to be that persons with a legitimate interest should also include press and civil society. [23] Privacy protection therefore remains at risk.

Upon request, the court will make information about beneficial ownership inaccessible about a UBO who is a minor or who is incapacitated. An exemption from access can also be requested in exceptional cases such as the exposure of the UBO to a risk of kidnapping, blackmail or violence, unless this would conflict with public interest.

8. Public opinion

The balance between the need for transparency and the fundamental right to privacy is perhaps different in the Czech Republic than in most western jurisdictions. In the Czech Republic the general attitude towards trusts is one of suspicion. The best-known example is the AB Private Trust formed by former Prime Minister Andrej Babiš, who in 2018 placed his chemical–food concern Agrofert in a revocable trust while remaining the only beneficiary. This resulted in a public outcry. The attitude of suspicion towards trusts is not only due to the fact that the use of trusts is very new – only 10 years old – but also that in developed western countries wealth is often admired and secrecy therefore suspect. In ex-communist countries, on the other hand, wealth is suspect and privacy is cherished. This suspicion is to some extent a result of the fact that some of the wealth in trusts has likely been created in dubious privatisation schemes during the 'wild 1990s' after the fall of communism.

---

22 *Supra* note 4.

23 Press release from the Council of the EU on 18 January 2024 (modified on 14 February 2024). Available at: www.consilium.europa.eu/en/press/press-releases/2024/01/18/anti-money-laundering-council-and-parliament-strike-deal-on-stricter-rules/.

9. Foundation register

While a trust is a legal instrument used in the Anglo-American legal system, in civil law countries like the Czech Republic it is more common to use actual legal entities to own property rather than contractual constructs. Asset management, asset protection and succession planning, as well as charitable endeavours, are often carried out by a foundation (or an endowment fund). A foundation is a separate and distinct legal entity. It is established by a public deed, which is either a foundation deed or a will in the event of death of the decedent, and by registration of the entity in the Foundation Register, managed by the relevant court. However, an endowment fund, which is basically a simpler form of foundation, can be established by drawing up a charter that does not need to be in the form of notarial deed.

As with trusts, the register is searchable by name of the foundation, registration number or file number. Other public information in the register includes the date of settling the foundation, an indication of the purpose of the foundation, and the identity of the members of its governing bodies – the management board, supervisory board and auditor. Unlike trusts, however, foundations are also searchable in the register by the name of the members of their governing bodies. In addition, the public part of the Foundation Register shows the amount of foundation capital, and there is a need to prepare annual reports which are also publicly accessible. Foundations are further obliged to publish their full charter. Details about the founder and about beneficiaries (if any) can be publicly accessed since these will be mentioned in the charter. The foundation can, however, request that data about beneficiaries is made unavailable to the public.

10. Foreign trusts

The UBO Registration Act provides that foreign trusts and foreign legal arrangements that are structurally or functionally similar to trusts are also required to register their UBOs in the Czech UBO Register under certain circumstances, unless the UBO is already registered in a UBO register of another EU member state. These circumstances include:

- where the foreign trust or legal arrangement has immovable property in the Czech Republic or its assets are predominantly located in the Czech Republic;
- where the foreign trust or legal arrangement is administered from the Czech Republic, or the trustee of the foreign trust is carrying out business in the Czech Republic; and
- where the purpose of the foreign trust or foreign legal arrangement is pursued and achieved in the Czech Republic.

Apart from the UBO, in the case of foreign trusts the Register of Trusts also records data and documents with identification details of the trust and the trustee, including:

- the trust's jurisdiction;
- its purpose and business activities (if any);
- its termination or the termination of its Czech activities; and
- whether it is subject to insolvency or bankruptcy proceedings.

The author would like to express sincere thanks to her business partner, mentor and friend Henk Goossen for his patience, his amazing ability to pass on experience and his many years of support in the field of estate planning. Without him and CEEtax, the author could not have gained the experience to participate in this book.

Taxation of trusts

Ivan Kovář
BDO Czech Republic

1. Introduction

As mentioned in previous chapters, under the Czech Civil Code a trust does not have a legal personality. However, for accounting and tax purposes trusts are treated as if they do have a legal personality, and are accounted for and taxed similarly to other legal entities. According to Section 20(3) of the Tax Regulations Act 280/2009,[1] as amended by later regulations, a 'trustee' is a person who fulfils all the obligations of a trust towards the tax authority.

The legal regulation of trusts in relation to taxes was introduced into the tax regulations and substantive tax law as part of a wide range of changes prompted by the adoption of the new Civil Code. Thus, the trust has been regulated in the domestic tax environment only since 2014. From an application of tax provisions standpoint, these regulations are recent and lack methodological guidelines, experience from tax audits, best administrative practices or case law.

Since then, there have been no significant developments in the tax legislation related to trusts. Domestic tax legislation completely omits provisions on trusts in relation to the new Private International Law Act. Furthermore, the current regulations do not address international treaties for the avoidance of double taxation; there are no provisions concerning non-resident taxation; and there are no regulations as to similar institutions, such as trusts, under foreign law. Although some areas have been clarified as a result of Coordination Committee talks between representatives of the Chamber of Tax Advisors and the General Financial Directorate (for example, in the fields of tax input prices for contributed long-term assets, acquisition costs and so on), dilemmas persist.

It is noted that this chapter solely addresses the taxation rules related to trusts – not to foundations, legal entities frequently used in the Czech Republic (for example, private family foundations). Although the basic principles of taxation are similar, there are differences in detail.

1 Available at: www.zakonyprolidi.cz/translation/cs/2009-280?langid=1033 (access requires registration).

2. Tax personality of trust

There are a number of approaches, in the context of substantive tax law, to deal with the tax personality of trusts. Undoubtedly, a trust is a standard taxable entity with respect to taxation. To illustrate this, Section 17(1)(f) of the Income Taxes Act 586/1992 ('the Income Taxes Act') provides that trusts are tax-paying entities and are liable to pay corporate income tax.[2]

Trusts are also considered legal entities for the purposes of value added tax (VAT). Section 4b(2) of the Value Added Tax Act 235/2004 states as follows: "For the purposes of this law, a trust shall be treated as a legal entity."

A trust is a taxpaying entity with respect to real estate tax under Section 3(2)(b) and Section 8(2)(b) of the Real Estate Tax Act 338/1992.

In the Road Tax Act 16/1993, however, there is no specific definition as to the tax personality of trust. Despite this, if registered as the operator in the vehicle registration certificate, the trust is liable to pay road tax.

It should be noted that the trust is not explicitly listed as a payer of excise duty and is not cited in the Gambling Tax Act 187/2016 or other tax-specific laws. Nevertheless, if the general terms are met, the trust will be subject to excise duty.

2.1 Tax registration and residence

Sections 125 *et seq* of the Tax Regulations Act 280/2009 provide that a trust has an obligation to register with the tax authority. As a fiduciary representative of a trust, a trustee is required to submit a registration application within 15 days of the trust's establishment. The obligation to register as a taxpayer has been specified in relevant substantive tax laws, such as in respect of real estate tax, road tax, withholding tax and others.

The application for registration must be submitted exclusively in electronic form. A separate application, containing certain information and attachments, must be submitted for VAT registration.

On 30 April 2014, the General Financial Directorate issued an instruction entitled Information on the Registration of Trust.[3] This instruction states that all trusts in the Czech Republic must be registered with the Financial Office in Prague, Administrative Office for Prague 7. An exemption applies with respect to a 'tax residence' for the purposes of real estate tax. A tax residence is determined by the tax office within whose district the specific real estate is located.

From 1 January 2018, a unified Register of Trusts was introduced as part of the public administration information system. Each trust is assigned a

---

2 The Income Taxes Act 586/1992 is available at: www.zakonyprolidi.cz/translation/cs/1992-586?langid=1033 (access requires registration).

3 Reference number: 22438/14/7001-41000-010450.

reference number which the tax administrator uses as the entity's tax identification number, with prefix 'CZ'.

It is important to note that if a trust is established according to the legal regulations of the Czech Republic (ie, the Civil Code), it is considered a Czech tax resident, even if the trustee is a foreign person. It follows that determining tax residence on the basis of the place of management (ie, the address where a taxpayer is established) does not apply. Section 17(3) of the Tax Regulations Act 280/2009[4] explicitly states the exemption:

> *If a taxpaying entity, which is not a legal entity, has been established or organised according to legal regulations of the Czech Republic, it is deemed to have its registered office in the Czech Republic.*

3. Accounting

3.1 The accounting obligation

The Accounting Act 563/1991 ('the Accounting Act')[5] and its related implementing regulations require a trust to maintain accurate financial records. Section 1(2)(i) of the Accounting Act defines a trust as an 'accounting entity'.[6] A trustee assumes an obligation of trust with respect to bookkeeping, including preparation of financial statements and fulfilling other obligations as outlined in Section 4a(1) of the Accounting Act.[7]

The Accounting Act does not impose any specific requirements on the trust; thus, trusts are subject to the same accounting rules as other accounting entities.

In addition, the Accounting Act does not include a trust in a list of entities with the right to use 'single-entry bookkeeping' when specific legal conditions outlined in Section 1(f) have been met. A trust, therefore, is obliged to maintain double-entry accounting. Under Section 2 of the act, accounting involves recording double entries on the status and movement of assets, liabilities, debts, expenses and revenues, as well as profits and losses.

3.2 Accounting procedures

The Accounting Act has several implementing decrees that specify the accounting procedures for different types of accounting entity.

For purposes of trust accounting, we will focus on two decrees issued by the Ministry of Finance:

- Implementation of Accounting Act 563/1991 for Entrepreneurs Decree 500/2002 ('the Decree for Entrepreneurs)'; and

---

4 *Supra* note 1.
5 Available at: www.zakonyprolidi.cz/translation/cs/1991-563?langid=1033 (access requires registration).
6 *Ibid.*
7 *Ibid.*

- Implementation of Accounting Act 563/1991 for Non-Commercial Entities Decree 504/2002.

According to Section 1449 of the Civil Code,[8] adherence to the binding accounting procedures and guidelines depends on the purpose for which a trust is established.

It is important to note that trusts established for private purposes, that is, for the benefit of a specific person or in his/her memory, must follow the Decree for Entrepreneurs. It adheres to the Czech Accounting Standards for Entrepreneurs, specifically the Czech Accounting Standards for Accounting Entities – covering entities that maintain accounting in accordance with the Decree for Entrepreneurs – which were published in the Financial Newsletter 11-12/2003.

The selection of applicable accounting procedures depends on the purpose for which the trust was established.

3.3 Categorisation of accounting entities

Determining the size of an accounting entity, also known as 'categorisation', is essential for ascertaining obligations under the Accounting Act. These obligations include:

- maintaining accounting records;
- creating financial statements;
- providing information; and
- fulfilling the audit obligation.

Categorisation is defined in Sections 1b to 1e of the Accounting Act.[9] Accounting entities are classified by size:

- **Micro:** A micro accounting entity does not exceed at least two of the following as of the balance sheet date:
  - net assets of CZK 9,000,000;
  - net annual turnover of CZK 18 million; and
  - 10 employees.
- **Small:** A small accounting entity does not exceed at least two of the following as of the balance sheet date:
  - net assets of CZK 100 million;
  - net annual turnover of CZK 200 million; and
  - 50 employees.
- **Medium:** A medium accounting entity does not exceed at least two of the following as of the balance sheet date:

8 See Appendix I.
9 *Ibid.*

  - net assets of CZK 500 million;
  - net annual turnover of CZK 1 billion; and
  - 250 employees.
- **Large:** A large accounting entity exceeds at least two of the following as of the balance sheet date:
  - net assets of CZK 500 million;
  - net annual turnover of CZK 1 billion; and
  - 250 employees.

It is noted that a new accounting act is currently being prepared and is expected to introduce changes to the aforementioned limits effective from 1 January 2026.

3.4 The extent of accounting

A trust compiles a financial statement in 'full form' or 'short form', depending on its categorisation. Trusts in the micro or small categories, which are not obligated to have their financial statements audited, may compile them in short form. As stipulated in Section 9 of the Accounting Act,[10] all other trusts are required to compile their financial statements in full form.

The majority of domestic trusts will be classified as micro accounting entities, unless they exceed an annual turnover of CZK 18 million, regardless of the value of contributed assets (the net asset condition), and have more than 10 employees. In this case, the trust will be required to prepare the financial statement in a simplified format only.

3.5 The audit obligation

The obligation for financial audit is outlined in Section 20 of the Accounting Act,[11] which provides the standard legal requirements for verifying the financial statement by an auditor. These conditions extend to trusts, meaning that all medium and large trusts are required to audit their financial statements without any additional conditions, as determined by their accounting entity categorisation.

Small trusts are only required to have their financial statements audited if they reach at least one of the following criteria for two consecutive accounting periods:

- total assets of CZK 40 million;
- annual net turnover of CZK 80 million; or
- an average of 50 employees during the accounting period.

10 *Ibid.*
11 *Ibid.*

If any of these criteria are met during the second accounting period, the financial statement must be verified by an auditor.

Micro trusts are not required to have their financial statements audited.

3.6 The opening balance

Upon registration of a trust in the Register of Trusts, the trustee is required to prepare an 'opening balance'.

Due to its inherent nature, a trust does not generate 'registered capital'. The contributed assets are detailed in the opening balance under standard balance asset items according to their type, while liabilities items are classified under other equity.

3.7 Operating accounting

Over the course of its existence, the trust follows standard accounting practices by recording double entries for the status and movement of its assets, liabilities, debts, expenses, revenues and profit and loss, in accordance with the rules and guidelines mentioned above.

3.8 Accounting for performance to a beneficiary

When accounting for a performance to a beneficiary from a trust, it is essential to determine whether it is a drawdown from the contributed assets or a performance from the trust's profit. Although both variants are treated similarly in the accounts as reduction in contributed assets versus reduction in equity, the classification is important as it has significant tax consequences, which are described later in the chapter.

4. Income tax

As previously mentioned, although a trust does not have a legal personality, Section 17(1)(f) of the Income Taxes Act states that a trust is a taxpaying entity with respect to corporate income tax, making it subject to taxation.[12]

An explanatory report[13] for the amendment to the Income Taxes Act (implemented by Act 344/2013) states in Point 194, referring to Section 17(1)(f) of the act, that the fundamental principles of trust taxation are as follows:

- a contribution of assets to a trust is not subject to income tax;
- a profit generated from administration of trust assets is subject to corporate income tax; and
- tax treatment of a performance from the trust depends on the beneficiary and the type of drawdown.

---

12 *Supra* note 2.

13 The report is available at: www.daneprolidi.cz/duvodova-zprava/duvodova-zprava-k-zakonnemu-opatreni-c-344-2013-sb-senatu-o-zmene-danovych-zakonu-v-souvislosti-s-rekodifikaci-soukromeho.htm.

Figure 1: Tax rates applicable to trusts in 2024

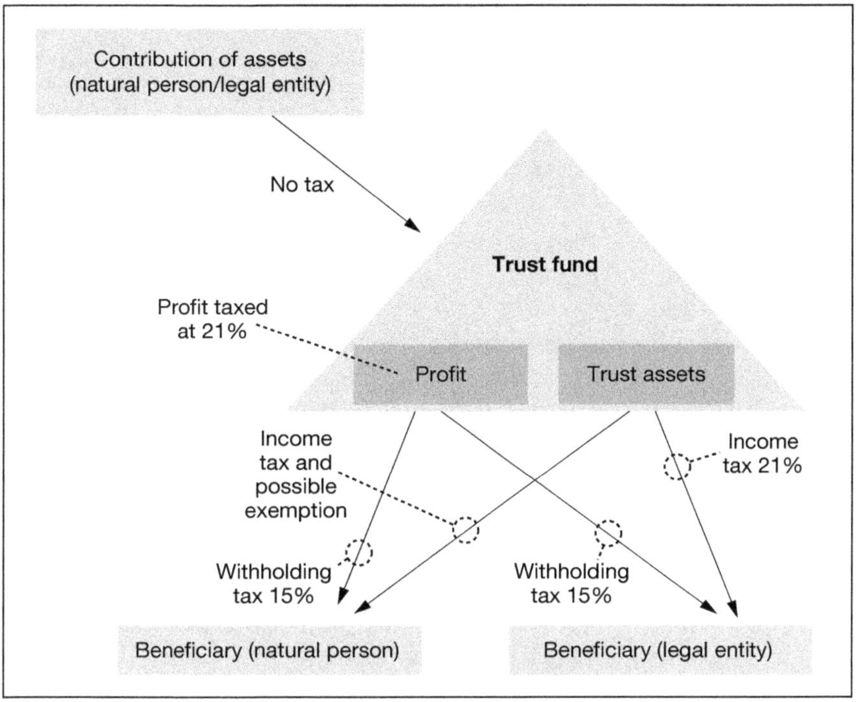

This overview assumes that the beneficiary is a tax resident in the Czech Republic. For residents from other countries, it is essential to adhere to the provisions stipulated in the international treaties on preventing double taxation.

The fundamental principle of taxing beneficiaries on their income through trusts is the 'tax neutrality' of gifts. The rationale behind this is explained in the reasoning report referred to above:

> *... [T]he trust's income shall be taxed continuously at the standard corporate income tax rate, and the performance provided to the beneficiary from the profit after taxation shall be subject to withholding tax, similar to other income derived from profit shares (eg, dividends). A different situation arises when the trust distributes a performance that is not an equitable profit-sharing interest but rather a part of the assets initially contributed or included in the trust through the trust deed. Such income is analogous to a gift or inheritance. The settlor or another contributor gratuitously set aside a part of their property to the trust, and this property is consequently transferred gratuitously to the beneficiary. When considering such income for the purposes of taxation, the same principles which apply to gift or inheritance tax should be used. For the trust termination, which occurs when the trustee*

surrenders the remaining trust property to the entitled person relevant to the trust statute, the same principles as when providing a performance to the beneficiary shall be applied.

The discussion highlights that if the purpose of a family trust is to hold family assets and change beneficiaries with the succession of generations, the tax implications of transferring assets in and out of the trust should be comparable to direct transfers between individual family members.

4.1 Contribution of assets to trust

Section 21f(1) of the Income Taxes Act contains the defining provisions:

For the purposes of income taxes, contributing assets to the trust and increasing trust assets through the trust deed or disposition upon death are treated as contributions to the commercial corporation. It follows that, according to relevant legislation, contributions to the trust are not considered 'gratuitous income' and are not subject to income tax.[14]

This conclusion is supported by the General Financial Directorate's information document from 23 October 2014 regarding Section 21f of the Income Taxes Act on trust contributions:

A new provision ... states that contributing assets to the trust and increasing trust assets through the trust deed or disposition upon death are treated, for the purposes of the act, as a contribution to the commercial corporation. This cannot be considered as gratuitous acquisition of assets, ie gratuitous income. This contribution is merely a balance sheet operation and therefore it does not ultimately affect the taxable base, ie it is not subject to taxation. The subject regulation eliminates restrictions related to the inability to depreciate trust assets and the inability to deduct amounts equal to accounting depreciation, or expenses when consuming non-depreciated assets, in the tax base of trust income for assets contributed to the trust, which arise from the application of Section 27(j), Section 25(1)(i),(zp),(zq) of the act.

A contribution of assets to a trust is considered a tax-neutral action from the perspective of income tax. If non-current assets eligible for tax depreciation from the settlor's business property are contributed to the trust, the trust will continue to receive tax depreciation, following procedures similar to those applied during transformations of business entities.

There has been debate historically regarding the possibility of claiming tax depreciation on assets contributed to a trust from private property (that is, assets contributed by non-business entities). After the amendment to the Income Taxes Act, which became effective in 2015, this inconsistency was resolved. Assets contributed to a trust can now be depreciated according to standard rules.

---

14 *Supra* note 2.

4.2 Taxation of trust income

All income derived from the administration of trust assets during a given period is subject to taxation. Section 1449 of the Civil Code provides that the purpose for which the trust is established determines its (significantly variable) taxation.[15] A trust may be subject to tax as:

- a standard (business) entity, provided that it was established for private purposes;
- a publicly beneficial taxpaying entity under Section 17a of the Income Taxes Act; or
- a basic investment fund according to Section 17b of the Income Taxes Act.

(a) Trust for private purposes

The tax base for trusts is determined by their economic results, with common tax adjustments such as additions or deductions, tax depreciation and other adjustments taken into account. Tax is then calculated using the same tax rate as for commercial companies, which is currently 21%.

The tax return must be submitted electronically in the format and structure specified by the tax administrator. The trustee is responsible for preparing and filing the tax return, including all required forms and attachments, particularly financial reports and attachments to the financial statement.

(b) Trust for public benefit

Section 38mb of the Income Taxes Act states that a publicly beneficial trust, as defined in Section 17a of the act, is exempt from filing an income tax return if it receives income that is not taxable, exempt from tax, or taxed at a special rate (withholding tax). This exemption also applies if a trust is not required to follow the procedure under the provisions of Section 23(3)(a)(8) of the Income Taxes Act (ie, it doesn't have to pay back previously claimed deductions).

The tax base of the trust is determined by calculating the profit, which is the difference between the trust's earnings and costs, for the relevant tax period. The accounting results of business activities must be adjusted in accordance with standard legal rules. Tax is then calculated from the tax base using the current tax rate of 21%.

Section 20(7) of the Income Taxes Act provides that if the trust purpose is for public benefit, the tax base may be reduced by up to 30%, with a maximum limit of CZK 1 million.

(c) Trust for investment

If a trust adheres to the regulations of the Investment Companies and Investment

15 See Appendix I.

Funds Act 240/2013 and operates as a basic investment fund, it may be subject to a special rate of 5% for investment funds as defined in Section 21(2) of the act.

It is noted that this type of trust has not yet been registered by the Czech National Bank in the Czech Republic.

The trust's corporate income tax return must be submitted electronically in the format and structure determined by the tax administrator. The financial statement is an obligatory attachment to the return. The deadline for submitting the return is four months from the end of the previous taxation period. If authorised by a tax adviser or lawyer, or in the case of an obligatory audit, the deadline for submitting the return is extended to six months.

4.3 Performance to beneficiaries

Performance to individuals and entities defined in the trust statute (both natural and legal entities) is considered taxable income in the hands of the beneficiaries. Beneficiaries may receive the performance from one of two sources: profit or contributed assets.

The following taxation principles apply:

- the trust's profit distributions to beneficiaries are always taxable; and
- if assets are transferred by disposition upon death or contributed by a close person, any benefits to beneficiaries from those assets may be exempt from income tax.

Section 21c of the Income Taxes Act (Common General Provisions on Property Rights) outlines the priority of sources for providing benefits to beneficiaries:

For the purposes of income taxes, it shall apply that performance from a trust shall be paid from the profit of the trust first and then from the other property of the trust.[16]

This provision is essential for income taxation of the beneficiaries. For the purposes of taxes, performance is derived first from the profit of the trust and then from the remaining assets, regardless of the type of transaction.

The General Financial Directorate provided its opinion on the issue on 24 March 2021, stating that Section 21c of the Income Taxes Act does not violate tax neutrality:

In other words, current wording of Section 21c considers a real and utterly logical approach which prioritises the provision of the created profit before drawing down the contributed assets. This is also related to preventing intentional tax avoidance when distributing profits created from contributed assets.[17]

---

16 *Supra* note 2.

17 General Financial Directorate, Minutes of the Coordination Committee meeting with the Chamber of Tax Advisers of the Czech Republic, "Gratuitous performance of assets from the family foundation and trust", reference no 572/24.03.21.

The trust's profit distributions to the beneficiaries are always taxable. If a beneficiary is a natural person, his or her income from a trust is considered income from capital assets, under Section 8 of the Income Taxes Act. Both natural persons and legal entities are subject to withholding tax on such income, with a current rate of 15%, under Section 36(2)(a) of the Income Taxes Act. Section 38d of the act regulates the obligation of the trust to return withholding tax. It follows that the trust is considered a taxpayer. This debate suggests that the taxation principles applied are comparable to those applying to the dividend and profit shares of commercial corporations.

Performance to the beneficiaries from assets contributed to the trust is also considered taxable income for the beneficiaries. However, in specific situations, it may be exempt from income tax. This occurs when assets that generate income are transferred to the trust, either by disposition upon death or directly by a close relative. From a tax perspective, contributions of assets to trusts are treated in a similar manner to inherited assets (from any individual) or gifts from a close person. For beneficiaries who are natural persons this is considered as other income under Section 10 of the Income Taxes Act. For beneficiaries who are legal entities this constitutes a tax base.

With regard to the points mentioned, it is necessary to thoroughly examine whether the contributed assets actually yield the stated income. If the beneficiary receives performance in the same form as the asset contributed, this is considered performance from assets and may be exempt from tax. For example, this is the situation when depositing monetary assets – the performance is directly related to the contributed assets. Likewise, performance from contributed receivables upon their realisation may be considered as provision of the performance from contributed assets, a position supported by the General Financial Directorate in one of its statements. If the beneficiary receives performance in the form of different assets, even if they are of equivalent value, it is considered as performance from profit and is always subject to tax.

Gratuitous income received by the beneficiary from trust assets is exempt from income tax if:

- it was either transferred to the trust by disposition upon death or contributed to trust assets through disposition upon death, under Section 4a(b) of the Income Taxes Act for natural persons and Section 19b(2) of the act for legal entities; or
- it increased trust assets or was contributed to the trust by an individual who was a relative of the beneficiary in the direct or collateral line, or a person from a jointly managed household (applicable only to natural persons), as outlined in Section 10(3)(c) of the Income Taxes Act.

According to Section 38v of the Income Taxes Act, a beneficiary who is a natural person is required to submit a notification of exempt income to the tax administrator if they receive exempt income exceeding CZK 5 million in a calendar year. The notification must be filed by the same deadline as the tax return.

4.4 Exemption for received dividends and profit shares

This situation often arises when shares or ownership interests of a commercial company are among the assets of the trust. If the commercial company pays dividends or profit shares to the parent trust, taxation follows the standard rules of the Income Taxes Act (in the case of withholding tax, under Section 36), including conditions for tax exemption under Section 19(1)(ze) of the act.

It is important to meet and maintain the conditions for the exemption of paid dividends or profit shares according to the principles in operation for parent and subsidiary companies. The legislation provides that if a trust is a parent company, it enjoys a tax-neutral status similar to that of a commercial corporation:

For the purposes of the act ... a 'parent company' is ... defined as a trust ... if it holds at least a 10% share in the registered capital of another commercial corporation continuously for a minimum of 12 months in its commercial property.[18]

This amendment is in accordance with Council Directive 2011/96/EU of 30 November 2011 on the common system of taxation for parent companies and subsidiaries of different member states.[19]

Under this definition, taxation of a commercial corporation and a trust that is a parent company will be the same in absolute amount, provided that:

- the profit is distributed in the form of dividends from the profits of the commercial corporation to a shareholder who is a natural person; and
- the profit was first transferred to trust assets, where the trust acts as the parent company, and subsequently paid out to a natural person by way of performance to a beneficiary.

In both scenarios, the company providing the financial benefit to the natural person is subject to withholding income tax at a rate of 15%.

4.5 Exemption of income from the sale of shares and ownership interests

If a trust sells contributed shares or ownership interests, the same exemption rules that apply to parent and subsidiary companies under Section 19(1)(ze) of the Income Taxes Act can be applied to income from the sale.

It is noted that contributing to the trust or buying shares or an ownership

18 The Income Taxes Act, Section 19(1)(ze). See note 2, *supra*.
19 Available at: https://eur-lex.europa.eu/legal-content/EN/TXT/?uri=celex%3A32011L0096.

interest triggers a new 12-month time limit for exemption under Section 19(1)(ze).

4.6 Assets declaration

Sections 38zc, 38zd and 38ze of the Income Taxes Act contain provisions on the declaration of assets. According to Section 38zd(3)(a) a taxpayer must declare "[t]he trust of which the taxpayer is the settlor or beneficiary, as well as known facts on assets of the trust". Such declaration is only required if requested by the tax authority.

4.7 Taxation of trustee's income

Any legally competent individual can act as trustee without obtaining any permission or business licence. However, if the trustee receives reimbursement for administering the trust, whether financial or non-financial, it is considered income from business under Section 7 of the Income Taxes Act.

The trustee is obliged to register with the relevant tax authority as a taxpaying entity and is subject to income tax as a natural person. Additionally, the trustee must register as a self-employed person for health and social insurance contributions. As a taxpayer, the trustee is required to file an annual income tax return for natural persons and health and social insurance statements within the specified deadlines. In compliance with standard regulations, an obligation for advance payments may arise for both income tax and health and social insurance contributions.

5. Value added tax

As mentioned above, a trust is considered a legal entity for purposes of VAT under Section 4b(2) of the Value Added Tax Act 2004. As such, the standard rules of the act apply to trusts if they perform a business activity as defined in the act. This applies to both mandatory and optional taxpayer registration.

Does the obligation to pay VAT arise when assets are contributed to the trust? The amendment to the Value Added Tax Act (enacted by Act 170/2017, effective from 1st July 2017) removed from the provision defining the supply of goods the limitation on the contribution of assets solely to business corporations, as provided by Section 13(4) of the Value Added Tax Act. After the amendment, any contribution of assets for which deduction of input VAT was claimed upon acquisition is now considered a supply of goods. This conclusion is supported by the explanatory report to the amendment:

> *This regulatory adjustment clarifies that the provision applies not only to commercial corporations, which is a commercial company and cooperatives, but also to other legal entities such as associations, institutions, foundations, endowment funds, and trusts.*

When contributing assets to the trust, it is crucial to carefully assess when and how any VAT deduction on the acquired assets was claimed, and whether the contribution qualifies as a taxable transaction or is eligible for any exemptions. The trust's eligibility for tax deduction on contributed assets is assessed on an individual basis, subject to certain conditions and provided that the contribution is associated with a taxable transaction and an obligation to pay tax.

The issue is not relevant in practice for a contribution of private property owned by an individual who is not registered for VAT (most commonly, for example, when it involves contributing private real estate to a family trust fund).

However, contributions of business assets to a trust require detailed analysis.

6. Property and other taxes

6.1 Real estate tax

As mentioned above, under Sections 3(2)(b) and 8(2)(b) of the Real Estate Tax Act 338/1992, trusts are subject to property tax on land and buildings. The financial office responsible for administering real estate tax is determined by the location of the property. Trusts must therefore comply with the same legal requirements, conditions and rules as other taxpaying entities.

6.2 Tax on acquisition of real estate

Currently, there is no tax in the Czech Republic on the transfer of real estate, though from the introduction of the Trust Institute in 2014 until its abolition in 2020, the potential impacts of such tax had to be examined. Real estate contributions to the trust and transfers of real estate from the trust to beneficiaries were exempt as they were considered gratuitous acquisitions. The tax only applied to paid transfers of property.

6.3 Road tax

As previously noted, trusts are not explicitly mentioned in the Road Traffic Act 16/1993 as being subject to road tax. However, if the trust is listed as the operator on the vehicle's technical certificate, it is still obligated to comply with the act.

Additionally, when the trust reimburses its employees for travel expenses related to the use of their private car, road tax is paid by the trust. The trust must adhere to the same legal requirements, conditions and regulations as other entities subject to road tax.

7. Tax comparability between foreign and Czech trusts

Tax rules for situations where a Czech tax resident contributes assets to a foreign trust or receives benefits from a foreign trust have not yet been defined by regulations or administrative practice.

In its minutes of the meeting of the Coordination Committee with the Chamber of Tax Advisers of the Czech Republic of 23 April 2014,[20] in the section, "Interpretation of the term 'trust' in relation to foreign comparable entities", the General Directorate of Taxes outlined six criteria that a foreign trust must meet to be comparable with a Czech trust established under the Czech Civil Code:

- The trust is created when a settlor entrusts assets to a trustee for a specific purpose through a deed or disposition upon death.
- The trustee undertakes to hold and manage the assets, to exercise proprietary rights in respect of the assets in its own name and on behalf of the trust, and to maintain the accounts of the foreign entity.
- Trust assets are not owned by the trustee, settlor or beneficiary.
- The trust does not have legal personality.
- Under the laws of the taxpayer's country of residence, they are subject to a tax similar to the income tax of legal entities, and their income is not attributed to other individuals, either wholly or partially.
- Profits from appreciation of assets and provision of performance to the beneficiary are considered taxable income in their country of residence.

The General Directorate of Taxes confirmed the comparability criteria for foreign trusts in its Minutes of the meeting of the Coordination Committee with the Chamber of Tax Advisers of the Czech Republic of 23 March 2022,[21] in the section, "Comparability of the foreign trusts and trust forms with the Czech trust". The penultimate criterion above may be interpreted more flexibly in justified cases.

8. Case study

The experience of our tax practice is that most family trusts face similar tax issues during their establishment and operation. This section aims to provide general solutions to the most common problems.

The following short case study assumes that the trust is private and that the settlor, trustee and beneficiary are all tax residents of the Czech Republic.

The trust was established by Mr and Mrs Smith as settlors. They contributed CZK 100,000 to trust assets. To avoid paying high notarial fees, they later contributed other assets to the trust, transferring assets from their marital property, which included a plot of land, a family house, money, a flat, works of art and an ownership interest in a private limited company.

The trust statute designates both settlors, as well as their three children, as the beneficiaries. Mr Smith and a family lawyer, Mr Turnbull, are designated as the trustees.

---

20 Reference number 421/26.02.14.
21 Reference number 588/24.11.21.

The financial contribution made at the establishment of the trust did not have any tax implications; nor do any other contributions. To determine the future tax acquisition cost of the contributions, a market expert conducted an appraisal of contributed assets. The contributions were recorded in the assets at the input prices as appraised, resulting in a corresponding increase in the trust's equity. According to the trust statute, all beneficiaries are entitled to reside in the family villa, and this free use of trust assets by the beneficiaries is not subject to taxation.

The trustees agreed to transfer the flat, which was contributed to trust assets by the settlors, to the youngest daughter as beneficiary. Providing assets to a beneficiary who is a direct relative of the settlors is considered performance from trust assets and is exempt from tax, the trustees recording the transfer as a reduction of non-current assets against a reduction of equity in the trust's accounting.

The tax acquisition cost of the flat for the beneficiary, the daughter, is equal to its fair market value at the acquisition date as determined by an appraiser, rather than its original value at the time of the contribution. This is important because if the daughter sells the flat before the end of the 10-year exemption period for income of a natural person, the tax base would be the difference between the selling price and the tax acquisition cost.

Would tax implications change if extensive repairs and technical improvements were made to the flat while it was owned by the trust and funded by it? The tax implications for this situation are the same, and the difference in fair market value between the time of transfer and the time of contribution does not affect exemption.

The trustees decided to use trust assets to purchase a car to be used by all beneficiaries. Such actions do not carry any income tax implications. Several years later, the trustees decided to transfer the car from the trust to the middle son as the beneficiary. This situation, too, is without tax implications. A non-monetary benefit in the form of a car, acquired with trust funds and provided to the direct relative of settlors, is exempt from taxation. The fact that a particular item may have a different market value at the date of its provision from the trust compared to its value at the time it was originally contributed, does not affect exemption.

The trustees in our case study supported the eldest son's studies by paying his tuition fees from trust assets. Whether any tax implications arise from this situation depends on whether the trust generated profit during its existence. If the trust did not generate any profit, payment of the tuition fees would be considered as performance from trust assets. This would reduce the trust's monetary assets and equity, and would be exempt from taxation as the beneficiary is a direct relative of the settlors. However, if the trust did generate profits, such as on profit shares received from a subsidiary company, it would be subject to taxation.

The trust must record such profits, equal to the profit shares it received, in its profit and loss account. However, income of the subsidiary company is exempt from tax. Therefore, the trust does not incur any tax liability for such income in its tax return.

The principle of prioritising performance from profits under Section 21c of the Income Taxes Act 586/1992 is applied in respect of the provision of the tuition fees to the beneficiary. The tuition fees are subject to withholding tax at a rate of 15% (in 2024). The trust, as a taxpaying entity, is responsible for deducting and remitting this tax. In what amount? The payment of the tuition fees cannot be reduced by tax and must be paid in full. Therefore, to calculate tax on the tuition fees, a gross up is necessary, which involves considering the value of the tuition fee as 85% and adding the 15% tax on top of that.

If the trust's profit recorded in its accounting does not cover the tuition fees, tax is withheld only in proportion to the profit, and the remainder is considered the performance from trust assets – which is exempt from taxation.

The trustees have decided to take advantage of a favourable offer and sell one of the paintings contributed to trust assets by the settlors. The transaction is recorded as profit. The selling price is recorded in revenues, and the input tax acquisition cost is recorded as cost. It is important to note that art objects are not subject to depreciation. The profit will be taxed in the trust's tax return in the standard manner, at a current rate of 21%.

This case study, provided for illustrative purposes, simplifies the various situations that may occur. However, real-life situations are often more complex, and to deal with specific scenarios it is recommended that the advice of an experienced tax adviser is sought.

Czech family foundations: an alternative to trusts

Štěpán Holub
Holubová advokáti s.r.o.

1. Introduction

This book focuses primarily on trusts. However, it would be remiss of us if we failed to mention family foundations, which in recent years have emerged as an increasingly interesting alternative to trusts.

In this chapter we look in more detail at Czech family foundations and highlight the differences between the two options, and the pros and cons of foundations relative to trusts.

2. Can a foundation be used for family estate planning?

Foundations (*nadace*) were introduced into the Czech legal system in 1991 by amendment to the Czech Civil Code.[1] Regulation of foundations was then significantly enhanced by a separate act in 1998.[2] In this act, alternative – and simpler – endowment funds were introduced alongside foundations. Until 2014, however, foundations and endowment funds could only be used "for the achievement of general benefit",[3] that is, as charitable organisations. Only under the new Civil Code 89/2012 Coll[4] was it possible to establish foundations and endowment funds even for "economically useful purposes".[5] Private foundations and private endowment funds that support the founders or their families can certainly be classified as economically useful.

The question of whether support of the founder and his or her family can be categorised as economically useful was clarified in 2017, when an amendment to the Income Tax Act introduced the term 'family foundation'.[6] The act included in the term both foundations and endowment funds that "according to their founding act, serve to support the founder or persons close to the founder, or whose activities are directed towards supporting the founder or persons close

1 Act No 509/1991 Coll, amending, supplementing and regulating the Civil Code.
2 Act No 227/1997 Coll on Foundations and Endowment Funds.
3 *Ibid*, Section 1.
4 An English translation of the Czech Civil Code is available at: http://obcanskyzakonik.justice.cz/images/pdf/Civil-Code.pdf.
5 *Ibid*, Sections 306, 394.
6 Act No 170/2017 Coll, amending certain acts in the field of taxation.

to the founder".[7] At the same time, the amendment established a similar tax regime for family foundations as for trusts.

Since 2017, therefore, both trusts and family foundations have been unequivocally available for family estate planning.

3. Differences between a family foundation and a family endowment fund

In principle, both foundations and endowment funds can be used for family estate planning – with each, it is possible to establish that their purpose is private and directed towards the support of the founder or those close to him or her.

The regulation of foundations and endowment funds is contained in the Czech Civil Code. While 90 sections are devoted to foundations,[8] only eight are concerned with endowment funds.[9] It is clear from the sheer scope of legal regulation that while foundations can be considered somewhat overregulated, the regulation of endowment funds can be considered insufficient. It should be emphasised that the literature on the topic,[10] subsequently confirmed by case law,[11] has concluded that the provisions governing foundations cannot be applied to endowment funds. Thus, endowment funds and foundations are different legal entities in Czech law and cannot be confused with each other, and automatic application of the legal regulation of foundations, on the basis of subsidiarity, to endowment funds is in practice excluded. However, case law reaches some similar conclusions for both forms in some cases where there are grounds for analogous application.

When deciding whether to choose a foundation or an endowment fund, it is important to consider whether, in one or other case, there are legal obstacles to effectively managing family assets. The legislation on foundations presents a few such obstacles; one example is the obligation of the foundation to make its annual report available to the general public.[12] This annual report must include, among other things, a list of persons to whom a distribution of more than CZK 10,000 has been made.[13] The fact that it is not possible to provide a distribution from the foundation to its founder, a member of its governing body or an employee of the foundation – or to a person close to such members or employees – may also be problematic.[14]

---

7 Section 17a of Act No 586/1992 Coll on Income Taxes ('the Income Tax Act'), as amended by Act No 170/2017 Coll. An unofficial translation of the Income Tax Act is available at: www.zakonyprolidi.cz/translation/cs/1992-586?langid=1033 (access requires registration).

8 Sections 306–393 of the Civil Code, *supra* note 4.

9 *Ibid*, Sections 394–401.

10 K Ronovská, "Endowment fund after the recodification of private law. Subsidiarity or analogy within foundation law?", *Právní Rozhledy* (*Legal Views*), 2013, Vol 21, 13–14, pp494–499.

11 Supreme Court, 29 Cdo 3225/2016 [R 54/2019 civ].

12 Section 360(1) of the Civil Code: "The Foundation shall publish the annual report within thirty days of its approval by the board of trustees and shall also make it available at its registered office. If the foundation is not established as a public benefit, it is sufficient to make the annual report available at its registered office." Section 361 of the Civil Code: "Anyone may consult the annual report in the public register and make extracts, copies or copies thereof. The same right may also be exercised at the registered office of the foundation."

13 Section 358(1)(d) of the Civil Code, *supra* note 4.

14 Section 353 of the Civil Code, *supra* note 4.

In contrast, an endowment fund has no such restrictions and appears much better suited to management of family assets. Therefore, for present purposes we will consider only endowment funds, indeed only family endowment funds, as an alternative to trusts. In doing so, we will focus on a comparison between a trust fund and an endowment fund and try to outline the basic differences in their legal regulation. When we use the term 'family foundations' in the following few pages, the term will include family endowment funds.

4. Differences between a trust fund and an endowment fund

A key difference between a trust fund and an endowment fund is again the extent of legal regulation. While an endowment fund is regulated by eight sections in the Civil Code, a trust fund is regulated by 27. Thus, an endowment fund generally offers a significantly more flexible solution than a trust fund, albeit it provides less legal protection.

It should also be noted that endowment funds are significantly less prevalent in the Czech Republic than trust funds. On the other hand, the case law on endowment funds is slightly more mature.

The differences, and their implications in terms of practical use, are discussed below.

5. The endowment fund as a legal entity

Probably the most obvious difference between an endowment fund and a trust fund is that an endowment fund is a legal person.

While trusts are classified in Part III of the Civil Code[15] among property rights, foundations and endowment funds are classified in Part II[16] among legal persons, in the general part of the Civil Code.

The endowment fund is a legal entity of the 'foundation type', in contrast to corporations. From this perspective, the endowment fund is a very standard legal entity, registered in a public register, and its recognition in continental Europe does not usually cause any problems in practice. The foundation is registered in the Foundation Register and the basic data is available free of charge and without restriction, as for other legal entities in the Czech Republic, on the website of the Ministry of Justice.[17]

For similar reasons, endowment funds are in practice more readily accepted by banks than trusts when setting up accounts.

However, even a trust fund has become much closer to being a legal person, especially thanks to the first ever amendment to the Civil Code, which introduced mandatory registration in the Register of Trusts as a condition for

---

15 Section 1448 *et seq* of the Civil Code, *supra* note 4.
16 Section 394 *et seq* of the Civil Code, *supra* note 4.
17 At: www.justice.cz.

the establishment of trust funds and assigned trust funds identification numbers. Nevertheless, trust funds are not, at least in theory, legal persons even after this amendment.

At first glance, therefore, an endowment fund and a trust fund may perform similar functions in the management of family property. However, the different legal basis is likely to lead to a different approach to the protection of assets in trusts. A trust fund will always act in legal relations only through its trustee, acting on behalf of the trust. On the other hand, the endowment fund will always act independently and in its own name.

In the case of an endowment fund, the assets in the fund are always registered as assets of the legal entity in all registers. As a matter of principle, with endowment funds there is no danger of mixing or confusing the personal assets of the trustee and the assets administered, as may be the case with trusts.

6. Establishment of the family foundation

An endowment fund is established in two steps, as is the case for certain other legal entities:

1. the establishment of the foundation fund; and
2. the proposal for registration and the actual registration in the Foundation Register.

The endowment fund comes into existence only once registered in the public register.

The initial establishment of the endowment fund is less formal than with a trust fund. In principle, it is possible to establish an endowment fund without a notarial deed. Typically, an endowment fund is established by a deed of incorporation, but it can also be established by a death grant, usually by will. Even though the law does not require establishment by a formalised legal act, establishment by way of notarial deed may be recommended. In addition to the presumption of compliance with the law, the notary can ensure direct registration of the endowment fund in the Foundation Register.

Unlike trust funds, endowment funds are not limited in time.

The instrument of incorporation must contain the usual elements such as the name and registered office of the endowment fund, the name of the founder and his or her residence or registered office. In addition, it must state the purpose for which the endowment fund is established; which, as mentioned above, may be a socially or economically useful purpose. In theory, charitable and family foundations can thus be combined. However, given the different tax treatment of family foundations,[18] we recommend not combining the purpose of a family foundation with other purposes.

---

18 See the Income Tax Act, *supra* note 7.

The instrument of incorporation must also contain the amount of the initial capital, or its non-monetary object, and the administrator of the deposit. It must also state the number of members of the board of directors together with the names and places of residence of the initial members,[19] and the manner in which members of the board act on behalf of the endowment fund. The endowment fund is required to have a controlling body – a role similar to a trust protector or supervisor – called a supervisory body or, in the case of an individual, a revisor. The instrument of incorporation must state the number of members of the supervisory board (or the revisor) and the names and places of residence of the initial members. Finally, the instrument of incorporation must contain the conditions for making contributions from the endowment fund's assets or a definition of the range of activities that the endowment fund may carry out in fulfilment of its purpose.

7. Amendment of the articles of incorporation

The Supreme Court explicitly stated in a 2017 ruling that amending the articles of incorporation of foundations and endowments is possible if the founder reserves such right in the deed of incorporation.[20] The Court thus favoured the autonomy of the founder's will and, as a consequence, the flexible nature of the foundation structure in Czech law.

One might be inclined to think that the above decision should be applicable, by analogy, to trusts.[21] However, a similar court decision explicitly confirming the possibility of changing the statute has so far been absent in the case of trust funds.

8. Founder of endowment fund

One or more founders are required to establish an endowment fund. A founder can be either a natural person or a legal entity.

The founder may then be either a beneficiary and/or a board member at the same time without restrictions. At the same time, the founder may retain certain controlling powers, for example, the power to appoint additional members of the board of directors or the supervisory board, or the power to amend the deed of incorporation.

However, the position of the founder is firmly linked to the founding of the endowment fund and, as such, the founder's actions are constrained by the creation of the endowment itself. This implies the impossibility of replacing the person of the founder with a new founder after the creation of the endowment fund.[22]

---

19 Though not in the case of *mortis causa* endowments funds.

20 Order of the Supreme Court of 27 March 2018, file no 29 Cdo 3225/2016, [R 54/2019 civ].

21 K Ronovská and V Pihera, "On the possibility of changing the foundation's charter (including changes to the purpose)", *Právní rozhledy* (*Legal Views*), 2018, Vol 157, 15–16, pp556–559.

22 Resolution of the High Court in Prague of 20 January 2020, file no 14 Cmo 325/2019.

9. Board of directors of the endowment fund

Members of the board of directors act on behalf of the endowment fund. The specific manner of acting is determined by the deed of incorporation. Although the statutory concept of a board of directors gives the impression of a collective body, the board of directors may have only one member.

Membership of the board of directors is not restricted in any way. Any person, both natural and legal, may be a member of the board. Regulations such as those for trusts, which limit the trustee to natural persons only or, in the case of legal persons, to investment companies,[23] do not apply in the case of endowment funds.

Members of the board of directors are liable as members of elected bodies under Section 159 of the Civil Code,[24] according to which, members are obliged to perform their duties with the necessary loyalty as well as the necessary knowledge and diligence. Under this provision, they may also be liable to the creditors of the endowment fund for damage caused by any breach of duty in the performance of their duties.

The High Court in Prague actually dealt with a situation where a member of the board of directors of an endowment fund, who had been removed from office, sought a declaration that the decision of the board of directors as to his removal was invalid. The Court addressed the question of whether a court can review the validity of a board decision and concluded that it could not.[25]

Effective control of the board of directors must therefore be carefully embedded in the deed of incorporation, as effective judicial oversight is not sufficiently regulated in law.

10. The supervisory board and the revisor

In contrast to the position for the board of directors, in the case of a supervisory body the law distinguishes between a collective supervisory body – the supervisory board – and an individual supervisor, referred to as the 'revisor'.[26]

As in the case of the board of directors, membership of the supervisory board, or the position of revisor, is not restricted in any way.

Since the law does not further define the supervisory board's or revisor's powers of control, attention must be paid to these powers in the deed of incorporation.

11. Beneficiaries of the endowment fund

As with the members of the board or the controlling body of the foundation,

---

23 Act No 240/2013 Coll, on Investment Companies and Investment Funds. Available at: www.mfcr.cz/assets/attachments/2023-04-13_Act-on-Investment-Companies-and-Investment-Funds.pdf.
24 Section 159 of the Civil Code, *supra* note 4.
25 Resolution of the High Court in Prague of 17 July 2018, Case No 7 Cmo 507/2016.
26 See section 6, above.

there is complete freedom as to the appointment or removal of beneficiaries. Moreover, there is so far no case law defining the role and rights of beneficiaries of the endowment fund. These mechanisms should thus be carefully enshrined in the deed of incorporation as appropriate – the courts cannot intervene in the affairs of the endowment fund in the way they can in a trust.

To summarise, the position of the beneficiaries highlights a fundamental difference between a trust and an endowment fund. This conclusion may be subject to revision in the future, however, as potential analogous treatment of endowment funds and trusts is debated.

12. Tax treatment of a family foundation

In the case of endowment funds, a distinction must be made between those funds that can be considered family foundations under the Income Tax Act, and other funds, typically charitable endowment funds. Given the different tax regimes, it is not entirely desirable to combine the two within a single endowment fund.

The definition of a family foundation is contained, somewhat unfortunately, within the definition of a public benefit corporation in Section 17a of the Income Tax Act.[27] A family foundation is, then, such foundation or endowment fund as, according to its founding act, serves to support the founder or persons close to the founder, or whose activities are aimed at supporting the founder or persons close to the founder. 'Close persons' are defined by the Civil Code as relatives in the direct line,[28] siblings and spouses or partners under the law governing registered partnerships. Other persons in a family or similar relationship shall be deemed close persons if harm suffered by one of them would reasonably be perceived by the other as harm to him or her. As a rule, persons who are married or living together permanently are also close persons.

Other foundations that do not meet the definition of a family foundation have a different tax regime, and are beyond the scope of this chapter.

From a tax perspective, a family foundation behaves much like a trust. First and foremost, this means that for income tax purposes the contribution and allocation of assets to a family foundation, as with a trust, is treated as a contribution to a business corporation.[29] In practice, this means that such income will not be subject to tax.

In the normal course a family foundation, like a trust fund, behaves similarly to a business corporation. Thus, there will normally be no difference from an income tax perspective whether the parent company is a corporation, a foundation or a trust – provided that they have held at least a 10% interest in the capital stock of another business corporation for at least 12 months continuously.[30]

---

27 Section 17a(2)(f) of the Income Tax Act, *supra* note 7.
28 Section 22 of the Civil Code, *supra* note 4.
29 Section 21f of the Income Tax Act, *supra* note 7.
30 Section 19(3)(b) of the Income Tax Act, *supra* note 7.

If there is a benefit from a family foundation, a distinction must be made between the benefit from the profits of the family foundation and the income contributed to the family foundation either by the founder or by a close person.[31] While income from profits is taxable, income from assets contributed to a family foundation is exempt from income tax.[32] In these respects, the treatment of a family foundation and the treatment of a trust are similar.

At the same time, it must be taken into account that performance from the family foundation is first from the profits, and only after that from other assets. In other words, contributions subject to tax are to be paid first, untaxed contributions thereafter.[33]

13. Ultimate beneficial owners of family foundation

The ultimate beneficial owner of the family foundation is the natural person who exercises decisive influence within it. It is always the founder, a member of the board of directors or of the supervisory board, or the revisor. If there is a legal person in any of these functions, the ultimate beneficial owner of the family foundation would be the ultimate beneficial owner of that legal person. In this respect, the definition does not differ in principle from the definition of beneficial owners in trusts. However, it should be stressed that the beneficiaries in a family foundation are not registered at all.[34]

Both family foundations and trusts may be subject to automatic transcription of persons registered in other registers,[35] in particular the names of founders, members of the board of directors, supervisory board or revisor. However, the situation is somewhat different in the case of beneficiaries. While registers of trusts record the beneficiaries, in the case of family foundations, as already mentioned, beneficiaries are not recorded in the Foundation Register at all. It follows that in the case of family foundations, the beneficial owners are not automatically entered in the register of the ultimate beneficial owners, as there is nothing from which to copy the data.

Some information about family foundations may be hidden in public records. In this respect, regulation is similar to that for trusts. However, the regulatory regime under which this is done is somewhat more complicated. Under the Public Records Act,[36] public disclosure may be avoided on the basis of a proposal by the family foundation. This can lead to hiding of personal details of the founder and the amount of their contribution, and the extent to

31 The exact definition of such persons is contained in Section 10(3)(c) of the Income Tax Act, *supra* note 7.
32 Section 10(3)(c) of the Income Tax Act, *supra* note 7.
33 Section 21c (2) of the Income Tax Act, *supra* note 7.
34 Section 6(1) of Act No 37/2021 Coll, on the Registration of Beneficial Owners. Available at: http://aplikace.mvcr.cz/sbirka-zakonu/ViewFile.aspx?type=c&id=39065. An unofficial translation into English is available at: www.zakonyprolidi.cz/translation/cs/2021-37?langid=1033 (access requires registration).
35 Section 37 of Act No 37/2021 Coll, on the Registration of Beneficial Owners, *ibid.*
36 Section 34(2) of Act No 304/2013 Coll on Public Registers of Legal and Natural Persons. Available at: www.zakonyprolidi.cz/translation/cs/2013-304?langid=1033 (access requires registration).

which the deposit obligation has been fulfilled, as well as the restrictions set by the donor for the treatment of his or her gift. Similarly, it is possible to hide from public inspection documents filed in the collection of deeds in which some of this data is included. Under the Act on the Registration of Beneficial Owners, information about the founders in the Czech Register of Beneficial Owners ('the UBO Register') is hidden from public inspection too.[37]

Thus, although the legal treatment of beneficial owners of trusts and family foundations may appear to be ultimately similar, a key difference is the recording of the beneficiaries.

14. Termination of the endowment fund

The Civil Code explicitly provides for the possibility of changing the legal form from endowment fund to foundation.[38]

Although it contains basic rules for the liquidation endowment funds, it only leaves the power to decide on the dissolution of the endowment fund, with liquidation and the election of a liquidator, to the board of directors if the endowment fund ceases to fulfil its purpose. Nothing more. Alternatively, it delegates a similar power to the court to order its liquidation on the application of a person who proves a legal interest.[39]

The general provisions of the Civil Code on liquidation therefore apply to the actual course of liquidation.[40] The question of how the liquidation balance is to be dealt with in the event of liquidation of the endowment fund must therefore be defined in the deed of incorporation of the endowment fund.

15. Conclusion

The characteristics of a family foundation and a trust look similar at first glance. Especially in tax matters, both solutions behave in a similar way. However, an interesting difference arises when it comes to the question of the status of the beneficiaries. Unlike in trusts, endowment fund beneficiaries are not registered in the UBO Register. At the same time, the beneficiaries of endowment funds do not have any legal rights, information rights or supervisory powers over the endowment fund or its board of directors.

The form of a family fund clearly has good use cases in multi-generational family estate planning. At the same time, limited legal regulation can serve as both an advantage and a disadvantage. With this in mind, it is highly advisable to pay close attention to the set-up of the deeds of incorporation and bylaws of family foundations.

---

37 Section 14 (4) of Act No 37/2021 Coll, *supra* note 34.
38 Sections 390–400 of the Civil Code, *supra* note 4.
39 Section 401 of the Civil Code, *supra* note 4.
40 Section 187 *et seq* of the Civil Code, *supra* note 4.

Part II: Trust laws in Hungary

History, implementation, peculiarities and adaptations

István Sándor
Kelemen, Mészáros, Sándor and Partners

1. Historical background

Hungarian private law has its roots in Roman law and belongs within the continental European civil law system, having significant similarities with the private law of a number of other European jurisdictions, in particular Germany, Austria and Switzerland.[1]

1.1 Hungarian society, economy, and private law in the second half of the 20th century

In Hungary, the codification of private law took place for the first time after World War II, during the era of socialism.[2] Despite the socialist features of the old Civil Code, it reflected the influence of the German BGB, Swiss OR and ZGB, and previous Hungarian judicial law. The codification of the old Civil Code took place in an economic environment where state ownership prevailed, and private ownership, as personal property, was limited.

Significant political and societal changes occurred in Hungary in the late 1980s. Formerly socialist state-controlled economic mechanisms were replaced with market-oriented economic regulations. This shift was accompanied by legislative changes. Alongside the creation of laws aimed at establishing a democratic political and social order, legislation sought to limit the state's involvement in the private sector. In the late 1990s, alignment with the legal standards of the European Union became another focus, with a view to facilitating accession.

As a consequence of the political transition, the constitutional guarantee of equality between private and public property was established, and compensation paid to the victims of World War II and those harmed by socialist nationalisations and cooperativisations, following much societal and political debate.

---

1 For a historical presentation of Hungarian private law, see Gábor Hamza, "Historical Development of Hungarian Private Law", in István Sándor (ed), *Business Law in Hungary*, Patrocinium, 2016, pp103–114. Considering the sole use of the Hungarian language in the work, for further scholarly references on specific topics, we have generally favoured foreign-language publications in this chapter.

2 Act No IV of 1959 on the Civil Code of the Hungarian People's Republic.

Foreign capital played a significant role in the transformation of the ownership system and the dismantling of state ownership, starting with privatisation, as Hungary offered one of the most investment-friendly regulatory environments of all Central and Eastern European countries. Economic laws necessary for the transition to a market economy provided the legal framework within which private ventures and operations with private capital could be established. Laws geared towards the market economy included the Company Law, the Competition Law and the Foreign Investment Law, as well as regulations establishing the foundations of the banking system and stock market trading.

1.2 The former legal framework for asset management

Under the old Civil Code, the management and administration of assets was primarily governed by the rights of asset managers, exclusively within the context of state-owned assets. The state entrusted certain assets to other entities, allowing them to exercise ownership rights under specific conditions defined by law. Under the old Civil Code, the right of management provided a mechanism for the state to act as owner, while certain public bodies and institutions could act as asset managers.

Before 2014, there was no legislative basis for establishing such legal constructions in the private sector. Consequently, attempts were made to address the deficit using alternative legal mechanisms,[3] including agency, mandate agreement and representation, and indirect representation (straw man), without formal regulation. A private asset management contract concluded in the private sector was inadequate in itself, within the legal framework provided by the old Civil Code, to establish proprietary rights for the asset manager towards third parties. The main reason for this was that, in accordance with Roman law traditions, ownership rights were treated as indivisible; only one ownership right could exist on a single object, and a dual or divided ownership situation could not be created. Ownership rights could only be encumbered with alien property rights having a *numerus clausus* (eg, servitudes, mortgage rights), meaning that it was not possible to apply asset management rights used for state-owned assets to the private sphere.

Wealth management based on mandate and representation, as above, resulted in financial vulnerability for asset managers since they could not have control over the managed property, making it impossible to sell it in their own name. In the context of wealth management they could not encumber the property, and they lacked an independent *locus standi* for asserting ownership protection.

As for a solution based on indirect representation, where the asset manager

---

3 For more information, see István Sándor, *Fiduciary Property management and the Trust. Historical and Comparative Law Analysis*, HVG-ORAC Publishing Ltd, Budapest, 2015, pp363–373.

acquired ownership rights over the managed property through contract, the principal could only take action against the asset manager based on contractual obligations, and the beneficiary's rights against the asset manager were governed solely by the rules of contracts for the benefit of third parties. Neither the principal nor the beneficiary could take action against third parties regarding the managed property. Furthermore, asset segregation could not occur, meaning the creditors, heirs, or spouses of asset managers could assert claims against the managed asset.

1.3 Direct predecessors of the regulation of fiduciary asset management

Following the regime change, and in a fundamentally altered economic environment, there was significant demand to introduce some of the asset management structures used abroad. Preparatory work on the new Civil Code began in the second half of the 1990s, and by the turn of the century, the shape of the new codex and the societal debate surrounding it had begun to resolve. At that time, the chief codification committee did not support the introduction of regulation of asset management as an independent legal institution, primarily because the concept of split ownership would not have aligned with Hungarian private law.

A significant breakthrough came with the adoption of the Civil Code in 2009, which regulated fiduciary asset management as an independent contractual institution.[4] By this time, the legislator had recognised the need for a legal structure in Hungary that would allow participants in the business sector to avoid placing Hungarian capital abroad due to the benefits offered by trusts established only in foreign jurisdictions. Although the parliament did pass the appropriate law, it did not come into effect due a decision by the Constitutional Court.[5]

Subsequently, however, the establishment of a fiduciary asset management contract, similar to a trust but in harmony with the principles of Hungarian property law, remained on the agenda and was incorporated into the Civil Code in 2013.[6] The new Civil Code regulates fiduciary asset management contracts at Chapter XLIII. Regulation followed the pattern for a trust established in English law, or a *Treuhand* in German law. The legislator placed fiduciary asset management within the framework of contract law, emphasising, however, that it originated from the legal construct of ownership (title) transfer similar to that pertaining in a trust.[7] Under the new Civil Code, a fiduciary asset management contract represents a legal construction with significant proprietary legal effects.

---

4 Act No CXX of 2009 on the Civil Code. For a detailed analysis, see Sándor, *Business Law in Hungary, supra* note 1, pp375–378.

5 Decision No 51/2010 (IV 28) of the Constitutional Court.

6 Act No V of 2013 on the Civil Code. The Hungarian Ministry of Justice's English translation is available at: https://njt.hu/jogszabaly/en/2013-5-00-00.

7 See István Sándor, "Different Types of Trust from an Ownership Aspect", *European Review of Private Law*, Vol 24, Issue 6, 2016, pp1189–1216.

1.4 Regulation of foundations in Hungarian law

To understand the current regulation of asset management in Hungary, we shall look briefly at foundations as well. In Hungarian private law, foundations have been known since the Middle Ages, primarily as institutions for public interest asset donations and, to a limited extent, for family purposes. Private law regulation of foundations did not occur until relatively recently; laws were only enacted for their state supervision. Following World War II, foundations were nationalised and only the state was authorised to establish them.[8]

Foundations were not regulated by the old Civil Code, regulations being introduced by decree in 1987,[9] at which time under the rules prevailing, foundations could only be established for enduring public benefit purposes.

The breakthrough came with the new Civil Code, which allowed the establishment of foundations for private purposes by removing the requirement of being for the public benefit, leaving only the criterion of having "long-term objectives".[10] The code also permitted the founder and the joiner (contributor) to be beneficiaries if the purpose of the foundation was to protect the founder's scientific, literary or artistic creations. In addition, the founder's and joiner's relatives could be beneficiaries if the purpose of the foundation included the protection of the relative's scientific, literary or artistic creations, their care and maintenance, their healthcare expenses, or support for their school studies through scholarships or by other means.[11] The new regulation created the conditions for foundations to become suitable for managing family assets, further movement in this direction being achieved by the adoption of a separate law specifically addressing asset-managing foundations.[12]

2. Concepts and terminology

2.1 Key concepts of asset management

The essential conceptual elements of a Hungarian fiduciary asset management contract are as follows:

- Ownership rights must be transferred to the trustee.
- The trust assets must be segregated from the trustee's other assets.
- A change in the person of the trustee does not automatically terminate the asset management relationship.
- The settlor and the beneficiary can assert claims against third parties if the asset manager gratuitously or in bad faith provided the asset(s) to third parties.[13]

---

8 Decree with the Force of Law No 2 of 1949.

9 The regulations governing foundations in the old Civil Code were introduced by the Decree with the Force of Law No 11 of 1987 on amending certain civil law rules.

10 Section 3:378 of the Civil Code, *supra* note 6.

11 Section 3:386(1)–(2) of the Civil Code, *supra* note 6.

12 Act No XIII of 2019 on Asset Management Foundations. See Appendix II.

2.2 Key terms

Hungarian regulations use the terms '*bizalmi vagyonkezelési szerződés*' and '*bizalmi vagyonkezelés*', which can be translated as 'fiduciary asset management contract' and 'fiduciary asset management'.[14] Analysis of the Hungarian regulations shows that the trust construct aligns with the concept of trust according to the Hague Convention and,[15] functionally and in the majority of its detailed rules, with the common law trust as well. Therefore, in this chapter we treat the concept of trust as synonymous with the Hungarian concept of fiduciary asset management, emphasising, of course, that in Hungarian law, there is no duality between common law and equity, so Hungarian fiduciary asset management cannot be considered identical to the common law trust.[16] Accordingly, for positions in the trust relationship we use the internationally accepted terms of 'settlor' ('*vagyonrendelő*'), 'trustee' ('*vagyonkezelő*'), 'beneficiary' ('*kedvezményezett*') and 'trust asset' ('*kezelt vagyon*'). Hungarian law also recognises a position similar to that of protector, but the Hungarian Civil Code does not name it;[17] only the Asset Management Foundations Act ('the AMF Act') does, but there the role is foundation-specific, known as the 'foundation asset supervisor' ('*alapítványi vagyonellenőr*'). Nevertheless, in the case of trust relationships we also use the term 'protector' to refer to the person appointed by the settlor to oversee the activities of the trustee and to exercise certain rights of the settlor towards the trustee.

2.3 The concept of a foundation

The term 'foundation', familiar in continental European legal systems, refers to a legal entity with an independent legal personality and a dedicated purpose. A foundation has a founder (and no owner) and operates with an independent governing body.[18]

In common law jurisdictions, the term often carries a different meaning. In US and English law, for example, the concept of a foundation *per se* was for a

---

13 For a detailed examination of Hungarian regulations on asset management in English, see István Sándor, *Property and Trust Law in Hungary*, Wolters Kluwer, Kluwer Law International, 2017, pp199–210; Ákos Menyhei and István Sándor, "Trust in Hungarian Law", in István Sándor (ed), *Fiduciary Property management and the Trust*, *supra* note 3, pp406–421; and Ákos Menyhei and István Sándor, "The Hungarian Trust Law", in Ákos Menyhei and István Sándor, *Introduction of the trust in Hungary and international practice. Selected studies on the lectures held on the conferences of STEP Hungary in the years 2014, 2015 and 2016*, HVG-ORAC Publishing Ltd, 2017, pp113–127. In the Hungarian language, see Gábor B Szabó, István Illés, Borbála Kolozs, Ákos Menyhei and István Sándor, *A bizalmi vagyonkezelés (Fiduciary asset management)*, 3rd ed, ORAC, 2023.

14 For the text of the Civil Code see note 6, *supra*. For an English translation of the Trustee Act, see the Hungarian Ministry of Justice's website at: https://njt.hu/jogszabaly/en/2014-15-00-00.

15 Convention on the Law Applicable to Trusts and On Their Recognition, 1985. Available at: www.hcch.net/en/instruments/conventions/full-text/?cid=59.

16 See Ádám Fuglinszky and Réka Somssich, "Language-bound terms–term bound languages: the difficulties of translating a national civil code into a *lingua franca*", *International Journal for the Semiotics of Law*, Vol 33, May 2020, pp749–770. Available at: https://doi.org/10.1007/s11196-020-09704-x.

17 Section 6:325(4) of the Civil Code, *supra* note 6.

18 See István Sándor, "Remarks about the History of Foundations", *Journal on European History of Law*, Vol 12 No 1, 2021, pp105–112.

long time not recognised. Its role was fulfilled by companies, trusts and corporations.[19] Even recently, especially in the United States, the term 'foundation' was primarily used as a tax category.[20] In 2017, New Hampshire became the first state to introduce a foundation with a legal nature similar to that under continental European law, and Wyoming was the second state to regulate private foundations.[21] The term 'statutory foundation' is used in the United States to distinguish it from the term 'foundation' as employed in the context of federal tax regulations.[22]

3. Introduction of trust rules

Regulation of the private law structure of trusts is covered by the new Civil Code, which came into force in 2014. Alongside the Civil Code, the Trustee Act was adopted,[23] together with a government decree regulating the financial guarantees of fiduciary asset management undertakings.[24] The new legal form also necessitated the modification of several other laws, including those relating to taxation, fees and the registration rules for certain assets (real estate, company shares, vehicles etc). In the first few years, practical issues arose, leading to refinements in the provisions of the Civil Code and the Trustee Act which took effect in 2017.[25]

In 2019, the legislature enacted a separate law specifically for asset management foundations ('AMFs').[26] AMFs represented another addition to the legal tools available for wealth planning, asset management, generational wealth transfer, and asset protection in Hungary. They combine elements of both foundations and fiduciary asset management, and remain a novelty in Hungarian private law, albeit a particularly welcome one. An AMF can serve the public interest, particularly in the sense of taking control of institutions that were previously under state control – for example, in the field of higher education. Additionally, AMFs can be established for private interests, where their primary function is the management of family assets.[27]

---

19 Anthony Viegas-Haws, "The Foundation as a trust substitute under US federal tax law", *Trusts & Trustees*, Vol 5, 2009, p281. István Sándor, "The Medieval History and Development of Company Law", *Journal on European History of Law*, Vol 8, No 1, 2017, pp34–49.

20 For usage in the context of taxation in the United States, see Inland Revenue Service, *Compliance Guide for 501(c)(3) Private Foundations*. Available at: www.irs.gov/pub/irs-pdf/p4221pf.pdf.

21 Wyoming Statutory Foundation Act, 2019 Wyo Sess Laws Ch 190 (HB 236).

22 Jordan S Chandler, Geoffrey Cone, Paolo Panico and Amy M Staehr, "Foundations in the wild west: the Wyoming Statutory Foundation Act", *Trusts & Trustees*, Vol 6, 2019, p617.

23 Act No XV of 2014 on trustees and the rules governing their activities. Available at: https://njt.hu/jogszabaly/en/2014-15-00-00.

24 Government Decree No 87 of 20 March 2014 on the rules of financial guarantees for trust management companies.

25 Act No LXI of 2017 on the necessary amendments to certain laws for the enhancement of legal competitiveness in the business environment.

26 Act No XIII of 2019 on Asset Management Foundations. See Appendix II.

27 On the regulation of AMFs, see: István Sándor, "The transformation of foundation law in Hungary, with particular regard to private foundations", *Trusts & Trustees*, Vol 29, No 6, July 2023, pp553–560; István Sándor, "Hungary for Change", *STEP Journal*, Vol 3, 2021, pp54–55; and Gábor B Szabó, Ákos Menyhei

The AMF Act was amended twice in 2020.[28] The primary purpose of the first amendment was to simplify the organisational rules for private interest AMFs. The amendment allowed private interest AMFs to have a three-member board, potentially led by a sole curator; and the requirement for a supervisory board was waived if the AMF had a foundation asset supervisor, and the founder delegated the powers of the board. The second amendment introduced public interest AMFs, performing a public duty with specific rules under a separate law.[29]

4. Possible types of fiduciary asset management

There are three main legal constructions for fiduciary asset management in Hungary today:

- *ad hoc* (occasional) trust;
- professional (business-oriented) trust; and
- asset management through an AMF.

The primary purpose of an *ad hoc* trust is to assist in family estate planning, especially for smaller asset portfolios. It can also be used for transactional purposes, for example in place of a deposit or for purposes of escrow. Through the regulation of professional trusts, the legislator opens up a new business sector where asset management specialists provide services to clients on a business basis. These services are primarily in demand for larger asset portfolios and unique assets requiring specific expertise, and they provide an opportunity for foreigners to manage their investments in Hungary.[30] The primary function of an AMF is to ensure unified asset management and simultaneously provide estate planning for larger family estates spanning multiple generations. While a trust is only a contractual relationship, the distinctive feature of AMFs is that they are independent legal entities, allowing for hybrid asset management. This means that, in addition to the capital provided by the founder and participants, AMFs can enter into trust agreements with third parties.

4.1 Distinguishing *ad hoc* and professional asset management

In the case of a simple trust, the starting point is that a person may act as a trustee in no more than one trust relationship. A person acting as a trustee in a

---

and István Sándor, *The Foundation: Historical, typological, operational, taxation and asset management omnibus (Az Alapítvány: Történeti, tipológiai, működési, adózási és vagyonkezelési omnibus)*, HVG-ORAC Publishing Ltd, 2021, pp149–183.

28 Act No LXXXI of 2020 on the administrative and incentive amendments to certain laws, as well as certain provisions affecting asset management, and Act No CXLVIII of 2020 on the regulation of higher education and the amendment of certain related laws.

29 Act No IX of 2021 on public interest asset management foundations performing public duties.

30 See Ákos Menyhei, "Development of the estate planning industry through the introduction of the trust in Hungary", *Trusts & Trustees* Vol 22, No 6, July 2016, p660.

trust relationship is required to conduct his or her activities in a professional manner.

Professional trustees require the approval of the National Bank of Hungary (NBH). To obtain approval, they must comply with numerous requirements related to the trust's capital, personnel, internal regulations, IT infrastructure and financial security. However, individual trust relationships established by professional trustees do not need to be approved.

On the other hand, *ad hoc* trustees' activities do not require approval, and anyone who meets the minimum legal requirements (individuals, for example, must have a clean criminal record regarding specified crimes, and legal entities must be transparent organisations with identifiable owners) can engage in such activities. Additionally, there are certain rules regarding incompatibility. For example, if the *ad hoc* trustee is a legal entity, then its owner, affiliated enterprises, executive personnel and their relatives cannot perform trust activities under the Civil Code. Moreover, executive personnel, natural person members and the actual owner cannot have a specified disqualification. *Ad hoc* trust relationships must be registered with the NBH.

In cases involving multiple settlors, it is often challenging to determine whether there is more than one asset management relationship. This issue has posed numerous challenges in legal practice, and the NBH has attempted to address it in its statements.

The NBH emphasised that defining businesslike conduct should not be limited solely to the perspective of the trustee,[31] despite the legislation primarily linking this notion to their role. The relationship between multiple settlors in the same legal relationship, and their varying contractual intentions, can also influence whether the legal relationship is characterised as businesslike. If the relationship, and the purpose of the asset disposition, between the settlors cannot be established, then before entering into the contract it is essential to examine whether there exists such a close relationship among the settlors as would exclude the pursuit of regular gain and the circumvention of the businesslike conduct rule. A good example is where four family members intend to establish a non-businesslike *ad hoc* trust.[32] They have been collaborating within the framework of a family business for decades to ensure the long-term preservation of family wealth. The NBH stated that in this scenario, when examining settlors, it is crucial to consider the nature of the relationship between them that justifies having multiple settlors in the same legal relationship without it being deemed businesslike. If the establishment of

31 Statement of the National Bank of Hungary, 14 August 2018. Available at: https://alk.mnb.hu/data/cms2466918/tmp643F.tmp(16138001).pdf.

32 Statement of the National Bank of Hungary, 3 August 2022, regarding the multiple asset allocation in the context of trust management relationships. Available at: https://alk.mnb.hu/data/cms2603451/247007_2022_kozzeteteli_peldany.pdf.

a trust contract is based on a close legal relationship between the settlors – such as a familial relationship – the necessity of a one-time contract makes the non-businesslike nature of the legal relationship non-problematic. If the settlors have a familial, or even corporate, legal relationship (eg, one settlor is also the owner of another), and this relationship is an essential characteristic of the asset disposition, it can be presumed that the trustee is not establishing the trust relationship with them with a view to regular profit-seeking.

In summary, the absence of a familial, business, or similar legal relationship among the settlors would result in the circumvention of the provisions of the Trustee Act regarding businesslike conduct when entering into a contract that involves multiple asset dispositions and creates multiple contractual relationships. Therefore, businesslike conduct is not just examined from the perspective of the trustee, notwithstanding that the legislation fundamentally associates this concept with their person – the relationship and contractual intentions between multiple settlors in the same legal relationship can also influence the characterisation of a relationship as businesslike.

On the other hand, the fact that a trustee invests the trust assets in various financial instruments for remuneration and makes payments to the beneficiaries does not necessarily imply that the trustee is professional.[33] It can only be determined on the basis of the trust contract, and the detailed fiduciary asset management activities, whether the trustee is actually engaging in an activity subject to the approval of the NBH. It cannot be ruled out that the parties intend to use the contract to disguise the performance of such activities.

4.2 Distinguishing contractual and AMF-based asset management

AMFs are established upon court registration, and their asset management activities can be bidirectional. The AMF primarily manages the initial assets (capital) provided by the founder. Additionally, the AMF is entitled to enter into trust contracts with the founder, the joiner or third parties, with the sole restriction that the beneficiary of these legal relationships must be the AMF itself.

The AMF does not require permission to carry out its activities, and it is not obligated to register *ad hoc* trust relationships with the NBH.

Table 1 below outlines the main differences between the three fiduciary asset management relationships, focusing on the type of trustee:

33 Statement by the National Bank of Hungary, 10 February 2021. Available at: https://alk.mnb.hu/data/cms2489418/allasfoglalas_kozzeteteli_peldany.pdf.

Table 1: Comparison of fiduciary asset management relationships

	***Ad hoc* trustee**	**Professional trustee**	**AMF**
Trustee	Natural or legal person, independent of nationality, address, place of business	Legal entity only (limited liability company, private limited company, branch office of an EEA-domiciled company in Hungary, law office)	Only AMF registered in Hungary
Permission/ registration	Trust relationship must be registered with NBH	Trustee can only conduct its activities with approval of NBH	Court registration required, but no requirement for approval or registration of trust relationships with trustee
Capital	No minimum capital requirement	Minimum HUF 70 million	Minimum HUF 600 million
Financial security	Not required	At least 20% of total trust assets, but not less than HUF 70 million and not exceeding HUF 1.5 billion	Not required
Duration of legal relationship	Maximum 50 years	Maximum 50 years	No time limit

5. The system of asset management regulations

5.1 The Civil Code

The regulation of Hungarian trust relationships is multilayered. The general private law rules are contained in the Civil Code, in the Sixth Book, on contractual relationships. The rules for trusts fall under Title XVI, which deals with mandate-type contracts, following the sections on mandate contracts, agency contracts, brokerage contracts and forwarding contracts in Chapter XLIII (Sections 6:310–330).

Regulation contained in the Civil Code pertains to substantive legal issues. It includes a statutory definition of the duties of a trustee: based on a fiduciary asset management contract, the trustee is obliged to manage the things, rights and claims entrusted by the settlor in their own name for the benefit of the beneficiary, and the settlor shall pay a fee. Encompassing the distinctive features of the legal institution, the definition effectively mandates as follows:

- The conceptual element of trust includes the transfer of ownership (or other rights or claims). Thus, a legal relationship is considered a trust only when the trustee becomes the owner (or entitled party) of the managed assets; otherwise, a different legal relationship exists between the parties (for example, mandate or agency).
- The trust assets can consist of any active asset element, including ownership of goods, other rights, or claims. Naturally, other sector-specific regulations must also be taken into account concerning the managed assets (for example, it is forbidden to entrust agricultural land,[34] and the purchase of claims as a business activity is subject to authorisation).[35]
- The position of the trustee is twofold. He or she becomes the legal owner of the trust assets, but these assets are entirely separate from their own, and they are obligated to manage the assets for the benefit of the beneficiary. Therefore, the trust assets constitute a special sub-asset of the trustee.
- There must be a beneficiary in the trust relationship; the creation of a trust for a purpose is not allowed. The regulations explicitly allow for specificity regarding the identification of the beneficiary or a reference to a circle of beneficiaries. The settlor can empower the trustee to designate the beneficiaries, in which case the trustee is entitled to determine the amount of benefits due to the beneficiaries.
- As a general rule, the trustee performs his or her activities in exchange for a fee, alteration of which may be provided for in the trust deed. The

34 Section 14(4) of the Act No CXXII of 2013 on agricultural and forestry land transactions.
35 Section 3(1)(l) of the Act No CCXXXVII of 2013 on credit institutions and financial enterprises.

settlor's obligation is to pay the fees (and costs) related to asset management, but he or she can authorise the trustee to settle these expenses of trust assets.

The Civil Code's rules also cover the following main topics:

- formal requirements related to the validity of establishing a trust;
- rights and obligations of the settlor, trustee and beneficiary;
- segregation and protection of trust assets;
- rules for designating beneficiaries;
- duty of care requirements for the trustee, and their liability;
- claims and cost demands of the trustee;
- rules applicable in the case of multiple trustees;
- termination of trust and distribution of assets; and
- in respect of trusts, provisions relating to mandate contract.

The specific rules in the Civil Code for trusts are underpinned by other provisions as well as those related to mandate contract, including provisions on contracts, general rules for obligations, guidelines applicable to wills and the principles and general clauses found in the First Book of the Civil Code. The guiding principle in this respect is *lex specialis derogat legi generali.*

5.2 The Trustee Act

The provisions of the Trustee Act complement the regulations of the Civil Code and are primarily of an administrative nature.[36] The structure of the act is three-tiered, as it contains general provisions (the scope of the law, interpretative provisions, compliance examination of the activities of the trustee, etc), followed by specific regulations for professional trust management undertakings and *ad hoc* trusts.

The Trustee Act establishes requirements for professional trustees, including:

- organisational, personnel and material conditions;
- procedures for approval and withdrawal of approval by the NBH;
- rules for the registration of professional trustee undertakings;
- regulations regarding fees related to licensing and registration; and
- rules for the conduct of professional trustees (maintenance of internal records, confidentiality, outsourcing, obligation to utilise, rules regarding cessation without a successor).

36 See note 23, *supra*.

The Trustee Act also includes separate rules for *ad hoc* trusts, covering:

- personal requirements related to the establishment of an *ad hoc* trust relationship;
- rules for reporting and registering the legal relationship and associated fees;
- requirements for the certificate of notification regarding registration; and
- regulations concerning access to information in the registry of trust relationships.

In summary, the Trustee Act provides detailed guidelines for both professional and *ad hoc* trustees, covering various aspects such as qualifications, registration procedures and fees, as well as rules governing the conduct of trust management activities.

5.3 Supplementary regulations

(a) *Fees and registration procedure*

Regulation No 32 of 2023 of the National Bank of Hungary, complementing the Trustee Act,[37] lays out the procedure for granting operating licences to trust management businesses, and the administrative service fee for registering *ad hoc* trust relationships.

(b) *Financial guarantees*

Decree No 87 of 20 March 2014 complements the Trustee Act on the rules for financial guarantees in the management of trust funds.

(c) *Others*

Numerous other sector-specific regulations include provisions relevant to trust management, such as tax laws, accounting laws, stamp duty laws and laws related to the registration of specific assets. Notable among these is the 2020 Arbitration Act, which includes the provision that there should be an arbitration clause in any legal relationship related to a trust management contract.[38]

---

37 Regulation No 32 of 2023 (VII 19) of the National Bank of Hungary concerning the administrative service fee for certain authorization and registration procedures carried out within the supervision of the financial intermediary system and for trust management companies.

38 This regulation was incorporated into Act LX of 2017 on Arbitration by Act CLXV of 2020 on modification of certain laws related to justice, in effect from 1 January 2021. This is of particular significance because under the previous regulations, in some cases the trust agreement could be classified as a consumer contract, in which case there was no room for an arbitration clause. For more on this topic see Péter Kun, István Sándor and Olivér Spiriev, "Adjudication by an arbitration court of legal disputes arising from trust relationships", *Trusts & Trustees*, Vol 29, No 7, September 2023, pp649–658.

We must also mention that Hungary is not a party to the Hague Convention, although the Hungarian trust complies with the criteria set out by the convention.

5.4 Legal background of AMFs

The regulation of AMFs is also complex.

The AMF Act defines special rules; however, it is nuanced as it includes general regulations applicable to all AMFs, and specific regulations for public interest and non-public interest (private interest) AMFs. The background regulatory provisions of the AMF Act come from the Civil Code, primarily the Sixth Part of the Third Book, which contains general rules for foundations.[39] Notwithstanding these rules, the Civil Code stipulates that members or founders of a legal entity, in matters concerning their relationships with each other and with the legal entity, as well as its organisation and operation, can deviate from the rules of the Civil Code in the founding document. Exceptions apply if the Civil Code expressly prohibits deviation, or if the deviation obviously violates the rights of the legal entity's creditors, employees, or the minority of members, or hinders supervision of the legal entity's lawful operation.

This results in the need to interpret individually the rules for foundations in the Civil Code, to determine whether they are mandatory or discretionary.

The AMF Act complicates matters further by specifically mentioning certain general rules of the Civil Code that cannot be deviated from in the case of public interest AMFs, including the following:

- The founder, joiner, foundation officer, foundation body members and their close relatives cannot be beneficiaries of the foundation, except under specific exceptions.
- The founder and joiner can only be beneficiaries if the foundation's purpose is the care of the founder's scientific, literary or artistic works.
- The founder and joiner's relatives can only be beneficiaries if the foundation's purpose is the care of their scientific, literary or artistic works, nursing, support for their health care costs, or support for their school studies through scholarships or other means.
- The beneficiaries of the foundation and their close relatives cannot be members of the board of trustees.
- The founder and close relatives cannot be a majority in the board of trustees.

---

39 Regarding the comparative legal regulations of private foundations, see István Sándor, "Key Features of Private Foundations in a Comparative Law Approach: With Special Emphasis on Asset Management", *European Review of Private Law*, Volume 29, Issue 6, 2021, pp885–912; and Gábor B Szabó, Ákos Menyhei and István Sándor, *The Foundation: Historical, typological, operational, taxation and asset management omnibus*, *supra* note 27, pp68–85.

Table 2: The regulatory framework for AMFs

<table>
<tr><th></th><th>Ad hoc trust</th><th>Professional trust</th><th>AMF's trust</th><th>Private interest AMF</th><th>Public interest AMF</th><th>Public interest AMF performing public duty</th></tr>
<tr><td rowspan="2">Special laws</td><td>Rules for ad hoc trusts in the Trustee Act</td><td>Rules for professional trustees in the Trustee Act</td><td rowspan="2">AMF Act</td><td>Rules for private interest AMFs in the AMF Act</td><td>Rules for public interest AMFs in the AMF Act</td><td rowspan="2">Rules for public interest AMFs performing public duty in the AMF Act</td></tr>
<tr><td colspan="2">General rules of the Trustee Act</td><td colspan="2">General rules of AMF Act</td></tr>
<tr><td rowspan="4">General laws</td><td colspan="3">Rules for trusts in the Civil Code</td><td colspan="3">Rules for foundations in the Civil Code</td></tr>
<tr><td colspan="3">Rules for contracts in the Civil Code</td><td colspan="3" rowspan="2">Rules for legal entities in the Civil Code</td></tr>
<tr><td colspan="3">General rules of obligations in the Civil Code</td></tr>
<tr><td colspan="6">General principles in the Civil Code</td></tr>
<tr><td>Additional rules in sectoral laws</td><td colspan="6">Acts on taxation, stamp duty, accounting, registration of immovables and movables, UBO registry, AML, etc.</td></tr>
</table>

- In the event of the foundation's dissolution without a successor, after satisfying creditors, the remaining assets go to the person specified in the founding document, with assets going to the founder, joiner and other donors and their close relatives, not exceeding the assets contributed to the foundation by them.

Deviations from these rules are allowed for private interest AMFs. On the other hand, there are additional, specific provisions for public interest AMFs performing a public duty, which can be considered a specific subtype of public interest AMF. However, the AMF Act's background regulation does not extend to them; only the Civil Code does.

It should be noted that AMFs can not only manage their own assets, but also enter into trust contracts with the founder or a third party. The rules of the Civil Code will apply to these contracts – except for the provision limiting the duration of the legal relationship to 50 years – but not the rules of the Trustee Act.

Finally, the regulations of each sector-specific law are naturally applicable to the asset management activities of AMFs.

Settlors, formalities and documents: contract, unilateral declaration, testament, changes

István Sándor
Kelemen, Mészáros, Sándor and Partners

1. Settlors

1.1 The identity of the settlor

A settlor may be any legal entity, or any natural person with legal capacity. Establishing a trust involves a legal transaction, so it is necessary for a natural person to be legally competent, which means meeting two conditions:

- being 18 or over; and
- not being under guardianship that restricts legal capacity.[1]

In the case of a legal entity, the rules of organisational representation come into play; so, a person authorised to represent the legal entity can enter into a transaction to establish a trust for the purpose of fiduciary asset management.

1.2 Multiple settlors

Several settlors together can establish a trust, in which case the general contractual rules of the Civil Code apply to the relationship between them, the starting point being whether or not the service specified in the obligation is divisible.

If the settlors are obligated in respect of a divisible service (eg, payment of fees to the trustee), each settlor is obliged to fulfil his or her share, and if the proportion is unclear, they are obliged to provide an equal level of service. If the specified service is not divisible (eg, handing over to the trustee a painting jointly owned by the settlors), the obligation is joint, meaning the entitled party can demand it from any of the settlors, and the settlors are jointly responsible for each other's breach of contract. In their internal relationship, a performing

1 In exceptional circumstances, a person with limited legal capacity can establish a trust – for example, where a minor has his or her own income or where a guardianship restricting the legal capacity of an adult does not extend to this particular area.

settlor can request reimbursement from the other settlors for an additional service provided by them.

The rights of the settlors follow a similar pattern. In the case of a divisible service, each settlor can demand their entitled share. If the specified service is not divisible, any of the settlors are entitled to demand it from a third party, and it must be fulfilled for all of them. The internal settlement obligation between the entitled parties will also apply.[2]

These rules can lead to differences in interpretation and therefore uncertainty as to whether joint or several liability exists among the settlors, so it is advisable to clarify the position when establishing a trust.

A common scenario is where only one spouse establishes the trust, but the asset contributed forms part of the marital community property. During the subsistence of the marriage, spouses can make decisions regarding common property jointly or with the consent of the other spouse. The consent does not need to be formal, but there is a presumption of consent only where one spouse disposes of property burdened with a return obligation. Establishing a trust results in a gratuitous alienation of property, so the consent of the spouse is always required if marital community property is included in the trust. A contract entered into without the consent of the spouse is ineffective as to their external legal relationship. In their internal relationship, the party establishing the trust without the spouse's consent is obligated to compensate the spouse for any resulting damage according to the rules of liability for tort damages, with the exception that liability is waived if it can be proven that the contract served the interest and presumed will of the other spouse, especially if the contract protected the common property from harm.[3]

Similar rules apply to the contribution to a trust of wealth accumulated during the cohabitation of life partners.[4]

1.3 Settlor succession

Changes in the position of settlor may occur during the life of the trust, upon the settlor's death or in the event of the settlor's cessation without a legal successor.

(a) Transfer of the settlor role

The settlor has the option to transfer their role to another person through a contractual transfer (*novatio*). The settlor and all other parties involved in the trust agreement must agree to the transfer. The consenting statement can be made in advance, even at the time of entering into the trust agreement, and it becomes effective when the exiting settlor notifies the remaining party of his or her

2 Sections 6:28–33 of the Civil Code. An English translation of the Civil Code (2013) by the Hungarian Ministry of Justice is available at: https://njt.hu/jogszabaly/en/2013-5-00-00.

3 Sections 445, 446, 450 and 452 of the Civil Code.

4 Section 6:516 of the Civil Code.

declaration. In the case of a contractual transfer, the incoming party is entitled to all the rights and is subject to all the obligations that belonged to the exiting party.[5]

It is also possible for the settlor to assign only certain rights or obligations to a third party. Notification to the trustee is required for any assignment, while consent is necessary for the assumption of obligations. In such cases the identity of the settlor does not change within the trust.

(b) Death of the settlor, cessation without a legal successor

In the event of the settlor's death, the rights and obligations arising from the settlor's contractual position become part of his or her estate. However, the trust ceases to exist if the settlor was the sole beneficiary.[6]

After the settlor's death, his or her heir assumes the settlor's role and can exercise the rights arising from the trust, while also being subject to the resulting obligations. This may be contrary to the settlor's original intentions, especially regarding termination of the trust relationship, removal and appointment of the trustee, and changes in respect of the beneficiaries. It may therefore be reasonable for the settlor to exclude, in the trust agreement, the right to terminate the relationship, remove the trustee and make changes in respect of the beneficiaries in the event of his or her death.

It is worth noting that if the settlor dies or withdraws without a legal successor, and no other settlor exists for the trust, if the trustee has been in serious breach of contract they can be removed from their position on application by the beneficiary to the court, which may simultaneously appoint a new trustee. This right can be exercised collectively by multiple beneficiaries, and upon the request of any of them the court will decide on termination of the trustee's mandate and the appointment of a new trustee. However, the court cannot appoint a trustee in the face of objections from all the beneficiaries.[7]

The rules described above can be assumed to apply in the case of withdrawal of a legal entity without a legal successor.

1.4 Rights and obligations of the settlor

According to the Civil Code, the rights of the settlor extend to defining the assets of the trust and appointing the trustee, which is in practice a bilateral legal transaction since it requires formal acceptance on the part of the trustee. The settlor transfers ownership, rights, claims and other transferable assets to the trustee and makes a statement regarding the manner of managing the assets. Within the trust relationship it is possible to set out other provisions, such as:

---

5 Sections 6:208–209 of the Civil Code.
6 Section 6:326(d) of the Civil Code.
7 Section 6:325(2)–(3) of the Civil Code.

- duration of the trust;
- trust terms;
- exclusion of the right to unilaterally terminate;
- determination of trustee compensation;
- appointment of additional trustees;
- regulation of the involvement of other intermediaries; and
- ensuring the right to transfer on the beneficiary side.

The main rights and obligations of the settlor are set out below.

(a) Allocation and transfer of assets

The settlor, at the establishment of the trust and thereafter, has the right to transfer assets to the trustee.

Hungarian private law follows the traditional approach to the transfer of ownership, meaning that both a valid method and formal title are required. The legal basis for the transfer of ownership is the trust relationship; however, the transaction establishing that relationship is not sufficient for the trustee to formally acquire trust assets. In the case of movable property, it is necessary to transfer possession of the object as well. Transfer of possession does not necessarily mean a change in the person exercising control over the object since, according to the Civil Code, in certain cases a transfer of possession agreement is sufficient for a change in possession.[8] For assets registered in a public register the transfer must be recorded in the relevant register – for example, a change of ownership of real estate must be recorded in the land register.[9] For other rights, a transfer of rights is required, while for the transfer of claims an assignment is required, both in addition to establishing the trust.[10]

(b) Termination of the trust

A trust established for an indefinite period can be terminated by the settlor at any time by declaration addressed to the trustee. It is possible for the settlor to exclude this right in the trust agreement.[11] This is particularly significant if the settlor wishes to prevent his or her successor from terminating the trust in the future with a view to thwarting the original transactional objectives of the settlor.[12]

If the trust is established by unilateral declaration and the settlor and trustee are one and the same, the right of revocation is inherently excluded.[13]

---

8 Section 5:3(2) of the Civil Code.
9 Section 5:38(1)–(2) of the Civil Code.
10 Sections 6:193(2) and 6:202(2) of the Civil Code.
11 Section 6:326(1)(e) of the Civil Code.
12 See the analysis in section 1.3(b) above.
13 Section 6:329(1) of the Civil Code.

(c) ***Removal of the trustee; appointment of a new trustee***

The settlor has the right to remove the trustee at any time without cause and is entitled to appoint a new one.[14] This is the default position; the parties may deviate from it, restrict it or even exclude it in the contract.

Removal of the trustee does not terminate the trust relationship; the trust remains in effect. This supports the notion that the trustee essentially holds an office, and a change in his or her person does not terminate the legal relationship between the parties.

Upon his or her removal the trustee is obliged to transfer the trust assets to the additional or new trustee designated by the settlor or, in the absence of such designation, to the settlor. If the trustee is removed or withdraws without a legal successor, the managed assets transfer to the designated additional or new trustee, or in the absence of designation, revert to the settlor. Any obligations assumed in respect of the managed assets are transferred to the additional or new trustee as part of the managed assets, or in the absence of a designation, to the settlor.[15]

(d) ***No right of instruction***

The settlor cannot instruct the trustee.[16] However, the settlor can express his or her wishes to the trustee (by letter of wishes), and although this does not have binding legal force, the trustee is not exempted from responsibility for fulfilling those wishes.

The prohibition on instructions does not extend to a stipulation in the trust deed that specific decisions or transactions of the trustee require the consent or even co-decision of the settlor. In such cases, the extent of the settlor's responsibility is an issue. For example, if the trust assets include a business entity and the settlor significantly influences decisions falling within its management scope, and as a result the business entity goes into liquidation, it may be argued that the settlor acted as a shadow director, resulting in personal civil liability.[17]

(e) ***Right to supervise; information; accountability***

The settlor has the right to oversee activities falling within the scope of the trustee's management, but bears the costs associated with such oversight.

Upon the settlor's request, the trustee must provide information about the managed assets, including:

---

14 Section 6:325(1) of the Civil Code.

15 Section 6:328 of the Civil Code.

16 Section 6:316 of the Civil Code.

17 The person who exercises decisive influence over the decisions of the business entity is considered the leader under Section 33/A(2) of Act No XLIX of 1991 on Bankruptcy Proceedings and Liquidation proceedings ('the Bankruptcy Code').

- the elements that make up the assets;
- their value and their actual and expected growth;
- the obligations assumed by the trustee in respect of the assets; and
- an account of the trustee's management of the assets.[18]

The trustee must also, on the settlor's request, settle any accounts with the settlor regarding the managed assets.[19]

The costs associated with fulfilling these obligations are borne by the settlor.[20]

Hungarian law does not specifically refer to a 'protector' or similar to oversee the assets but allows for the possibility of appointing such a person. In the event of the settlor's death or withdrawal without a legal successor, the settlor may designate someone to exercise the settlor's rights and fulfil their obligations. Upon acceptance, the designated person will acquire the rights and obligations of the settlor, except where restricted by the terms of the contract.[21] Such appointment may be made during the settlor's lifetime.

(f) *Exemption from confidentiality*

The trustee is obligated to keep confidential any fact, information, or other data acquired in the course of his or her role as trustee. This obligation is independent of the establishment of the trustee relationship and persists even after the termination of the trustee's position. The settlor and his or her legal successors have the authority to exempt the trustee from the obligation of confidentiality.[22]

(g) *Tracing*

A settlor has the right to take action against third parties to whom the trustee, in violation of the trust, gratuitously or in bad faith, has provided assets from the trust estate or who, without authorisation, have burdened the trust assets to their advantage.[23] This aligns fundamentally with the principles of common law tracing.

(h) *Fee payment and cost reimbursement*

As a general rule, the settlor is obligated to pay a fee for the services of the trustee, but the parties can deviate from this and it is open to the trustee to provide its services for free. The trustee is entitled to reimbursement of its costs from the settlor even if it performs its duties for free.

---

18 Sections 6:315 and 6:320 of the Civil Code.
19 *Ibid.*
20 *Ibid.*
21 Section 6:325(4) of the Civil Code.
22 Section 6:319 of the Civil Code.
23 Section 6:318(3) of the Civil Code.

The trustee is authorised to satisfy their fee, justified expenses, and other claims arising from the trust relationship directly from the managed assets.[24]

Compensation of the trustee is subject to free agreement by the parties, both in terms of amount and the manner of performance. It is possible to stipulate a fixed fee, lump-sum fee, hourly rate or, in some cases, a success fee tied to achieving certain results.

(i) *Other rights and obligations*

The settlor's rights and obligations are naturally subject to the general rules of contractual and obligatory law. Accordingly, the settlor is obligated to cooperate with the trustee and provide necessary information, among other standard contractual and legal obligations.

2. Establishment of the trust

2.1 General rules

It is a general requirement that the establishment of the trust relationship must be in writing.[25] In this regard, it is important to highlight the regulations regarding written declarations.[26]

If a declaration must be made in writing, it is valid if at least its essential content is recorded in writing, and as a general rule the declaring party must also sign it. A declaration is considered to be in writing if its content is reproduced unchanged in a form suitable for eliciting both the identity of the declarant and the timing of the declaration, even if the actual act of conveying the content of the declaration involves electronic means. A document with a qualified electronic signature is considered to be in writing, in line with the development of information technology.[27]

Unless the law provides otherwise, an electronic declaration made regarding real estate or in connection with inheritance law, family law, corporate law or financial service relationships is considered to be in writing only if its content is recorded with characters and meets the legal requirements for creating an electronic document.[28]

The written declaration of a person who cannot write or is unable to do so is valid if it is included in a public document or a private document with probative force, certified by a court or notary, or endorsed by a lawyer or two witnesses to state that the declarant signed or acknowledged his or her signature before them. For those who cannot read or understand the language in which the

---

24 Sections 6:310(1) and 6:322 of the Civil Code.
25 Section 6:310(2) of the Civil Code.
26 Section 6:7 of the Civil Code.
27 In this connection see the provisions of Act No XXXV of 2001 on electronic signatures.
28 Section 6:7(3a) of the Civil Code.

written declaration is made, an additional condition for the validity of the declaration is that the document itself shows that one of the witnesses or the authenticating person explained the content to the declarant. In such cases, invalidity can only be claimed for the benefit of the declarant.

(a) ***Public document***

A public document is considered as such if it is issued by a court, notary or other authority or administrative body within their jurisdiction, in compliance with legal provisions. The public document is presumed authentic until proven otherwise; however, the court may call on the issuer of the document to make a statement as to its authenticity.

(b) ***Private document***

A private document with probative force is one where:

- the signatory writes and signs the document by hand;
- two witnesses confirm that the signatory signed the document before them, or that they recognise the signature;
- the signature or handwriting of the signatory is certified by a judge or notary;
- a person authorised to represent a legal entity signs according to the relevant rules;
- a lawyer or a 'chamber legal adviser' (*kamarai jogtanácsos*), with a proper countersignature, proves that the signatory signed the document before them;
- the electronic document bears the qualified electronic signature or stamp of the signatory and – if required by law – a time stamp;
- the electronic document is authenticated by a document authentication service based on identification specified in the relevant government decree;[29] or
- the document is electronically signed in accordance with the E-Government Act.[30]

If the signatory cannot read or understand the language in which the document is written, a private document with probative force is only created if it is evident from the document itself that one of the witnesses or the authenticating person has explained the content to the signatory.[31]

A private document with complete probative force, until proven otherwise,

---

29 Section 16(A) of Government Decree No 451/2016 (XII 19) on the detailed rules of electronic administration.

30 See the provisions of Act No CCXXII of 2015 on the general rules of electronic administration and trust services ('the E-Government Act').

31 Sections 323 and 325 of Act No CXXX of 2016 on civil procedure.

fully proves that the signatory made, accepted or recognised the declaration contained therein.

All other documents are considered simple private documents.

Breach of the formalities renders a contract void, but acceptance of performance under an otherwise void contract makes the performed part valid. However, if the law prescribes a public or a private document with probative force or a special form for the transfer of ownership of real estate, acceptance of the performance does not cure the invalidity of the contract.[32]

In the context of establishing the trust relationship, the regulations differentiate depending on the type of declaration and the type of trustee, as discussed below.

2.2 The trust contract

The Trustee Act requires an *ad hoc* trustee to have the trust agreement notarised by a lawyer or a chamber legal adviser or to be drawn in the form of a notarial deed. In the case of a trust agreement concluded with a professional trustee, there are no additional formal requirements prescribed by law,[33] and for an asset management foundation (AMF) to enter into a trust agreement there are no additional requirements beyond the need for written documentation.

When considering the formalities, the nature of the assets held in the trust is important. For transfer of trust assets whose ownership is required to be registered in a public register, it is logical to consider the formalities required for such transfers. This may involve not only simple written documentation but also 'attorney at law' (*ügyvéd*) or chamber legal adviser endorsement or notarisation, which may not be a condition for the validity of the trust agreement but could be necessary for the transfer or registration of ownership (eg, a transfer in respect of real estate). Additionally, the parties themselves may stipulate a required formality for probative force private documents or public documents, particularly if the trust agreement is part of a complex transaction.

2.3 Establishing a trust by unilateral declaration

The trust relationship can also be established through unilateral declaration, but in such cases the declaration requires notarisation.[34] Since the legal relationship established by unilateral declaration involves the same person as settlor and trustee, notarisation is necessary to prove the fact and timing of the separation of assets. In other respects, the normal rules of trust contracts must be applied to trusts formed through unilateral declarations.

---

32 Section 6:94(1) of the Civil Code.
33 Section 18/A(1) of the Trustee Act.
34 Section 6:329(1) of the Civil Code.

2.4 Establishing a trust by will

To determine the testamentary nature of the document it is necessary that, at the very least, it outwardly appears to originate from the testator and contains a declaration related to death that indicates its testamentary character. In the absence of either of these conditions, the document cannot be considered a will. Testamentary disposition can be made through a public will, a written private will or, exceptionally, an oral will.[35]

(a) *Public will*

A public will is a testament made before a notary public in accordance with the formal requirements for notarial deeds.[36] It is distinct from a private will deposited with a notary, where the deposit is in the interests of preservation and security only.

(b) *Private written will*

Concerning the formal requirements, a private written will can take two forms:

- a holographic will, which is entirely handwritten by the testator; and
- an allographic will, which is written by someone else.[37]

Under the Civil Code,[38] a will deposited with a notary is also equivalent to a private written will.

There are numerous substantive and formal rules applicable to a private written will, and failure to adhere to them may result in invalidity. The private written will must be made in a language that the testator understands and is capable of reading and writing.[39] The quality of the will, as well as the time of its creation, must be evident from the document itself. In the case of a multi-page will, continuous numbering is required, and the necessary signatures must appear on each page.[40] If the testator does not write the entire will or a part of it by hand, the will is valid only with the participation of two witnesses, and this requirement cannot be replaced by the countersignature of an attorney at law.[41]

(c) *Oral will*

An oral will is exceptional and its validity is only temporary. A trust cannot be validly established by an oral will.

By way of summary, the minimum formal requirements for establishing a trust are set out in Table 1.

---

35 Section 7:13 of the Civil Code.
36 Section 7:14(1) of the Civil Code.
37 Section 7:16(1) of the Civil Code.
38 Section 7:17(1)(c) of the Civil Code.
39 Section 7:15 of the Civil Code.
40 Section 7:17(2)–(3) of the Civil Code.
41 Section 7:17(1)(b) of the Civil Code.

Table 1: Minimum formal requirements for a trust

	Ad hoc trust	Professional trust	Trust with AMF
Trust contract	Countersigned by an attorney at law or chamber legal adviser	Simple private document	
Unilateral declaration	Public document	–	–
Testament	Probative private document[42]		

2.5 Creditor protection rules in asset allocation

As a general rule, creditors of the settlor cannot make claims against the trust assets. However, an exception arises where the settlor is also a beneficiary. In such cases, the rules for creditors of the beneficiary apply, allowing them to assert a claim on trust assets when the assets are due to be released. Creditors of the settlor may enforce their claims against the trustee based on the modern rules of *actio Pauliana*, following the general principles of contract law.

The Civil Code does not offer explicit provisions regarding the illegitimacy of asset allocation within the rules of the trust relationship. However, general civil law regulations are applicable in such cases. Therefore, asset allocation is considered unlawful if its aim is to divert assets from the creditors of the settlor *in fraudem creditorum* or if it violates the prohibition of abuse of rights. These aspects will be discussed further in the following sections.

(a) Contract aimed at concealing assets

A contract is considered to conceal assets if it partially or entirely diverts resources that would otherwise be available to satisfy the claims of third parties.[43] This applies to both natural and legal persons acting as settlors. Establishing a trust can be disadvantageous for the creditors of the settlor since the collateral for their claims is reduced. The diversion of resources can occur through the transfer of assets, claims or rights.

For the transaction to be considered concealment of assets, the claimant

42 In such cases, the formalities required for the registration of the *ad hoc* trust are replaced by the notary's inheritance transfer decree.

43 Regarding the concealment of assets, the contract's terminology should be interpreted broadly, encompassing unilateral legal transactions as well. See point 1 of legal statement No 1/2011 (VI 15) of the Civil Law Collegium of the Supreme Court. Available in Hungarian at: https://kuria-birosag.hu/hu/kollvel/12011-vi-15-pk-velemeny.

must already have a claim against the obligor at the time the contract is concluded. In other words, the trust provides full protection against future creditors of the settlor. In addition, it is a condition that the obligor does not provide other assets as collateral for the claim of the claimant. And a final essential element is the bad faith of the contracting party benefitting from the contract, or the creation of gratuitous benefits for them.[44] If all these elements are proven, the contract will not provide protection against the claims of third parties.[45]

In a lawsuit to determine asset diversion, the claim must be quantified in monetary terms. The claimant must submit a claim for determination of relative invalidity, along with a claim for performance of the obligation if there is no final judgment or other enforceable document regarding the obligor's denial of the claim.[46] On request by the claimant, the contracting party must accept satisfaction from the acquired asset and tolerate enforcement on it. The claim extends to others who have benefited from the contract through the immediate contracting party. If the contracting party, acting in bad faith, has transferred or lost the acquired asset through the asset-diverting contract, they are obligated to compensate the third party for the value of the acquired asset. The claim can be asserted against a person who was not originally a party to the asset-diverting transaction.

In summary, in the case of an asset-diverting transaction, a claim for determining relative invalidity arises. However, the asset allocation and the trust contract remain valid. The creditor of the settlor can only rely on the relative invalidity of the transaction. From a different perspective, the asset-diverting transaction is treated as a special provision compared to invalidity. Therefore, in judicial practice, if the claim seeks invalidity, as long as the facts of asset concealment are present, the court will not establish invalidity. A significant advantage of Hungarian law is that creditors emerging after the establishment of the trust cannot make claims against the trust assets.

---

44 The provisions of the Civil Code on contracts aimed at concealing assets are similar to Roman law rules concerning harm to creditors (*in fraudem creditorum*). The *interdictum fraudatorium* issued by the praetor and the *actio Pauliana* resulting from the legal remedy of *in integrum restitutio* were means of seeking damages against a colluding debtor, while a *bona fide* debtor could initiate an *actio de in rem verso* for unjust enrichment. See András Földi and Gábor Hamza Gábor, *A római jog története és institúciói* [*The History and Institutions of Roman Law*], 27th ed, Novissima, 2023, p196.

45 The Civil Code presumes bad faith in cases where someone enters into a contract aimed at concealing assets with his or her close relative or a legal entity in which he or she has a controlling interest (Section 8:1(1) of the Civil Code); or where a legal entity enters into such a contract with its member or executive officer or their close relative. Bad faith and gratuitousness must also be presumed in the case of contracts between legal entities under the operational control of the same natural or legal person, even if direct or indirect majority control is not present (Section 8:2(1)–(3) of the Civil Code).

46 See points 7–8 of legal statement No 1/2011 (VI 15) of the Civil Law Collegium of the Supreme Court – note 43, *supra*.

(b) ***Bankruptcy regulations***

If the settlor is a business organisation,[47] the provisions of the Bankruptcy Code apply to asset allocation. Creditors or the insolvency administrator (liquidator) can challenge in court, within a one-year prescriptive period from the date of publication of the order for commencement of insolvency proceedings, any contract or legal statement by the debtor within the following time limits:

- five years before the date of taking effect of the court's decision to initiate insolvency proceedings which resulted in a reduction of the debtor's assets, if the debtor's intention was to circumvent the creditor or creditors, and the other party knew or should have known about this intention;
- three years before the date of taking effect of the court's decision to initiate insolvency proceedings which involved the gratuitous alienation of the debtor's assets, the gratuitous assumption of an obligation encumbering the assets, or a transaction with a disproportionately large value difference concluded to the detriment of the debtor;
- ninety days before the date of taking effect of the court's decision to initiate insolvency proceedings which were aimed at favouring one creditor, especially the modification of an existing contract in favour of the creditor or providing security to a creditor without security; or
- three years before the date of taking effect of the court's decision to initiate insolvency proceedings which involved the transfer of ownership or rights for security purposes or the transfer or exercise of a pre-emptive right for security purposes, in which the entitled party exercised its acquired right against the debtor in such a way that it did not fulfil, or inadequately fulfilled, its settlement obligation, or did not provide the debtor with collateral exceeding the secured claim.

If, therefore, it is suspected within five years after the establishment of the trust that the settlor intentionally created the trust to circumvent creditor claims, the trust can be challenged in insolvency proceedings. Since the asset allocation in the trust is gratuitous, the three-year challenging deadline will be applicable without examining other conditions. The three-year deadline also

47 A business organisation ('economic operator') is defined by the Bankruptcy Code, at Section 3 (1)(a)(aa), as a legal entity with a registered office in Hungary, including economic companies, non-profit companies, law firms, notary offices, patent attorney offices, judicial enforcement offices, European joint stock companies, cooperatives, housing cooperatives, European cooperatives, forestry associations, voluntary mutual insurance funds, private pension funds, sole proprietorships, associations – including European economic interest groupings – European regional associations, associations, foundations; and (ab) any other legal entity or entity engaging in economic activities based on personal rights, not possessing legal personality, whose principal interests' centre – pursuant to the Regulation (EU) 2015/848 of the European Parliament and of the Council of 20 May 2015 on insolvency proceedings (hereinafter: Regulation 2015/848 EU) – is located within the territory of the European Union, and insolvency proceedings that can be initiated against it fall within the scope of Regulation 2015/848 EU Section 3(1)(a) of the Bankruptcy Code.

applies if the settlor established the trust for the purpose of providing fiduciary collateral, and the beneficiary did not fulfil, or inadequately fulfilled, its settlement obligation. The 90-day deadline is applicable in the case of favouring a creditor.

In the event of a successful challenge, the provisions of the Civil Code on invalid contracts must be applied. The general rules for asset diversion will not be applicable, meaning that the court will not declare relative ineffectiveness. The insolvency administrator (liquidator) and the creditor may request the restoration of the *status quo ante* and the deletion of the right established and registered in the public registry after the alienation of the asset. Within sixty days from the date of publication of the court's decision to initiate insolvency proceedings, the insolvency administrator can reclaim any services provided by the debtor if the result was the favouring of a creditor and the service did not fall within the scope of ordinary management.

If the debtor enters into a contract with a business under its majority control, or if the business concludes a contract with a business member or executive officer, or their relatives, bad faith and gratuitousness must be presumed. Bad faith and gratuitousness must also be presumed in the case of contracts between business organisations operating under the influence of the same person or business, even if they are not directly or indirectly interlinked.[48]

(c) Abuse of right

In cases of abuse of right, it cannot be claimed that the person abusing the right acts explicitly unlawfully. In fact, in such disputes the defendant typically asserts that they acted within the bounds of the law, exercising their entitled right. Consequently, while the action may seem lawful, it contradicts the societal purpose of the law and the fundamental objectives and ideals of the legal system. The nature of an act conflicting with the prohibition of abuse of right can only be determined by weighing all the circumstances of the case.

In the context of trusts, abuse of right may manifest as the misuse of a limited liability sub-fund. As there is no precedent for this in Hungarian law, analogies can be drawn primarily from corporate law. In the case of companies with limited liability and legal personality, the liability of the company itself extends only to its assets, and its members usually risk only their financial contributions. However, it is conceivable that a member of a limited liability company will abuse this liability structure. For example, in the knowledge that limited liability will shield them from accountability, they may intentionally enter into transactions in respect of which the company will be unable to fulfil its obligations. Abuse of right, as a non-autonomous basis for liability, results in breach of the separate liability of the legal entity and the transfer of

48 Section 40 of the Bankruptcy Code.

responsibility. The reason for this is that when a member operates within the scope of the legal entity's activities, they severely abuse the entity's independent liability.[49]

Use of a trust can theoretically constitute abuse of right in exceptional cases. A good example from foreign legal practice is the case of a so-called 'sham trust', where a trust is established to create the appearance of a legal transaction, deceiving outsiders. In such cases, the rules of piercing the corporate veil may be applied. As with a limited liability company, the structure of a trust or other form of fiduciary asset management does not provide protection for an individual if it is used abusively.

2.6 Relationship between asset allocation and inheritance

In the system of inheritance law under the Civil Code, there are three additional areas where the relationship between trust and inheritance may arise:

- the obligation of collation;
- lineal family property; and
- the compulsory share.

(a) *The obligation to collate and the trust*

If multiple descendants inherit jointly, each heir is obliged to include in the value of the estate any gratuitous donation received during the lifetime of the testator, provided that the inclusion was stipulated by the testator or can be inferred from the circumstances surrounding the donation. Where a donation is made to an heir through a trust, as a beneficiary, it is generally considered a gratuitous benefit. However, in cases where a trust is part of a back-loaded legal transaction, it is not the asset reservation that becomes back-loaded – if the deceased grants a beneficiary position as part of an onerous transaction, collation does not apply.[50]

Naturally, in the context of an obligation to collate, it must be considered whether the testator, as the settlor, made any gratuitous donations to one of the heirs during their lifetime. In our opinion, this question can only be answered with knowledge of the contents of the trust deed and on examination of all relevant circumstances.

Another condition for the obligation to collate is that the gratuitous donation received from the testator should only be included in the value of the estate if the testator stipulated it or if circumstances indicate an obligation to include it. If the settlor explicitly excludes inclusion in the trust deed, the rules of the obligation to collate do not apply. To avoid potential disputes after their

---

49 Recommendation No 1/2005 (June 17) of the Civil Law Collegium of the Szeged Court of Appeals on the piercing of the corporate veil.

50 Section 7:56 of the Civil Code.

death due to different interpretations of these rules, the settlor should address the issue definitively in the trust deed.

(b) ***Relationship between lineal family property and the trust***

To ensure that family wealth remains within the family, Hungarian law recognises the institution of lineal, or agnatic, inheritance. If an intestate heir is not a descendant of the deceased (the estate leaver) then assets inherited or gifted from the estate leaver's ascendants are subject to lineal inheritance.[51] If the estate leaver placed such assets in trust before his or her death, they might be considered as lineal property within the trust. However, the rules of lineal inheritance do not apply to assets that the testator no longer possesses at the time of his or her death. These rules also extend to assets that have replaced or been acquired in lieu of such property.

The heir inherits lineal property in kind, but if inheriting in kind is impossible or impractical, the court may order a cash settlement equal to the value of the lineal property.

While the application of lineal inheritance may not be an everyday occurrence, it is still worth considering when establishing a trust from the perspective of determining the assets of the trust.

(c) ***Relationship between compulsory share and the trust***

Hungarian private law recognises the institution of compulsory share, and the legislator gives it preference over the trust. Compulsory share entitles the descendants, spouse, and parents of the deceased to a share of the inheritance at the time the inheritance is opened, if the deceased did not allocate at least the compulsory share to the person entitled to it in their will, or gave gratuitously to third parties during their lifetime, thereby partially or wholly reducing the basis of the compulsory share.[52]

The applicability of inheritance rules concerning compulsory share in the case of assets placed in trust has historically sparked much professional debate. As a result, the 2017 amendment to the Trustee Act[53] explicitly stipulated that the basis of compulsory share is the net value of the estate, as well as the net value of any gratuitous gifts by the deceased to anyone among the living, including the value of assets placed in trust by the deceased.[54] Accordingly, although the trust assets are not part of the estate, the value of assets placed in

51 The parent inherits those assets that originally came from them or their ancestors. If the parent dies, their descendants inherit according to the general rules of intestate succession. If both the parent entitled to inherit the lineal (agnate) assets and their descendant are disqualified from inheriting, the grandparent will inherit. If they too are disqualified, a more remote ancestor of the deceased will inherit the assets that originally came from them or their ancestor. If there is no lineal heir, the lineal assets are considered part of the general estate of the deceased. See Section 7:67 of the Civil Code.

52 Sections 7:75–7:86 of the Civil Code.

53 Act LXI of 2017. Available (Hungarian only) at: https://njt.hu/jogszabaly/2017-61-00-00.0.

54 Section 7:80(1) of the Civil Code.

trust by the deceased must be factored into the calculation of the compulsory share.

While assets transferred during a trust created at least ten years before the testator's death are considered gratuitous gifts, not all gifts must be taken into account when calculating the net value of the estate. Certain types of gift made by the deceased are excluded from the calculation of compulsory share, including:

- gratuitous gifts made more than ten years before his or her death; and
- gratuitous gifts made before the creation of the relationship establishing the entitlement to the compulsory share.[55]

A separate interpretation is required for a provision in the Civil Code stating that a gratuitous gift whose inclusion in the calculation of the compulsory share has been waived by the deceased cannot be counted towards the entitlement of the beneficiary's own compulsory share.[56] This provision can only be applied if the beneficiary had previously received a gratuitous gift from the deceased, and the inclusion of the gift in the calculation of compulsory share had been waived by the deceased before the creation of the relationship establishing the entitlement.

Satisfaction of the compulsory share is primarily accomplished through inclusion;[57] however, if it is not completely satisfied on this basis, the compulsory share may be disbursed. Those receiving a share of the estate are primarily responsible for satisfying the compulsory share, followed by those who received gratuitous gifts from the deceased within the ten years preceding his or her death. However, the latter are only responsible for that part of the compulsory share that cannot be satisfied from the estate.

The 2017 amendment to the Trustee Act allowed the application of a no-contest (*in terrorem*) clause.[58] According to this, the beneficiary's entitlement ceases if they assert a claim against the trust assets on a ground other than those specified in the trust deed. This rule seemingly has no direct connection to compulsory share; however, its primary purpose is to ensure that the compulsory share beneficiaries respect the testator's intentions. In the event that a compulsory share beneficiary seeks to enforce their compulsory share against the trust assets, they forfeit their beneficiary position and cannot receive any further distribution from the trust assets on this ground. If the testator does not want this rule to apply, he or she must expressly exclude it in the trust deed.

55 Section 7:81(1) of the Civil Code.
56 Section 7:81(3) of the Civil Code.
57 Section 7:83(1) of the Civil Code.
58 Section 6:311 of the Civil Code.

3. Modification of the trust

Modification of the trust contract is possible based on general civil law rules, and requires agreement between the parties.[59] As a general rule, a beneficiary is not a contracting party, therefore their consent is not necessary.[60] In addition, there is the option for the parties to authorise one of their number in the contract to unilaterally modify the agreement.

A practical issue may arise if the settlor dies without a successor, and there is no person who can exercise the settlor's rights. Hungarian law does not contain a specific rule as to whether the trustee can turn to the court for modification of a trust in cases where economic or other circumstances have changed over time. However, the court's discretion (similar to the common law notion of *nobile officium*) may be invoked to ensure that the trust can serve the interests of the beneficiaries to the extent possible, even when economic conditions change.

Hungarian law recognises the general concept of the amendment of a contract by the court.[61] Accordingly, any party can request the court's modification of the contract if, in a long-term legal relationship between the parties, performance of the contract under the conditions prevailing at its conclusion would significantly harm their interests. The court may modify the contract from such date as it determines, starting from the earliest possible date but not earlier than the date when the claim for modification of the contract is brought before the court. For the court to intervene in this way, certain conditions must be satisfied, namely:

- that the change in circumstances was unforeseeable at the time of the conclusion of the contract;
- that the party making the application did not cause the change; and
- that the change does not fall within the parameters of ordinary business risk.

Since the introduction of the trust in Hungary is relatively recent, there is not yet sufficient practical experience to determine the extent to which this provision of the Civil Code offers a suitable tool for trust modification.

---

59 Section 6:191 of the Civil Code.
60 It is possible that the beneficiary may also be a contracting party; in such a case, logically, their consent is also required for modification of the contract.
61 Section 6:192 of the Civil Code.

How trusts are used in Hungary

Ákos Menyhei
Primus Wealth; Aliant-Menyhei-Molnár-B. Szabó Law Firm

1. Introduction

Even before the introduction of trusts under the new Civil Code, Hungarian law included various legal instruments (wills, gifts, mandates) that could be utilised and combined to achieve the legal effects of a trust.[1] Furthermore, since its enactment in 1979, the International Private Law Act ('the IPL Act') required the application of foreign law in cases not recognised by Hungarian law.[2] In addition, the IPL Act has allowed contracting parties the freedom to select the governing law for their civil law relationships,[3] eliminating any private law obstacles to establishing a trust relationship in the Hungarian jurisdiction under foreign law. While it was possible to create a trust under civil law in Hungary in the past, obstacles such as limited awareness of the legal instrument and unfavourable tax and duty regulations impeded its widespread adoption, even after the regime change.

Since the mid-2000s, a subtle yet discernible push has emerged within professional circles, advocating for the introduction of trusts in Hungary.

This shift has been influenced by Hungary's increasing prominence in international tax planning through its holding, royalty and financing structures.[4] Despite a decline in interest in royalty and financing structures due to recent changes in domestic tax regulations, Hungarian holding companies remain highly favoured among international tax planners. However, Hungary has lagged behind major competitor countries, for example Luxembourg,

---

1 See István Sándor, *Property and Trust Law in Hungary*, Wolters Kluwer, 2017; Dániel Deák (ed), *The Financial Law of Asset Management*, research report, Budapest, 1998; and Norbert Csizmazia and István Sándor, "Models of fiduciary asset management and the reform of the Civil Code", in *Codification of Civil Law 2002/4*. See also István Sándor, *Regulation of asset management rights*, Economy and Law (publishers), 2000 and 2003.

2 While the IPL Act is no longer in effect, it was crucial to the development of Hungarian legal thinking. Paragraph (2) of Article 3 of the act:

> *If Hungarian law does not recognise a legal instrument or recognises it with a different content or by a different name, and it cannot be determined by interpreting the rules of Hungarian law, the legal classification shall also take into account the foreign law governing the legal instrument.*

3 Section 25 of the IPL Act:

> *The contract shall be governed by the law chosen by the parties at the time of the conclusion of the contract or subsequently, either for the whole contract or for only part of it.*

4 Balázs Horváth, "Hungarian and International Taxation of Fiduciary Trusts through Examples", at the STEP Hungary Conference in Budapest on 24 April 2014.

Malta, the Netherlands and Cyprus, where trusts are well established. Trusts and similar legal structures are common globally,[5] including in Russia[6] and China.[7] Nearer home, Romania[8] and the Czech Republic[9] have also embraced the concept.[10] Even France, a bastion of continental law, incorporated trusts into its domestic law in 2007 under the term '*fiducie*'.[11] These international examples underscore that what originated as a quintessentially English law instrument has evolved into a globally recognised and utilised legal framework.[12]

Internally, economic and social transformations following the regime change, such as the proliferation of family businesses and the concentration of substantial wealth within single families, highlight the limitations of succession law in addressing the complexities of generational wealth transfer. As individuals involved in the privatisation process approach the end of their careers, the need for a regulated approach to planned generational transfers becomes apparent. International examples show that unregulated generational wealth transfer is often associated with significant wealth loss.[13] Trusts offer a viable solution to this challenge, driven by significant demographic factors, and provide wealthy families with an alternative legal avenue for managing planned generational transfers in various contexts.

In conclusion, trusts represent a breakthrough in Hungarian law by conferring upon the trustee a *de facto* ownership position. Trusts can include the exercise of all partial ownership powers without any restrictions on property rights, fully aligning with the reasons for their introduction.

2. Use of trusts in common law systems

The trust, within common law systems, is a versatile legal institution designed to address a myriad of social needs, distinguished by its diverse typology. Trusts can be used to manage assets during the settlor's lifetime, address medical and

5 See István Sándor, *Property and Trust Law in Hungary, supra*, p231.

6 In Russia, the trust was first introduced into the legal system by presidential decree in 1993, mainly for privatisation purposes. For more information, see István Sándor, *Property and Trust Law in Hungary, ibid*, p286.

7 Trust Law of China, 2001. See István Sándor, *Property and Trust Law in Hungary, ibid*, p297.

8 The new Romanian Civil Code was drafted in 2011 and introduced the legal institution of *fiducia* in Romania. See István Sándor, *Property and Trust Law in Hungary, ibid*, p278.

9 Almost at the same time as Hungary, the Czech Republic introduced the trust with the entry into force of the new Czech Civil Code on 1 January 2014. See István Sándor, *Property and Trust Law in Hungary, ibid*, p12.

10 See István Sándor, *Property and Trust Law in Hungary, ibid*, p279

11 The introduction of the *fiducie* in France in 2007 was preceded by an extremely lengthy professional and political debate. For further details, see István Sándor, *Property and Trust Law in Hungary, ibid*, p271.

12 Charles E Rounds Jr and Charles E Rounds III, *Loring and Rounds: A Trustee's Handbook*, 2014, pp11–14.

13 There are no fully reliable statistics, but several studies show that in around 70% of cases, there is a loss of wealth in the event of a disorderly generational change. See Karen File and Russ Prince, "Attributions for Family Business Failure: The Heir's Perspective", *Family Business Review*, Vol 9, No 2, 1996, p171. Other sources, based in part on surveys of private firms, have found that the probability of a successful generational change in family firms and of the second generation successfully continuing the family business built by the first generation is only 33%, while the probability of the third generation successfully continuing the family business is only 10%. See Christian Stewart, "Finding the harmonious pathway: where a trust owns a family firm", *Offshore Investment*, April 2014, p13.

burial needs, settle debts, provide posthumous services to beneficiaries and even support pets. Trusts can also offer financial support for household members, facilitate estate distribution, discretionary payments and annuity arrangements, provide for marital deduction, and more.[14]

The primary motivation for establishing a trust is to ensure legal protection for assets.[15] This includes safeguarding against creditors,[16] deviating from inheritance rules, enhancing asset management and optimising taxation. Hayton identifies numerous commercial applications of trusts, showcasing their role in preserving family wealth across generations.[17] Commercial uses include pension earmarking, collective investment schemes, managing bonds and facilitating various trusts in project finance, securitisation[18] and syndicated lending. Trusts are also used to manage shareholding, separate voting rights, secure bills of lading and ensure legal security in subcontractor fee payments.[19] Overall, trusts are universally recognised in English legal literature as a pivotal means of wealth transfer during generational change.[20]

3. Use of trusts in Hungary

Among professionals, there is a consensus that the trust is an extremely versatile, varied and flexible legal instrument. However, given the unique features of the Hungarian legal system, which is rooted in European continental principles, and the regulation of the Anglo-American capital market, adapting Anglo-American trust methods to the Hungarian legal environment requires careful consideration and caution. Despite this, even before the introduction of specific trust rules and detailed trust regulations around tax, duty and accounting, Illés identified six areas where trusts could be employed in Hungary.[21]

In the sections below, following the rules of the Hungarian legal system and partially following Illés' categorisation,[22] we outline the most significant potential uses and types of trust in Hungary, which are as follows:

---

14 William Franklin Fratcher, article 5, *International Encyclopedia of Comparative Law, Vol VI: Trust and Property*, JCB Mohr (Paul Siebeck), 1973.

15 "It is understandable that someone, faced with the uninsurable risks already mentioned, would want to secure parts of their assets from their creditors": Milton Grundy, John Briggs and Joseph Field, *Asset Protection Trusts*, Key Haven Publications, 1997, p27.

16 This is essentially the case for special purpose and discretionary trusts, as the beneficiary's right to trust property can be used by the beneficiary's creditors to seek satisfaction. See Maurizio Lupoi, "Introduction, Trusts – Some observations from a Civil Law Perspective", in Rosalind F Atherton (ed), *Estates, Taxes and Professional Ethics. Papers of the International Academy of Estate and Trust Law*, Kluwer Law International, 2003, p6.

17 David Hayton, "English Trusts and Their Commercial Counterparts in Continental Europe", in David Hayton (ed), *Extending the Boundaries of Trusts and Similar Ring-Fenced Funds*, Kluwer Law International, 2002, p35.

18 Edoardo Andreoli, "Trusts and Company Law – The Italian Experience", in RF Atherton (ed), *Estates, Taxes and Professional Ethics*, *supra*, p7.

19 Harold J Ford and William A Lee, *The Law of Trusts*, Thomson Reuters (Professional) Australia, 2012, pp1–54.

20 Charles E Rounds Jr and Charles E Rounds III, *Loring and Rounds: A Trustee's Handbook*, *supra*, p26.

21 István Illés, "*Mire jó a bizalmi vagyonkezelés?*" ("What is the purpose of trust management?"), *Jogtudományi közlöny* (*Journal of Legal Studies*), Vol 11, 2011, p4.

22 *Ibid*.

- generational wealth transfer planning including:
  - family business trusts;
  - internal systems of family firms;
  - issues concerning the family business life cycle; and
  - long-term intergenerational operation of the family business;
- business uses including:
  - quasi-representation;
  - joint ventures and unit trusts;
  - transactional trusts, acquisitions; and
  - warranty rights;
- collateral;
- active and passive asset management;
- asset protection;
- financial operations including:
  - syndicated lending;
  - corporate reorganisation; and
  - securitisation;
  - pension fund/pre-savings; and
  - charity; and
- tax panning.

3.1 Generational wealth transfer

Mortality prompts a universal question: how to transfer accumulated wealth to the next generation or, in the absence of an heir, to redirect it, often for charitable purposes. Hungarian inheritance law, while theoretically well developed, falls short in addressing the practical and swift decision-making requirements of economic life. The dogmatically closed system, whereby a person's estate immediately passes to the heir upon death, does not align with the needs of everyday life. Despite this immediate transfer, legal certainty regarding the estate's content and the identity of the heir or new owner takes time to materialise. State approval of the estate and its owners in succession cases introduces significant delays, ranging from months to years and leaving assets in limbo during probate proceedings.

This delay poses particular challenges for family-owned micro, small and medium-sized enterprises (SMEs), where ownership and management functions are often intertwined. The death of the owner or manager renders day-to-day decision making impossible until probate is finalised, risking the viability of the business. Anticipating this, legal solutions like executors[23] and trusteeships have emerged. Trusteeships, in particular, facilitate asset transfer by the appointment of a trustee responsible for estate administration.

Consequently, the trust is ideally suited to wealth planning as an alternative to the will, preventing the loss of assets during the lengthy probate process.

In Hungary, trusts can serve as an alternative to gifts, wills, inheritance contracts or prenuptial agreements for intergenerational wealth transfer in various scenarios, including:

- *Flexible asset allocation:* Trusts allow for flexible and differentiated asset distribution based on gift or inheritance conditions, will provisions or intestacy rules, allowing varied distribution among beneficiaries as to timing and proportion.
- *Preventing dissipation:* Trusts can address issues of dissipation or unworthiness by allowing for instalment payments, suspension, or termination based on specified conditions.
- *Deviating from mandatory succession rules:* Trusts enable the settlor to determine beneficiaries, timing, and extent of property and proceeds utilisation, creating sophisticated structures beyond statutory rules.
- *Multijurisdictional families:* Where family members are resident in different jurisdictions, trusts can effectively navigate jurisdictional conflicts following the settlor's death.
- *Caring for dependent relatives:* As a pre-planned and institutionalised solution for caring for dependent relatives without independent income, trusts ensure the wellbeing of surviving spouses, minors or incapacitated family members.
- *Avoiding disputes between heirs:* Trusts can prevent disputes and asset loss among heirs with complex family dynamics or relationships from multiple marriages.
- *Protection of pre-marriage assets:* Trusts can protect assets placed in trust before marriage, excluding them from matrimonial community property in the event of divorce.
- *Succession in family businesses:* Trusts are a crucial tool for succession in family-owned businesses, enabling planned and managed generational wealth transfer while maintaining the settlor's influence over assets.

Given the significance of trusts in these areas within a socio-economic context, further exploration of the benefits, risks and challenges of running a family business as a trust, along with the importance of wealth planning, is undertaken in detail below.

---

23 Although the new Civil Code does not mention this legal institution either, the provisions of the earlier Decree 6/1958 (VII 4) of the Interior Ministry on the procedure of probate have been adopted and partially extended in Sections 6 (4) and 99–101 of Act XXXVIII of 2010 on the procedure of probate. See further, Attila Tikász, *"Néhány gondolat a végrendeleti végrehajtóról"* ("Some thoughts on the executor of the will"), *Közjegyzők Közlönye* (*Notaries' Bulletin*) Issue 7–8, 1998, p68; and Tibor Anka, *A megújult hagyatéki eljárás* (*The new probate procedure*), HVG-Orac, 2011, p68.

(a) *Placing the family business in trust*

Wealth planning for family businesses represents one of the most important domains of trust, yielding positive outcomes at the individual level – for both the settlor and the beneficiary – and also at the national economic level. As mentioned above, Hungary boasts a considerable number of family businesses that employ more than 50 individuals. When combined with the small business sector, comprising entities with fewer than 50 employees, the SME sector constitutes the largest employer in Hungary.

Ensuring the successful continuation of these businesses after the retirement or death of their owners serves the interests of both the individuals involved and the state, which collects taxes and social security contributions. Trusts add a significant legal tool to facilitate a smooth generational transition. However, like any tool, trusts must be employed judiciously and strategically to attain the intended outcomes.

Drawing on practical experience, Christian Stewart succinctly outlines the key considerations, challenges and potential solutions for structuring and managing a family business trust,[24] placing the key elements, or sub-systems, of family, ownership and management within three-circle Venn diagrams to illustrate how the relationship between those elements varies depending on the particular business trust ecosystem in question.[25]

(b) *Internal systems of family firms*

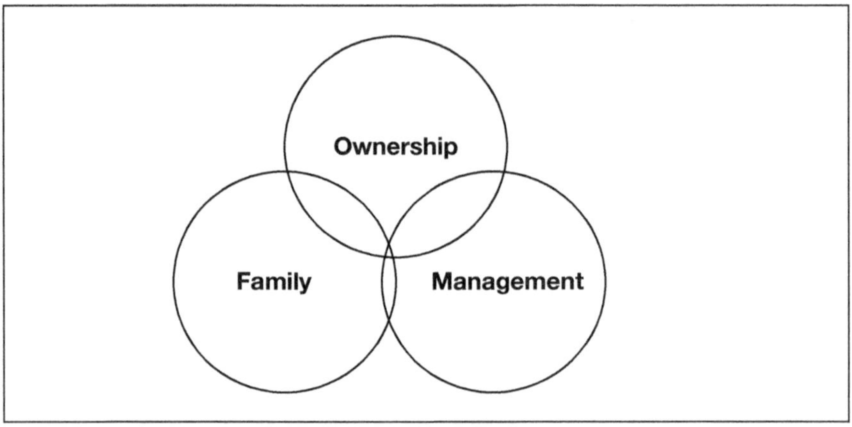

In the context of the three elements, the family functions as an emotional relationship sub-system, ideally fostering positive relations among its

24 Christian Stewart, "Finding the harmonious pathway", *supra*, p124. Following Stewart's line of thought, we summarise below the dangers to family businesses in the long term in terms of generational change, as well as possible solutions.

25 Christian Stewart, *ibid*, p124.

members. In the ownership sub-system, proprietors form emotional attachments to the business, believing the interests of the business, and by extension their own interests, to be served by their decision making. In the management – or governance – sub-system, the company operates with expertise and efficiency.

From a trustee's perspective, the family and ownership sub-systems pose the greatest challenges. Unlike the management sub-system, where the trustee exercises quasi-ownership through management powers, the trustee assumes an executive role in the first two sub-systems. Moreover, the family and ownership sub-systems are often more complex than the management sub-system, driven more by emotional than rational factors. Analysing the family sub-system requires gaining an understanding of family habits, values, emotions, stress tolerance and risk-taking appetite. And in the ownership sub-system, motivational factors such as return on investment, dividend rates, business value preservation, liquidity assurance, exit strategy, and the need for additional capital investment, must be carefully evaluated.

Establishing clear boundaries and maintaining balance between the three sub-systems is crucial for a trust structure supporting the long-term, harmonious operation of the family business. Operational guidelines for trust management should be meticulously defined, incorporating decision-making mechanisms into the trust. Key considerations will include the following:

- The trustee must be an independent and professionally operated entity.
- Beneficiaries should be defined through a discretionary trust for enhanced flexibility, with the settlor specifying governance principles, asset distribution and named beneficiaries in a 'letter of wishes'.
- It is essential to involve a protector or board of protectors to provide checks and balances against the trustee's powers.
- The protector should have the authority to approve certain decisions, remove and appoint a new trustee and select and change investment board members.
- Larger and more diversified businesses may benefit from establishing an investment council to assist the trustee and involve family members in decision making.
- Integrating all elements of the interconnected business system into the trust structure will help avoid divergent and conflicting decisions.
- An operating mechanism must be established that clearly defines the trustee's responsibilities, investment control, decision-making powers and beneficiary benefit decisions.

When designing the operating mechanism, it is crucial to recognise that family members within a particular sub-system may share common interests, while those in different sub-systems may have partly or wholly divergent interests. Special attention should be given to the different motivations as between family members who perform owner/manager functions, and those who are solely owners. Balancing these sub-systems requires addressing any potential conflict of interest between the groups, ensuring communication and joint decision making. Failure to reconcile conflicting motivations may lead to a disconnect between the ownership and management sub-systems, potentially resulting in business failure or less than ideal sale terms.

To maintain balance among the interconnected sub-systems, each sub-system should have its own decision-making forum, along with clearly defined boundaries and decision-making powers. Although this is more straightforward in the management and ownership sub-systems due to legal requirements for distinct decision-making bodies, creating informal forums for discussion and decision preparation is advisable to enhance efficiency. This is more challenging in the family sub-system. In the absence of legal constraints, institutionalising annual family meetings, including business discussions, in the form of a family council is a practical approach.

(c) ***Issues related to the family business life cycle***

During the initial phase of the family business life cycle, the three sub-systems largely or entirely converge and cannot be easily separated. Typically, the founder who builds the business up is a dominant individual who, even with the establishment of an appropriate trust structure, positions him or herself in all pivotal roles, rendering the roles of the investment board and protector (or protector board) redundant. The trustee often assumes a purely formal role.

The main drawback of this setup is its failure to educate and involve the next generation in decision-making processes, leading to a lack of the emotional

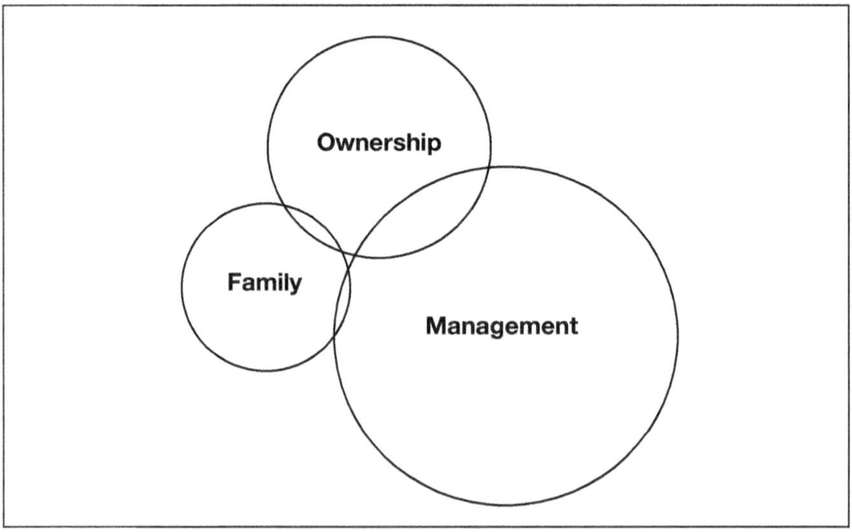

attachment essential for the ongoing success of the family business. This may result in the dissolution or sale of the business following the founder's death. It is common for the founder to perceive the ownership sub-system as significantly more important than the family sub-system, with the management sub-system holding even greater importance.

This founder mindset may prompt the settlor, while carefully crafting a trust scheme, to overemphasise the management function and confer decision-making authority upon family members holding managerial roles in the family business. Consequently, the investment board may be bereft of family members who solely serve as beneficiaries, causing them to lose any influence in the family business and gradually become detached from it. This increasing gap between family members in different positions often results in those in managerial roles exerting control not only in the business but also within the trust itself, through the investment and protection boards.

Ironically, in contrast to the settlor's primary intentions, the family and ownership sub-systems may become entirely disconnected from the management sub-system and the family cease to be actively involved in day-to-day business management, which is then overseen by professional managers.

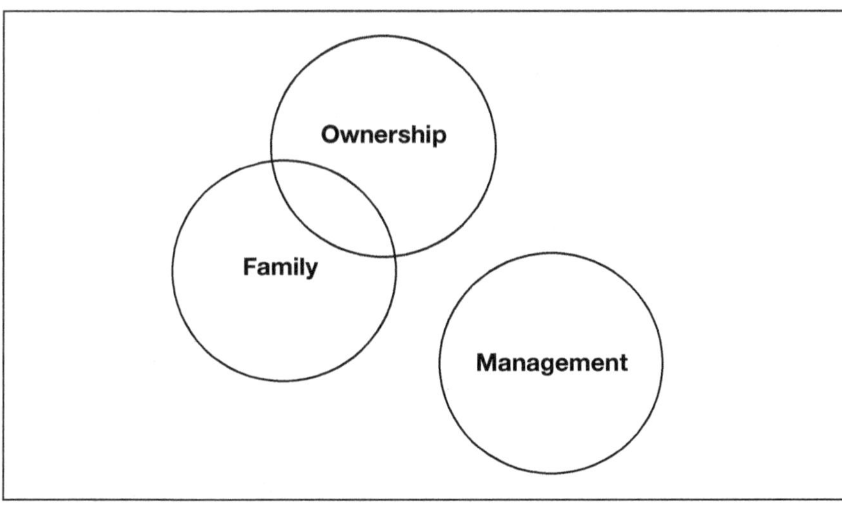

This scenario is likely to unfold in the following circumstances:

- the investment board comprises only family members who are not actively involved in the day-to-day management of the family business;
- the investment board is predominantly composed of family members who are not engaged in the day-to-day management of the family business and do not prioritise management concerns; and
- the trust was initially established without an investment board or a similar mechanism, and the trustee, responsible for exercising voting

> rights in the family business on behalf of the family, faces pressure from an increasing number of family members/beneficiaries who receive a smaller *per capita* benefit and no longer hold management roles.

When decision making tilts towards the ownership sub-system at the expense of the management sub-system within the family business, a growing number of beneficiaries may lose interest in new capital-intensive investments. Instead, they may seek to extract escalating amounts of capital from the firm in the form of dividends. With diminishing support for management decisions and the absence of a prepared exit mechanism for discretionary trust beneficiaries, conflicts between trustee, management and beneficiaries are likely to ensue.

(d) Contribution of trusts to the long-term operation of the family business

These systemic shortcomings raise a fundamental question: how can a trust structure and a trustee ensure the long-term, multigenerational operation of the family business? How can trusts facilitate effective communication between the family, ownership and management sub-systems while balancing divergent interests over the long run?

Given the complex and dynamic nature of the sub-systems constituting the family business, coupled with the evolving legal and business landscape, no single, static solution can address the problem through organisational trust structures alone. Nonetheless, a well-conceived trust structure and decision-making mechanism can provide invaluable assistance. The crux is flexibility, continuous adaptation to changing circumstances, and decision-making mechanisms that factor in the interests of diverse sub-systems. The trustee must be aware of potential threats and respond adeptly to a changing environment, while considering the long-term interests of the beneficiaries. This requires wisdom and restraint on the part of the trustee and their advisers, as well as the integration of the principle of due process into the trust's decision-making processes.

One potential solution involves including a predetermined number of family members, with and without managerial positions, on the investment board. To avoid indecision, there could be an additional mechanism in the trust with clearly defined roles and responsibilities, complemented by a procedural framework for decision making. Flexibility should be retained to adapt to unforeseen changes, allowing for a bespoke arrangement based on detailed knowledge of the family and business.

Another plausible solution is to expand the protector's role, to enable communication between board members and consider divergent interests in decision making. The protector could also be empowered to remove an uncooperative investment board member and appoint a replacement from the family. This approach could be complemented by an informal beneficiary forum, where non-management beneficiaries can articulate their perspectives and engage in discussions with members of the investment board and the board of directors.

Establishing an effective board of directors with the right mix of independent professionals and family members is crucial for a business trust. This aids decision making in a multigenerational family trust, preserves and transmits family values, fosters responsible ownership education and maintains commitment within a family business. In addition to meeting the legal and trust deed requirements, the trustee's role extends to that of mediator – someone who facilitates conflict resolution and assists both the settlor and, subsequently, the family members and business management in implementing a combination of the solutions mentioned above.

3.2 Business use

The use of trusts for business purposes can be extraordinarily diverse and varied due to the flexibility of the trust and the highly regulated nature of trust activities. Flexibility promotes diversity of use, while regulation provides the necessary framework for utilising trusts in business.

The most common uses are outlined below, recognising that numerous variations of business use can be developed.

(a) Quasi-representation

Quasi-representation[26] should, in our opinion, be classified as a subcategory that can be subdivided into further categories. Simultaneously, the fiduciary nature of the legal instrument prevails in the representative use of trusts, as the settlor and beneficiary remain concealed from third parties. However, the extended EU anti-money laundering rules and the UBO Register increasingly limit confidentiality and security.

Since the trustee appears as the owner of the assets held in trust, they execute tasks on behalf of the beneficiaries, not the settlor and the beneficiary. Unlike in a traditional trust, they are performing their duties in their own name but for the benefit of the beneficiaries. This solution may entail broader powers than a traditional trust, covering a wider range of property without the need to specify for whom and on whose behalf the trustee is acting.

A trust is among the most formalised methods of preserving commercial confidentiality, given the trustee's duty of confidentiality, presenting to the outside world as the owner of the assets in trust. This approach can be employed to keep critical business interests confidential during acquisitions, concerted

26 István Illés, "*Mire jó a bizalmi vagyonkezelés?*" ("What is the purpose of trust management?"), *supra*, p4.

market action,[27] joint voting in a company or ownership of specific high-profile assets. This use of fiduciary trusts is closely related to asset protection, a category that can be considered separately.

A subcategory of quasi-representation is a trust established to effectively exercise rights over common property, where property rights that are otherwise fragmented or under threat of fragmentation can be effectively exercised. This solution is suitable for the effective exercise of ownership rights by small shareholders in companies, each of whom has an insignificant ownership interest on its own. It ensures unity of action and the necessary level of ownership required to exercise minority rights under company law or the company's articles of association. Another way to address common ownership difficulties is through a trust, where owners living at a distance can entrust the trustee with the management of an asset, such as a property. In general, trusts are well suited to situations where the value of jointly owned property to one owner does not justify the investment required to effectively manage it, or where owners lack the expertise to manage the property properly.

Finally, fiduciary management through the use of trusts can ensure the involvement of employees in the exercise of employer ownership rights. This solution, unlike direct ownership, has the advantage that if an employee who is included in an employee share ownership scheme leaves the company, they can be removed from ownership by excluding them from the beneficiaries without additional cost or administrative burden.

(b) Joint venture and unit trust

In business, it is often the case that individuals or companies with limited familiarity will initiate a joint business venture, with the risk that over time, some owners may develop interests that diverge from those of the joint venture, or they may not wish to fulfil their commitments for other reasons. This challenge has led to the creation of the syndicate contract, still not mentioned in the Civil Code, where parties typically commit to managing the undertaking, exercising voting rights, determining dividend and investment levels, recalling directors and so on. However, due to the contractual nature of the syndicate contract, enforcement is challenging except through legal proceedings, with rare exceptions where parties include deposits and property options.

The use of a trust addresses these issues by clarifying rights and obligations through the involvement of the trustee, preventing any unilateral deviation from commitments. This type of common ownership and management of a partnership can be achieved through a unit trust, where beneficial owners hold units in a trust rather than a direct ownership interest, and the units may be transferable.

27 The use of trusts does not avoid compliance with competition rules, so in all cases market conduct must comply with the competition rules.

(c) ***Transactional trusts, acquisitions***

Business-type uses include employing a trust in connection with a takeover or contingent legal matters to provide mutual assurance to the parties. Transactions frequently involve obligations not immediately fulfilled, where a deposit would typically serve as security for subsequent performance, but physical or legal constraints prevent it, putting the leading party at a disadvantage. A typical example is a takeover, where a considerable time gap exists between the contract date and the transaction closing, typically several months. During this period, the seller must continue to manage the company in the usual way, but the parties' interests may be divergent. The seller might try to diminish the assets of the business in their favour, resulting in the buyer receiving less value than initially agreed. Determining a moment in time to define the economic object of the purchase is challenging as the shares or share capital are only indirectly linked to the assets of the business. A similar challenge arises in complex real estate sales (eg, an office building sold with a tenant) or the sale of geographically dispersed and constantly moving assets (eg, railway wagons, cargo vessels).

A solution acceptable to both parties may be the use of a trust. An independent trustee, not under the control of either contracting party, takes ownership of the transaction object and manages it with the diligence of a good steward for the interim period. When this period ends, the trustee releases the transaction object according to the trust deed. Due to the dispositive nature of the Civil Code, the trust deed is flexible and can be tailored to meet practically any transactional need. If the transaction succeeds, the purchaser receives the assets held in trust. If for some reason the contract fails, the seller, as the beneficiary settlor, reclaims the assets. This ensures a low-risk solution in the interest of all parties to the contract, potentially reducing transaction risks and costs.

(d) ***Warranty rights***

A trust can also be used to manage the performance of a contract's ancillary obligations. A common example is withholding the purchase price or fees to secure warranty[28] obligations.[29] This provides the buyer or the party using the service with insurance, but there is little guarantee that the other party will receive the amount due after the warranty period if it is not enforced. Involving a trustee to retain the funds to fulfil warranty obligations ensures that both parties will have sufficient assurance as to contractual performance.

---

28 Section 6:15-6:170 of the Civil Code.
29 Section 6:171-6:173 of the Civil Code.

3.3 Use for collateral purposes

Trusts, notwithstanding the prohibition against fiduciary security,[30] can still serve as a unique form of security in complex lending relationships, specifically for subordinated loans. The prohibition against fiduciary collateral prevents the transfer of ownership, other rights or claims, or the assignment of the right to purchase if the contract involves a consumer. However, from our perspective, trusts can be employed as security in financing transactions involving non-consumer parties.

In the context of collateral, the debtor or the debtor *in rem* pledges the property, right, or claim securing the loan to a trust. The trustee holds these assets for the benefit of the parties as beneficiaries, ensuring the future enforceability of the loan. If the debtor defaults on repayment, the trustee will act on behalf of the creditor as a beneficiary. This involves utilising the proceeds from the trust assets and, if necessary, the assets themselves. When collateral enforcement is triggered by the loan agreement's termination, the trustee sells the trust assets, settles the debt from the proceeds, and releases the remaining assets to the settlor. By adhering to the trust deed's provisions, this quasi-execution circumvents the need for court proceedings or notarisation, and subsequent enforcement proceedings. This approach can significantly reduce the time and cost of enforcement, providing greater security and liquidity for the creditor and more favourable credit terms for the debtor. An additional major advantage of this collateral arrangement is its applicability to assets that were not included, or were challenging to include, in the existing collateral arrangements.

The use of trusts as described in the context of loan collateral has similarities with leasing, where the lender retains ownership of the asset purchased with the loan. However, it differs significantly in two key respects. First, the owner is an independent third party, which assures the debtor that the creditor will not misuse ownership or leave the debtor vulnerable in the event of the creditor's bankruptcy, provided the debtor has fulfilled their contractual obligations without receiving ownership. Secondly, unlike with a lease, collateral can encompass any property, right, or claim eligible for security, resulting in a much broader range of applications.

3.4 Asset management

With the introduction of trusts in Hungary, it became possible for settlors to transfer ownership in their assets to the trustee, for a defined purpose and for the benefit of the beneficiary. It's important to note that the settlor transfers full

---

30 Section 6:99 of the Civil Code, Nullity of fiduciary collateral:
A clause in which the consumer undertakes to transfer ownership, other rights or claims or to establish a right of purchase in order to secure a claim is void.

ownership *in rem* to the trustee, but that the transfer of ownership is limited by the specific terms of the trust.

Due to the flexible rules of the trust arrangement, the diverse needs of settlors, and the variety of entrusted assets, from the asset management perspective trusts can be categorised as either active or passive.

(a) Active asset management

Active asset management primarily involves investing assets under management with the goal of accumulation, utilising the specialised expertise of the trustee, often a commercially operating trust company. This use of trusts closely resembles mutual funds, where an investor, relying on the knowledge of the fund manager, transfers funds in exchange for securities that can be redeemed or sold at a higher value if the investment is successful. There is also a significant similarity with portfolio management, where a professional manager is authorised to conduct transactions in the owner's securities account, subject to contractual limits.

Trusts, however, offer broader and more sophisticated options. They encompass a wider range assigned assets, and allow for definition and limitation of possible operational areas, beneficiary diversity and timing of benefits. Another advantage of active investment through a trust is the complete discretion that the trustee has in the market, as they do not need to disclose for whose benefit they are acting. The trustee can therefore invest without revealing their identity to the market, appearing as the true owner behind the investment.[31]

(b) Passive asset management

Asset management may also focus on safeguarding assigned property and preserving its value and condition, referred to as passive asset management. Passive trusts share similarities with active trusts but differ in several key respects. Unlike active trusts, which can involve any marketable, possessable thing, the object of a passive trust is relatively limited. Additionally, a trust relationship imposes obligations on the trustee, who must actively manage the entrusted property rather than merely holding it in custody.

Passive asset management offers a tailored solution for individuals transitioning from a business career to the civil service or politics. In such cases, a 'blind trust' is common in the United States,[32] involving an independent trustee conducting business in a commercial manner, not controlled by the settlor. The trustee must have full power to manage and dispose of the assets and may not

---

31 Trusts do not hide the settlor and the beneficiaries from the taxation perspective, because trusts are transparent to the authorities.

32 Charles E Rounds Jr and Charles E Rounds III, *Loring and Rounds: A Trustee's Handbook*, *supra*, p26.

consult the settlor on matters within their competence. A blind trust can also be applied in the private sector when there is a conflict of interest between an employee's or officer's new position and their previous investments.

Since passive trust management overlaps significantly with several uses categorised separately, the use of trusts for asset protection, acquisition and common property are discussed individually in the sections that follow.

3.5 Asset protection (limitation of liability)

Preserving and conserving existing assets is a common concern for all businesses and their owners. Trusts provide a means for individuals exposed to high business risks, such as lawyers or senior executives, to secure part of their assets for beneficiaries by placing them in trust.[33] Trusts can also serve as an alternative to prenuptial agreements, ensuring that assets placed in trust remain separate from the settlor's or beneficiaries' own assets and are not considered community property. Establishing a trust before marriage can prevent disputes and litigation in the event of a divorce.

Trusts are also effective in protecting against fraudsters, offering a security firewall for beneficiaries by keeping the assets and their benefits confidential, shielded from the public eye. Asset protection is a crucial use of trusts, especially given the absence of provisions that previously allowed the termination of a trust agreement at the request of the settlor's creditors. In summary, assets held in trust enjoy full protection against both the settlor's and beneficiaries' creditors, provided the asset transfer to the trust is not a fraudulent transaction.

3.6 Financial operations

Fiduciary relationships can be utilised in a diverse range of financial transactions, provided the involved parties recognise the legal safeguards and adhere to the relevant financial rules. Examples are examined below.

(a) Syndicated lending[34]

A trust can be employed as a credit protection instrument, safeguarding the interests of both the debtor and the creditor. In syndicated lending, where multiple creditors often lend to a single debtor, the trust can act as an intermediary. In this scenario, the debtor fulfils obligations for the trustee, who represents all creditors, thus consolidating the creditor interests and the collateral for the loan in one entity.[35] This set-up, supported by specific rules of

---

33 See István Sándor, *A vagyonvédelem jogi eszközeinek legújabb nemzetközi tendenciái* (*The latest international trends in legal instruments for asset protection*), HVG-ORAC, 2019, p126.

34 At present, this is a theoretical possibility – Hungarian financial institutions have not yet fully explored the potential of fiduciary asset management.

35 This use of trusts requires careful legal consideration due to the rules on the nullity of fiduciary transfers of ownership.

trust administration and the fiduciary's duty of loyalty, ensures a high degree of assurance for the contractual performance of the loan agreement. Moreover, reduced risk and streamlined lending administration can lead to cost savings. Despite the numerous advantages and potential cost reductions associated with this use of the trust, financial institutions have not yet begun using it in Hungary.

(b) *Corporate reorganisation*

A specialised form of trust can be employed in corporate reorganisation scenarios where the debtor is economically insolvent. In such cases, a new loan can be extended to revive the business and facilitate debt repayment.[36] While Hungarian bankruptcy law does not prioritise new liabilities, a well-drafted trust deed could offer a solution. The debtor, acting as a trustee under the trust deed, receives the new credit, making the credit and associated purchases the property of the trustee instead of the debtor. This positions the creditor, taking on the additional burden, more favourably as the beneficiary of the trust in the event of a liquidation procedure.

(c) *Securitisation*

Trusts can be instrumental in securitisation transactions, where managed assets are securitised economically, and the beneficiary position is securitised legally. This approach enables the marketability of assets that may be challenging to sell due to their nature (eg, large or high-value assets or membership rights subject to securities issuance prohibitions).[37] With this approach, the settlor may place the tangible or intangible asset or receivables into a trust for sale, issuing and placing a security related to the beneficiary position in collaboration with the trustee. The success of the trust arrangement is ensured by the trustee's expertise and the closely defined system of rules governing its operation. The legal restrictions specified in the Civil Code and the rules of the capital market must be adhered to for this use of trusts.[38]

3.7 Pension fund/pre-savings

A viable approach to retirement preparation involves using a trust where an individual trustee establishes a trust exclusively for the benefit of an individual beneficiary, entering into a permanent investment contract. This method combines unique tax advantages with a high level of security. Families, groups of friends, workforces, or employers aiming to benefit their employees can, with

---

36 In English legal literature, this type of trust is known as a 'Quistclose trust', named after the 1970 case of *Barclays Bank Ltd v Quistclose Investment Ltd.*

37 Section 3:11 of the Civil Code: Prohibition to issue securities on membership rights: "Except for a joint stock company, no securities may be issued on membership rights."

38 An analysis of the detailed rules and guidelines is beyond the scope of this book, but in all cases it is important to seek professional assistance regarding the desired construction.

the assistance of an expert trustee, allocate long-term investments through trusts. This form, with suitable modifications, could also serve as a means for employers to reward loyal employees, encouraging long-term savings as part of a loyalty programme alongside annual bonuses. Fiduciary trusts offer greater flexibility and reduced administrative burden compared to currently available savings options.

3.8 Charity

Before the enactment of the new Civil Code in Hungary, foundations were the sole means of institutionalising charitable donations. Despite their numerous advantages, foundations suffered from costly and cumbersome administration. Trusts present an alternative for charitable donations, especially when the assets allocated for charitable purposes are modest or intended to support a specific, time-limited cause.

The settlor can outline the charitable purpose in the trust deed, directing the trustee to support this purpose using the assets or their income. Alternatively, the trust agreement can specify both a private and charitable purpose. After the beneficiaries' death or termination of the relationship, the remaining assets or a portion predetermined during the beneficiaries' lifetime can be directed by the trustee for charitable purposes according to the settlor's wishes. Once the assets are used or the designated purpose ends, the trust can be terminated with relatively straightforward administration.

Utilising an occasional trustee allows swift and cost-effective support for charitable purposes, presenting a significant advantage over the rigid structure of a trust. However, it is important to note that the Civil Code requires specifying the identity of the beneficiary in the trust agreement, necessitating the naming of specific individuals as beneficiaries, rather than relying solely on defining the purpose.

3.9 Tax planning

Hungary offers substantial advantages for tax planning, competing with other EU member states that offer optimal tax conditions. A key benefit of the trust taxation regime in Hungary is that trust assets are treated as a separate taxable business entity under the Corporate Income Tax Act. Consequently, those elements of the Hungarian tax system that offer relief or exemption to companies are also applicable to trust assets. This makes trusts a valuable tool for designing effective tax-planning structures. Moreover, a qualified trust[39] is permitted to open a long-term savings account, resulting in tax exemption after a five-year holding period.

---

39 A trust is qualified if all the beneficiaries and settlors are private individuals and the trust has income only from investment activity.

Professional trustees

István Illés
APELSO Trust

1. Introduction

As explained in the opening chapter on the history of trusts in Hungary, there are two different types of trustee – *ad hoc* and professional. The distinction recognises two very different classes of trustee:

- 'amateur' or family trustees, typically family members or friends who, often gratuitously, take on the role of the trustee to preserve family wealth and look after the interests of minors and/or incapacitated family members; and
- professional organisations, who conduct trust business as a profession and may provide not just trusts-related services, but also comprehensive tax, legal, investment and other services (eg real estate management) as part of a comprehensive wealth management or family office portfolio.

It is self-evident that professional trustees should face stricter regulatory requirements than *ad hoc* trustees. But why should one regulate trustees at all, and where lies the golden line between the *ad hoc* and the professional trustee?

The reason for regulation stems from the fact that ownership is the most powerful property right one can have. Although, as we shall see below, the trustee is bound by a strict duty of loyalty towards the beneficiaries and the settlor, he or she is considered an owner and ownership offers numerous opportunities for abuse. As the saying goes, with great power comes great responsibility.

This is, however, only one side of the coin. The office of trustee is a complex one requiring a high degree of knowledge and skill in a number of fields. As Charles E Rounds points out (about US trusts):

> *[T]aking care of somebody else's wealth is a serious task and yet, it is only one of the trustee's non-delegable duties.*[1]

A typical trustee, even if they outsource many of their responsibilities (for example, investment management or accounting) still has a lot of work to do internally. Among other things, they have to:

1 Charles E Rounds Jr and Charles E Rounds III, *Loring and Rounds: A Trustee's Handbook*, Wolters Kluwer Law & Business, 2014, p78.

- identify the beneficiaries and the trust property;
- separate trust property from their own;
- decide on what is in the best interests of the beneficiaries; and
- deal with distribution.

These are all complex tasks requiring key competencies, and a set of minimum requirements should apply to ensure that every trustee is capable of discharging their obligations. Nevertheless, it would be unjust to apply the same set of standards to family members (if they manage their own wealth as *ad hoc* trustees) and professional trust companies (who make a business out of managing others' assets). This is why the Trustee Act regulates *ad hoc* and professional trustees differently.

If a trustee holds their position under more than one trust agreement, they automatically become a professional trustee.[2] The classification remains unchanged even if a family establishes two trusts and appoints the same family member as trustee in both. He or she may even not charge a fee. The only determining factor is the number of appointments that the same trustee has at the same time. One might think that such a rigid rule is unfair under certain circumstances – for example, where a family wants to set up two different trusts for two children under the management of the same family member trustee – but it is sometimes hard to separate amateur and professional trustees (notwithstanding that efforts were made to do so under previous Hungarian law).

Before the comprehensive overhaul of the Trustee Act in 2017, a trustee was considered professional if they were appointed regularly (more than twice a year) or their trustee fees (or other gains acquired as a result of the trusteeship) exceeded 1% of the value of the trust fund at the conclusion of the trust agreement.[3] This regime, however, proved impractical. Questions arose from the fact that trust agreements are usually intended to endure for a relatively long period: *ad hoc* trustees might fall under the professional trustee regime simply because, over the years, their fees ultimately exceeded the starting value of the trust fund; and the regime favoured established market players because a trustee who had been longer in the business might be permitted to have more clients than a trustee at the start of their career.

The current regime resolves many of the impracticalities surrounding the definition of a professional trustee and provides clear rules that everyone can follow. The regime also requires trustees to obtain a licence if they plan to take on the role a second time,[4] which means that they have to build a robust

2 Section 3(1) of Act XV of 2014 on trustees and the rules governing their activities ('the Trustee Act'). Available at: https://njt.hu/jogszabaly/en/2014-15-00-00.

3 Section 3(1) of the Trustee Act before 23 June 2017.

4 Without supplementary provisions, this requirement would be easy to circumvent. A trustee could establish a company and appoint it as trustee for another client. This is why there are other conflict of interest laws in place for *ad hoc* trustees. We discuss them in the next section.

organisation, with financial safeguards and proper infrastructure. This aligns with clients' interests – the more assets a trustee manages, and the more clients they serve, the better service level they must provide.

2. Licensing of professional trustees

2.1 Licensing requirements

Professional trustees do not form a homogenous group globally. In common law jurisdictions, they tend to be private individuals like lawyers, accountants and tax advisers. In other countries, corporate trustees like banks, wealth management companies and family offices are more common. The latter have their advantages – while individuals are generally known to, and trusted by, the settlor, corporate trustees come with elaborate structures, long-term stability (in contrast to individuals, who can get sick, become old and die) and replacement plans should individual trustees be out of action.

Hungarian law allows only corporate entities to obtain a licence and become professional trustees.[5] An organisation can be considered a professional trustee if it meets the following criteria:[6]

- it is a limited liability company ('Kft') or a private company limited by shares ('Zrt') with a registered office in Hungary, a branch office in Hungary of an enterprise with a registered office in the European Economic Area (EEA), or a law firm;
- it qualifies as a 'transparent' organisation as described in the Act on National Assets;
- it has a good business reputation;[7]
- except in the case of law firms, it performs trust management as its main activity and, as a secondary activity, functions that are directly related to the fulfilment of trustee duties;
- except in the case of law firms, its trade name in Hungarian clearly indicates its trust management status;
- it is listed in the tax debt-free taxpayer database, or does not have any outstanding debts with the state tax authority;
- it is not subject to the exclusionary condition where the supervisory body has withdrawn its operating licence *ex officio* in the ten years preceding the licence application;
- its owner or 'member' does not engage in professional or non-professional trust management activities;

---

5 Section 3(2) of the Trustee Act.

6 Section 3 of the Trustee Act.

7 Good business reputation is not positively defined; however, there are some criteria that would rule out certain individuals (eg, convicted criminals).

- it possesses the necessary National Bank of Hungary (NBH) licence for conducting trust activities; and
- it meets the personal, material, and organisational requirements set out in the Trustee Act.

According to the National Assets Act,[8] an organisation is considered to be 'transparent' if:

- its ownership structure and ultimate beneficial owner (UBO) can be identified;[9]
- it is tax resident in a member state of the European Union, the EEA, or the Organisation for Economic Co-operation and Development (OECD), or in a state with which Hungary has a double taxation treaty;
- it is not considered a controlled foreign corporation (CFC);[10] and
- the foregoing conditions are also met by a legal entity, or an economic entity without legal personality, that directly or indirectly holds more than 25% ownership, influence, or voting rights in the organisation.

If all the above conditions are met, the company is considered a trust management company or a professional corporate trustee. Failure to meet the licensing requirements not only has adverse effects on the trustee, but is detrimental to the settlor and the beneficiaries, because if a trust agreement breaches a licensing requirement (usually where an *ad hoc* trustee accepts a second appointment), the whole trust will be deemed null and void.[11]

2.2 Requirements for staff, owners and UBOs

Corporate form and structure account for only a few of the many requirements professional trustees must consider. Another set of rules pertains to the professional trustee's personnel:

- *Number and composition of employees:* The professional trustee must employ at least the following:[12]
  - one person having a master's degree in economics;
  - one lawyer who has passed the bar examination; and
  - an independent auditor (employed by way of standard engagement, not an employment agreement);
- *Ethical requirements:* All employees, as well as members and UBOs of the professional trustee, must comply with the following ethics and reliability criteria:[13]

---

8 Section 3(1)1(b) of the National Assets Act.
9 Hungarian AML law defines 'UBO' in line with EU AML directives.
10 Section 4(11) of the Corporate Tax Act defines a controlled foreign corporation.
11 Section 48/A(2) of the Trustee Act.
12 Section 4(5) of the Trustee Act.
13 Section 4(1) of the Trustee Act.

- They must have a clean criminal record.
- They must not be subject to any ban prohibiting them from conducting trustee activities or other activities under the supervision of the NBH.
- They must not have worked as a senior manager or executive, nor been a sole or majority owner, of a professional trustee whose licence was revoked within ten years prior to the licence application (excluding revocations at the applicant's own request).
- They must not have worked in a financial institution as a senior manager or executive, nor been a sole or majority owner of a professional trustee whose licence to operate was revoked by the NBH or other financial supervisory authority for violating legal regulations within ten years prior to the date of the application.
- They must not have been subject to a personal supervisory fine by the NBH or its predecessor within ten years prior to the date of the application.
- There must be no doubt as to their good business reputation. It is up to the applicant to demonstrate good business reputation. The NBH may require additional documents in this respect. This requirement does not apply to non-management employees or contractors.[14]

- *Conflict of interest requirements for board members and senior management:* These requirements are extensive, aimed at preventing collusion between professional trustees and self-dealing between the trustee and the trust fund, both of which are potentially detrimental to settlors' and beneficiaries' interests. Under these rules neither the relevant person nor their spouse can:[15]
  - own any stake (directly or indirectly) in another professional trustee;
  - be part of the senior management of another trust company or any other company having direct or indirect ownership in another professional trustee; or
  - be an employee of any of the foregoing.

  The professional trustee's senior management and its executives are also barred from holding key positions in any company belonging to a trust that the professional trustee manages. This means that they may not:
  - be a member (directly or indirectly) of a company belonging to a trust fund that the professional trustee manages, or part of the senior management of such a company;
  - be part of the senior management of a company belonging to a trust fund; or

14 Section 4(3) and Section 4(3a) of the Trustee Act.
15 Section 5(1) of the Trustee Act.

- be an employee of any of the foregoing entities above.[16]

Conflict of interest does not arise if the executive is the settlor or beneficiary of the trust and there is no other settlor or beneficiary,[17] or if there is informed and written consent from all settlors and beneficiaries of all trusts (in the case of holding interests or positions in another professional trustee) or the affected trust (in the case of holding interests or positions in a company belonging to the trust fund).[18]

2.3 Infrastructure requirements

A professional trustee is obliged to maintain a website and to publish thereon:[19]

- its founding document;
- its company registration number (or, in the case of a law firm, its bar association registration number);
- its tax number;
- its organisational and operational rules;
- its financial statements;
- a list of its direct and indirect owners, and in the case of a legal person their company registration number and registered office; and
- its registration number in the HNB Register of Professional Trustees.

A professional trustee is obliged to maintain such IT system, internal regulations and records as will ensure fulfilment and verification of its obligations under the trust agreements, and prevent their violation.[20] The professional trustee's systems must be adequate for the timely preparation of the trust fund's financial statements, as well as the management and accounting of all assets belonging to the fund. This is usually achieved electronically (for example, to manage accounting for different trust funds), but sometimes requires physical intervention (for example, to protect valuable artwork).

2.4 Financial requirements

Like other regulated entities in the financial sector, trustees must be adequately capitalised at all times to ensure the stability of their operations. In the case of a professional trustee, the obligation is doubly important.

First, the professional trustee must provide security equal to at least 20% of the aggregate assets under management, but always at least HUF 70 million (around €175,000) and not exceeding HUF 1.5 billion (around

---

16 Section 5(2) of the Trustee Act.
17 Section 5(3) of the Trustee Act.
18 Section 5(4) of the Trustee Act.
19 Section 6 of the Trustee Act.
20 Section 8(1) of the Trustee Act.

€3,750,000).[21] The actual form of the security may vary from one service provider to another,[22] but the most common is liability insurance. The legislation sets out strict rules for the contents of the insurance policy.

In addition to the provision of security, the professional trustee's capital[23] must at all times exceed HUF 70 million (around €175,000).

2.5 Licensing procedure and the Register of Professional Trustees

Provided a professional trustee complies with all the requirements, it may apply for a licence from the NBH. The licensing procedure is fully electronic and takes up to nine months.[24] It begins with the filing of the trustee's application and follows a procedure very similar to that of other financial institutions. The process is governed by the standard rules of administrative procedure and the NBH may – conceivably multiple times – require the trustee to file additional documents. Stamp duty for the filing is HUF 1,000,000 (around €2,650).

As soon as the NBH issues a licence the professional trustee may commence its activities. As mentioned above, if a trustee is appointed prior to this date, in violation of the licensing requirement, the trust agreement will be considered null and void. Although there are no court decisions on the matter, we think that subsequent licensing does not retrospectively remedy invalidity and a fresh application will have to be made.

On issuing the licence, the NBH enters the trustee into the Register of Professional Trustees.[25] The register is a public[26] database containing the basic data relating to the trustee (for example, name, address and list of permitted activities).[27] If the data changes, the trustee must report the change within eight days to the NBH unless it concerns the professional trustee's senior management or UBO,[28] in which case the trustee must file the updated data as part of the annual renewal process.

Although the licence is issued for an indefinite period, all professional trustees must renew their licences annually on 30 July.[29] As part of the procedure, trustees must demonstrate that they still comply with the licensing

---

21 Section 2(1) of Regulation No 87/2014 on the rules relating to professional trustee's financial guarantees ('the Trustee Guarantee Regulation').

22 According to Section 1(1) of the Trustee Guarantee Regulation, the following can also be accepted as security:
- guarantee provided by a financial institution;
- suretyship undertaken by a financial institution; or
- deposit account held at a credit institution.

23 The trustee's capital for the purposes of the capital requirement is the combined amount of the trustee's registered capital, capital reserves and profit reserves, per Section 7(2) of the Trustee Act.

24 Section 11/A of the Trustee Act.

25 Section 13(2) of the Trustee Act.

26 Under Hungarian law 'authenticity' means that any data entered into an authentic database or registry must be considered true and valid until proven otherwise in a formal court procedure.

27 The database is available at: https://intezmenykereso.mnb.hu/en/Home/Index. For professional trustees the category must be set to 'Capital markets/trust'.

28 Section 14(1) of the Trustee Act.

29 Section 32(1) of the Trustee Act.

requirements.[30] This usually entails the trustee filing their new insurance policy (if the policy previously filed has expired) and declaring that no material changes have occurred over the year.

2.6 Revocation of the licence

The NBH may revoke a professional trustee's licence if:[31]

- the trustee no longer complies with the licensing requirements (usually as part of the annual renewal procedure);
- the licence was wrongfully obtained; or
- the professional trustee seeks revocation.

Usually, revocation takes place only if the professional trustee has settled third-party debts (including those of clients and creditors of trust funds) and/or another professional trustee takes over the obligations. This means in practice that if a professional trustee wants to cease its operations in respect of a trust, it must first transfer the trust to another professional trustee.[32] This can be done at the direction of the settlor, who at any time may replace the trustee.[33]

3. Appointment, replacement and termination

There is essentially no difference between the appointment of a professional and an *ad hoc* trustee. Hungarian trust law considers the trustee's position to be an office rather than a mere contractual relationship. This comes from the provision that the trust agreement remains in effect if the trustee dies or resigns.[34] In such cases the settlor may appoint a new trustee within a grace period of three months.[35] This power is not limited to where the trustee is unable to perform their duties, one of the settlor's inherent powers being that he or she may, at any time, revoke the trustee's mandate and appoint a new trustee. No reasoning is required and the decision may not be challenged in court. The settlor can even delegate this power to the protector and/or designate a successor trustee if certain conditions are met.

Appointment is a two-step process: first the trustee is designated and then they accept the appointment. In most cases, designation and acceptance come hand in hand because the settlor and the designated trustee conclude a trust agreement. In the case of testamentary trusts, however, the settlor usually designates the trustee in a will,[36] so acceptance comes at a later stage, during

---

30 Section 34 of the Trustee Act.
31 Section 12(1) of the Trustee Act.
32 Section 12(2) of the Trustee Act.
33 Section 6:324(1) of the Civil Code. An English language version of the 2013 Civil Code is available at: https://tdziegler.wordpress.com/wp-content/uploads/2014/06/civil_code.pdf.
34 Section 6:326(5) of the Civil Code.
35 After the three months the trust agreement terminates by law under Section 6:326(1)(c) of the Civil Code.
36 Testamentary trusts are defined in Section 6:329(2) of the Civil Code.

probate. In many cases, the settlor appoints a professional trustee only as a successor, should the settlor die or become incapacitated. In these cases, years can pass before the trustee even learns about the existence of their appointment. Another slightly different situation arises when the settlor replaces the trustee. In such cases the new trustee not only accepts the role by becoming a party to the trust agreement, but also has to conduct a formal handover-takeover procedure with the previous trustee.

The settlor may also decide to appoint several trustees simultaneously. If more than one accepts the appointment, they all become trustees and own the trust fund as joint tenants.[37] The trust agreement may regulate the division of their rights and obligations; however, unless provided otherwise, they must act together in every aspect of their mandate[38] and their liability is joint and several against the settlor, the beneficiary and third parties.[39] It should be noted that it is quite uncommon in Hungary to nominate more than one trustee at the same time.

The above are, however, not the only ways to appoint a trustee. As is usual in common law jurisdictions, courts have certain powers when it comes to trusts. In Hungary, beneficiaries may unanimously request the court to replace the trustee if the trustee commits a material breach of contract, for example, by violating the duty of loyalty, or if the NBH removes an *ad hoc* trustee from the register.[40] The beneficiaries may also request the court to appoint a new trustee where there is no trustee in place (for example, where the trustee dies or resigns).[41] In this case, unanimity is not required and even a single beneficiary is enough to invoke the court's assistance. The only restriction is that the court may not appoint a trustee to whom the beneficiaries unanimously object.[42]

Once the trustee is designated, he or she must accept the appointment in order for it to take effect. Just as Hungarian trusts may only be created in writing,[43] the trustee must accept the appointment in writing. The acceptance must cover the appointment in its entirety; thus, an acceptance in which the trustee refuses to accept certain conditions of the appointment (eg, with regard to fees) is considered invalid. In such cases it is possible for a successor trustee to step in (usually in the case of testamentary trusts, provided, of course, that the settlor designated a successor trustee), otherwise the trust is not created. For existing trusts, only the appointment fails and, depending on the

37 Section 6:324 of the Civil Code.
38 Section 6:324(1) of the Civil Code.
39 Sections 6:324(2) and (3) of the Civil Code.
40 Sections 6:325(2) and (3) of the Civil Code.
41 Section 6:325(2) of the Civil Code. Only beneficiaries with vested interests are permitted to ask for court assistance. Contingent beneficiaries and members of a class of beneficiaries are barred from doing so until the trustee declares them actual beneficiaries.
42 Section 6:325(3) of the Civil Code.
43 Section 6:310(2) of the Civil Code.

circumstances, the previous trustee remains in office or the trust is left without a trustee. As we have seen previously, the settlor and/or the beneficiaries may appoint or request the appointment of a new trustee within a grace period of three months.

Once the acceptance is received, the trustee may take possession of the trust fund and begin their duties. In the case of testamentary trusts the appointment is retrospective, becoming effective as from the date of death of the settlor.[44]

As a trust is usually created for an extended period it is important to provide convenient and flexible ways to terminate a trustee's mandate. Hungarian law recognises this by allowing both the settlor and the trustee to unilaterally terminate the trustee's appointment at any time by serving written notice (the length of the notice period is up to the parties). Termination does not require a stated reason and may not be challenged in court. If all trustees resign or are removed, the settlor and/or beneficiaries have three months to appoint a new trustee.

One interesting feature of the settlor's unconditional termination right is the seeming impossibility of creating irrevocable trusts in Hungary. If the settlor is, by law, allowed to change the beneficiaries[45] and terminate the trustee's mandate at any time, and this leads to the termination of the trust itself, it follows that all Hungarian trusts are revocable. Prior to 2017, academic opinion confirmed this by questioning whether the settlor's unilateral termination right could be excluded from the trust agreement.[46] The 2017 reforms, however, settled the debate and now Section 6:326(1)(e) of the Civil Code stipulates that the settlor's unconditional termination right applies only if the trust is established for an indefinite term (up to a maximum of 50 years) and the trust agreement does not exclude the settlor's termination right. This means that the settlor can indeed create an irrevocable trust. However, it should be noted that there is no real difference between revocable and irrevocable trusts under Hungarian law. Both instruments have the same taxation regime and offer the same level of asset protection, which is almost unique in the context of jurisdictions globally.

Besides unilateral termination, standard contractual rules offer other means of terminating the trustee's mandate. The settlor and the trustee may, at any time, agree on termination, and the trustee's death or dissolution will also result in the termination of their appointment.[47]

Where the trustee's appointment ends, the trustee must provide a full account of the trust fund to the settlor and beneficiaries, and transfer the entire

44 Section 6:329(2) of the Civil Code.
45 Section 6:311(1) of the Civil Code.
46 See, for example, Péter Miczán, "*A bizalmi vagyonkezelés visszavonhatóságáról I*" ("On the Revocability of Trust Management I"), *Gazdaság és Jog* (*Economy and Law*), No 11, 2017, pp25–29.
47 Section 6:326 of the Civil Code.

trust fund, including all assets, rights and obligations, to the successor trustee (or the settlor/beneficiaries if the trust is terminated).[48] This is usually done by submitting closing financial statements and handing over the paperwork (eg, accounts and contracts) to the new trustee. Even during this procedure, the trustee's duty of loyalty remains intact, meaning that it is the trustee's duty to give notice in a way that is not incompatible with the interests of the beneficiaries, and must protect the beneficiaries' interests during handover.[49] This is obviously not applicable if the trustee's appointment terminates due to death or dissolution – in such cases the trust fund is passed on to the successor trustee as part of the deceased/terminated trustee's probate or dissolution procedure.[50] As professional trustees are necessarily corporate bodies, special rules determine who can be a liquidator of a professional trustee.[51]

One last thing should be noted concerning termination of the trustee's mandate. Naturally, if there is more than one trustee, and one ceases to be a trustee, the others' share in the trust fund increases proportionately.[52] The more interesting fact is that, unless the trust agreement provides otherwise, the trust fund must be handed over to the settlor (rather than the beneficiary) if the trust terminates due to the lack of a trustee.[53] This is another indication that Hungarian legislation has treated the revocable trust as the model for the trust regime.

4. Outsourcing

Professional trustees often rely on the services of other service providers.[54] This is unsurprising, since they usually manage large and complex wealth funds, which often include assets requiring specialist knowledge or care (for example, real estate, art or niche investments like hedge funds). It is almost impossible for a trustee to provide all the necessary expertise in-house, so there will be a need for outsourcing. The question is, which activities can a professional trustee outsource?

There is no general rule or prohibition concerning outsourceable activities, so theoretically a trustee can outsource every aspect of their operation. The one thing that a trustee must keep in-house, however, is title to the trust fund itself.

48 Sections 6:327–328 of the Civil Code.

49 Section 6:317 of the Civil Code.

50 In order to preserve and protect the trust fund, the main rule is that the trust fund does not form part of the trustee's estate or liquidation assets (Section 6:313 of the Civil Code).

51 Liquidators of professional trustees are the same corporations licensed to liquidate financial institutions, under Section 46(2) of the Trustee Act.

52 Section 6:328(4) of the Civil Code.

53 Section 6:328(1)–(2) of the Civil Code.

54 Although *ad hoc* trustees are not barred from outsourcing – general civil law principles allow them to do so – the Trustee Act regulates only professional trustees' outsourcing activities. This is probably because *ad hoc* trustees usually manage their own family wealth and therefore there is no need to impose special restrictions on their activities. The position is entirely different for professional trustees, who are required to clearly state to their clients which activities are carried out in-house, and which by third parties.

If the trustee is not the owner of the trust fund, the trust loses its very essence, therefore title to the trust fund must always reside with the trustee. General civil law rules support this interpretation, as they prohibit outsourcing if someone is obliged to provide a service personally.[55] It stands to reason that because the trustee is appointed to manage the trust fund, they cannot outsource the entirety of the trusteeship to third parties. It also follows that the trustee cannot outsource their obligation to separate the trust fund from other trust funds and their own property. Any other activities, however, may be outsourced to service providers. Even such key aspects as accounting or investment decisions can be outsourced to appropriate third parties.

Also relevant is the difference between outsourcing and obtaining professional advice, for example, on legal, tax or investment matters. It is common for a professional trustee to rely on the advice of a third-party expert. But how is this different from outsourcing? The similarities between the two are certainly clear enough. For example, if an adviser gives inaccurate advice or a service provider of an outsourced activity causes loss to the trust fund, the trustee remains equally liable towards the settlor and/or the beneficiaries. However, an adviser does not participate in actual asset management (that is, it does not make decisions on behalf of the trust fund), while the provider of an outsourced activity has some degree of autonomy and is allowed to make decisions for and on behalf of the trust fund.

The Trustee Act provides that a professional trustee may outsource certain activities at their own discretion provided their duties may be discharged more effectively by outsourcing.[56] The service provider must ensure:

- there is no conflict of interest with the trustee or its clients;
- it has the appropriate licence if licensing is required; and
- it will observe a strict duty of confidentiality.[57]

It is also imperative that the outsourcing can neither disrupt supervision over the trustee's activities nor have an impact on the liability of the trustee. The outsourcing agreement must also not contain provisions that have an adverse effect on the trustee's right to instruct the service provider or supervise its activities, or limit the trustee's right to terminate the outsourcing agreement with immediate effect in the event of the service provider's breach of contract.[58]

As a customer protection rule, the Trustee Act stipulates that certain advisory and other services not directly related to trust management, as well as

55 Section 6:57(1) of the Civil Code.
56 Section 44(1) of the Trustee Act.
57 Section 44(3) of the Trustee Act.
58 The activities include legal and tax advice, IT-related and educational services, and accounting and payroll (Section 44(5) of the Trustee Act).

employment relationships with the trustee, may not be considered outsourcing. This only applies if the professional trustee can demonstrate unequivocally that the costs incurred as a result of these activities form no part of the fees or costs paid by the client to the trustee or third parties.[59]

5. Trustee's powers, rights, duties and obligations

The trustee's relationship with the trust fund, the settlor and the beneficiary is usually determined by their powers, rights, duties and other obligations. While clearly a number of powers derive from the mere fact of having title over the trust assets, certain duties and obligations are designed to prevent the trustee from abusing those powers and putting their own interests before those of the beneficiaries. Conversely, certain rights give protection to the trustee, enabling them to take possession of the trust fund and secure their remuneration.

5.1 Trustee's powers and rights

All of the trustee's powers and rights stem from the fact that in a civil law sense the trustee is considered the owner of the trust assets. Therefore, the trustee has the power to do everything a civil law owner is permitted to do with his or her own property. Ownership is unrestricted, meaning that the trustee can take possession of the trust assets, use and invest them, and in certain cases dispose of them.[60] These three powers are considered the three facets of civil law ownership. Theoretically the trustee may also be able to gratuitously transfer certain assets to third parties; however, doing so typically results in a breach of trust as it is unlikely that a gratuitous transfer will be in the best interests of the beneficiaries.[61] This, however, does not mean that such a transfer is invalid under proprietary law rules.

The duty of loyalty and other trustee duties (which we analyse in the next section) are fundamentally contractual, and therefore *in personam*, in nature. This means that a breach of trust does not render the act of a trustee invalid *per se*. Nevertheless, unlimited powers would leave the settlor and the beneficiary unfairly unprotected, so supplementary provisions reinforce the rights of the settlor and beneficiary against the trustee and even extend them to third parties. The most important restriction is the *bona fide* purchaser rule[62] that allows the settlor and the beneficiaries to recover trust assets which the trustee has alienated to a third party, acting wrongfully or without consideration. The third party acts wrongfully if he or she knows or should have known that the trustee is committing a breach of trust with the alienation of the trust property. An important qualification is that the settlor and the beneficiary may not

59 Section 44(5) of the Trustee Act.
60 Sections 5:21 and 5:30(1) of the Civil Code.
61 One notable exception is charitable activity, where the trust agreement or the beneficiaries permit it.
62 Section 6:318(3) of the Civil Code.

invalidate the transfer solely because improper consideration was given. If the purchaser did not act in bad faith and gave at least some consideration, then the settlor and beneficiary may sue the trustee for breach of trust, but will be unable to recover the trust asset.

In summary, the trustee's powers cover the entirety of civil law ownership, but their duties and the specific provisions of the trust agreement require them to provide adequate protection to settlors and beneficiaries.

Two of the trustee's powers are regulated in more detail and bear closer investigation.

(a) Power (and duty) to obtain professional advice

The Trustee Act expressly empowers the professional trustee to obtain advice during the course of managing the trust fund.[63] This does not mean that *ad hoc* trustees cannot do so, but the Trustee Act stipulates that it is not only a power but a duty to obtain the necessary expertise if the trustee does not possess it themselves. As discussed above, the trustee remains liable if they act on the advice obtained, but may charge their costs to the trust fund.[64] Lastly, a reasonableness clause leaves it to the trustee to decide whether the costs of the advice are proportionate to the value of the trust fund.[65]

(b) Powers concerning beneficiaries (in discretionary trusts)

If a settlor so decides, he or she can grant the trustee authority over matters concerning the beneficiaries and the distribution of assets to them. Such 'discretionary' trusts are analysed in depth elsewhere in this book. Here it need only be noted that the settlor may provide the following powers to the trustee under the Civil Code:[66]

- to decide on a beneficiary's share from the trust fund (for example, the trustee might decide to distribute the trust capital to the two beneficiaries, allocating 50% to each);
- to appoint or modify beneficiaries (for example, the trustee might decide to give the whole trust fund to only one of two beneficiaries, thus excluding the other); or
- to distribute to the beneficiaries in their respective shares.

The trustee's powers may also include revising and changing either the beneficiaries or their shares.

---

63 Section 45(1)(d) of the Trustee Act.
64 Section 6:322 of the Civil Code.
65 Section 45(2) of the Trustee Act.
66 Section 6:311(3) of the Civil Code.

(c) *Rights of the trustee*

As mentioned earlier, trustees' rights should be distinguished from their powers. Although there are certain rights that are also considered powers (for example, the right/power to take possession of the trust fund), the purpose of the trustee's rights is to protect the trustee and allow them freedom to exercise their powers and discharge their obligations.

The most important right of the trustee is to take possession of the trust fund.[67] One might wonder why this right is also considered a power. It is because the trustee may use this right against the settlor as well as the beneficiaries – although the trustee owes a duty of loyalty towards the beneficiaries and the settlor, who may hold them accountable, the trustee must also observe the provisions of the trust agreement itself. This is why this right is not subordinated to the beneficiaries' interests and the trustee may exercise it to fulfil the trust agreement even against the will (though not necessarily the interests) of the beneficiaries.

Besides the right to take possession of the trust fund, the trustee has the right to seek satisfaction of their fee and cost claims directly from the trust fund.[68] These two rights might also be contrary to the interests of the beneficiaries, but protect those of the trustee. Of course, the trustee may claim fees only if the trust agreement is not gratuitous in nature.

5.2 Trustee's duties

As was seen in the previous section, the trustee's powers over the trust fund put them in a strong legal position, almost equivalent to outright ownership. The qualification suggested by 'almost' alludes to the duties of the trustee. These duties limit the trustee's powers and define the boundaries of what a trustee can do with the trust property. If they are in breach of their duties they become liable to the settlor, the beneficiary and even third parties. That is why duties are the essence of the trust relationship.

(a) *Duty of specific performance*

Although this duty is not specifically stipulated in any of the trust law provisions, it takes precedence even over the trustee's duty of loyalty (see section 5.2(b) below). This stems from fundamental contract law rules, which require contracting parties to follow the letter of the agreement.

The duty of specific performance means that if the settlor so provides in the trust agreement, the trustee may decide (or be obliged) to depart from or simply go against the interests of the beneficiaries in certain situations. The duty of specific performance, in this sense, overrides even the duty of loyalty.[69]

---

67 Section 6:310(1) of the Civil Code.
68 Section 6:322 of the Civil Code.
69 This comes from the principle of freedom of contract, covered by Section 6:1(3) of the Civil Code.

It is worth noting that not only the settlor, but sometimes even the legislation, requires the trustee to depart from the interests of the beneficiaries. Anti-money laundering (AML) rules, for example, require the trustee under certain circumstances to freeze assets.[70] This obligation may override the beneficiaries' interests should they want an immediate distribution from the trust fund.

(b) *Duty of loyalty*

If one were to single out the trustee's most important and unique duty, it would undoubtedly be the duty of loyalty. This duty underpins every other duty owed to the settlor and the beneficiary by the trustee. Other duties, such as to provide accounts and separate the trust fund, make sense only because the duty of loyalty exists. Without it the trustee would be considered the unrestricted owner of the trust fund, indistinguishable from the civil law owner of a property. The duty of loyalty is the foundation of the trust institution and establishes the trustee's unique fiduciary position.

Under Hungarian law the duty of loyalty is fundamentally the same as in common law trusts. It requires the trustee to always act fairly and in good faith to foster the interests of the beneficiaries. It encompasses both a positive (active) obligation involving monitoring and consideration of the beneficiaries' interests during investment, asset management and wealth distribution activities, and a negative (passive) duty to avoid conflicts of interest or obtain the informed consent of the settlor and the beneficiaries if such conflicts nevertheless arise.

The duty itself is formulated in a way that the trustee must always exercise their powers in compliance with the confidential nature of the trust relationship, primarily by taking into account the interests of the beneficiaries.[71] But what does this mean in practice?

As mentioned above, the negative aspect of the duty of loyalty requires the trustee to avoid conflict of interest situations arising during their service. This usually goes beyond the written requirements laid down in the various statutes. The main principle is that the trustee should avoid self-dealing or profiting from the trustee mandate, other than by charging a fee for their services. For example, if commercial real estate belongs to the trust fund and the trustee wants to rent it out, self-dealing may occur if the trustee has an interest in the lessee. The problem is that the trustee potentially benefits from a lower rent, while the trust fund suffers a loss of profit that is against the interests of the beneficiaries. In the case of common law trusts the no-further-inquiry rule[72] provides a clear solution: if there is even a slight chance of a conflict of interest,

---

70 Section 32(1) of the Anti-Money Laundering and Counter-Terrorism Financing Act.
71 Section 6:317(1) of the Civil Code.
72 Charles E Rounds Jr and Charles E Rounds III, *Loring and Rounds: A Trustee's Handbook*, *supra* note 1, p446.

then the trustee is already in breach of trust. The Hungarian regime, however, is more relaxed in the sense that the trustee may prove that they did not benefit from the deal (ie, rent out the property on below standard market terms) and therefore that the beneficiaries' interests suffered no harm. If they fail to do so, then just as is the case with their common law counterparts, the trustee must surrender all gains to the trust fund.[73] This is why the rule cited above requires the trustee to proceed only by primarily taking into account the beneficiaries' interests. (If the legislation had intended to introduce a strict rule like the no-further-inquiry rule, it would have changed the word 'primarily' to 'exclusively'). Naturally, just as in common law jurisdictions, the settlor and/or the beneficiaries may give their informed consent to the trustee's planned act and relieve them of the negative consequences of self-dealing.[74]

The other (positive) aspect of the duty of loyalty requires the trustee to actively foster the interests of the beneficiaries. In practice, this usually means that the trustee must seek investment vehicles corresponding to the risk-bearing appetite and investment timeframe of the beneficiaries, and acquire or sell trust assets in line with their needs (for example, if a beneficiary wants to settle down somewhere, the trust may buy the property he or she wants to live in). This obligation still exists even during termination of the trustee's mandate. Under standard Hungarian civil law principles, fair and honest behaviour is expected from the trustee, who must always act in good faith.[75]

But what if there are beneficiaries whose interests collide? This can readily occur if there is a life beneficiary and a remainderman. The former wants short-term profits to be distributed immediately, while the latter is more interested in long-term wealth accumulation with no immediate distributions at all. In these cases, unless the trust agreement provides otherwise, the trustee must act impartially and by balancing out the different interests. This is sometimes one of the hardest things to do in a trust relationship.

(c) Duty of care

While the duty of loyalty tells the trustee what to do, the duty of care describes how to do it. As the trustee is a fiduciary, they must act with special care during all aspects of their mandate. This derives directly from their unique position of trust.

Hungarian law recognises this requirement and stipulates that the trustee should proceed, at all times, in compliance with the "elevated requirements stemming from the confidential nature of the legal relationship".[76] These

73 Section 6:321(3) of the Civil Code.
74 This can be done under standard contract law principles and/or under the specific provisions of the Trustee Act (Section 5(4)).
75 Section 1:3 of the Civil Code.
76 Section 6:317(1) of the Civil Code.

standards remain the same, unlike in any other contractual relationship, if the trustee acts free of charge.

There is little help in the statute itself as to the meaning of 'elevated requirements'. The matter has yet to be developed and will depend on judicial practice, which could mean either a strict and rigid interpretation permitting only a cautious and prudent approach, or more relaxed standards on the basis of reasonableness. It seems that the legislator tended towards the second interpretation, as the Civil Code expressly sets a standard of 'commercial reasonableness' concerning protection of the trust fund.[77]

The Trustee Act provides additional guidelines for the duty of care of professional trustees. Although the parties can expressly rule out their applicability in the trust agreement, these provisions provide a clear view as to the essential elements of the professional trustee's duty of care:[78]

- *Prudent investing:* The first requirement is the duty of prudent investing. When utilising the trust fund, the trustee should refrain from acts as a result of which the chance of incurring loss to the trust fund exceeds the chance of increasing its value. This general rule is intended to set a risk-averse standard for investing, rather than explicitly allow or prohibit particular types of investment. The trustee must therefore conduct a full evaluation of the possibilities before deciding for or against a specific investment.
- *Correct procedure:* The second requirement is procedural in nature. Once an investment is made, the trustee must periodically review and assess whether it is still prudent to keep the investment or whether it would be wiser to sell it or replace it with another. The emphasis is on the timeframe: the trustee is not allowed to do nothing – the law requires the trustee to conduct the assessment from time to time as long as the given investment forms part of the trust fund portfolio.
- *Diversity of investments:* The trustee is required to diversify the investments of the trust fund. As most trusts contain significant family wealth, they are usually complex in nature, perhaps including financial assets, real estate and family businesses. This, however, is not necessarily the same as diversification. If, for example, a trust fund owns real estate directly and at the same time shares in a real estate fund, these are different asset classes that increase complexity but do not make the fund diverse. It is up to the trustee (and the trust fund as the case may be) to do what is necessary, but the principle is reasonable risk reduction through diversification.
- *Lack of expertise:* Finally, professional trustees are required to resort to

77 Section 6:317(2) of the Civil Code.
78 Section 45 of the Trustee Act.

professional advice if they lack the necessary expertise in a field required to manage the trust fund. The trust fund may cover the costs, as described above.

(d) ***Duty to protect trust assets***

As mentioned above, the Civil Code sets commercial reasonableness as the standard for protecting trust assets.[79] This means that the trustee must take all reasonable measures to protect the trust fund against all foreseeable risks in a commercially reasonable matter.

The Civil Code does not elaborate as to what exactly the trustee should do in this context. Protection measures may include physical protection (for example, setting up an alarm system), legal protection like taking out insurance, or choosing a reputable service provider as account holder of the trust fund securities. Setting commercial reasonableness as a standard does seem inappropriate, as most trust funds hold family assets and do not operate as commercial entities, and many trustees lack experience in commercial operations.

Another limit on the duty to protect assets is foreseeability. If a risk is not foreseeable, the trustee is not required to protect against it. But the timing is important – even if a risk is not foreseeable at the time of the conclusion of the trust agreement, it appears that the trustee is required to review the trust fund from time to time, to assess potential risks and adjust protection accordingly.

(e) ***Duty of confidentiality***[80]

Another important consequence of the trustee's fiduciary position is their duty of confidentiality towards the settlor and the beneficiaries. This duty is similar to that of a lawyer or a doctor, but sometimes even stricter. The reason is that the trustee may have extensive knowledge of the entirety of a family's affairs, which makes them potentially the most important third party in the life of many families. Any information shared with the trustee requires adequate protection. Therefore the trustee, unless the settlor or the beneficiaries relieve them of the obligation, must treat all information learned during or in connection with their mandate as confidential, even after the termination of their appointment.

Nevertheless, an unlimited duty of confidentiality could lead to the abuse of the trust institution and cause public harm (for example, through the disguising of certain criminal offences like money laundering or tax evasion). For that reason, the following organisations may relieve the trustee of the duty of confidentiality during the course of their investigations:[81]

- the NBH;

79 Section 6:317(2) of the Civil Code.
80 Section 6:319 of the Civil Code.
81 Section 42 of the Trustee Act.

- the tax authority;
- the Hungarian Competition Authority;
- the governmental control body checking the regularity and appropriateness of the use of central budgetary funds;
- the national security service;
- a body performing internal crime prevention and detection tasks, as well as counter-terrorism tasks, as defined in the Police Act; and
- an authority operating as a financial intelligence unit.

Some other public organisations may also require certain information from the trustee (for example the courts, the office of the public prosecutor, court bailiffs or the European Anti-Fraud Office (OLAF)), albeit strictly in connection with the matter they are hearing or investigating at the time.

An important restriction on the above limitations is proportionality. None of these organisations are free to learn whatever they want. They have to specify what data they require and on what grounds. If, for example, a court bailiff, in a procedure against the settlor, asks for the trust agreement in full, the trustee must reject the request, because the case likely has nothing to do with details like what happens to the trust fund when the settlor dies. The bailiff must confine their request to particular dates and circumstances. It is the trustee's duty to decide on the lawfulness of a public authority's request, and the trustee is liable if they disclose too much information.

(f) ***Duty to give proper accounts***[82]

Hungarian law is unique in the sense that both the settlor and the beneficiaries can supervise the trustee. This right, however, is ineffective if they lack the information necessary to decide on the trustee's performance. This is why the Civil Code gives them the right to request information from the trustee as to the following:

- the actual and expected growth of the trust fund;
- the individual assets belonging to the trust fund, and their respective values; and
- the duties undertaken on behalf of the trust fund.

In addition, accounting and tax procedure rules require the trustee to obtain a tax number[83] for the trust fund and prepare annual financial statements, just like companies.[84] The only difference is that these financial statements do not become public – their purpose is to provide information to the settlor and the beneficiaries, and serve as a basis for tax calculations.[85]

---

82 Section 6:320 of the Civil Code.
83 Section 16(3) of the Tax Procedure Act.
84 Section 7/B of the Accounting Act.
85 Section 154(1a) of the Accounting Act.

Naturally, the trust agreement may contain other requirements as to the contents or regularity of the trustee's reporting (for example, quarterly reporting on the performance of the financial portfolio) and the settlor or beneficiaries may also require the trustee to provide other information about the trust. By default, the settlor and the beneficiaries must bear the cost of all inquiries (usually through the trust fund).[86] If the information that the trustee provides is inaccurate or incomplete, the settlor and/or the beneficiaries may turn to the court and/or hold the trustee liable.

(g) Miscellaneous obligations

The above comprise the most important obligations of the trustee. However, the list is not exhaustive. Many administrative and other rules impose additional duties or obligations on the trustee. The most important are the Know Your Customer (KYC) and AML rules, which are common and standard in the world of the professional trustee but seem slightly odd for *ad hoc* trustees (who in many cases manage only their own wealth). Nevertheless, most of the regulations do not differentiate between professional and *ad hoc* trustees and impose the same requirements and fines or other adverse consequences on both in the event of non-compliance.

5.3 Trustee's liability

If a trustee violates any of the duties above or commits a breach of contract in some other way, they may be found liable for their act or omission. The direction and extent of this liability defines who can file what kind of claims against the trustee, and the rules on liability also determine the available remedies.

Under Hungarian law the trustee's liability is twofold:

- 'internal liability' towards the settlor and the beneficiaries; and
- 'external liability' towards third parties who have dealings with the trustee during the existence of the trust.

(a) Internal liability

Hungarian trusts diverge in this area from the standard English common law trust. In many jurisdictions, the beneficiary is the person 'holding the gun', that is, the person who may find the trustee liable if they commit a breach of trust. While Hungarian law too recognises that the beneficiary suffers most from a breach of trust, the settlor may also hold the trustee accountable.[87] This is because Hungarian law gives a similar role to the settlor as to the founder of a foundation. They each have a significant impact on the organisation and

86 Section 6:320(3) of the Civil Code.
87 Section 6:321(1) of the Civil Code.

operation of the trust or foundation. In the latter case, however, the founder is exclusively entrusted with enforcing the terms of the foundation and holding the management responsible. Hungarian trust law places the settlor in a very similar position – thus, both settlor and beneficiary can sue the trustee for breach of contract. This can put the trustee in a difficult position. In the case of the duty of loyalty, for example, the settlor and the beneficiaries may have very different views as to where the beneficiaries' real interests lie. Often, they each expect a different approach from the trustee. The position becomes even worse if the beneficiaries do not form a homogenous group (for example, there are life beneficiaries as well as remaindermen). In an atmosphere of tension, such divisions often fall on the shoulders of the trustee and can lead to extensive litigation.

As to the extent of the liability of the trustee, this depends on the nature of the trust. If the trustee receives remuneration, the amount of damages payable is much higher. If the breach of trust is deliberate, the trustee may be found liable for all losses including direct losses (for example, a decrease in the value of the trust fund), consequential losses (for example, due to the decrease in value the trust fund is unable to renovate a beneficiary's house, which later collapses), and loss of profit (for example, due to the decrease in value the trust fund is unable to make a lucrative investment and loses potential returns).[88] Negligence results in damages only for foreseeable losses stemming from indirect losses and loss of profit.[89] There has been insufficient litigation to work out the details, but it seems that the reference point for foreseeability is the date of the conclusion of the trust agreement – which seems unfair for long-term trust relationships.

If the trustee does not receive consideration for their services (gratuitous mandate), loss of profit is excluded from damages, but direct losses and direct consequential losses are still covered.[90] Deliberate wrongdoing results in damages for all consequential losses as well.[91]

Various options are available for trustees to relieve themselves of liability. In the case of non-gratuitous trust agreements, the trustee can avoid payment of damages only in the rarest of cases (if the circumstances leading to the breach of trust were beyond the trustee's control, the breach was unforeseeable, and it would be unreasonable to expect the trustee to avoid the breach).[92] Trustees without remuneration may also rely on absence of culpability when it comes to a breach of trust.[93]

---

88 Section 6:143(3) of the Civil Code.
89 Section 6:143(2) of the Civil Code.
90 Section 6:147(2) of the Civil Code.
91 Section 6:147(1) of the Civil Code.
92 Section 6:142 of the Civil Code.
93 Section 6:147(1) of the Civil Code.

In all cases, the trustee is liable for outsourced activities, and in most cases if an adviser commits a breach of contract.[94]

(b) *External liability*

As a general rule, the trustee is liable to third parties only with the trust fund. However, to protect third parties who may be unaware of the trustee's capacity or the limited resources of the trust fund, the trustee may also be liable with their own personal property if they fail to inform a contracting party that the trustee's commitment exceeds the trust fund's resources.[95]

If the trustee's liability is non-contractual, for example in cases of environmental harm, they are liable primarily with their own personal property.[96] It is also possible that the injured party may seek remedy from the trust fund; however, the law is unclear on this question and there is no established authority from judicial practice.

6. Supervision over professional trustees

As mentioned above, the NBH is the authority that issues and reviews licences for professional trustees. At the same time, it acts as a supervisory body for all trustees (both *ad hoc* and professional) concerning their AML and KYC obligations.[97]

Other powers of the NBH, however, are rather limited. *Ad hoc* trustees are subject to a registration requirement only (as discussed at the beginning of this chapter). Professional trustees, on the other hand, have to comply with complex and detailed licensing rules (like other members of the financial sector), and some of their activities fall outside the NBH's general oversight powers. Thus, while the NBH may investigate a professional trustee's compliance with the licensing requirements,[98] it is barred from scrutinising the general activities of the trustee. This does not, however, prelude the NBH from conducting a so-called 'market supervisory procedure' against the trustee if it detects violations of other regulations, such as under the Bank and Financial Institutions Act.

As part of the annual supervision, the professional trustee must demonstrate compliance with all registration requirements. The deadline for filing a licence renewal is 30 July each year. As part of the procedure, the trustee is required to file its annual financial statements.[99] If the NBH approves the trustee's motion, it renews the licence; otherwise, it revokes the licence and removes the trustee from the Register of Professional Trustees.[100]

---

94 Sections 6:148(2) and 6:542 of the Civil Code.
95 Section 6:323(2) of the Civil Code.
96 Section 6:522(1) of the Civil Code.
97 Section 1(b) of the Trustee Act and Section 5(g) of the Anti-Money Laundering and Counter-Terrorism Financing Act.
98 Section 32 of the Trustee Act.
99 Section 32(1) of the Trustee Act.
100 Section 34 of the Trustee Act.

Ad hoc trustees

Sára Seszták
Seszták Ügyvédi Iroda

1. Introduction

As seen in earlier chapters, trusts have become an integral part of the Hungarian legal landscape in the years since their codification. In addition, the establishment of the asset management foundation in its various forms has meant that fiduciary activities can now be carried out by a separate legal entity.

Although these legal institutions have much in common and their objectives may be similar, there are inherent differences between the two, as discussed in the chapter on asset management foundations.

2. Requirements for *ad hoc* trustees

Whether dealing with professional or non-professional trusts, a crucial aspect of the fiduciary relationship is trusting the trustee to manage the trust assets to the best of their ability and for the intended purpose of the contractual relationship.[1]

However, the liability and administrative burden associated with the role of trustee can vary from case to case, as illustrated by the distinction between professional trusts – discussed in the previous chapter – and *ad hoc* trusts, which are the subject of this chapter.[2]

A non-business or *ad hoc* trustee may only carry out their fiduciary activities for a single trust, in accordance with the provisions of Section 3(1) of the Trustee Act.[3]

The National Bank of Hungary (NBH) has established principles for determining whether multiple trusts are considered professional or *ad hoc*. The NBH's objective in this regard is to detect whether multiple trusts in a single trust contract conceal a fiduciary relationship that is businesslike and thus subject to authorisation.

The NBH states that the mere presence of multiple settlors or beneficiaries in a contractual relationship, as well as the management of multiple assets,

1 Gábor B Szabó *et al*, *A bizalmi vagyonkezelés* (*Fiduciary asset management*) (2nd ed), HVG-ORAC, 2018. Available at: https://jogkodex.hu/doc/6064674.
2 *Ibid*.
3 Act XV of 2014 on Fiduciary Managers and on the Regulations Governing Their Activities.

does not necessarily imply the businesslike nature of a trust. While the trustee should be the main consideration in such an assessment, it is also important to examine the relationship between the settlors. If the trust is based on a close association between the settlors – such as a familial or corporate relationship – establishing the non-commercial nature of the fiduciary relationship should not be an issue.

The legal environment for *ad hoc* trusts is less regulated than its professional counterpart, making it more permissive. This is evidenced by the fact that while *ad hoc* trusts also fall within the scope of the Trustee Act, there is a narrower set of specifically applicable rules.

Ad hoc trusts tend to involve a smaller volume of assets and therefore require less regulation, and they are often based on personal or family acquaintance rather than on professional expertise.[4] In addition, there is no requirement under the Trustee Act for *ad hoc* trustees to have any financial, legal or other qualifications or training.

The law does not offer an explicit definition of a person who may act as an *ad hoc* trustee. Therefore, unless otherwise specified, both a natural or legal person and an organisation lacking the legal status of a legal person – as long as they have general legal capacity to act – may be appointed.

This broad scope is balanced by public law requirements concerning grounds for exclusion as set out in the Trustee Act. Until the date of exemption from the adverse legal consequences of a criminal record, the Trustee Act excludes from the role of *ad hoc* trustee any person convicted of certain offences defined in Section 18/A(1)(a)[5] and (b) of the act.[6]

---

4 The concept of the 'family office' shows that this is not always the case: in a family office, substantial family assets are managed by a professional trustee. See Gábor B Szabó *et al, A bizalmi vagyonkezelés, supra.*

5 This refers to the following criminal offences set out in Act IV of 1978 on the Criminal Code:
- a crime against the integrity of public life under Title VII of Chapter XV;
- any crime against international justice;
- acts of terrorism;
- violation of international economic sanctions;
- unlawful seizure of an aircraft, of any means of railway, water or road transport or of any means of freight transport;
- participation in a criminal organisation;
- taking the law into one's own hands;
- the forging of administrative documents;
- the forging of private documents;
- misuse of document under Title VIII of Chapter XV;
- an economic crime under Chapter XVII; or
- an offence against property under Chapter XVIII.

6 This refers to the following criminal offences set out in Act C of 2012 on the Criminal Code:
- a crime of corruption under Chapter XXVII;
- acts of terrorism;
- terrorist financing;
- unlawful seizure of a vehicle;
- participation in a criminal organisation;
- violation of international economic sanctions;
- forgery of administrative documents;
- use of a forged private document; or
- criminal offences with official documents or records under Chapters XXXV–XLIII.

For legal persons (business entities), the conditions for carrying out *ad hoc* trust activities are as follows:

- They must comply with the requirements for a transparent organisation set out in Section 3(1)(1) of Act of 2011 CXCVI on National Assets.[7]
- Fiduciary activities cannot be conducted by any member (owner), affiliated company[8] (as defined in Section 4(23) of Act LXXXI of 1996 on

---

7 'Transparent organisation' is defined by the act in the following terms:
(a) *the state, a budgetary body, a public body, a local government, a national minority government, a partnership, a religious legal person, an economic entity in which the state or a local government, individually or jointly, holds a 100% share, an international organisation, a foreign state, a foreign local authority, a foreign state or local authority and a public limited liability company listed on a regulated market of a state party to the Agreement on the European Economic Area;*
(b) *a domestic or foreign legal person or business entity lacking the legal status of a legal person that meets the following conditions:*
(ba) *the ownership structure and the beneficial owner, as defined in Act LIII of 2017 on the Prevention and Combating of Money Laundering and Terrorist Financing;*
(bb) *is tax resident in a member state of the European Union, a state party to the Agreement on the European Economic Area, a member state of the Organisation for Economic Cooperation and Development or a state with which Hungary has a double taxation convention;*
(bc) *is not a controlled foreign company as defined in the Act on Corporate Tax and Dividend Tax;*
(bd) *a legal entity, a business entity lacking the legal status of a legal person, which directly or indirectly holds more than 25% of the ownership, influence or voting rights in the entity, meets the conditions under (ba), (bb) and (bc);*
(c) *NGOs and water associations that meet the following conditions:*
(ca) *its leading officials are known;*
(cb) *the NGO and the water board and their managing directors do not hold more than 25% of the shares in a non-transparent organisation;*
(cc) *the registered office is in a member state of the European Union, a state party to the Agreement on the European Economic Area, a member state of the Organisation for Economic Cooperation and Development or a state with which Hungary has a double taxation convention.*

8 'Affiliated company' is defined by the act in the following terms:
(a) *the taxpayer and the person in which the taxpayer directly or indirectly holds a majority interest, with relevant application of the provisions of the Civil Code;*
(b) *the taxpayer and the person who directly or indirectly has a majority influence in the taxpayer, with the relevant application of the provisions of the Civil Code;*
(c) *the taxpayer and another person, if a third person has, directly or indirectly, a majority influence in both of them, with the relevant application of the provisions of the Civil Code, with the condition that close relatives who have a majority influence in the taxpayer and the other person shall be considered third persons;*
(d) *the foreign enterprise and its domestic establishment, and the foreign enterprise's establishments, as well as the foreign enterprise's domestic establishment and the person who has a relationship with the foreign enterprise as defined in (a)–(c);*
(e) *the taxpayer and its foreign establishment, as well as the taxpayer's foreign establishment and the person who has a relationship with the taxpayer as defined in (a)–(c);*
(f) *the taxpayer and another person, if there is a decisive influence between them on business and financial policy in view of the congruence of management;*
(g) *in addition to (a)–(c), an affiliation is also established if:*
(ga) *in relation to (11.), (53.) Section 8(1)(f) and Section 16/A, if there is a direct or indirect holding of at least 25% of the voting rights, or a direct or indirect holding of at least 25% of the equity participation, or a direct or indirect holding of at least 25 % of the profit participation between the taxpayer and another person, or where a third person is entitled to hold, directly or indirectly, in the taxpayer and in another person, a direct or indirect voting interest of at least 25%, or a direct or indirect equity participation of at least 25 %, or a direct or indirect profit participation of at least 25%, provided that for the purposes of these provisions, the fulfilment of the conditions of (f) need not be examined;*
(gb) *in relation Section 2(7) and Section 16/B, if the taxpayer and another person have a direct or indirect voting interest of at least 50%, or a direct or indirect equity participation of at least 50%, or a profit participation of at least 50%, provided that for voting rights and equity participation, the influence of persons acting in concert shall be aggregated and, in the case of taxpayers belonging to a group of companies preparing consolidated financial statements, the factors in (f) shall also be considered.*

Corporate Tax and Dividend Tax), senior executive, or any of their relatives.[9]

- None of the above grounds for exclusion apply to any of its senior executives, members who are natural persons, or beneficial owners.

The *ad hoc* trustee benefits significantly from the absence of public law requirements for financial securities and equity capital like those set out in Section 7 of the Trustee Act. Notably, while a professional trustee requires authorisation from the NBH to commence their activities, an *ad hoc* trustee does not. This key difference provides the latter with a significant advantage. Section 19 of the Trustee Act requires only the registration of the trust. For an *ad hoc* trustee, it is sufficient to notify the NBH of the relationship within 30 days of concluding the contract. Notification must include the deed and any information necessary to identify the parties to the trust.

3. Registering an *ad hoc* trust

To mitigate the risks inherent in *ad hoc* trusts, the legislator has institutionalised their transparency. The NBH is responsible for maintaining a register of fiduciary asset management relationships.

3.1 Notification method

A natural person trustee is not required to communicate electronically and may choose to file the trust information either on paper or in electronic form. Paper filings can be made by filling out the notification form available on the NBH's website. The filing can also be done electronically via the General Form Completion Programme using the form also available on the NBH website.

To comply with Section 58 of Act CXXXIX of 2013 on the National Bank of Hungary, legal representatives and business entities must communicate electronically. These notifications must be submitted via the electronic form provided in the NBH's electronic filing system (ERA system).[10]

3.2 Content and attachments of the notification

In their notification, the trustee, as the notifier, must state their own contractual status and that of the settlor and the beneficiary, as well as the data referred to in Section 20(1)(a)–(b) of the Trustee Act:

- *For legal persons and organisations lacking legal status:* name, type, registered office, registered number (or other similar identifier), phone

9 'Relative' is defined at Section 8:1(1) (1) and (2) of the Civil Code as the spouse, the lineal relative, the adopted child, the stepchild and the foster child, the adoptive parent, the step-parent and the foster parent and the sibling, the cohabitant, the spouse of a lineal relative, the lineal relative and the sibling of the spouse, and the spouse of the sibling.

10 Once registration is complete, the electronic form can be accessed through the E-Administration Authorisation service via the NBH's ERA portal.

number, email address and – exclusively for the notifier – senior executive,[11] member[12] and beneficial ownership data.

- *For natural persons:* name, birth name, mother's name, home address, place and date of birth.

Under Section 20(2) of the Trustee Act, the notifier must enclose a statement, in the form of at least a private document representing conclusive evidence provided for in the Code of Civil Procedure, confirming their status as a non-professional fiduciary and that they meet the conditions set out above.

It is important to note that Article 5m of Council Regulation (EU) No 833/2014 of 31 July 2014 concerning restrictive measures in view of Russia's actions destabilising the situation in Ukraine includes sanctions measures that apply to fiduciary activities. Consequently, the *ad hoc* trustee must make specific declarations regarding these measures on the hardcopy or electronic form, failing which registration will be impeded.

In general, pursuant to Section 20(3) of the Trustee Act, the *ad hoc* trustee is required to submit the following with the notification:

- the trust deed;
- a statement, in the form of at least a private document, representing conclusive evidence provided for in the Code of Civil Procedure that they are acting as a non-professional fiduciary;
- a statement, in the form of at least a private document, representing conclusive evidence provided for in the Code of Civil Procedure that they meet the conditions set in Section 18/A of the Trustee Act. In this connection, a business entity *ad hoc* trustee must declare in a properly signed document that it is a transparent organisation, that its members, its affiliated companies, its senior executives and their relatives as defined by the Civil Code do not carry out fiduciary activities, and that its senior executives, natural person members and beneficial owners have no criminal record. These declarations can be made in a single document that meets the formal requirements, or in the trust deed itself;
- where the trustee acts through a legal representative,[13] a declaration that neither the trustee nor the settlor or beneficiary of the trust to be registered is subject to the prohibitions set out in Article 5m of Council Regulation (EU) No 833/2014 of 31 July 2014 concerning restrictive

11 According to Section 2(2) of the Trustee Act, 'senior executive' includes executive officers and supervisory board members, a person appointed by a foreign-registered company to lead a branch, his or her deputy, the office manager in law firms, or the person who provides representation at the organisational level, and any person so designated in the instrument of constitution or in internal operational policy.

12 A 'member' is defined as an individual or organisation registered with the company.

13 If the trustee is undertaking the notification procedure, this declaration can be made on the hard copy or electronic form itself and does not need to be submitted separately.

measures in view of Russia's actions destabilising the situation in Ukraine;
- where relevant, confirmation that the trustee, settlor or beneficiary affected by the prohibitions set out in Article 5m has been exempted pursuant to Article 5m(3)–(6);
- proof of payment of the administrative service fee for notification;
- a statement on the adoption of internal regulations to comply with obligations in relation to money laundering and terrorist financing, and the implementation of any restrictive measures imposed by the European Union and the UN Security Council relating to liquid assets and other financial interests; and
- in the case of legal representation, the power of attorney of the legal representative.

If filing on paper, the original documents must be attached. In the case of electronic filing, the electronic form and annexes must be submitted in an electronically certified form.

It should be noted that the provisions of Chapter XLIII of the Civil Code on Trust Contacts also apply to *ad hoc* trusts. Such trusts may be created by a trust agreement executed in an authentic instrument or a private document countersigned by an attorney or registered legal counsel, by a unilateral declaration executed in an authentic instrument, or by a will (and acceptance).[14]

The person drafting the trust deed must adhere to the client due diligence and notification obligations outlined elsewhere in this book. Furthermore, notarisation or countersignature requires a criminal conflict of interest check conducted by a notary public, attorney, or registered legal counsel based on a certificate of clean criminal record. Under Section 18/A(3) of the Trustee Act, the trust deed must include the name, mother's name and home address of the senior executive, natural person member, and beneficial owner of the *ad hoc* trustee if it is a legal person or an organisation lacking legal status. The deed (and countersignature) attests to the completion of this examination, therefore the NBH does not verify this requirement during registration. However, the NBH will annually verify compliance and take necessary measures against the *ad hoc* trustee if there are grounds for exclusion.

If an incompatible person or entity is appointed as a trustee, their actions will be considered unlawful. However, this alone will not render the trust null and void.[15] On the other hand, a contract that does not meet the formal

14 Under Section 6:329(3) of the Civil Code, the rules of the trust contract also apply to trusts established by unilateral act. Therefore, when this chapter refers to trust contracts, it also means unilateral statements and wills.

15 Lajos Vékás and Péter Gárdos (eds), *Nagykommentár Polgári Törvénykönyvről szóló 2013. évi V. törvényhez (Commentary on Act V of 2013 on the Civil Code)*, Wolters Kluwer, 2023.

requirements is null and void under Section 6:6(1) and Section 6:94 of the Civil Code.[16]

During the registration process, the NBH only examines the notification and its annexes. The *ad hoc* trust will be registered within 60 days if it meets the conditions set out in the Trustee Act.[17] These conditions, pursuant to Section 21(1)–(1a) of the Trustee Act, are:

- a valid submitted deed;
- the trustee not acting in a commercial capacity; and
- the contents of the notification and its annexes being appropriate.

If the notification does not comply with the provisions of the Trustee Act, the NBH will issue a deficiency notice within 45 days of receiving the notification submission. The notice will invite the notifier to submit a correction pursuant to Section 49(3) of Act CXXXIX of 2013 and warn of the legal consequences of non-compliance. The 60-day time limit will restart as soon as the deficiencies have been fully remedied.

Although the chapter on registers details the rules for the Register of Trusts, it is important to emphasise that the purpose of the register is to ensure the traceability of trust assets and the conduct of investigations under Act LIII of 2017 on the Prevention and Combating of Money Laundering and Terrorist Financing. The register therefore contains only the most basic information on trusts, the accuracy of which is not guaranteed by the Authority,[18] given its purely administrative role. The notifier is responsible for ensuring the trust deed is truthful and the data contained in the notification correct, per Section 22(3) of the Trustee Act. Therefore, the register of fiduciary asset management relationships does not qualify as a public register.[19]

Pursuant to Section 28 of the Trustee Act, the Authority must issue a certificate of notification to the notifier, which is recognised as an official instrument. Registration does not have a constitutive effect. Failure to notify the Authority does not affect the legal status of the trust agreement, except in cases provided for by law, per Section 23 of the Trustee Act.

3.3 Notification of data changes

The register must accurately reflect the status of the trusts notified. Therefore, the notifier must inform the Authority of any changes within eight days of the occurrence that caused the change. The notifier must also inform the Authority if the conditions for registration no longer exist, per Section 24(1) of the Trustee

16 Gábor B Szabó *et al*, *A bizalmi vagyonkezelés*, *supra*.

17 Although the NBH does not perform civil law validity checks, it will inform the client of any deficiencies it detects. This may be done through a deficiency notice or as a note at the end of the official certificate.

18 In the Trustee Act, the NBH is referred as 'the Authority'.

19 Gábor B Szabó *et al*, *A bizalmi vagyonkezelés*, *supra*.

Act. The *ad hoc* trustee must comply with the registration notification rules, noting that:

- if the trust is amended or terminated, such notification must take place within eight days of the amendment or termination (Section 24(1) of the Trustee Act);
- the notification must be accompanied by the amended or terminated contract (Section 20(3)(a) of the Trustee Act); and
- if the amendment to the trust only involves a change of the trustee, a declaration by the settlor in accordance with Section 20(3)(d) of the Trustee Act must be attached along with the annexes mentioned above.

There is no specific paper or electronic form for these filings; they can be made in a free-form document for hard copy filings or on the general application and filing form available within ERA (under 'Other applications and filings') for electronic filings.

The Authority will either register the change in the data or delete the registered data if the conditions set out in Section 25 of the Trustee Act apply.

4. Provisions for performing the function of an *ad hoc* trustee

From a private law point of view, the rules applicable to professional trusts and *ad hoc* trusts are essentially the same – the main differences can be found in the rules of public law. The chapter on professional trustees provided a thorough summary of the regulations governing the establishment, termination, succession, rights, duties, care and liability of the professional trustee.

This chapter outlines the key rules that highlight the different regulations as between professional and *ad hoc* trusts.

4.1 Establishing the *ad hoc* trust and duty of care of the trustee

There is a two-step process to becoming an *ad hoc* trustee: the entitled person appoints the trustee, and the trustee accepts the appointment. The form in which the trust is created will determine this process.[20] Once appointed, trustees must familiarise themselves with the contents and background of the trust, including any previous trustees, and arrange for the transfer of the trust assets, including updating the relevant records and registers. Additionally, trustees must notify the NBH as described earlier in this chapter.[21]

In the case of an *ad hoc* trust, several trustees can act on behalf of a single trust under Section 6:324 of the Civil Code. The notification to the NBH must reflect this arrangement, otherwise the trustees will be jointly and severally liable, pursuant to Section 6:324(1) and (3) of the Civil Code.

---

20 For further discussion, see Gábor B Szabó *et al*, *A bizalmi vagyonkezelés*, *supra*.
21 *Ibid*.

The Trustee Act, given its commercial nature, imposes strict requirements on the fiduciary activities of professional trustees, but does not require the same for *ad hoc* trustees. The Act provides a more flexible framework for *ad hoc* trustees, enabling non-professional trustees to fulfil their roles despite having different resources and expertise compared to their professional counterparts. In *ad hoc* trust management, it is more common for the trustee to have less professional experience and knowledge, and in the case of assets requiring special handling (eg, works of art), trustees may lack relevant expertise altogether.[22]

In view of the differences in expertise, the *ad hoc* trustee is held to a lower standard of care compared to the professional trustee; however, the *ad hoc* trustee must nevertheless exercise an enhanced level of care in the management of the trust assets. The fiduciary nature of the legal instrument means that, while serving the best interests of the beneficiary, the trustee is obligated to protect the managed assets from foreseeable risks under the principle of reasonable commercial practice, per Section 6:317 of the Civil Code, and to ensure that the risks to the trust assets are minimised.[23]

As part of their principal contractual obligation, the trustee must manage the trust assets in a way that ensures their growth in value. In this context, the *ad hoc* trustee must act with the due care and diligence (and professional standards, if any) expected of a non-commercial trustee. This means complying with the expectations set out in the trust deed,[24] while following general investment practices and adhering to the Civil Code's standard of assuming and mitigating risk. However, this does not constitute an investment obligation under Section 45 of the Trustee Act.[25]

In *ad hoc* trusts, it is common for the trustee to have to consider the interests of multiple beneficiaries. This is particularly true for family trusts, where the trust contract may stipulate that the interests of the entire family must be taken into account. The trustee is obligated to act in the best interests of the beneficiaries and cannot prioritise one over the other unless otherwise stipulated in the trust contract. However, this can be particularly challenging if the trustee is also a family member or beneficiary.[26]

Since the standard of care applicable to an *ad hoc* trustee is different from that of a professional trustee, and because they must also act in accordance with reasonable commercial practice, it is particularly important that, if they do not have the necessary expertise for the decision in question, the *ad hoc* trustee

---

22 *Ibid.*

23 Lajos Vékás and Péter Gárdos (eds), *Commentary on Act V of 2013 on the Civil Code, supra.*

24 Once again, the trustee's dual duty to serve interests is reflected in the fact that the establishment of the trust is essentially intended to serve the interests of the settlor, whilst the interests of the beneficiary must take precedence during the life of the trust. See György Wellmann (ed), *Polgári Jog I-IV. - új Ptk. - Kommentár a gyakorlat számára* (6th ed), ORAC, 2023.

25 György Wellmann (ed), *Polgári Jog I-IV. - új Ptk. - Kommentár a gyakorlat számára, ibid*; and Lajos Vékás and Péter Gárdos (eds), *Nagykommentár Polgári Törvénykönyvről szóló 2013. évi V. törvényhez, supra.*

26 Gábor B Szabó *et al*, *A bizalmi vagyonkezelés, supra.*

should – in accordance with the provisions of Section 6:129(2) of the Civil Code – appoint a person with the necessary qualifications as executing agent (assistant or adviser) in order to avoid damage, unless the trust deed provides otherwise. Section 44 of the Trustee Act contains rules on outsourcing that apply solely to professional trusts – in the case of an *ad hoc* trustee, the framework for the use of an executing agent can be freely determined by the trust contract. However, despite the absence of cogency, when designing the contractual framework it is important to consider the prohibitions set out in Section 44(4) of the Trustee Act[27] and to assess whether the risk of outsourcing is proportionate to the need to protect the assets and mitigate loss, given the more personal relationship between the *ad hoc* trustee and the settlor or beneficiary.[28] It should be noted that the *ad hoc* trustee is liable for the conduct of the executing agent as if it had acted itself, under Section 6:148(1) of the Civil Code.

The costs of the executing agent may be recovered from the trust assets under Section 6:322(3) of the Civil Code.[29]

4.2 Powers and rights of the *ad hoc* trustee

Although the *ad hoc* trustee has full and exclusive power over the transferred property under the general rules of the Civil Code,[30] they must still adhere to the conditions and limits set out in the trust deed, including the interests of the beneficiary,[31] and focus on preserving and increasing the value of the trust assets. However, these obligations do not prevent the trustee from acting independently and in their own name, given that Section 6:316 of the Civil Code expressly excludes the right of the settlor and the beneficiary to instruct the trustee.

The trustee has a duty to maintain the integrity of the trust in the best interests of the beneficiary. This includes refraining from unauthorised transfers or encumbrances of trust assets to third parties in violation of the trust deed's terms or restrictions. According to Section 6:318(3) of the Civil Code, both the settlor and beneficiary are entitled to reclaim such property, provided that the third party did not act in good faith[32] or acquired the property free of charge.

---

27 Section 44(4) of the Trustee Act. Upon entering into outsourcing arrangements:
(a) the mandate shall not prevent the effectiveness of supervision over the fiduciary asset management company;
(b) the mandate shall not affect the liabilities of the fiduciary; and (c) the mandate shall not prevent the fiduciary manager:
(ca) from giving further instructions to and supervising the activities of the outsourcing service provider; and
(cb) from terminating the outsourcing arrangements with immediate effect in the event of any breach of the outsourcing arrangements.

28 Lajos Vékás and Péter Gárdos (eds), *Nagykommentár Polgári Törvénykönyvről szóló 2013. évi V. törvényhez, supra.*

29 For further discussion, see Gábor B Szabó *et al, A bizalmi vagyonkezelés, supra.*

30 Section 5:13(1) of the Civil Code.

31 Section 6:318(2) of the Civil Code.

32 An acquirer is considered *bona fide* if it did not know, and with the care ordinarily required in the circumstances should not have known, that it had acquired the trust property in breach of the trust contract.

Ad hoc trusteeship is typically a transaction for consideration,[33] but due to its personal nature it is sometimes performed free of charge, especially for family members. In such cases, the *ad hoc* trustee is still entitled to claim reimbursement of the normal costs of asset management, which can be satisfied directly from the trust assets pursuant to Section 6:322(1) of the Civil Code.

4.3 Obligations of the *ad hoc* trustee

The full property rights of the trustee *in rem* are limited by the terms of the trust deed and the duty to act in the best interests of the beneficiary.[34]

To achieve the trust's purpose, it is essential to fully implement the separation of property in the case of *ad hoc* trusts as well. *Ad hoc* trustees act on the basis of a single trust, but the obligation to keep separate records imposes a significant administrative burden.[35] Under Section 6:312 of the Civil Code, assets transferred under a trust do not add to the personal assets of the trustee. Instead, they constitute a separate and limited liability economic entity with its own tax number, books and accounts. As a general rule, liabilities can only be satisfied from trust assets. However, if claims are not covered by the trust assets, the trustee is also liable without limitation with their own assets, provided the other party did not know, and could not have known, that the trustee's liability extended beyond the trust assets, as per Section 6:323 of the Civil Code.[36]

It is important to note that the separate accounts discussed above are distinct from the internal accounts and registers regulated by Sections 39–40 of the Trustee Act. Their purpose is to enable the monitoring of trust relationships with professional trusts so as to facilitate official property search procedures and support the client's right to information and control. The *ad hoc* trustee's record-keeping obligation ensures that the assets held on behalf of the beneficiary are distinguished from the trustee's own assets. This ensures that the assets held in trust and their benefits are released to the beneficiary in accordance with the trust deed's terms, while also serving to protect capital and creditors.

The beneficiary has a claim on the trust assets until the requirements of the trust deed are fulfilled. Afterward, the Civil Code grants the beneficiary the right to enforce its claim for the release of the assets against the trustee. The law protects the interests of the beneficiary against their creditors until the assets or their benefits are released to the beneficiary. After the due date, creditors can seek satisfaction from the released assets under the general rules on

---

33 Section 3:310(1) of the Civil Code.

34 Gábor B Szabó *et al, A bizalmi vagyonkezelés, supra.*

35 Trust assets should be recorded as external assets or liabilities on the balance sheet. Separate accounts must be maintained for them, and they should be treated differently according to their nature.

36 However, all this can be avoided if the trustee informs its contracting partners of these circumstances in an appropriate manner.

enforcement under Section 6:314(2) of the Civil Code, as the benefit is then part of the beneficiary's own assets.

Because of the relative nature of the trustee's ownership, the trust assets are protected from the claims of the trustee's spouse, cohabitant and personal creditors. In addition, they are not considered part of the trustee's estate under Section 6:313 of the Civil Code.[37] Therefore, any liquidation or enforcement proceedings against the trustee will not compromise the integrity of the trust assets.[38] Both the beneficiary and the settlor have the right to take legal action against the spouse, cohabitant and personal creditors of the trustee. They can also request the separation of the trust assets from the settlor's personal property, as stated in Section 6:313(2).

If a trustee fails to adequately separate trust assets from their own property, it constitutes a breach of contract. Assets that are part of the trust and kept separately from the trustee's own assets will be considered part of the trust assets. Conversely, assets not recorded as part of the trust will be considered part of the trustee's personal assets unless proven to the contrary.

Under Section 6:312(2)–(4) of the Civil Code, individual assets replacing certain assets, security deposits, reimbursement, or any other value of the like, and their proceeds, will form part of the managed assets, even if not shown in the records.[39]

The trustee's statutory obligations emphasise the primacy and protection of the beneficiary's interests. These obligations allow for verification that the trustee is fulfilling their duties in accordance with the trust contract as outlined in Section 6:315 of the Civil Code. Both the settlor and beneficiary have the right to check the trustee's activities within the scope of the trust. The primary means of control is the trustee's obligation to provide information and account for their activities. This requires the trustee to inform the settlor[40] of their activities and, when requested, to provide the settlor and beneficiary with appropriate information regarding the managed assets. This information should include the actual and foreseeable growth in the managed assets, the individual assets managed and their value, and the liabilities undertaken against the managed assets.[41] Under Section 6:320 of the Civil Code, the *ad hoc* trustee is also required to provide an account of the management of assets upon request, to both the settlor and the beneficiary.

A protector may be appointed alongside an *ad hoc* trustee. The function of a protector is discussed elsewhere in this book.

---

37 However, if the heirs become the successors of the trustee, they will acquire ownership of the assets held in trust through this mechanism.

38 For further discussion, see Gábor B Szabó *et al*, *A bizalmi vagyonkezelés*, *supra*.

39 The settlor can also provide in the trust deed for these benefits to be released or managed in a different way from the rest of the trust assets.

40 Section 6:275 of the Civil Code.

41 The information may vary as between the settlor and the beneficiary, but for the beneficiary it usually relates to the most significant events occurring in administering the trust.

The framework for the right of control described above is not set out in the Civil Code – the parties are free to determine the detailed rules in the trust contract. However, the costs of information and accounting obligations to be borne by the settlor or the beneficiary may limit the right of control. It should be noted, however, that Section 40 of the Trustee Act does not apply to *ad hoc* trusts, meaning *ad hoc* trustees are not required to keep records of trust declarations made during the performance of the trust to facilitate the exercise of control powers.

Given the legal nature of trusteeship, the trustee is subject to a strict duty of confidentiality in respect of all facts, data and information obtained in the course of their activities. This duty of confidentiality is independent of the trusteeship and survives the termination of the trust relationship. Because of its fiduciary nature, the trustee or their successor has the right to waive the duty of confidentiality. The duty of confidentiality of an *ad hoc* trustee does not fall under the scope of Section 42 of the Trustee Act.[42]

4.4 Liability of the *ad hoc* trustee

The trustee has both criminal and civil liability for any breach of obligations described in this chapter towards both the settlor and beneficiary, either of whom may be entitled to bring a claim against the trustee. It is important to note that the trustee is primarily responsible for the performance of the trust contract, and the interests of the beneficiary can only be enforced within the contract's limits.[43]

From a contract law perspective, the *ad hoc* trustee is liable for any breach of obligations towards the settlor and/or the beneficiary in accordance with the general provisions on liability for non-performance of an obligation.[44] If the trustee is not remunerated for their services, the provisions on liability for damages relating to any breach of gratuitous contracts apply.[45]

A trustee is in breach of contract – and liable for damages – if their conduct does not meet the standard of care normally required of an *ad hoc* trustee or as

42 The Civil Code does not specifically sanction breaches of confidentiality, so the general civil law sanction regime applies, but the trust deed may also set out the consequences of such breaches of contract. See Lajos Vékás and Péter Gárdos (eds), *Nagykommentár Polgári Törvénykönyvről szóló 2013. évi V. törvényhez, supra*.

43 Gábor B Szabó *et al, A bizalmi vagyonkezelés, supra*.

44 Under Section 6:142 of the Civil Code, the person who causes damage to the other party by breaching the contract shall be liable for such damage. They shall be relieved of liability if they can prove that the damage occurred in consequence of unforeseen circumstances beyond their control, and there had been no reasonable cause to take action to prevent or mitigate the damage.

45 Under Section 6:147 of the Civil Code, in the case of gratuitous performance of a contract, the obligor is liable for damages related to the service if the obligee can prove that the obligor's non-performance was due to actionable conduct, or that the obligor failed to disclose material characteristics of the service, of which the obligee was unaware. In addition, the obligor shall be liable to provide compensation for any damage caused to the obligee's property during performance. However, the obligor is relieved of liability if they can prove that their conduct was not actionable.

expressly imposed on them by the trust deed.[46] In such cases, under Section 6:321(3) of the Civil Code both the settlor and the beneficiary have the right to lay claim to any financial advantage the trustee has gained through the breach of their fiduciary liability, and to add such financial advantage to the trust assets.

4.5 Termination of the *ad hoc* trusteeship

The rules for termination set out in the chapter on professional trustees also apply to the termination of an *ad hoc* trust. In particular, the trustee must act in the interests of the beneficiary and the trust does not end with the death or resignation of the trustee, as set out in Section 6:326(2) and (5) of the Civil Code. The trustee must apply to the NBH for removal of the trust from the register within eight days of termination.

The *ad hoc* trustee is also required to provide an account and disburse the assets in accordance with Section 6:327 and Section 6:328 of the Civil Code. This means that the trustee must fulfil its obligation to provide information and account for the assets as before. During the settlement of accounts, the trustee must disclose all the property acquired for the purpose of or as a result of the trust, as per Section 6:279 of the Civil Code. Additionally, upon termination the settlor must exonerate the trustee from obligations assumed in dealings with third parties on the basis of the trust, and must reimburse necessary and justified expenses per Sections 6:276 and 6:279 of the Civil Code.[47] Pursuant to Section 6:328(1), (3) and (4), the *ad hoc* trustee must, upon termination of their mandate, release the trust assets to an additional or replacement trustee appointed by the settlor, or to the settlor or settlors in proportion to their original contribution.

Regarding the termination of a trustee's mandate, it is important to consider the case of termination without succession of an *ad hoc* trustee. The procedures outlined in the chapter on professional trustees apply to *ad hoc* trusts, with the exception of the provisions related to dissolution without succession under Section 46 of the Trustee Act. As a result, *ad hoc* trustees may be subject to bankruptcy or compulsory liquidation proceedings.

---

46 A disposition by the trustee with the beneficiary's consent does not result in a breach of the trustee's obligations, even if the beneficiary cannot otherwise modify the content of the trust deed. This is because the trust must be administered primarily for the benefit of the beneficiary.

47 As the Civil Code rules on mandate contracts also apply to the *ad hoc* trustee, the trustee is entitled to a lien on the assets in their possession up to the amount of their legitimate claim for costs and fees, per Section 6:277 of the Civil Code.

Beneficiaries and protectors

Gábor B Szabó
Aliant-Menyhei-Molnár-B. Szabó Law Firm

1. Beneficiaries

The beneficiary is the person who gives the trust its meaning. Whatever the settlor's original motivation and the type of trust used, the ultimate goal is always to ensure that the named beneficiary or beneficiaries – whoever they may be – benefit from the trust at the end of the day, receiving the assets at the right time and in the right way, without depreciation and preferably with a return.

Ultimately, all the features of the trust discussed in this book serve this ultimate purpose, and all other elements are subordinated to it. The beneficiaries' interest is the red line that runs through the trust from creation to termination, and in relation to which the other parties must position their own operations. The trustee's ownership of the trust assets is limited by the interests of the beneficiary, and the resolution of legal disputes between the parties and the elimination of operational disruptions can only be achieved by means that cause the least damage to the rights and interests of the beneficiary. And all this is independent of who appoints the beneficiary, because, as we shall see, it is by no means only the settlor who is entitled to do so.

These expectations of the parties to the legal relationship are by no means static, as trusts are dynamic in nature and can vary over time. For example, the beneficiary may change several times during the term of the trust and a new beneficiary may introduce new expectations into the relationship. However, the lodestar of the trust remains the interest of the beneficiary, notwithstanding the beneficiary is not in a position to exercise their rights as a contracting party.

1.1 Status of the beneficiary

(a) *Identity of beneficiary*

Two key elements of a trust deed are the identity of those who will benefit from the trust assets and the conditions under which those beneficiaries' entitlement arises and ceases. Both are typically determined by the settlor. This is treated as a general rule in the Civil Code,[1] but it is by no means a hard and fast rule. In line with international practice, the Civil Code permits the trustee to designate the beneficiary or beneficiaries where the settlor makes a decision to that effect.[2] In fact, the Civil Code does not even require the settlor to provide the trustee with guidance as to the identity of the beneficiary; to fix in advance the date of the appointment of the beneficiary; or to determine the beneficiary's share of the trust assets.

The identity of the beneficiary is connected to confidentiality concerns related to the creation of the trust. Although the scope of beneficiaries typically extends to immediate relatives (for example, spouse, descendants or ascendants), it is not uncommon to designate persons outside the circle of relatives as beneficiaries, depending on the settlor's wishes. The designation of beneficiaries is a key element in the use of trusts as an alternative to succession and will. In many cases, persons who, simply by virtue of their status, cannot be the subject of a legal succession or who, for personal, emotional or even intimate reasons, cannot be beneficiaries of a will, may be beneficiaries of the trust.

Corporate beneficiaries are common in charitable non-profit trusts. In common law jurisdictions, museums, hospitals, and welfare and educational institutions managed and run by trusts are widespread. In many cases, these institutions are created by the trust, making them trust assets rather than beneficiaries. This is typical in common law charitable trusts, where the scope of beneficiaries is undefined, or defined only in general terms, such as the general population, people who love the arts, and so on.

The settlor can define the scope of beneficiaries. In such cases, it is important that the beneficiaries are identifiable. English law uses the 'is or is not' test, which examines whether the beneficiaries of the trust assets can be clearly identified based on the criteria. In Hungarian practice, when defining groups of beneficiaries it is important to determine whether a person falls within the scope of a particular group. It is therefore important to define the group as precisely as possible when settling the trust property.

A trust can also be created by the settlor giving the trustee authority to appoint beneficiaries. This gives the trustee discretionary powers to determine the identity of the beneficiaries and their respective shares.[3] This type of trust is highly fiduciary in nature and provides the legal framework for an asset protection trust, as only the creditors of the beneficiary can claim against the trust assets. In the case of a discretionary trust, the trustee may choose not to make an asset distribution to certain beneficiaries, meaning those individuals are not yet beneficiaries. Consequently, the creditors of potential beneficiaries

---

1 Section 6:311(1) of the Civil Code. An English language version of the Civil Code of Hungary is available at: www.refworld.org/legal/legislation/natlegbod/1960/en/74370.

2 Section 6:311(3) of the Civil Code.

3 *Ibid.*

will not be able to claim against the beneficiary position or the benefits due to the beneficiary.

The tripartite nature of the trust is based not on persons but on contractual positions. The legislation therefore allows for both the settlor and the trustee to be beneficiaries. However, there is a safeguard preventing the trustee from being the sole beneficiary. This is in line with the principle that while the trustee can be a beneficiary, if they were the sole beneficiary there would be a different contractual relationship, such as a gift.

(b) *Who can be a beneficiary?*

The Civil Code does not impose restrictions on who can be a beneficiary. Accordingly, a beneficiary can be a natural person, a legal entity, an entity without legal personality or even the state or its smaller administrative units.

As regards beneficiaries, only legal capacity is relevant, capacity to act being of secondary importance. It is possible to designate an incapacitated person as a beneficiary, but exercising the beneficiary's rights must take into account the rules of legal representation due to the lack or limitation of capacity. Questions about capacity to act become particularly relevant in relation to the beneficiary at the time of asset transfer. The role of legal representative, guardian or trustee may be of particular importance in relation to the makeup of the assets to be disposed of, and whether there are associated obligations.

An intriguing question is whether a person who has not yet been born can be designated as a beneficiary. There are no specific provisions on this in the trust rules. Since the beneficiary is not a party to the contract, having legal capacity is not a prerequisite for the creation of a trust deed. While the Civil Code addresses the legal capacity of the unborn child,[4] what happens when the person designated as the beneficiary has not yet been conceived at the time the trust is created? In such cases, the trust has no legally qualified beneficiary. If such a beneficiary is subsequently conceived or born, the trust continues to operate within its contractual framework, and the beneficiary acquires their rights. If, however, the beneficiary is never born, the trustee must decide how to handle the assets already entrusted to him or her, by carefully examining the circumstances to settle them appropriately. One thing is certain: the trust can only be maintained for as long as there is a possibility of having at least one legally capable beneficiary. Once this possibility no longer exists, the trust must be terminated and the assets distributed to those entitled to them under other legal provisions, such as the settlor or, in the event of death, the beneficiary's legal heirs.

From a legal doctrine perspective, it is important to clarify that the above scenario does not fall under the Civil Code regulations in relation to the establishment of contractual effects conditional on an uncertain future event,

---

4 Sections 2:2 and 2:3 of the Civil Code.

where the contract takes effect when the condition occurs.[5] The trust deed has already entered into force and the parties have performed their obligations (ie, the settlor has transferred ownership of the trust asset and the trustee continues to fulfil their fiduciary duties). Only the legal beneficiary is missing – for the time being.

(c) *Benefits payable to the beneficiary*

The settlor may designate one or more beneficiaries. If more than one beneficiary is appointed, it must be specified:

- when and under what conditions the appointment is made;
- how long the appointment is to last; and
- to what extent trust assets are to be used to make allocations.

The settlor may determine the benefits to which the beneficiaries are entitled, typically as follows:

- beneficiaries receive equal shares of the trust assets at the same time;
- beneficiaries benefit from the trust assets at the same time but in different shares;
- beneficiaries receive the same or different proportions of the trust assets at different times or subject to different conditions;
- beneficiaries receive trust assets consecutively (eg, one beneficiary until a certain age, then another until a certain age, and so on);
- beneficiaries receive trust assets under the foregoing regime but also subject to meeting certain conditions (eg, marriage or the attainment of a degree); or
- one beneficiary receives a periodic benefit until the death of the other (eg, a child in care), then the other beneficiaries share the entire remaining assets.

Thus, the settlor has a number of options as to when, under what conditions and to what extent beneficiaries can benefit from the trust assets.

(d) *Purpose of the trust*

The trust law of the United States may seem extreme to professionals accustomed to continental legal systems, particularly as regards the person of the beneficiary. There is nothing to prevent, for example, a deceased person being named the beneficiary of a trust, even though they lack legal personality at common law, if the trust also covers the ongoing care of their place of burial.[6]

---

5 Section 6:116(1) of the Civil Code.

6 Charles E Rounds Jr and Charles E Rounds III, *Loring and Rounds: A Trustee's Handbook*, Wolters Kluwer, 2014, p282.

An even more extreme aspect of US trust law is the designating of animals, usually pets, or even inanimate objects, as beneficiaries, without any charitable intent.[7]

In Hungarian law, on the other hand, a trust can only be created if a beneficiary or a specific group of beneficiaries is designated; without this designation, a trust cannot be established. A trust cannot be created for a specific purpose under Hungarian law.

Hungarian law requires that the beneficiary of a trust be a specific person, similar to the position in common law jurisdictions. The principle that a trust cannot be created for abstract purposes is also generally applied in English law. For example, in a case where the settlor had allowed a memorial to be built for them without benefitting a particular person, the trust was held to be invalid. Similarly, a trust designating 'a nun's order' was also deemed invalid.[8] The purpose of this rule is to prevent the creation of a trust under which the trust assets are not alienable and no natural person benefits (the 'rule against inalienability'). Another important legal reason for the rule is that, in the absence of a beneficiary, there is no one to enforce the trustee's performance.

Exceptionally, a trust may be created for a specific private purpose, without specifically identifiable beneficiaries, and despite such abstractions these trusts are considered valid in court practice as there are people available to enforce the trust.[9] There are currently two such cases in English and Welsh law,[10] one relating to the care of animals[11] and the other to the maintenance of gravestones, statues and monuments.[12] Of course, these cases are not about animals and memorials in general but about specific animals and memorials, otherwise the trust would be considered charitable. The question arises, however, who will be the beneficiary in these cases, and if there is no specific beneficiary, who will enforce the trust?[13] In 1952, Judge Roxburgh concluded in

---

7 *Ibid*, p284.

8 *Leahy v Attorney-General for New South Wales* (1959) 2 WLR 722.

9 In *Re Denley's Trust Deed* (1969) 1 Ch 373, the purpose of the trust was the development of a sporting estate, Judge Goff concluding that although the trust was created for a specific purpose, it was indirectly and directly for the benefit of specific people. See Thomas Glyn Watkin, "Changing Concepts of Ownership in English Law During the Nineteenth and Twentieth Centuries", in Martin Dixon and Gerwyn LLH Griffiths (ed), *Contemporary Perspectives on Property, Equity and Trusts Law*, Oxford University Press, 2007, p154; and PJ Millett, "Equity's Place in the Law of Commerce", *The Law Quarterly Review*, 1998, p114. Cf Grant MR: "[T]here must be somebody in whose favour the court can decree performance", *Morice v Bishop of Durham* (1804) 9 Ves 399 at 405. See also David Hayton (ed), *British Legal Developments in the 21st Century*, Hart Publishing, 2000, p443.

10 Originally there were five of these, but over time trusts for funerals have been classified as charitable trusts, trusts for the benefit of unincorporated associations as trusts for the benefit of the association's members, and trusts for miscellaneous purposes as discretionary trusts. See Thomas Glyn Watkin, *Changing Concepts, ibid*, p817.

11 As early as 1842, in *Pettingal v Pettingal* (1842) 11 LJ Ch 176, such a private purpose trust was held to be valid, and was upheld by Judge North in *Re Dean* (1889) 41 Ch D 552. In the latter case, the testator had transferred his property to the trustee by requiring him to pay an annual fee for the care of his horses and dogs.

12 A trust for the maintenance of gravestones was first recognised as valid in 1856 in *Trimmer v Danby* (1856) 25 LJ Ch 424. This was followed by other cases such as *Musset v Bingle* (1876) WN 170, *Pirbright v Salwey* (1896) WN 86 and *Re Hooper* (1932) 1 Ch 38.

his judgment that private purpose trusts were "anomalous and exceptional" and should be regarded as a "concession to human weakness and sentiment". He concluded: "A court of equity does not recognize as valid a trust which it cannot both enforce and control. This seems to me to be good equity and good sense."[14] The Court of Appeal Master of the Rolls, Lord Evershed, came to the same conclusion, as did Judge Harman, who described the trust for the benefit of animals and tombs as "troublesome, anomalous and aberrant" and called for a reconsideration of its validity.[15]

In English law, therefore, only in exceptional cases will a purpose trust be accepted by the courts.[16] Another key requirement for a trust is that there must be someone who can enforce it. In addition, the trust must be established for a legitimate purpose and not for a futile or whimsical purpose.[17] An extreme case of the private purpose trust is found in Jersey, Bahamas and Cayman Islands law, among others, often referred to in the literature as 'hypermodern trusts'.[18] Other countries have also made attempts to provide statutory recognition for purpose trusts.[19]

In English law the concept of a charitable trust is recognised, where the beneficiary cannot be a specific person. This form of trust has been allowed for four purposes:

- poverty alleviation;
- the advancement of education;
- the advancement of religion; and
- other purposes beneficial to society (for example, public health provision).[20]

---

13 Alec R Anderson, "The Statutory Non-Charitable Purpose Trust: Estate Planning in the Tax Havens", in Donovan WM Waters (ed), *Equity, Fiduciaries and Trusts*, Thomson Canada Limited, 1993, p100.

14 *Re Astor's Settlement Trusts* (1952) Ch 534. Cited in Thomas Glyn Watkin, Thomas Glyn, *supra*, p150.

15 *Re Endecott* (1960) Ch 232. Cited in Thomas Glyn Watkin, *ibid*, p817.

16 Anderson criticises this, saying that there are many cases where we cannot speak of a trust serving the purposes of society as a whole, but where a community or part of a community benefits from the trust. On the other hand, in such a case the settlor is in a much better position to describe the purpose for which the assets are to be used than if he were to name only a beneficiary. See Alec R Anderson, "The Statutory Non-Charitable Purpose Trust", *supra*, p821.

17 An example of a whimsical purpose is the trust set up to lock up all the apartments in a house for twenty years so that four of them could be used exclusively by the landlord and his wife. *Brown v Burdett* (1882) 21 ChD 667. It has also been held that a trust for the erection of statues and artistic towers (*M'Caig v University of Glasgow* 1907 SC 231) and a trust for the erection of eleven bronze statues in memory of family members (*M'Caig's Trustees v Kirk-Session of United Free Church of Lismore* 1915 SC 426) were both whimsical and therefore invalid. See Paul Lásd Baxendale-Walker, *Purpose Trust*, Butterworths, 1999, p237.

18 "New-fangled kinds of trust": Paul Matthews, "The Comparative Importance of the Rule in *Saunders v Vautier*", *The Law Quarterly Review*, Vol 122, 2006, p266.

19 On the Canadian initiative, see Karen A Beauchamp, "Law Reform in Canada: The Proposed Introduction of the Non-Charitable Purpose Trust into Canada", in Donovan WM Waters (ed), *Equity, Fiduciaries and Trusts*, *supra*, p111.

20 The four objectives are based on the decision of Lord Justice MacNaghten in the House of Lords in *Commissioners for Special Income Tax v Pemsel* (1891) AC 531. Lord MacNaghten based his choice of purposes on those listed in the preamble to the Statute of Charitable Uses. These purposes have now been extended under the Charities Act 2006. See Thomas Glyn Watkin, *supra*, p817.

The Charities Act 2011 now lists a total of 13 purposes that can be included in the fourth category, building on previous case law.[21] The public interest, in which area the Attorney General is empowered to act, is therefore a defining element of the charitable trust. Hungarian legislation has not allowed for the creation of a trust with an express public interest purpose, on the basis that the institution of the foundation is available for the same purpose.

1.2 Beneficiaries' multiple contractual position

(a) *The 'beneficiary-settlor'*

The typical case of a 'beneficiary-settlor' coincidence occurs between professions with higher exposure to unlimited or increased liability for their activities (lawyers, doctors in private practice, and so on) or for entrepreneurs who wish to earmark some of their assets for an activity involving a higher risk, or to protect them from that risk.

(b) *The 'beneficiary-trustee'*

The combination of 'beneficiary-trustee' presents an intriguing issue. The Civil Code does not exclude this combination, only specifying that "the appointment of the trustee as sole beneficiary is void".[22] That is, a trustee can be a beneficiary of a trust but not the sole beneficiary. However, it is clear that this possibility – particularly in light of the trustee's right to designate themselves as beneficiary where appropriate – could potentially lead to trustee abuse. It is therefore advisable to preclude this situation by a carefully considered and drafted trust deed.

The question arises as to why the Civil Code allows for this possibility. It should be noted that the trustee's claim for fees and expenses does not confer beneficiary status, even though, under the Civil Code, the claim may be satisfied from the assets under administration. What circumstances, then, could justify the trustee being a beneficiary of the trust at all? For the time being, we can only answer this question on the basis of foreign practice and experience.

In other jurisdictions, one of the most common applications of the trust is the family trust, specifically, a trust created for family assets or a specific group of family assets. It is not at all uncommon for family trusts to combine settlor, trustee and beneficiary in one person. In this case, the owner or owners – typically the head of the family or the spouses – place the family assets in trust

---

21 These include the development of health and life-saving, the development of community life, the development of art, culture, heritage and science, the development of amateur sport, the development of human rights, the development of environmental protection, the protection of the disadvantaged, the protection of animals, support for the Crown's armed forces, assistance to the police, fire and rescue services, and all the objectives already accepted in case law. Charities Act 2011, Section 3(4).

22 Section 6:311(4) of the Civil Code.

by designating themselves or one of their number as trustee and, typically alongside their children, designating themselves as beneficiaries, perhaps because they want to share in the income from the assets during their lifetime. This creates a separately administered sub-trust which will no longer, for example, form part of the settlor's estate. The death of the settlor-trustee-beneficiary does not disrupt the trust, which can continue without interruption. In the event of the death of a single trustee, the person entitled to appoint a new trustee (for example, the protector), and in the case of multiple trustees, the surviving trustee, will continue to administer the estate. Obviously, the risk of a trustee-beneficiary as described above is not present in this scenario.

Thus, the only restriction under Hungarian law is that the trustee cannot be a sole beneficiary, and this is a relatively easy condition to meet. The big question, however, is what happens when two trustees have been appointed and they are the only two beneficiaries? Does this situation not conflict with the prohibition under the Civil Code? In our opinion, it could very easily collide with it; however, a definitive answer to the question can only be given after examining all the circumstances of the specific case. It is relatively easy for a situation to arise where the two beneficiary-trustees are not objectively in a position to abuse this dual position.

(c) The 'beneficiary-protector'

The 'beneficiary-protector' combination is also an interesting one. The protector is discussed below, in section 2, so for now we will note only that, while the combination carries considerably less risk than that of 'beneficiary-trustee', framing the trust deed with care can prevent unpleasant surprises.

It is not objectionable in principle for the settlor to reward the protector's time-consuming and responsible fiduciary work by designating them as a beneficiary of part of the trust assets. However, designating the protector as the sole beneficiary would be as contrary to the purpose and characteristics of the trust, as it would be in the case of a trustee. However, a contractual provision to that effect, unlike the exclusive designation of the trustee as a beneficiary, would not be null and void under the dispositive regime of the Civil Code.

1.3 Legal status of the beneficiary

The beneficiary's ability to enforce their rights depends on their awareness of the existence of the trust deed and their status as beneficiary. For various reasons, the settlor may prohibit the premature disclosure of this information to the beneficiary, and may even prevent the trustee from identifying themselves to the beneficiary during asset distribution. If the beneficiary is unaware of their position, the only means of enforcement open to them is through the asset distribution. Of course, there is nothing in principle to prevent the settlor from imposing in the trust deed certain fiduciary obligations in favour of the beneficiary (for example, sending an annual report on the status of the assets under management), but in practice this is rarely done. The beneficiary therefore typically gains enforceable rights at the time of asset distribution. In this context, it is an important requirement that the beneficiary can only claim the release of the assets under management and their benefits from the trustee according to the contract. The beneficiary's creditors can claim these assets from the moment the release of the assets or their benefits become due to the beneficiary.

In cases where the beneficiary is aware of their position, they can monitor the activities of the trustee in the management of the trust, with the costs incurred borne by the beneficiary. However, despite this oversight the beneficiary, like the settlor, cannot instruct the trustee.

(a) The relationship between multiple beneficiaries

The beneficiary is often not one specific person, but several individuals or a well-defined group of individuals. The relationship between them is primarily determined by the trust deed between the settlor and the trustee.

The various individuals may be specifically named, but the Civil Code also allows beneficiaries to be identified by reference to a "circle of beneficiaries".[23] In this case it is not necessary to designate the beneficiaries by name; it is sufficient merely to refer to the 'circle' that binds them together in some cohesive sense. The Civil Code gives no guidance as to how strong this cohesive force must be; that is, weak cohesion between individuals does not exclude them from constituting a circle of beneficiaries.

The scope of beneficiaries can therefore be very broad, and the broader the scope, the greater the likelihood that the beneficiaries will change significantly (the scope narrowing or even expanding) between the creation of the trust and the transfer of assets. It is therefore recommended that the position of the beneficiaries in relation to the trust assets and their distribution be covered in as much detail as possible in the trust deed. It is advisable to stipulate at least the following:

- which elements of the assets each beneficiary may receive, and in what proportion to the total;
- the relative timing of the transfer of assets to the beneficiaries – simultaneously, consecutively according to some temporal sequence, or linked to the occurrence of some event; and
- the applicability of internal or external successions between beneficiaries at the time of the transfer of the assets.

23 Section 6:311(1) of the Civil Code.

The relationship between multiple beneficiaries as to asset distribution should, then, be defined primarily in the trust deed. However, the Civil Code also allows the transfer of trust assets from one beneficiary to another on the occurrence of a specified condition or after a given lapse of time.[24] Assets may, under the same section of the Civil Code, be transferred not only to another beneficiary but also to the beneficiary's successors in title. A typical scenario might be the death of a beneficiary before the asset distribution. However, the narrow possibility of post-inheritance in the event of the death of a beneficiary must also be taken into account.[25] As a general rule, the Civil Code prohibits post-inheritance,[26] but still allows it for spouses and life partners, as well as in cases where the primary heir is unable to make a valid will (*substitutio pupillaris*) due to age or other reasons.

The question arises as to how multiple beneficiaries can exercise their rights under the Civil Code beyond asset distribution. The Civil Code provides an explicit answer in one instance: where beneficiaries jointly exercise their right "on the application of any of them" to request the court to terminate the trustee's mandate and appoint a new trustee.[27] At first reading, this seems contradictory, but the same section states that "the court may not appoint as trustee a person to whom all the beneficiaries object". This underscores the need for joint action by the beneficiaries, at least in this particular scenario. However, it is uncertain whether joint action is required in the exercise of other rights. Is the trustee obliged to comply separately and individually with the requests of several beneficiaries for control, accounting and disbursement of assets? In the absence of a statutory provision in this regard, the reasonableness of the circumstances of the case must be relied upon.

(b) Relationship between the beneficiaries and other actors in the trust

Although the beneficiary is not bound by a contractual obligation to any of the actors, the Civil Code nevertheless imposes on them a number of obligations within the legal relationship.

Relationship between settlor and beneficiary: There is no actual legal relationship between the settlor and the beneficiary. However, settlor declarations made at the time of the creation of the trust may impose a quasi-obligation on the beneficiary by making the release of assets conditional on something to be achieved by the beneficiary (for example, obtaining a degree or getting married). Presentation of the result provides the beneficiary with a legal basis for claiming the disbursement of the assets.

---

24 Section 6:311(2) of the Civil Code.

25 The institution of post-inheritance and substitution *in fidei comissum* was a legal institution in our private law before the Second World War.

26 Section 7:28 of the Civil Code.

27 Section 6:325(3) of the Civil Code.

If the settlor is also a beneficiary, the capacity in which they act in relation to their individual rights must be examined. The beneficiary's relationship with the settlor can best be described by their rights as to information and proposal. They can communicate to the settlor their comments and suggestions on the administration of the assets, but cannot assert any claims against the settlor.

Relationship between trustee and beneficiary: The beneficiary has the right to legally enforce the trustee's obligations. The question in this context is what rights the beneficiary may exercise against a debtor in the case of contracts for the benefit of third parties. The beneficiary has the right to the release of the assets held in trust and their benefits; to information; and to remuneration and reimbursement of expenses by the trustee. The beneficiary, like the settlor, does not have the right to instruct the trustee.

The beneficiary therefore has the right to enforce the trustee's performance of their obligations by legal action, even if there is no contractual relationship between them. The Civil Code, however, as indicated above, bridges this 'gap' by imposing an obligation on the trustee to satisfy the beneficiary's rights to control, information, accountability, disbursement of assets and protection against creditors. The beneficiary, on the other hand, should be aware that, like the settlor, exercising certain of these rights may incur costs for the trustee. Like a settlor, the beneficiary does not have the right to reject the trustee or – unlike a settlor – to recall the trustee.

Relationship between beneficiary and protector: While there is no formal relationship between them, a balanced relationship between the beneficiary and the protector is perhaps the greatest guarantee of the stability of the trust. A harmonious relationship will positively affect the trustee's effectiveness, whereas tensions between them may result in the trustee becoming uncooperative, or 'closed'.

The beneficiary, not being a contracting partner of the protector, cannot instruct the protector. Their relationship can best be described as one of consultation and advisory rights. The beneficiary informs the protector of their position on the administration of the assets and may request the protector's intervention, either at the settlor's or the trustee's direction. However, the protector is under no obligation to act on such requests and has discretion as to how to deal with them.

The relationship between beneficiaries and their creditors: The creditors of the beneficiary have a clear right of action against the trustee, as if he or she were the beneficiary. They have a right of satisfaction, up to the amount of their claim, out of the trust asset and its benefits. However, this right of satisfaction arises only on the release of the assets and their benefits to the beneficiary.[28] The settlor alone can determine the date of the release of the assets. This right of disposition may be vested in the settlor not only at the creation of the trust, but also at a later date by amendment of the trust deed.

However, the trustee can also influence the satisfaction of a creditor's claim against the beneficiary if the settlor has given the trustee discretionary power, allowing them to decide all trust matters, including the date of the release of assets to the beneficiary. Since in such a case the beneficiary's claim is uncertain and indeterminate, the position of their creditor will be similarly weak.

It may be difficult to determine the claim of the beneficiary's creditors to the trust assets if the trustee is given discretionary rights to manage the assets, as in this case too the beneficiary's claim is uncertain and indeterminate.

The questions arise as to the depth of the information to which the beneficiary's creditor is entitled under the trust deed in order to enforce their rights effectively, and to whom this request can be addressed. While the creditor can approach the beneficiary, the beneficiary, not being a contracting party, will in most cases not be able to provide relevant information even if they wish to, due to lack of awareness of the trust deed, especially given common settlor clauses. The creditor may, of course, approach the trustee, but the trustee is expressly bound by their statutory duty of confidentiality. If the trustee breaches this obligation, they will be liable for damages.

A creditor might hope to succeed by going to court and naming the trustee as a defendant, claiming that the trustee's discretionary power is being used to avoid having to release the assets to the debtor-beneficiary. However, in the absence of concrete case law, such an action would be speculative, probatively challenging and unlikely to succeed. It would require the court to disregard the legal basis and purpose of the trust, that is, that the trustee, especially in a discretionary trust, cannot be motivated by any other considerations than compliance with the law and the settlor's contractual will.

Relationship between the beneficiary and other creditors: The creditors of the other two main actors in the trust, the settlor and the trustee, do not pose a risk to the release of trust assets and thus to the beneficiary, because these creditors cannot enforce their claims against the trust assets.

Beneficiary's claim for compensation from trust assets: The beneficiary has the same right of action as the settlor against third parties to whom the trustee has made a gratuitous or bad faith grant in breach of the trust deed. The rules in this regard are essentially in line with common principles of English law.

---

28 Section 6:314(2) of the Civil Code.

Transferability, succession: The general rules on the law of obligations in the Civil Code apply to the transfer of rights to the beneficiary. We consider that the rules on the assignment of contracts do not apply to the beneficiary of the trust as the beneficiary is not a party to the contract. Under the rule regarding a contract for the benefit of a third party, the beneficiary is only entitled to claim the release of the assets from the trustee when they fall due. However, unlike under that rule, this right does not arise from the time either party has notified the other that a contract for their benefit has been concluded, but only from the time of the asset distribution as set out in the trust deed.[29] From that date, we consider that the beneficiary has the right to assign the claim in favour of a third party. Nevertheless, the asset distribution, with all its tax consequences, can only be made for the benefit of the beneficiary – that is, the trustee is only accountable to the beneficiary and not to the assignee. Of course, during the asset distribution process the actual settlement (eg, transfer of money) can be made directly to the assignee, with the appropriate assignment title indicated. While the settlor may exclude assignments in the trust deed, this will be ineffective *vis-à-vis* third parties.[30]

A trust does not terminate on the death or dissolution of the beneficiary, unless the settlor was the sole beneficiary.[31] If the beneficiary dies intestate or ceases to exist, the trustee cannot transfer the trust assets to anyone other than the settlor, and only upon termination of the trust.[32] In our view, during the interim period, the settlor has the option of appointing a new beneficiary by amending the trust deed. To avoid disruption due to the death of a beneficiary, it is advisable to appoint an additional beneficiary at the time the trust is created. In the absence of an additional beneficiary, the rules on succession or inheritance will apply in the event of the death of the beneficiary or their termination.

1.4 Rights and obligations of the beneficiary

Although the trust is based on the trinity of settlor, trustee and beneficiary, the beneficiary is not a party to the trust, since the trust contract is concluded between the settlor and the trustee. This remains the case even if the beneficiary holds another contractual position within the legal relationship, such as being a settlor, a trustee or both, in addition to their position as beneficiary. In these cases, the contractual rights and obligations are distinct from those of the non-contractual beneficiary.

This does not mean that asset distribution from a trust to a beneficiary is equivalent to performance of a contract for the benefit of a third party.[33] In the

29 Section 6:136(2) of the Civil Code.
30 Section 6:195(1) of the Civil Code.
31 Sections 6:326(5) and 6:326(1)(d) of the Civil Code.
32 Section 6:328(1) of the Civil Code.
33 Section 6:136 of the Civil Code.

latter case, the third party may claim performance of the service contracted for as soon as they are notified of a contract concluded for their benefit. In contrast, under a trust, the beneficiary's right to claim performance typically arises only on the occurrence of some future date or event specified in the trust deed. The beneficiary's obligations in relation to the trust are therefore established not by the trust deed but by law, specifically the Civil Code.[34] These obligations primarily position the beneficiary *vis-à-vis* the trustee, essentially affording them a guarantee.

With regard to the beneficiary's powers, it is recommended to start from the premise that their identity is the most important limitation on the trustee's exercise of ownership rights. Indeed, the trustee may only exercise their property rights, derived from the settlor, for the benefit of the beneficiary. Any deviation from this rule is contrary to the purpose of the trust and as such may constitute a serious breach of contract. Consequently, the Civil Code has conferred on the beneficiary rights identical to those of the settlor, but without specifying precisely when and by whom these rights may be exercised. The ambiguity leaves room for regulation in the trust deed and ultimately for future case law to provide clarification. The rights in question are as follows:

- right of control;
- right of access;
- right of withdrawal;
- right to compensation;
- right to claim the surrender of property; and
- right of defence against foreign creditors.

The beneficiary does not have the right to recall the trustee and appoint a new one, but can apply to the court in the event of the death or dissolution of the settlor and serious breach of contract by the trustee.[35] Additionally, since the beneficiary is not a party to the trust deed, they cannot initiate modifications to the contract or terminate it in the event of poor administration of the trust. Instead, they can only make such proposals to the settlor or protector.

The Civil Code also prohibits the beneficiary from giving instructions to the trustee, like the restrictions placed on the settlor.[36] The beneficiary cannot therefore take over the role of master during the settlor's lifetime, nor automatically replace the settlor after their death or dissolution. The beneficiary can only enforce their objections against the trustee in court.

These legal limitations on the beneficiary must be taken into account when framing the trust deed.

34 Section 6:2(3) of the Civil Code.
35 Section 6:325(2) of the Civil Code.
36 Section 6:316 of the Civil Code.

1.5 Right to dispose of the assets under management

An important provision of the trust contract is that the beneficiary can claim release of trust assets and their benefits. The creditors of the beneficiary may claim the assets of the beneficiary from the time the release of those assets or their benefits to the beneficiary becomes due.

1.6 Right of control

The beneficiary has the right to monitor the trustee's activities, the costs of doing so being borne by the beneficiary. However, the beneficiary cannot instruct the trustee.

2. Protectors

The role of the protector is not directly referred to in current Hungarian law. Instead, the role is indirectly regulated by the Civil Code. Despite this, the use of protectors has spread rapidly because they give considerable stability to the fiduciary relationship.

A 2017 amendment to the Civil Code allows the settlor to appoint, by contract, a person to exercise the settlor's rights and obligations upon their death. Although professional opinion is divided as to whether this amendment implicitly refers to the protector (the Civil Code still does not use this term or even a related term) or whether it was intended to create a kind of 'supplementary settlor' to enhance the long-term stability of trust administration, it is clear that the amendment introduced elements of protector functions into domestic law. Regardless, the institution of the protector, whether or not mentioned in the Civil Code, could quickly become established in Hungarian trust practice due to the dispositive nature of the Civil Code. We are of the opinion that this amendment to the Civil Code explicitly refers to the role of the protector.

Due to the lack of legal regulation, there is no proper Hungarian term for 'protector'. Despite its well-established use, the foreign-sounding term 'protector' is considered unacceptable in a domestic legal context.

The question arises as to how an actor not regulated by the fiduciary provisions of the Civil Code can play the stabilising role mentioned and enhance the effectiveness of the fiduciary relationship. There follows a summary of the various international regulatory techniques applicable to the protector, including the concept itself, the status of the protector, their relationship with other parties in the relationship, and their rights and obligations.

2.1 International rules for protectors

Regulatory approaches for protectors are grouped according to Ulmann's classification along three main lines:[37]

---

37 Kristóf Ulmann, "The legal institution of the protector", *Lawyers' Journal*, Vol 4, 2017.

- regulation based on case law;
- formal written legislation; and
- full regulation.

(a) ***Regulation based on case law***

This category applies to countries where the legal institution of the protector is not explicitly regulated by law but is still governed by general principles of equity,[38] and according to common law. The countries include England, Bermuda, Cayman Islands, Guernsey, Isle of Man and Hong Kong.

(b) ***Formal written legislation***

This category includes countries where laws address the role of the protector, but the institution itself – as in Hungary – is not explicitly named. These laws allow for the trustee to exercise certain powers only with the approval of a specific person, provided this is stipulated in the trust document. Jersey is a typical example.

(c) ***Full regulation***

This category includes financial centres such as the Bahamas and the British Virgin Islands, and some smaller ones such as Labuan, Anguilla, Belize and the Cook Islands, which have no comprehensive legislation on protectors and their status, rights and obligations.

It is evident that countries with a traditional trust culture use various regulatory approaches, but all of them recognise and regulate the role of protector. As will be seen below, in our domestic context, 'permissive silence' best describes the current approach to regulation and non-regulation. This has its disadvantages, but also undoubted advantages. The greatest benefit is that by the time the issue comes to the legislature's attention, the institution of the protector will be well defined and informed by a wealth of practical experience.

2.2 The concept of protector

A protector is a person who, acting on behalf of the settlor, exercises the settlor's rights or a specified range of rights to ensure that the trust's objectives are

---

38 Equity is the third pillar of English law, alongside common law and statute law, which from the 12th and 13th centuries onwards was developed by the royal chancery court to compensate for the rigidity and injustice of the other two pillars. It is equity that brings justice based on practical experience and common sense into a world of law that is strict and intolerant of exceptions.

In the work Ulmann cites, he draws on these principles as a bundle. Although no English jurist has yet dared to undertake a taxonomic list, they include principles, mostly developed by life experience, such as the following:

- Equity will not suffer a wrong to be without a remedy.
- Equity follows the law, but not always slavishly.
- He who comes to equity must come with clean hands.
- Equity looks to the intent rather than the form.
- Equity will not assist a volunteer.

achieved. The protector accomplishes this by overseeing the trustee's activities and exercising additional powers to ensure compliance with the trust deed or declaration. Their appointment is not a mandatory requirement of a valid trust deed and is solely at the discretion of the settlor.

In US trust literature, the protector is more succinctly described as "a party who has overriding discretionary powers with respect to the trust but who is not a trustee".[39] The English common law and offshore jurisdictions' understanding of a protector is better described as follows:

> *[N]on-judicial third-party oversight of the trustee's activities is often effected through an express appointment in the governing instrument of a trust protector.*[40]

However, despite these confident definitions, the practice is far from clear. The duties of the protector are not precisely or even generally defined, which is why one of the definitive American handbooks of the trust profession makes the following observation:

> *Because of scope of trust protector's duties tends to fall somewhere between the nonexistent or limited scope of duties of the holder of a special power of appointment and the broad scope of duties of a full-fledged trustee, extreme caution should be exercised by anyone contemplating serving as a trustee or a trust protector of a trust that provides for both offices if that trust is to be subject to the jurisdiction of a state of the United States.*[41]

The critical language suggests that the protector's authority is not generally defined by state law, although Alaska, for example, is cited as a refreshing exception,[42] and thus the functional distinctions between protector and trustee are often blurred.

An example of the protector's 'overriding power' is the role of 'enforcer' in some common law jurisdictions, who not only oversees the trustee's operations but can compel the trustee to take certain actions when necessary. The Alaskan example cited above is one such case. However, this presupposes that the trustee can be instructed, which would be entirely contrary to Hungarian trust law, since it would violate one of the core principles: the prohibition against instructing the trustee.

---

39 Charles E Rounds Jr and Charles E Rounds III, *Loring and Rounds: A Trustee's Handbook, supra*, p26, quoting Alexander A Bove Jr.

40 *Ibid*, p26.

41 *Ibid*, p26.

42 *Ibid*, p26. Alaska law gives the protector very broad dispositive powers. Among other things, they have the power to recall the trustee and appoint a new one, to amend or supplement the trust instrument to obtain a more favourable tax status (!), and to reduce or increase the share of each beneficiary.

2.3 Status of the protector

(a) *Who can be a protector?*

In principle, the protector can be any of the same entities as the settlor and the beneficiary, that is, a natural or legal person, a non-legal entity, a body with civil legal personality conferred by law, and the state. In practice, however, for *ad hoc* trusts, individuals with a close relationship of trust with the settlor, such as relatives or friends, are often chosen as protectors. For professional trusts, where asset management requires a higher level of expertise and coordination, professionals such as lawyers, accountants, investment or financial specialists and their companies are more likely to be appointed.

The legal position of the protector within the trust is identical to that of the beneficiary in that the protector is not a contracting party with the trustees, but the obligations related to the protector's role ensure they are included in the trust. Unlike the passive role of the beneficiary, the protector has a more active role, involving control and mediation role in the settlor–trustee relationship.

(b) *The protector's relationship with other parties in the trust*

The status of the protector can be understood by comparing their position with that of the other actors in the trust.

Relationship with the settlor: Only the settlor may appoint a protector. Without the settlor's intention to do so, the protector cannot exist. The settlor's intention to appoint a protector can take several forms, depending on whether the intention is meant to apply during the settlor's lifetime or after their death; whether the intention is total or partial; and whether the intention can be modified later:

- *Protector for life or after death:* The most common way to appoint a protector is for the settlor to appoint a third party through a contract separate to the trust deed. This relationship is governed by the rules of the Civil Code on the contract of appointment. One of the pillars of the fiduciary relationship is the right to instruct the trustee. However, this right has a significant limitation compared to the Civil Code rules on trusts: it cannot involve delegating instructions to the trustee.

  A trust contract thus created terminates on the death of the settlor-principal, a critical time for the trust, rendering the protector's claim less effective.

  Efficiency can be increased by using delegation instead of a trust,[43] that is, by contractually transferring to the protector the rights he or she has under the trust deed. In this case, the protector's status is not

---

43 Section 6:202 of the Civil Code.

affected by the death of the settlor, since the protector can exercise the settlor's powers after their death. The rules on assignment apply *mutatis mutandis* to the transfer. However, the transfer of rights remains independent of the trust deed and, like a power of attorney, can be effected by a separate contract between the settlor and the protector.

An important rule for the transfer of rights is that, if the existence of the right is attested by a public register, a change in the right holder, that is, the settlor, must also be recorded. Typically, this is done at the Companies Register, where the settlor's identity must be notified in accordance with company procedure rules. However, the question may arise whether, in the case of an *ad hoc* trust, the identity of the settlor (changed following the transfer of rights) must be notified to the National Bank of Hungary (NBH), which registers trust deeds. Our view is that since the Civil Code refers to a 'public' register and the register kept by the NBH cannot be considered public, the obligation to notify is not applicable.

The 2017 amendment to the Civil Code[44] allowed for the creation of a direct protector in the event of the death or dissolution of the settlor by permitting the settlor to designate in the trust deed a person entitled to exercise the rights and obligations of the settlor.

- *Full protector or protector light:* Regardless of which protector appointment approach a settlor chooses, the extent of the protector's authorisation requires further decision making. The protector's powers may be limited compared to those of the settlor, or they may be comprehensive. The Civil Code accommodates these variations, providing rules for both delegation and direct appointment.
- *Recallable or permanent protector:* When a protector is appointed based on a mandate, there is no doubt as to their recallability. However, in the case of a transfer of rights, the settlor must give more careful consideration to the implications, since the only ways to recover the settlor's rights are to unilaterally terminate the contract containing the transfer, or terminate it by mutual agreement. In the case of a direct appointment of a protector on the settlor's death, the question of revocability does not apply.

The relationship between settlor and protector is inherently more trust-based than between settlor and trustee, for the simple reason that the protector's role is not extensively regulated by law. Although this fiduciary relationship can be formalised by one of the means outlined above, the fiduciary element will always be central to the relationship between the settlor and the protector, due to the nature of their interaction.

44 Section 6:325(4) of the Civil Code.

Relationship with the beneficiary: The relationship between the protector and the beneficiary is unique and not governed by civil law. Within the relationship, the protector must be able to leverage their interpersonal skills – it is where their stabilising role will be most apparent, despite the absence of a civil law relationship.

The starting point is that perfectly satisfied beneficiaries are as rare as white ravens. Almost invariably, beneficiaries feel the need to exert some influence over the trust, and this need increases significantly with the death of the settlor. However, a professional protector with the right life experience can mitigate this by helping the typically lay beneficiary understand the purpose of the trust, the original reasons for its creation and its long-term benefits.

The question arises whether the beneficiary is also entitled to appoint a protector. In our opinion, the beneficiary is not entitled to do so, since they are not a party to the trust deed, despite having certain rights in relation to it under the Civil Code. These rights do not extend to appointing a protector. However, the trust deed itself can confer this power on the beneficiary. For example, the beneficiary might be given the power under the trust deed to appoint a protector in the event of the death of the settlor. However, the protector must still act in accordance with the trust deed and not primarily in the interests of the beneficiary, since the protector, like the trustee, serves within the framework of the trust deed and the law.

Relationship with the trustee: In practice, especially in more complex trust matters, the protector and not the settlor maintains day-to-day contact with the trustee. As the protector's role and powers are determined by the settlor, the trustee must accommodate the protector's involvement. In most cases the trustee and the protector will work together harmoniously, the protector providing assistance and advice as they will have more intimate knowledge of the settlor and their family.

The Civil Code only explicitly prohibits the trustee taking instructions from the settlor and beneficiary,[45] but not from the protector, and it is tempting to interpret this absence as permission for the protector to instruct the trustee. Yet we believe that this interpretation is misplaced. The existence and authority of the protector are based solely on the settlor's decision. It would be unacceptable, perhaps even an abuse of law, for a settlor to create a protector merely to circumvent the prohibition on instructing the trustee. This prohibition is a fundamental and integral pillar of the trust, the disruption of which would jeopardise the integrity of the legal institution.

The protector's role is to monitor the trustee's activities in accordance with the criteria and guidelines in the trust deed, to make comments, objections and

45 Section 6:316 of the Civil Code.

suggestions and to discuss them with the settlor. If the trustee does not accept the protector's input or fails to adjust the administration of the trust accordingly, the protector should communicate their proposals for amendment of the trust contract or recall of the trustee to the settlor, who will then act at their discretion.

A harmonious relationship between trustee and protector is central to the success of the trust. It is important that the protector is not just the eyes, ears and voice of the settlor, but an expert focused on solving operational problems and creatively removing obstacles.

(c) *The protector's multiple positions*

The combination of roles involving the protector should be considered carefully due to the legal implications:

- The coincidence of protector–settlor is legally meaningless, since it would imply a self-contract of the settlor, which is not permissible.
- The coincidence of protector–beneficiary requires the settlor's explicit decision, documented in the trust deed, since the trustee's involvement is necessary for the beneficiary to exercise their powers, such as in connection with asset disposition. A typical case might be where the settlor wishes to reward the protector's efforts through benefits from the trust assets.
- The protector–trustee coincidence is conceptually excluded in trust law.

(d) *Additional protector, protectors' committee*

Significant assets or complex settlor tasks may justify assigning the protector's tasks to multiple individuals with diverse expertise, or even to a board, committee or investment committee. The added perspective of an extra pair of eyes may reduce the risk of error and miscalculation by the settlor, countering any concern that too many cooks spoil the broth. Multiple protectors hold no more power than one – organisational details and procedural protocol will not give them extra powers over the trustee. Nevertheless, organisation, division of areas of expertise, cases, tasks and powers between them is useful and desirable for efficient working.

In practice, it is always desirable to have a representative of the trustee at protectors' committee meetings. These meetings can be a regular and organised forum where the trustee can give an oral account of their activities, justify and, if necessary, defend their actions. Of course, to function efficiently the committee should not merely focus on the input side in the form of reports from the trustee, but should actively manage the output side and contribute with substantive information and proposals to the most effective asset management possible, keeping the trustee and settlor informed as to the progress and status of the trust.

2.4 Rights and obligations of the protector

The protector's rights and obligations have been discussed above, but some important issues need to be addressed for a more complete understanding.

The existence of the protector can be inferred from the control powers held by the settlor (and the beneficiary).[46] This means that in the Hungarian context, the protector is likely to play a primary role in the mechanism of the trust. However, control is only one of the protector's possible roles within the trust. The right of control may serve as a guide in determining the protector's status, but it is not sufficient on its own. We must start from the dispositive nature of the legal relationship, meaning the settlor can in principle confer on the protector any broad powers within the rights available to them.

Generally, a settlor cannot validly confer on a protector powers that are not theirs by law. This raises the question of whether the protector can exercise all the rights of the settlor. The answer is far from clear, given the lack of statutory regulation of the protector's position. As the Civil Code does not regulate the protector, their role is governed by the trust deed to be created between the settlor and the protector, the trust deed between the settlor and the trustee, the provisions of the Civil Code relating to trustees and the general provisions of the Civil Code's Book of Obligations. Their duties and powers under the Civil Code must be set out in detail in these two instruments, failing which the protector's role, far from increasing the stability of the legal relationship, could create instability. If the contract does not set out the duties and powers of the protector, merely providing for their appointment, the protector will not be able to carry out their duties effectively, eventually leading to tensions between the protector and the trustee, as well as between other parties to the trust.

In addition to the control powers already mentioned, the protector may have the right to demand accountability and disbursement of assets, subject to appropriate contractual authorisation. In this respect, the protector must in practice act as analysed in the sections elsewhere on the settlor and the beneficiary.

The details of the protector's duties should be set out in the trust deed to be concluded with the settlor, including the powers granted to the protector. The trust deed should specify the protector's powers, the services that they are to provide, and their remuneration. The latter is particularly important for expert supervision in long-term or more complex fiduciary relationships. In such cases, the protector's remuneration and/or reimbursement of expenses should be taken into account by the settlor, similar to how they would be for the trustee.

The protector's remuneration can be agreed between the settlor and the protector in the trust deed. Their fees and expenses can be reimbursed directly

46 Section 6:315 of the Civil Code.

by the settlor from sources outside the trust, or from the trust assets themselves, subject to appropriate authorisation in the trust deed. Indeed, in the latter case, the issue of the protector's remuneration must be addressed in the trust deed. Alternatively, the settlor may remunerate the protector by designating them a beneficiary in the trust deed for a specific part of the trust assets. In either case, the amount of the share in the trust assets and the timing and frequency of the release of the assets must be specified in the trust deed.

The trust deed should also include all the duties and powers of which the trustee should be aware, such as the scope of the protector's powers or the method of the protector's remuneration, or which cannot be fulfilled without the active involvement of the trustee (for example, remuneration from the trust assets). This does not mean that the protector becomes subject to the trust deed, which they – like the beneficiary – do not need to sign.

Generally speaking, although the protector may have powers related to the operational activities of the trust, their primary focus should be on advising the settlor on strategic decisions related to the existence and future of the trust (for example, recall of the trustee and appointment of a new one, initiation of contract amendments and termination of the contract). There may be specific situations in which it is appropriate to grant the protector some 'constitutional' powers. Such situations typically arise in the event of the death or incapacity of the settlor, or their long-term absence from work, which may lead to the need to appoint a new trustee. The 2017 amendment to the Civil Code can be seen as a step in this direction, allowing someone to take settlor decisions, exercise settlor powers and discharge settlor obligations in the event of the death or dissolution of the settlor. However, this relatively new rule of the Civil Code allows for a new settlor only in the event of the death of the settlor, *post mortem*, while the protector's role must be filled *inter vivos*. If we were to predict who the *post mortem* protectors would be, the most likely candidates would be the already active protectors. We can, therefore, see a certain functional overlap between the positions of settlor and protector, and the Civil Code amendment can be seen as a first step towards a possible merger of the two positions.

In relation to the settlor's or beneficiary's right to compensation, the protector's standing to sue is worthy of separate discussion. This question should be examined on the basis of whether the settlor has this right against the trustee. The Civil Code only explicitly mentions the right to sue the trustee in one place, where it states that the beneficiary may ask the court to recall the original trustee in the event of the death of the settlor, and if there is no other settlor, to appoint another trustee at the same time, if the settlor has committed a serious breach of contract.[47] On the face of it, the Civil Code has left very narrow scope and strict conditions for bringing an action. But clearly this does

47 Section 6:325(2) of the Civil Code.

not imply that the settlor lacks the right to bring an action against the trustee, for example on the basis of a claim for settlement or disgorgement. The silence of the Civil Code should not be regarded as a prohibition. If the settlor has the right to bring an action, it would seem reasonable to confer this right on the protector. This would not conflict with the original purpose of the trust.

It should be borne in mind that the protector pays a crucial role in complex asset management schemes, where a professional trustee must be able to rely on a professionally qualified specialist with similar skills – that is, they must be given the necessary legal tools. This also means that the protector, as the third active participant in the trust, must be included in the trust deed, and should acknowledge the provisions of the contract (not only those that apply to them) and accept those parts that apply to them as legally binding.

Although the Code of Civil Procedure does not explicitly address the matter, domestic procedural practice does not recognise the institution of delegation of authority in the context of trusts, that is, the possibility of bringing an action when a contracting party does not give a non-party to the contract the right to bring proceedings on its behalf, but transfers the right to bring proceedings. By means of a litigation trust, the contracting party, as the substantive rightholder, allows the litigant to claim performance in the action in their own name or directly on behalf of the principal, without assigning or transferring the claim arising from the legal relationship in question. Therefore, under current legislation, it cannot be expected that a protector's action against a trustee in their own name will be accepted by the court. In the absence of an independent right of action, the protector could only sue on behalf of the settlor with the appropriate power of attorney.

However, we would not exclude the possibility of a protector bringing a direct action if they have been granted this ability either by a transfer of rights or by direct protector status introduced by the 2017 amendment to the Civil Code. In these cases, there should be no obstacle to the protector bringing an action against the trustee.

We recommended the introduction of the institution of delegation in Hungary, *de lege ferenda*, many years ago. This has not been done at the codification level in the new Civil Procedure Code, although the need for it is no less today than it was then. In English legal literature, for example, Hayton argues that the existence of a protector is linked to the existence of a person who enforces the obligation of the trustee (the 'enforcer principle'). The settlor may appoint themselves as the enforcer of the trust or, in the event of their death, designate others entitled to do so. This is particularly important where the beneficiary is unborn or a minor. It is crucial that the trust has a person who has *locus standi*, and this role could be fulfilled by the protector. Without such a person, the trustee is ultimately unaccountable.

With regard to the obligations of the protector, we would draw attention to the duty of cooperation and information as laid down in the Civil Code.[48] While the protector, by virtue of their position as an 'outsider', cannot breach the trust deed in any way, they are nevertheless bound by the duty to cooperate, provide necessary information, and more broadly to exercise their rights in good faith and fairness.[49] Under their agreement with the settlor, the protector may also have more specific and detailed obligations, such as regularly reporting to the settlor on the current status of the trust and the performance of the trust deed. In addition, the protector has a duty of loyalty not only to the settlor but also to the beneficiary.

48 Section 6:62 of the Civil Code.
49 Section 1:3 of the Civil Code.

Register of Trusts and UBO Register

Ákos Menyhei
Primus Wealth; Aliant-Menyhei-Molnár-B. Szabó Law Firm

---

1. Who can be a trustee?

The eligibility criteria for a trustee fall into two categories: legal capacity and professional competence.[1] Both are examined in detail below.

1.1 Regulatory aims

When formulating the Civil Code, the legislator envisioned two main business models and types of trustee:

- *Corporate trustees:* These so-called 'trust companies',[2] predominantly wealth managers specialising in holistic private wealth management such as the establishment of family offices catering to the personal and property needs of one or more families, were expected to administer trusts in a more flexible manner than previous structures. Although professionals like lawyers, tax advisers and wealth management specialists could potentially be ideal trustees based on international practice, such a hybrid arrangement has not yet become commonplace in Hungary. Given the substantial asset management responsibilities in the hands of the trustees – akin to investment fund management – it was considered necessary to closely regulate professional trustee companies.
- *Family and* ad hoc *trustees:* This category includes trustees of family trust companies and other smaller scale or transactional trusts. The trustees are bound by a duty of care but are not necessarily specialised in trust management. Many family trusts and almost all transactional trusts involve trustee compensation.

To accommodate both market models, Hungarian regulators devised a two-tier system. General rules governing trustees are set out in the Civil Code and apply to all trustees, whereas specific criteria for more regulated trustees are

---

1 See: Charles E Rounds Jr and Charles E Rounds III, *Loring and Rounds: A Trustee's Handbook*, Wolters Kluwer, 2014, sections 3.1 and 3.2, pp71–84.
2 *Ibid*, p26 *et seq*, p79.

contained in the Trustees Act.[3] It is noted that none of the rules in the Trustees Act apply to trusts administered by asset management foundations.[4]

1.2 Civil law requirements

The Civil Code imposes no restrictions on potential trustees. Consequently, any entity, whether a natural or legal person, can become a trustee, the sole condition being the possession of legal capacity. Furthermore, the trustee must be able to effectively execute their duties, requiring the capacity to act.

While earlier legislation embodied the liberalism of the Civil Code, even permitting trust relationships that did not comply with public law requirements, the 2017 amendment to the Trustees Act introduced a provision[5] rendering null and void trust relationships deemed as 'businesslike' conduct and concluded with non-licensed trustees.[6] This necessitated scrutiny regarding the number of trusts a trustee is concurrently administering, given the new public law regime defining the concept of 'businesslike' according to the trustee's functions.[7]

The question of whether the trustee must possess capacity arises. Since the Civil Code does not mandate such a requirement, there is no legal impediment to the appointment of an individual with partial or fully restricted capacity (minor) by the settlor. However, the formation of the trust relationship or the appointment of a trustee in an existing trust hinges on acceptance. Consequently, for individuals with fully restricted capacity[8] the consent of the guardian or legal representative is invariably required. In the case of partial restriction, consent is required if the limitation extends to trust management activities.[9] While a full or partial restriction of capacity theoretically allows such individuals to be appointed as trustees, practical considerations might limit such appointments. Challenges may emerge if the capacity of an acting trustee becomes restricted, rendering them unable to perform their duties.

---

3 Act XV of 2014 on trustees and the rules governing their activities. Available at: https://njt.hu/jogszabaly/en/2014-15-00-00.

4 Under current legislation, there is a third type of trustee in Hungary, the asset management foundation, which can also act as trustee. In terms of their business role and organisation, asset management foundations can be classified as professional trustees, even if they manage the assets of a single family. Nevertheless, they are subject to the most liberal regulation. Under Article 2, Section 2(3)(c) of the Asset Management Foundation Act (see Appendix II), trusts administered by an asset management foundation are not subject to the Trustees Act. Trust management by a (private) asset management foundation is dealt with in detail in the chapter, "Private asset management (family) foundations – an alternative".

5 Trustees Act, Section 48/A(2).

6 Paragraph (1) of Article 48/A of the Trustees Act also requires the application of the new definition of businesslike conduct for trust arrangements concluded prior to the amendment, so a new trustee must be appointed instead of a trustee who does not meet the new criteria, or the trustee must obtain an NBH licence to carry out the activity.

7 See Trustees Act, Section 3(1).

8 Section 2:14(1) and Section 2:22(1) of the Civil Code.

9 Section 2:20(1) of the Civil Code.

1.3 Public law duties

(a) Accrual of ad hoc *and businesslike trust*

As discussed earlier, any person or entity with legal capacity under civil law can assume the role of trustee. However, the Trustees Act, delineating the public law framework for trusts, introduces additional requirements contingent upon the nature of the trust activity.

If a trustee, adhering to the conflict of interest requirements outlined in the act,[10] has no more than one trust relationship, their activities do not qualify as businesslike for the act's purposes. This streamlined and more efficient approach, tailored to practical needs, supersedes the prior concept that relied on multiple factors (eg, trustee fees). The revised definition of 'businesslike' now liberates *ad hoc* trustees, allowing them to effectively implement the business model proposed earlier for family and other small-scale trusts.

In its guidance of 14 August 2018,[11] the National Bank of Hungary (NBH) clarified that acting in a commercial capacity is not exclusive to the trustee. The relationship and contractual intentions among several beneficiaries within the same legal relationship can also impact its businesslike character. The NBH emphasised the need to scrutinise relationships between settlors to ascertain whether a close relationship precludes a systematic profit motive or circumvents regulations relating to businesslike trusts.

The NBH's guidance of 3 August 2022 on multiple trusts[12] further stresses the examination of settlors' relationships. In a scenario involving four family members establishing a family non-businesslike trust, the NBH highlighted the significance of familial connections in justifying the non-businesslike character of the trust relationship. However, if the trust relationships were extended to a broader circle of family and relatives, creating multiple trusts formally in one arrangement and attempting to disguise several trust relationships, the non-businesslike nature of the arrangement could be questioned.

Legally, the distinction between *ad hoc* and licensed trustees is highly significant, impacting not only the trustee but also the trust relationship. Trusts concealing their commercial, businesslike nature and managed by a non-licensed trustee are null and void under the Trustees Act.[13]

Given these NBH guidelines, it is important to note that the mere act of a trustee investing assets in various instruments against remuneration, and making payments to beneficiaries in a trust relationship, does not in itself

10 See Trustees Act, Section 18/A(2).
11 Available in Hungarian at: https://alk.mnb.hu/data/cms2466918/tmp643F.tmp(16138001).pdf.
12 Available in Hungarian at: https://alk.mnb.hu/data/cms2603451/247007_2022_kozzeteteli_peldany.pdf.
13 Trustees Act, Section 48/A(2).

denote commercial, businesslike activity as defined by the Trustees Act.[14] The specific trust deed and the actual trustee activities govern whether the trustee is engaged in businesslike activities. There is a need for caution to prevent parties from disguising regulated activities through contracts.

So-called *ad hoc* trustees, falling outside the businesslike activity definition, are subject to less stringent rules. However, if a trustee administers more than one trust, they operate in a commercial, businesslike capacity, subjecting them to stricter regulations and to licensing.

(b) *Requirements for* ad hoc *trustees and registration*

If a trustee does not meet the commerciality criteria of the Trustees Act, they are obliged to notify the NBH of the trust arrangement within 30 days.[15] The law requires that a trust deed, concluded by a trustee not acting in a commercial capacity, must be recorded either in a public deed or in a private deed countersigned by a bar member lawyer or a chamber counsel. This record must include the name, mother's name, and address of a private person, and the company data and beneficial ownership data of a legal person, acting as trustee.[16] Recording serves to screen individuals whose conflicts of interest have been verified during the verification process under the Trustees Act.

Although the Trustees Act does not impose a penalty of nullity for failing to fulfil formal requirements, trust arrangements of this nature are deemed null and void by application of Sections 6:6(1) and 6:94(1) of the Civil Code, and such nullity is not cured even by subsequent fulfilment.[17]

Since 2020 the Trustees Act has included new conflict of interest rules for trustees. For example, a natural person or a manager, member or beneficial owner of a corporate trustee, may not have a criminal record for certain offences.[18]

Under the transparency requirements of the Act on National Assets,[19] entities must refrain from engaging in trustee activities if they do not maintain transparency. In addition, under the Civil Code trustees' members (owners), affiliated companies, senior management and their relatives are prevented from engaging in trustee activities.

In summary, a trust relationship qualifies as a regular *ad hoc* (non-businesslike) trust if the following conditions are met:

---

14 Trustees Act, Section 3(1). The NBH guidance is available in Hungarian at: https://alk.mnb.hu/data/cms2489418/allasfoglalas_kozzeteteli_peldany.pdf.

15 Trustees Act, Section 19. On the official procedure, see Péter Miczán, "Hungarian property law and official regulation of trust asset management", *Számviteli tanácsadó* (*Accounting Consultant*), 2014/5, p2.

16 Trustees Act, Section 18/A(3). This requires a clean criminal record.

17 Although the Civil Code, at Section 6:94, excludes the possibility of *ex post* remedy in the case of a public deed or a private deed with full evidentiary value, while the Civil Procedure Act requires a public deed or a countersignature by a bar member, lawyer or a chamber consultant, violation of the stricter formal requirements also excludes the possibility of *ex post* remedy on the basis of the principle of 'more is less'.

18 Trustees Act, Section 18/A(1) and (2)(c).

19 The Act of 2011 CXCVI on National Assets, Section 3(1).

- The trustee holds a trusteeship under a trust deed.
- The trust relationship, which includes specific elements, is documented in a public deed or in a private deed countersigned by a bar member lawyer or a chamber counsel.
- The trust relationship is notified to the NBH.
- Where the trustee is an entity, it is considered transparent and meets all conflict of interest requirements.

At time of writing, NBH notification must include provision of the following:

- the details of the settlor;
- certain details of the trustee (if a legal entity, the registered and ultimate beneficial owners);
- the details of the beneficiary or beneficiaries specified in the contract;
- a declaration affirming that the trustee is not acting in a commercial, businesslike capacity and that the conditions for not so acting have been met;
- the trust deed;
- certification of payment of the administrative fee;[20]
- a declaration that the trustee accepts the (model) regulations under AML laws;[21]
- a declaration that individuals involved in the trust relationship are not subject to sanctions related to the Russia–Ukraine war; and
- if the trustee acts with legal representation, a power of attorney.

A certificate of clean criminal record in respect of the trustee must be provided to the notary public or the attorney at law who prepares the trust deed, but does not need to be attached to the notification.

Only the details of beneficiaries named in the trust deed need to be reported. Thus, if the trust deed does not specify a beneficiary but refers to a range of potential beneficiaries,[22] giving the trustee the right to choose,[23] there is no need (nor even an option) to reveal the identity of the beneficiary.

Following electronic submission of the notification, if the NBH determines within a 60-day administrative period[24] that the commerciality criteria of the Trustees Act do not apply, it registers the trust deed and the parties' details in

20 Trustees Act, Section 20(1). An administration fee of HUF 50,000 is payable for the notification, and changes to *ad hoc* trusts.

21 The Uniform Model Rules issued by the NBH are available at: www.mnb.hu/felugyelet/szabalyozas/penzmosas-ellen/szabalyzatok-segedletek/bizalmi-vagyonkezelok-egyseges-szabalyzata.

22 Section 6:311(1) of the Civil Code.

23 Section 6:311(3) of the Civil Code.

24 Trustees Act, Section 21(1a).

the Register of Trusts.[25] The register is non-public, accessible only to authorities specified by law.[26] Concurrently with the notification, the NBH issues an official certificate attesting to the notification.[27] The trustee can use this certificate to register the trustee's interest in other registers (eg, the land register and the National Business Registry).[28]

Amendments and terminations of the trust deed, and terminations of the conditions of registration, must likewise be notified[29] – the Trustees Act allows eight days for notification.[30] However, failure to notify does not render the trust relationship null and void.

(c) Control over non-businesslike trustees

For trustees operating on a non-businesslike basis under a notified trust relationship, the NBH can monitor compliance with registration obligations concerning the prevention of money laundering and terrorist financing,[31] and may remove the trust from the register if these are no longer met.[32,33] The NBH notifies the National Tax and Customs Office of the removal, which leads to cancellation of the trust's tax number and termination of the trust.[34] The NBH may also request criminal record information from the Ministry of Interior Affairs as part of the verification process.[35]

To mitigate the legal consequences of termination, the NBH must simultaneously notify the settlor (or, in the absence of a settlor, the beneficiary) when removing the trust from the register.[36] Within 90 days of notification, the settlor(s) may recall the trustee and appoint a new trustee, or the trustee may make good the reason for removal.[37] In the absence of a settlor, beneficiaries may initiate trustee removal and appointment before a court within 60 days of the NBH's decision.[38] The court examines whether grounds exist to disqualify the trustee acting in a non-commercial, non-businesslike manner.[39] The legislation pertains only to cases where the settlor or the beneficiary appoints an *ad hoc* trustee – the appointment of a commercial trust company is not addressed. Based on the logic of the regulation, however, there is no obstacle to

---

25 Trustees Act, Section 22(3). In contrast to the position under earlier legislation, the register is not public. The notifier is responsible for the truthfulness and accuracy of the data pursuant to Section 22(3) of the Trustees Act.

26 Trustees Act, Section 29.

27 Trustees Act, Section 28.

28 Article 25(1)(z) of the Company Registration Act.

29 Trustees Act, Section 24(1).

30 *Ibid.*

31 Trustees Act, Sections 21(2) and 31(1)(b).

32 Trustees Act, Section 31(1).

33 Trustees Act, Sections 25(c) and 31(3).

34 Trustees Act, Section 36(5).

35 Trustees Act, Section 36(1).

36 Trustees Act, Section 36(2).

37 Trustees Act, Section 36(3).

38 Trustees Act, Sections 37(2) and 36 (4).

39 Trustees Act, Section 37(1).

the appointment of a licensed trustee, though of course the disqualifying reasons cannot be judged according to the regulations applicable to *ad hoc* trustees.

(d) ***Failure to register***

The Trustees Act does not specifically outline how the NBH should act if the trustee fails to register the trust relationship. The law states that failure to notify information does not affect a contract's validity, except in cases otherwise specified by law, such as where a trustee acts as a businesslike trustee without a licence.[40]

However, the detailed procedure above cannot be followed in this scenario, because the NBH cannot establish that the conditions for registration are not met. Conversely, the registration conditions may be met, but registration does not occur. Nevertheless, there are several compelling reasons for a non-businesslike trustee to register the trust relationship, one being that the registration certificate[41] is essential for the trustee to register ownership in public registers. Since NBH registration is a prerequisite for obtaining the notification certificate, trustees cannot circumvent the requirements of the Trustees Act if the trust involves real estate or a company.

1.4 Register of ultimate beneficial owners (UBOs)[42]

The legal status of trust assets needs evaluation not only from the creditor's standpoint but also in the context of the broader environment. Under the Civil Code, the trustee acquires ownership of the trust assets. Nonetheless, to provide additional assurance, certain public registers note the trustee's specific legal capacity and may include details of key individuals such as the settlor. The NBH's register, while not public, records detailed information about the individual actors involved.

Until the Money Laundering Act implemented the 4th EU Anti-Money Laundering Directive, the scope of information available concerning trusts was limited. The introduction of the UBO Register altered the landscape, simplifying the identification process for service providers subject to anti-money laundering (AML) compliance and enhancing data accessibility for law enforcement agencies. The 5th EU Anti-Money Laundering Directive extended access to certain data of beneficial owners to "any member of the public".[43]

---

40 Trustees Act, Section 23.

41 Trustees Act, Section 28.

42 See Ákos Menyhei, "The impacts of the beneficial owner register on Hungarian asset management foundations, trusts, and hybrid trusts", Oxford Journals, *Trusts & Trustees*, Vol 28, No 6, 2022, pp1–9.

43 Directive (EU) 2018/843 of the European Parliament and of the Council of 30 May 2018 amending Directive (EU) 2015/849 on the prevention of the use of the financial system for the purposes of money laundering or terrorist financing, and amending Directives 2009/138/EC and 2013/36/EU. Available at: https://eur-lex.europa.eu/legal-content/EN/TXT/?uri=celex%3A32018L0843.

The Hungarian legislature implemented the 5th EU AML Directive through Act XLIII of 2021 ('the BOR Act').[44] The act establishes a legal framework that makes the beneficial ownership information of companies and foundations covered by the act accessible to the public.

When requesting information on trusts, the requester must first demonstrate and document the intended purpose of use in accordance with the BOR Act and establish a legitimate interest. This implies that beneficial owners of trusts may have some level of privacy, albeit constrained. Authorised authorities[45] now have unrestricted access to information on the beneficial owners of trusts, eliminating the need to obtain such information from the trustee or the NBH, as was the practice prior to the introduction of the UBO Register.

The BOR Act, in line with the AML Directive, includes the following objectives:

- establishing the beneficial ownership data service;
- ensuring transparency in the ownership of economic and social actors; and
- combating money laundering and terrorist financing.

The BOR Act divides its scope into two categories – data providers and service providers:

- Data providers are required to maintain accurate and current information about their beneficial owners and transmit the details to financial institutions where the respective data provider holds payment accounts. Data providers include, among others:
  - all types of company available in Hungary, including Societas Europaea (SE);
  - cooperatives;
  - associations;
  - foundations; and
  - trustees, if the trustee provides its services in Hungary, establishes a business relationship in Hungary or acquires real estate in Hungary.

  Although the BOR Act tries to focus on trust relationships and their beneficial owners, it actually classifies the trustee as a data provider.
- Service providers play a technical role in the process of transmitting data to the UBO Register. Their responsibilities involve either collecting beneficial ownership data from the data providers and conveying the information to the register, or using the register for their extended 'know your customer' (KYC) and compliance procedures.

---

44 The act is currently not available in English. The original Hungarian version is available at: https://net.jogtar.hu/jogszabaly?docid=A2100043.TV.

45 That is, any authority performing its statutory duty, the prosecutor's office, the court and any supervisory authority.

> The BOR Act defines service providers by reference to the AML Act,[46] which has extensive lists of entities dealing with clients' assets. Financial institutions have specific obligations under the BOR Act, requiring them to collect beneficial ownership data related to their payment accounts from data providers, and transmit this information to the UBO Register.

The definition of 'beneficial owner' is crucial to an understanding of the functioning and scope of the UBO Register. The definition is highly technical, it is crafted exclusively from an AML perspective, and it does not comprehensively align with the concept of a civil law owner. For instance, from a civil law standpoint, a trustee is considered the absolute owner of an asset. However, the AML legislation introduces the possibility of different beneficial owners associated with the same asset owned by the trustee.

The BOR Act does not itself furnish a definition of the beneficial owner of the data provider; rather, it defers to the AML Act,[47] in which the beneficial owner is determined according to criteria outlined in its Article 3.[48] Establishing the beneficial owners in a trust relationship is straightforward: the settlor, the trustee, the beneficiary and the protector (if the protector wields control over the trust assets) are acknowledged as beneficial owners in a trust.

(a) Operation of the UBO Register

Entities falling within the personal scope of the BOR Act, known as data providers, are required to maintain accurate and current information about their beneficial owners. They must then transmit the information to financial institutions where the data provider holds payment accounts. If there is a change in the beneficial owner information, the data provider is obligated to receive the updated details from the beneficial owner within 15 days, responsibility for fulfilling this obligation lying with the data provider. This places a significant burden on the management of data providers, who must determine the beneficial owners in accordance with the AML Act.

Financial institutions, guided by their KYC and compliance obligations under the AML Act, are required to collect and maintain accurate, up-to-date beneficial ownership information for data providers with whom they have a business relationship. This information is transmitted to the UBO Register through a secure electronic transmission channel by the fifth day of each month. The National Tax and Customs Office is responsible for maintaining and managing the register.

46 Article 3, Sub-paragraph 12 of the BOR Act.
47 Article 3, Sub-paragraph 13 of the BOR Act.
48 Article 3, Sub-paragraph 38, points a, b and d–f of the AML Act.

As previously mentioned, trustees, rather than trust relationships, are designated as data providers under the BOR Act. This means that trustees must maintain accurate and current information about their beneficial owners. However, a literal interpretation of this rule poses a challenge, as it implies that trustees must provide their own beneficial ownership information rather than that of the trust relationships they manage. This interpretation runs counter to the overarching objectives of the AML Directive and the BOR Act, under which the intention is for trustees to furnish beneficial ownership information regarding trust relationships.

Misclassification in this regard leads to a technical issue of implementation. Financial institutions find it challenging to transmit beneficial ownership information separately for different trust relationships managed by the same trustee. Despite the trustee providing beneficial ownership information for different trust relationships individually to the financial institution, processing can only occur in connection with the trustee, as the trustee is the designated data provider, which poses complications. Moreover, the tax authority assigns a national registration number to each data provider, exacerbating the technical problem. Under one national registration number, there may be a commingling of beneficial ownership information from several trusts, as there is no differentiation on a trust-by-trust basis.

The register includes various data related to data providers, including national registration, company registration and tax numbers, name, address and EU individual identification number (if any). Concerning the beneficial owner of the data provider, the register includes full birth name, citizenship, place and date of birth, address, and type and share size of ownership interest in the data provider, along with the index of the beneficial ownership information.

(b) Access to beneficial ownership information

Access to information on the register depends on the status of the applicant, as set out in Table 1.

(c) Third-party access for trust relationships

A third party may, on payment of a fee, request individual data on the beneficial ownership information of a trust relationship if the third party documents the purpose of its intended use of the data and its legitimate interest in obtaining it.

Legitimate interests are:

- combating money laundering or terrorist financing;
- that the third party obtaining the data and any beneficial owner in the trust relationship are family members as defined in the Civil Code; or
- that the third party and any beneficial owner in the trust relationship are both beneficial owners of the same legal entity, and these individuals are in a close business relationship or engaged in a property lawsuit.

Table 1: Levels of access to UBO Register

Applicant	Level of access	
Authorities, prosecutor's office, courts	Free, immediate online access to beneficial ownership information during the performance of their duties without informing the data provider.	Can transfer beneficial owner information to an authority, prosecutor's office or court of an EU member state, or a third country if the latter complies with data processing regulations equivalent to EU regulations.
Service providers	Free access as determined by the tax authority, excluding access to the beneficial ownership index and deviation reports from authorities, prosecutor's office, court or other service providers.	
Data providers and beneficial ownership	Can request a free, individual data service on their beneficial ownership information and deviation reports from authorities, prosecutor's office, court, or other service providers.	
Third parties (fee-based access) – general	Can request individual data service on the beneficial ownership information of any data provider (excluding trust relationships) against a fee by providing the name of the data provider. Deviation reports from authorities, prosecutor's office, court or service providers are excluded.	
Third parties (fee-based access) – trust relationships	See section 1.4(c) above.	

If the trust assets include assets held by a legal entity registered in a third country outside the European Union, and the assets give rise to a controlling interest in said entity, the third party may request in writing data on the beneficial owner in the trust relationship. The third party must obtain the prior approval of the competent minister before submitting the data request to the tax authority.

Although the UBO Act came into effect as recently as May 2021, making it hard to assess its success in practice, the registry is operational, containing data supplied by account holders. Service providers have commenced using it as part of fulfilling their money laundering obligations. However, a recent decision by the Court of Justice of the European Union raises doubts about the availability of access to the UBO Register. In joint cases C-37/2020 and C-601/20,[49] the ECJ ruled that allowing anyone access to beneficial ownership data is incompatible with the protection of personal data and fundamental privacy rights. Although it is too early to gauge the judgment's impact on UBO registers, and in particular Hungarian regulations, the ruling has led several countries to withdraw access to public UBO registers.[50] Despite this, the ruling does not conclusively end the trend towards transparency, and a refinement or restructuring of the regulatory landscape is anticipated.

49 The unofficial press release of the European Court of Justice on the judgment is available here: https://curia.europa.eu/jcms/upload/docs/application/pdf/2022-11/cp220188en.pdf.

50 Member states making the register inaccessible are Luxembourg, Malta, the Netherlands, Austria, Germany and Belgium. See www.investigate-europe.eu/en/2022/public-access-to-ubo-abolished-by-european-court-of-justice/.

Taxation of trusts

Csaba Magyar
Crystal Worldwide Law Firm

1. Areas of taxation

1.1 Taxation of trust settlement

Ownership of assets is transferred to the trustee simultaneously with the conclusion of the trust contract. This transfer is typically made without consideration. The trust fee paid to the trustee is not considered consideration, given that it is payment for the provision of services rather than the price of the assets. Under the Hungarian Duties Act of 1990 ('the Duties Act'), any transfer of assets without consideration is generally considered a gift, and therefore subject to gift tax in relation to the transfer of ownership. However, the Trustee Act amended the Duties Act[1] such that the transfer of assets under a trust contract is exempt from gift tax. Gift tax exemption applies if the following conditions are satisfied:

- the trustee has reported its status to the state tax authority;
- the parties entered into a trust contract pursuant to the Civil Code; and
- the transfer of assets is made without consideration.

If these conditions are met, the trust settlement will not be subject to gift tax, regardless of the tax status of the settlor and whether the settlor is a natural or legal person.

Trust settlement: Example 1
A natural person transfers their corporate shares and residential property into trust, without consideration to the trustee. The trustee notifies the tax authorities of the establishment of the trust. This transfer of assets is not liable to gift tax.

However, the question of whether or not the settlor is a taxable person subject to VAT is relevant since, under the VAT Act, free transfer is in certain cases treated as a sale of goods, in which case the trust settlement may give rise

1 Section 17/D of the Duties Act.

to a VAT liability. However, a sale of goods will not be deemed to occur if the assets are transferred under a trust contract pursuant to the Civil Code.[2] This presupposes that the trustee:

- is a taxable person subject to VAT and registered in Hungary;
- undertakes, as legal successor, to assume the rights and obligations arising from the settlement from the moment of acquisition; and
- does not have a legal status, at the time of acquisition or thereafter, that would be inherently incompatible with the fulfilment of its VAT liability.

The above rules only apply if the settlor is subject to VAT and the asset transferred falls within the scope of the VAT Act – for example, it is possible that no VAT liability will arise in relation to the transfer of business shares.

Trust settlement: Example 2

A company subject to VAT transfers its software into trust. In connection with the purchase of such software, it has exercised the right to deduct the VAT. The software is transferred without consideration to the trustee. The trustee is also a Hungarian company subject to VAT.

The trustee notifies the tax authority of the settlement of a trust, and thus no gift tax arises on the transfer of assets. Free transfer of the software – in respect of which the VAT paid had previously been deducted – is not deemed as a sale of goods, as the trustee is considered a taxable person subject to VAT and undertakes to act as a successor for the purposes of VAT.

If the settlor is subject to the Accounting Act, consideration should be given to the value at which the trust assets are settled. The asset value (contractual value) should be recorded in the trust contract. There are no legal regulations for determining the contractual value – in practice, the determination should be based on either the market value or the book value. If the contractual value is higher than the book value recorded in the settlor's accounts, the difference generates 'other income' for the settlor.[3] Conversely, if the contractual value is lower than the amount recorded in the settlor's accounts, the difference is treated as 'other expense'.[4]

Trust settlement: Example 3

A Hungarian company transfers into trust an office space, the book value of which is €1 million. The settlor is subject to corporate income tax (CIT). The settlor decides to transfer the real property into trust at market value, that is,

2 Section 17(5) of the VAT Act.
3 Section 77(3)(i) of the VAT Act.
4 Section 81(2)(i) of the VAT Act.

€5 million, under a trust contract compliant with the Civil Code, without consideration.

The trustee notifies the tax authorities of the settlement of the trust. Upon settlement, the settlor earns income of €4 million, the income being calculated as the difference between the book value and the market value.

Transfer of the property is exempt from gift tax (and VAT).

1.2 Taxation of trust management

During management of the trust, under the asset separation rule the administered assets must be separated from the trustee's own assets. Accordingly, it is advisable to divide the taxation of trusts into two parts.

On the one hand, the trustee – whether acting in a professional capacity or not – is considered an independent taxable person, and as such must pay taxes according to the applicable rules. This also applies to any consideration received for management of the trust. Professional trustees are subject to CIT (and local business tax (LBT)) in any case, since they can only carry out their activities in a specific legal manner, while *ad hoc* trustees are able to meet their tax liabilities according to the rules on personal income tax (PIT), given that even a natural person may act in this capacity.

On the other hand, the trust is classified as an 'artificially created' taxable person, regardless of whether the trustee is a professional or an *ad hoc* one. This concept is based on the provisions of the Tax Administration Act, which stipulates that a trust shall be considered a taxable person.[5] The Act also provides detailed rules on reporting and the issuance of a tax number for the trust.

The trustee is regarded as the representative of the trust,[6] and must notify the tax authority of the establishment of the legal relationship on conclusion of the trust contract. The trust should be specified on the dedicated form, including the date the contract was concluded. It is advisable to name the trust within the contract itself. Thereafter, the tax authority will issue a tax number for the trust and record it as a taxable entity distinct from the trustee. However, the trust will be subject to CIT, even if the trustee is a natural person. The trustee is responsible for fulfilling all tax obligations associated with the trust; for example, the trustee must submit a tax return in their own name, using the tax number of the trust.[7] If the trustee administers multiple groups of trusts under multiple trust contracts, a separate tax number must be requested for each group of trusts.

The trust is considered an individual taxable person subject to CIT,[8] so it will

5 Section 11(2) of the Tax Administration Act.
6 Section 21(1) of the Tax Administration Act.
7 Section 21(2) of the Tax Administration Act.
8 Section 2(6) of the CIT Act.

be subject to the rules of the Corporate Income Tax Act ('the CIT Act') as if it were a company. The trust will have its own taxpayer ID number, and the trustee must prepare financial statements, since the Accounting Act considers the trust an independent entity equivalent to a company.[9] The financial statements form the basis of the CIT return, but do not have to be submitted to the Company Court for the purpose of disclosure, since the Company Court does not keep records of trusts.

A trust is not subject to CIT if the settlor and beneficiary are both natural persons. An additional condition for tax relief is that during the fiscal year, income from asset management is derived exclusively from financial investments, receivables, securities or cash and cash equivalents, or from their profits and disposal.[10] In cases where both the settlor and the beneficiary are natural persons, a simplified procedure applies: the trustee is only required to make a declaration in lieu of CIT return for the trust, provided that the trustee did not earn any income in the fiscal year, or only earned tax-exempt income.[11]

Under the Local Business Tax Act, a trust administered under a trust contract compliant with the Civil Code shall be considered a company.[12] The registered office of the trust will be the registered office or place of residence of the trustee. In addition, any real estate used as part of the trust will be considered a branch.

Trust management: Example 1

The settlor is the father, and the beneficiary his son. The trustee managing the trust is a friend of theirs. The trust assets include shares in a Hungarian company and Hungarian government bonds. In the fiscal year, the company paid €1 million in dividends, and €1 million in interest was paid on the government bonds.

Given that both the settlor and the beneficiary are natural persons, the shares in the company are considered a financial investment and government bonds are considered securities, the trust is not liable to CIT on the received dividends and interest. Instead of filing a CIT return, it is sufficient for the trust to submit a declaration to the tax authority of the trustee's place of residence.

The basis of assessment of LBT is net turnover, which is calculated from the net sales revenue as defined by the Accounting Act. Dividends and interest received are not considered net sales revenue, therefore the trust did not incur LBT liability in this regard; however, an LBT return must be submitted to the tax authority of the trustee's place of residence.

---

9 Section 7/B of the Accounting Act.
10 Section 20(1)(b) of the CIT Act.
11 Section 5(7a) of the CIT Act.
12 Section 52(26) of the Local Business Tax Act.

A trust is not regarded by the VAT Act as an independent taxable person;[13] this is therefore the only area where the trust has the same VAT status as the trustee.

Trust management: Example 2
A natural person settlor transfers real property into a trust. Previously, the settlor had rented the property without charging VAT. The trustee is considered a taxable person for VAT purposes and had previously chosen to charge VAT on real estate rental activity. Following the trust settlement, the trustee must charge VAT when renting out the property (although the settlor had rented the property without charging VAT).

The trustee must issue VAT invoices to the tenant for rent. The trust need not submit a VAT return on these transactions, but the trustee must include the VAT payable in connection with the rental of the property in its own VAT return. The trust must include the rental income in its CIT and LBT returns, but the income need not be included in the trustee's CIT return.

1.3 Taxation of trust distributions

Provided that the criteria set out in the trust contract are met, the beneficiary may claim both the trust assets (capital) and any increase in the capital (yield). During trust distribution, different rules apply depending on whether the beneficiary receives the capital or the yield.

If the capital is distributed without charge to the beneficiary and the trust assets did not appreciate during the trust settlement, the Personal Income Tax Act ('the PIT Act') considers the transaction to be tax exempt, unless the yield cannot be distinguished from the capital.[14] As a result, the beneficiary may be liable to pay gift tax for this acquisition, although logically, this will not apply if the capital is returned to the settlor or received by them as a beneficiary. As regards capital distributions, the Duties Act treats the trustee as 'transparent', that is, acquisition of the trust assets is considered as if the beneficiary had acquired them directly from the settlor.[15] The current exemption rules under the Duties Act remain applicable to such transactions, for example exemptions for distribution to a spouse, sibling or lineal relative.[16]

Trust distribution: Example 1
A father transfers his residential property into a trust. The beneficiaries of the trust are the father, his friend, and their child together.

---

13 Pursuant to Section 5(1) of the VAT Act, only a person or entity having legal capacity can be a taxable person; however, a trust does not have legal capacity.
14 Section 7.26 of Annex 1 and Section 66(5) of the PIT Act.
15 Section 17/D(2) to (3) of the Duties Act.
16 Section 17(1)(p) and (w) of the Duties Act.

After a few years, the property is distributed to the beneficiaries (giving a one-third share to each). The husband and the child will not be liable to gift tax; the father's friend, however, will have to pay gift tax based on the market value of the residential property.

In the case of transactions not carried out without charge, that is, where the beneficiary had previously provided compensation to the settlor in exchange for distribution of the assets, the compensation will be considered as consideration for the given activity and taxed accordingly.[17]

In the case of yield distribution, a distinction is made depending on the beneficiary's status as a taxable person. If the beneficiary is a taxpayer subject to the PIT Act, that is, a natural person, the yield distribution on the trust assets will be regarded as equivalent to dividend payments,[18] and the beneficiary will be subject to tax as though they were a shareholder. In the event that the settlor is subject to CIT and is also a beneficiary, the yield will also be considered a dividend, although the rules governing CIT will apply to taxation of the dividend. If the settlor and the beneficiary are different persons, but the beneficiary is subject to CIT, the payment will be classified as 'other income'[19] and a tax liability will be incurred according to the general rules of taxation.

Trust distribution: Example 2
A natural person transfers his shares in a Hungarian company into a trust. The beneficiaries of the trust are the settlor and his wife.

The company that is part of the trust assets pays a dividend, after which the trustee makes a yield distribution to the beneficiaries from the received dividends. The yield paid to the settlor and his wife is considered a dividend payment, on which they will incur tax.

The legislator has extended the favourable tax provisions of the PIT Act, which govern long-term investment contracts, to include yield from trusts. This means that a trustee is able to conclude such long-term investment contracts.[20] In summary, if the trustee invests the trust assets under a long-term investment contract with an investment service provider or credit institution as defined by law, the PIT payable on the yield will only be 10% after three years and 0% after five years.

Even when made without consideration, the distribution of trust assets may be deemed a sale of goods falling within the scope of the VAT Act, regardless of

---

17 Section 17/D(2) of the Duties Act.
18 Section 66(1)(ae) of the PIT Act.
19 Section 84(1) of the Accounting Act excludes the possibility of the payment being regarded as a dividend, where it is not made to the settlor.
20 Section 67/B(14) of the PIT Act.

whether it is capital or yield distribution, if the asset contributed is considered a product (or service) and the trustee is a taxable person subject to VAT. On the other hand, distribution of trust assets to a beneficiary that is the same person as the settlor will not be considered a sale of goods.[21]

2. Recent changes in the taxation of trusts

The tax package adopted in summer 2023 significantly changed the provisions of the PIT Act applicable to trusts. Below, we outline the gap that brought about this legislative change, and briefly review the key elements of the new legislation.

As explained in section 1.1 above, although under the Duties Act a transfer of property without consideration is considered a gift and subject to gift tax, the free transfer of assets under a trust deed is exempted from gift tax.

The trustee must notify the tax authority of the legal relationship established on conclusion of a trust deed. The tax authority will issue a tax number for the trust and record the trust as a taxable person distinct from the trustee. At the same time, the trust will become subject to CIT and LBT, as a result of which the rules of the CIT Act will apply to it as if it were a company.

Under the Accounting Act,[22] the trustee must record the initial assets (capital) transferred, at the value specified in the trust deed. There is no requirement (besides under general legal principles) to record the value of assets in the trust deed, which provides the opportunity to set – within reason – any value.

Appreciation: Example 1

The nominal value of the shares of Company A Ltd is €10,000, but the company's estimated market value is €1 million. A private individual shareholder transfers shares in Company A to a trustee. The parties decide to set the value of the shares, that is, the trust assets, at €1 million in the trust deed.

Due to the flexibility within the Accounting Act mentioned above, the trustee can record the value of the transferred shares at a level higher than the nominal value by €990,000. No tax liability arises for either party in respect of this appreciation in value.

If the trustee later sells the shares, €1 million will be considered the acquisition value, rather than €10,000. If the shares are sold for €1.1 million, the taxable amount will be only €100,000.

This is significantly more favourable than if the value of the shares had been recorded at the original nominal value of €10,000.

---

21 Section 17(5) of the VAT Act.
22 Sections 40/A(1) and 50(9) of the Accounting Act.

This method of calculation will be important in the next phase – trust contribution – since similar methods could be applied to the proceeds of the sale to achieve tax relief. For example, the capital gain on participation exemption reduces the taxable base,[23] and in the case of trusts, returns on financial instruments are tax free.[24]

Provided the criteria set out in the trust deed are fulfilled, the beneficiary may claim both the initial assets (capital) and any increase in the capital (yield). During trust contribution, different rules apply depending on whether the capital or the yield is contributed to the beneficiary.

If a capital contribution is made to the beneficiary, the transaction is considered tax free under the PIT Act.[25] Thus, a gift tax liability may arise due to the free contribution of capital. As regards capital contributions, the Act on Duties considers the trustee to be 'transparent', that is, acquisition of the trust assets will be considered as if the beneficiary had acquired the assets directly from the settlor.[26] The current exemption rules set out in the Act on Duties remain applicable to this transaction – a capital contribution is not subject to gift tax where it is made to the settlor or their spouse, sibling or any lineal relative.[27] In all other cases, gift tax is payable on capital contributions.

Where the beneficiary is a natural person, the yield contribution on trust assets will be treated as dividend[28] and the tax liability fulfilled according to the general rules of taxation as if the beneficiary were a shareholder receiving a dividend from a company.

Appreciation: Example 1 (continued)
The trustee sells the shares in Company A Ltd for €1.1 million. The trustee pays €1.1 million to the beneficiary, who is the spouse of the settlor.

Thus, a capital contribution of €1 million and a yield contribution of €100,000 are made to the beneficiary from the trust assets. In respect of the capital contribution of €1 million, the beneficiary does not incur liability to gift tax, since they are the spouse of the settlor. The beneficiary, however, is subject to PIT on the €100,000 yield contribution which is considered as dividend.

The taxation of the trust contribution would have been much less unfavourable if the trust assets were registered at a value of only €10,000 upon trust settlement. In the present case, however, while there is no liability to gift tax on the capital contribution of €10,000, the beneficiary is required to pay PIT on the €1.09 million yield as if it were dividend.

23 Section 7(1)(dz) of the CIT Act.
24 Section 20(1)(b) of the CIT Act.
25 Section 7.26 of Annex 1 and Section 66(5) of the PIT Act.
26 Section 17/D(2) to (3) of the Act on Duties.
27 Section 17(1)(p) and (w) of the Act on Duties.
28 Section 66(1)(ae) of the PIT Act.

We can assume that an increasing number of people have used trusts for tax optimisation when selling business shares, taking advantage of the gap mentioned above. With the tax package introduced in 2023, the legislator intended to address the issue by imposing a tax liability on the settlor, based on the appreciation of the assets to be transferred upon trust settlement and treating the transfer as if it were made for a consideration.

The relevant part of the tax package applies to trust deeds executed after 12 September 2023.

Change on appreciation: Example 1

The nominal value of the shares of Company A Ltd is €10,000, but its estimated market value is €1 million. A private individual shareholder transfers their shares in Company A to a trustee. The parties decide to set the value of the shares, that is, of the trust asset, at €1 million in the trust deed.

Due to the above-mentioned legislative change, the settlor incurs a tax liability on the €990,000 difference, even though the transaction is carried out without consideration.

The next change to the PIT Act related to the tax package adopted in autumn 2023. While the summer tax package had introduced stricter rules, the autumn tax package was less stringent, restoring the old rules with one exception. The new rules took effect from 30 December 2023, and can be applied retroactively.

No tax is payable on the appreciation of the assets; it is sufficient for the trustee to maintain records of the appreciation of assets it administers. If the trustee does not distribute the assets to the beneficiaries within five years, the distribution will be tax-free, as it was before the initial legislative change. Conversely, if the assets are distributed within five years, then the portion subject to appreciation will be liable to tax, just as if the beneficiary had received a dividend. There is no need to determine appreciation upon settling assets to be distributed after death and on contribution assets at the death of the settlor.

Change on appreciation: Example 2

The nominal value of the shares of Company A Ltd is €10,000, but its estimated market value is €1 million. A private individual shareholder transfers their shares in Company A to a trustee. The parties decide to set the value of the shares, that is, the trust assets, at €1 million in the trust contract.

On the difference of €990,000, the settlor does not incur a tax liability, but the trustee must record the appreciation in its books.

If the capital (ie, trust assets) subject to appreciation is distributed to the beneficiary more than five years after the trust settlement, no tax liability arises. (This tax exemption does not override the gift tax rules applicable to capital distributions.)

The fact that, after six months, the tax provisions applicable to trusts were changed again – and favourably – is an important message to family-run businesses that they should not lose interest in this estate planning solution. For those looking to make asset transfers within the family while also seeking asset protection, trusts can offer a favourable tax-free solution from 2024. By refraining from accessing the assets for five years, a trust can ensure the protection of family assets within a regulated framework. In addition, trusts offer a more flexible solution to the distribution of assets after death than a last will and testament.

Private asset management (family) foundations – an alternative

Ákos Menyhei
Primus Wealth; Aliant-Menyhei-Molnár-B. Szabó Law Firm

1. Evolution of Hungarian foundations[1]

The new Hungarian Civil Code of 2013 transformed the estate planning landscape by introducing two legal solutions.[2] First, it incorporated an English law-style trust.[3] Secondly, it changed the fundamental nature of Hungarian foundations.[4] In the past, establishing a foundation in Hungary was contingent upon the purpose of serving the long-term public interest.[5] However, under the new rules, setting up a foundation for private purposes became permissible, and in 2019, the Asset Management Foundation Act ('the AMF Act') dramatically extended the scope of private foundations.[6]

Despite, however, sharing the general concept of a foundation – a legal entity without an owner – with, for example, Austria or Germany, the Hungarian private foundation's application scope remains relatively narrow. Unless otherwise specified, the Civil Code explicitly prohibits the establishment of private foundations in the interest of:

- the founder;
- any current or future member;
- a foundation officer; or
- members of a foundation body, or their family members.[7]

There are two exceptions to this rule. First, the Civil Code allows the founder and co-founder to be beneficiaries if the foundation is established for the

1 See Gábor B Szabó, Ákos Menyhei and István Sándor, *The Foundation*, HVG-Orac, 2021.
2 Act V of 2013 on the Civil Code of Hungary. Available in English at: https://njt.hu/jogszabaly/en/2013-5-00-00.
3 Ákos Menyhei, "Development of the estate planning industry through the introduction of the trust in Hungary", *Trusts & Trustees*, Vol 22, No 6, 2016, p659.
4 See Ákos Menyhei, "The use of the Hungarian Foundation for asset protection and private purposes", *Trusts & Trustees*, Vol 23, No 6, July 2017, pp673–677.
5 Act IV of 1959 on the Civil Code of the Republic of Hungary, Section 74/A. Available in English at: https://gss.unicreditgroup.eu/sites/default/files/markets/documents/Civil%20Code%20_effective%20on%2024%20July%202012_.pdf.
6 Act No XIII of 2019 on Asset Management Foundations – see Appendix II. And see Ákos Menyhei, "The new Hungarian asset management foundation", *Trusts & Trustees*, Vol 25, No 6, July 2019, pp599–610. Available at: https://doi.org/10.1093/tandt/ttz047.
7 Section 3:379(4) of the Civil Code.

purpose of preserving their scientific, literary and artistic works.[8] Secondly, family members of the founder and co-founder may be beneficiaries if the foundation is established to care for their scientific, literary and artistic works, or to provide care, nursing or maintenance, cover medical expenses or support education through scholarships or otherwise.[9]

The above significantly altered the law on asset management foundations (AMFs) as set out in the AMF Act, which was originally created with the fundamental purpose of changing the intended use of private foundations. It aimed to transform the objectives of private foundations, essentially establishing them as cornerstones of wealth planning for larger family estates.

Beyond wealth planning, there is the asset protection advantage associated with transferring assets into an AMF. Access by potential creditors to the assets held in the foundation is extremely limited, as the foundation creates complete asset separation. Once the founder sets up the foundation and transfers assets into it, the founder loses ownership of those assets. Registration of the foundation creates a new legal person,[10] and this new entity is the owner of the assets transferred to it.

It may seem that despite its usefulness, the AMF is a dead-end street, providing no means for the founder to claim the return of the foundation's assets. However, taking into account that the founders have the power to appoint themselves as beneficiaries and even to dissolve the AMF, this is far from the case.

The foundation's assets are protected from beneficiaries' undue claims, as well as from the creditors of the beneficiaries. The Civil Code limits the designated beneficiary's potential claims against the foundation to the following two cases:[11]

- the charter document properly specifies the person of the beneficiary, the benefits due to such person, and the date when the benefits are due; or
- the board of trustees has adopted a decision to provide benefits to the beneficiary and delivered this decision to the beneficiary, and the beneficiary has accepted the applicable conditions.

Naturally, the beneficiaries' creditors cannot assert any claims or demands against the assets of the AMF until the beneficiary has received them, either partially or in full, as a distribution of assets.

---

8 Section 3:386(1) of the Civil Code.
9 Section 3:386(2) of the Civil Code.
10 Section 3:378 of the Civil Code.
11 Section 3:387 of the Civil Code.

2. Private foundations and AMFs – the key differences

The most significant features that distinguish AMFs are as follows:

- The primary purpose of an AMF, unlike a private foundation, is to conduct economic activities, namely, asset management.[12]
- An AMF can be specifically established for the benefit of the founder, the founder's family members, and individuals designated by the founder, providing financial benefits and distributions to these individuals.[13]
- The founder and family members can directly participate in the work of the board of trustees responsible for managing the AMF.[14]
- The AMF can act as a trustee without being subject to the law on trustees.[15]
- The founders may control the AMF, change the composition of the board of trustees and the beneficiaries at any time, and dissolve the AMF. In this event, the founder is entitled to receive both the capital and yields of the AMF's assets.[16]
- The founders can transfer their founders' rights to the AMF or the board of trustees, or delegate to them the exercise of their founders' rights.[17]
- The board of trustees should not become dysfunctional upon the founder's death or incapacity, as the founder can allow the board to appoint new members.[18]

3. Decoding the AMF: structure, governance and legal dynamics

The AMF Act introduced a specialised form of foundation designed to engage primarily in the management of assets assigned by the founder and to achieve specific aims and tasks outlined in the founding charter. An existing foundation can be transformed into an AMF with the appropriate modification of the founding charter, provided that the minimum capital requirement is met.[19] The primary role of the AMF is to provide distributions for the beneficiary or beneficiaries identified in the founding charter, and the AMF Act offers the possibility of establishing an AMF for public interest purposes, allowing for a wider circle of beneficiaries.[20] In contrast to a trust, an AMF comes into existence upon registration. The creation of the founding charter only initiates the process, and the legal entity is formed with the court resolution to register the AMF.

12 AMF Act, Article 1(2).
13 AMF Act, Article 4 Section (4).
14 AMF Act, Article 4 Section (4).
15 AMF Act, Article 2 Section (3)C.
16 AMF Act, Article 11 Section (1).
17 AMF Act, Article 5 Section (1).
18 AMF Act, Article 5 Section (3).
19 AMF Act, Article 1 Section (1).
20 AMF Act, Article 4 Sections (1)–(3).

3.1 Laying the financial foundation: minimum capital requirements

As the AMF is positioned as the premier asset management structure in Hungary, the AMF Act sets a minimum capital requirement of HUF 600 million for its establishment.[21] The founder can meet this requirement through various types of contributions, encompassing both liquid (bankable) and non-liquid (non-bankable) assets (contributions in kind). To ensure proper control of asset management activities, the founding charter must precisely describe the assigned assets so they are identifiable at any time. The Civil Code requires an auditor to value the non-bankable assigned assets before the application for AMF registration is submitted.

This minimum capital requirement must be maintained throughout the existence of the AMF. If the AMF's capital falls below the minimum amount, the board may suspend or reduce distributions to beneficiaries. If the AMF fails to meet the minimum capital condition for three consecutive years, it must be liquidated.[22]

3.2 Navigating authority: the transfer of founder's rights

An additional significant feature of the AMF is the ability of the founder to transfer founder's rights to the foundation and empower the board of trustees to exercise them.[23] This transfer can encompass the entire spectrum of founder's rights or be restricted to specific ones. This underscores the necessity for a mandatory supervisory board for an AMF. To safeguard against unwarranted changes, the AMF Act mandates that the board of trustees can only amend the foundation charter if expressly authorised by the founder.[24] In the absence of such authorisation, amendments are permissible only if changing circumstances or legal requirements necessitate them to achieve the foundation's objectives.[25]

The AMF Act also provides that if the founder has transferred the founder's rights to the foundation or empowered the board of trustees, they must appoint an external person – the protector – in addition to the supervisory board. This individual is responsible for overseeing the activities of the board of trustees, exercising the founder's rights and managing the foundation's assets. The protector is empowered to exercise the rights of the supervisory board and can, among other things, initiate enforcement procedures.[26]

The primary objective of the AMF Act is to empower AMFs to operate as 'self-driven' entities, ensuring their independent operation for a prolonged period – up to a decade – free from founder intervention. This implies that an

---

21 Currently, around €1.5 million.
22 AMF Act, Article 11 Section (2).
23 AMF Act, Article 5 Section (1).
24 AMF Act, Article 9 Section (6).
25 AMF Act, Article 9 Section (6).
26 AMF Act, Articles 7–8.

AMF should function autonomously, without reliance on its founder, and the founder should refrain from intervening through the exercise of founder's rights. Autonomy is at the discretion of the founder, and the AMF Act offers an avenue for the founder to opt for it, relinquishing the full extent of their founder's rights and enabling the appointment of a foundation body, including a board of trustees, to exercise these rights.[27]

Furthermore, the AMF Act allows the founder (including the founder of an existing AMF) to delegate founder's rights to the AMF without amending the foundation charter. In such cases, the board of trustees assumes responsibility for exercising the founder's rights. The same regulations apply when the founder designates the board of trustees in the founding charter to exercise the full range of these rights. The appointment of the board of trustees to exercise founder's rights can be revoked, contingent upon the modification of the founding charter, a right reserved by the founder. If the founder delegated founder's rights to the AMF without charter amendment, this decision becomes irrevocable.[28]

While the Civil Code permits the appointment of a foundation body, including the board of trustees, to exercise founder's rights only in specific circumstances, such as the founder's demise, the lack of legal successor, or the founder's incapacity to exercise the rights, the AMF Act extends the possibility with no such restrictions. However, the general rules of the Civil Code continue to apply in the case of an AMF. Even if the founder has not designated any person or foundation body to exercise founder's rights in an AMF, or if the founder is unable to do so due to death, lack of legal successor or other reasons, the board of trustees exercises founder's rights within the limitations set by the Civil Code.

The Civil Code restricts the exercise of certain founder's rights by the foundation body. In contrast, the AMF Act offers flexibility by allowing the board of trustees, the supervisory board or both, to retain the exercise of these founder's rights, ensuring complete independence of the AMF from its founder. This flexibility extends to the election of members and chairs of an AMF's corporate bodies by the bodies themselves.

3.3 Structural components and governance

In relation to the organisational structure of AMFs, the AMF Act includes a few mandatory provisions, while the majority of rules are discretionary, governed by the Civil Code.

Under the AMF Act, it is a requirement to have at least one individual member on the board of trustees. In addition, given the significant economic

27 AMF Act, Article 5 Sections (3)–(4).
28 AMF Act, Article 5 Sections (1)–(2).

activities and capital of AMFs, the act requires the establishment of a supervisory board and the appointment of a permanent auditor.[29]

It is possible for the founding charter of an AMF to stipulate particular qualifications and other professional prerequisites for the chairs and members of both the board of trustees and the supervisory board.[30]

As a precautionary measure, decisions regarding the filling of vacant seats on the board of trustees or the appointment of the chair are jointly made by the board of trustees and the supervisory board; likewise for the members and chair of the supervisory board. No individual may join either body against the majority vote of the members. The AMF Act specifies that if the board of trustees exercises founder's rights and a vacancy occurs, the new member is elected by majority vote of both bodies and the body with the vacancy.[31] Alternatively, the founding charter may stipulate a qualifying majority for this decision.

The AMF Act outlines rules for the dismissal of members and chairpersons of the board of trustees and the supervisory board, which mirror the rules for the appointment process, subject to conditions or restrictions as outlined in the founding charter.[32]

3.4 Guardianship and oversight: the role and powers of the protector

If the founder's rights are exercised by the board of trustees, extending beyond the supervisory board, there is no external body or individual with the authority to counteract activities jeopardising the interests or prudent management of the AMF and restore its lawful operation. Consequently, there is a need for an external entity or individual to safeguard the assets of the AMF, ensure compliance with internal regulations, protect the interests of the beneficiaries and preserve the founder's purpose. To answer this need, and provide an additional layer of operational assurance, the AMF Act introduced the concept of 'protector' into the Hungarian legal system.[33]

When the founder designates, in the founding charter, the board of trustees to exercise the founder's rights, the founder must also appoint a protector, beyond the supervisory board, to oversee the exercise of those rights.[34] Although the role of protector had been common in Hungary in the context of trust relationships, the introduction of a protector's rights and powers is a novel addition to the legal system as it relates to AMFs.

Under the AMF Act, the protector is responsible for ensuring and restoring the foundation's integrity in case of deviation from the asset management policy, founding charter, or the AMF's purpose. The protector has robust rights

29 AMF Act, Article 6 Section (2).
30 AMF Act, Article 6 Section (3).
31 AMF Act, Article 5 Section (3).
32 AMF Act, Article 5 Section (4).
33 AMF Act, Articles 7-8.
34 AMF Act, Article 7 Section (1).

and powers granted by the AMF Act, and the founder has the option to extend further rights and powers to the protector through the founding charter. These include the ability to:

- monitor the activity and decisions of AMF bodies;
- inspect documents;
- participate in meetings;
- offer opinions before resolutions are made; and
- in the event of a conflict between a resolution and the founding charter or other governing document, initiate court proceedings to block the execution of an unlawful resolution.[35]

The AMF Act requires the appointment of a protector in the founding charter. Responsibility for this appointment lies with the founder, who must also specify the protector's remuneration. Alternatively, the founder may authorise the foundation itself to appoint a protector, an authority that must be explicitly included in the founding charter. In cases where the AMF exercises this founder's right, joint appointment of the protector by the board of trustees and the supervisory board is required, with court approval necessary to ensure independence and impartiality.[36]

This provision remains applicable in cases where the founder's rights are exercised by the board of trustees, and the protector resigns, dies, is terminated without a legal successor, or no longer possesses the necessary qualifications for the role. Such instances require the appointment of a new protector.

The AMF Act establishes specific eligibility criteria for a protector, including qualifications such as being a chartered auditor, an audit company, an attorney at law who is also a bar member, a law firm, or a natural person with a clean criminal record and meeting the professional requirements outlined in the founding charter.[37] To address conflicts of interest related to the protector, the court of registration is tasked with reviewing compliance with these requirements during the AMF registration process or the approval of corporate decisions.

The protector's most potent tool is the authority to initiate enforcement proceedings, compelling the AMF's bodies to restore the lawful operation of the foundation. This extends to situations where the asset management of the AMF deviates from the asset protection obligation.[38] Additionally, the protector can intervene if corporate bodies fail to resolve a vacancy in the board of trustees or supervisory board within 90 days, proposing a suitable appointee for court approval.[39]

35 AMF Act, Article 8 Sections (1) and (4).
36 AMF Act, Article 7 Section (1).
37 AMF Act, Article 7 Section (3).
38 AMF Act, Article 8 Section (3).
39 AMF Act, Article 8 Section (5).

Furthermore, the AMF Act grants the protector the right to exercise additional powers or fulfil further obligations specified in the founding charter. This includes the ability to challenge resolutions of the board of trustees and the supervisory board, requesting annulment if the resolution is deemed unlawful or non-compliant with the founding charter or investment policy.[40]

To ensure the proper exercise of these rights, the AMF Act provides the protector with access to all information concerning the AMF's operation, equivalent to that available to the supervisory board.[41]

Lastly, the AMF Act entitles the protector to remuneration, the cost to be borne by the foundation's assets.[42]

3.5 Structuring the foundation's blueprint: a look at the founding charter

The objectives for managing the AMF's assets must be explicitly defined in the founding charter. Additionally, an investment policy needs to be formulated, and at the founder's discretion, it can be included in the founding charter or accepted by the board of trustees within six months from the date of registration. In either case, the investment policy serves as the cornerstone for asset management.[43]

Except where the AMF Act specifies otherwise, the regulations on foundations outlined in the Civil Code and other legislation apply to AMFs.

Under the AMF Act, the founding documents must be incorporated into a public deed, or a private document countersigned by an attorney at law. A crucial legal requirement is the inclusion in the founding charter of the fundamental aims and principles governing the management and utilisation of the AMF's assets.[44]

The AMF Act requires the inclusion of portfolio descriptions, risk management strategies and investment decision-making methods. If the founder chooses not to append an investment policy to the founding charter, the AMF must prepare one within six months after registration and approval. This responsibility falls on the foundation (specifically, its board of trustees), guided by the supervisory board and the person exercising the founder's rights. If the board of trustees exercises the founder's rights, joint approval by both the board of trustees and the supervisory board, following the protector's opinion, is required under the AMF Act.[45]

The rules for modifying the founding charter are contained in the Civil Code. Deviation from these rules by the founder is permitted. If the founder's

---

40 At the founder's discretion, the investment policy can be included in the founding charter or accepted by the board of trustees within six months from the date of registration. See section 3.5.
41 AMF Act, Article 8 Section (2).
42 AMF Act, Article 8 Section (6).
43 AMF Act, Article 9 Section (2).
44 AMF Act, Article 9 Section (1)–(2).
45 AMF Act, Article 9 Section (3)–(4).

rights are exercised by the board of trustees, modification is allowed only if the founding charter allows it or if changes in the broader legal framework require it. The board of trustees is not permitted to change the AMF's objectives. It is essential to consider the founder's aims and decisions, which can only be altered by the board of trustees if explicitly authorised by the founder. Without such authorisation, amendments are restricted to specific circumstances. The AMF Act acknowledges changed circumstances since registration, including changes in the legal environment. Any modification must be justified by these changed circumstances; that's to say, without the planned modification the AMF's objectives and asset management would be in jeopardy.[46]

In certain scenarios, amendments to the founding charter cannot be initiated by the board of trustees. In such cases, modifications are only permissible if required by legislative changes. If the amendment concerns the AMF's objectives, the authority for such changes is limited to the founder and applicable only if the AMF is not for public interest, or if the board of trustees does not exercise the founder's rights.[47]

Modifications to the founding charter may have implications for beneficiaries, and the AMF Act requires that pre-existing obligations for the benefit of beneficiaries must be fulfilled. Consequently, such modifications cannot exempt the AMF from previously assumed obligations.[48]

3.6 Preservation and distribution: constraints on asset management

The founder has the authority to determine the minimum value of assets that the AMF must maintain throughout its existence, and this must be explicitly outlined in the founding charter. If the founder does determine a minimum, it becomes a requirement under both the law and the AMF Act.[49]

The obligation to retain assets implies that if the AMF's assets fall below the designated value specified in the founding charter or the AMF Act, the distribution intended for the beneficiaries will be proportionally reduced in line with the loss. Alternatively, the distribution may be withheld until the asset value rebounds to meet the prescribed amount set out in the founding charter.[50]

3.7 Termination of the AMF

The AMF Act empowers the founder, in their capacity as the holder of founder's rights, to petition the court for the termination of a non-public interest AMF. This marks a significant departure from the general provisions of the Civil Code, which lack provision for such termination. Importantly, a court decision to terminate the

46 AMF Act, Article 9 Section (6).
47 AMF Act, Article 9 Section (7).
48 AMF Act, Article 9 Section (8).
49 AMF Act, Article 10 Section (1).
50 AMF Act, Article 10 Section (2).

AMF does not hinder the fulfilment of previously established obligations, which persist and must be met for the benefit of the beneficiaries. The removal of the AMF from the registry is contingent upon satisfying these obligations.

The AMF Act explicitly bars the founder from seeking the termination of a public interest AMF.[51]

In addition to the termination grounds outlined in the Civil Code, the AMF can be terminated under the AMF Act if, for three consecutive fiscal years, its assets fail to meet the minimum capital requirement. This specific termination provision is justified by the impracticality of sustaining an AMF that has not reached the minimum capital threshold for an extended period. In such a scenario, the AMF is unable to fulfil its purpose and distribute benefits to the beneficiaries. Consequently, the AMF Act, adopting a legal construct, deems this circumstance equivalent to the impossibility of achieving the foundation's objectives, warranting the termination of the AMF.[52]

4. A hybrid legal solution: trusts managed by an AMF

The AMF has the authority to engage in the economic activity of managing assets placed in a trust, either for its own benefit or for the purposes outlined in its founding charter. Notably, the AMF Act explicitly exempts the AMF from the provisions of the Trustees Act.[53] Consequently, the AMF has the flexibility to provide trust services simultaneously to multiple parties without the requirement for licensing. Crucially, however, this trustee activity is restricted solely to the defined purpose of asset management as specified in the founding charter of the AMF.

In practical terms, this means that the settlor of a trust relationship can transfer assets to the AMF, as long as the objectives of the trust align with the purposes outlined in the AMF's founding charter.[54] This legal framework represents a hybrid solution, integrating aspects of the common law trust and the German foundation. The result is an AMF that not only manages assets but can also act as a trustee, offering a distinctive and versatile approach to wealth management. There is a dual effect, requiring separate accounting for assets managed under the trust and resulting in distinct corporate tax numbers for the trust assets. Externally, the AMF is the registered owner, but internal accounting must distinguish its assets from those held in trust.

While trusts managed by an AMF are not subject to the Trustees Act, the rules of the Civil Code on trusts, with some deviation provided by the AMF Act, apply to the AMF as trustee. Hungarian law recognises three forms of trust management:

---

51 AMF Act, Article 11 Section (1).
52 AMF Act, Article 11 Section (2).
53 AMF Act, Article 2 Section (2)c.
54 AMF Act, Article 2 Section (2).

- businesslike trust management;
- non-businesslike (*ad hoc*) trust management under the Trustees Act; and
- trust management under the AMF Act.

Despite relying on the Civil Code, significant differences exist between trust relationships governed solely by the Civil Code and those under the AMF Act. The AMF Act outlines five crucial deviations from trust relationships governed by the Civil Code:

- The AMF Act allows the establishment of a trust relationship through the founder's unilateral declaration in the foundation deed.[55] This differs from the Civil Code, where a trust created by a will requires the trustee's acceptance. It creates a unique situation where the founder contributes assets to the trust, forming a separate pool of 'trust assets'. The AMF Act permits various methods of trust creation, either directly by the founder or through a separate contract. The legislation also allows a third party to contribute assets to the foundation, expanding possible relationships beyond just the founder.
- The AMF Act establishes a statutory presumption that the AMF is the sole beneficiary of assets held in trust.[56] This contrasts sharply with the Civil Code, which deems invalid the appointment of the trustee as the sole beneficiary. The AMF Act specifies that benefits can only be paid directly to the AMF from the trust property as a separate asset. The legislation therefore requires careful drafting of the trust instrument regarding the functions and beneficiaries where a direct beneficiary cannot be designated.
- The Civil Code stipulates that a fiduciary relationship established for an indefinite period, or a fixed term exceeding fifty years, terminates after fifty years, with any contrary agreement deemed void. However, the AMF Act allows trusts managed by an AMF to last until the termination of the foundation itself.[57] Consequently, an AMF-managed trust can potentially extend for centuries. Although perpetual trusts may be theoretically viable, practical considerations informed by international experience suggest that many face erosion over time due to various factors, potentially leading to the dissolution of the foundation or trust.
- When the founder entrusts the property through a unilateral declaration in the deed of foundation, they may, within the specified bounds and conditions of the deed, override the Civil Code's implicit provisions

55 AMF Act, Article 2 Section (4).
56 AMF Act, Article 2 Section (3)a.
57 AMF Act, Article 2 Section (3)b.

prohibiting instructions to the trustee. The AMF Act enables the founder to issue instructions to the trustee, provided the trust instrument allows it.[58] This dual legal situation allows the founder to intervene directly in managing the trust assets, providing a safety valve for exceptional circumstances. However, daily intervention is seen as an extreme measure that could hinder professional asset management in the short term.

- A pivotal provision in the AMF Act is the exemption of trusts managed by an AMF from the Trustees Act.[59] This has significant consequences, such as the freedom to perform trust activities without notifying the National Bank of Hungary (NBH). The AMF can manage multiple assets without a businesslike trustee licence and is not subject to specific rules on trustee-related procedure apart from those in the Civil Code and the AMF Act. This exemption ensures confidentiality in the trust relationship, as the Trustees Act defines those public bodies in respect of which the trustee is not bound by the obligation of confidentiality laid down in the Civil Code. Since the AMF Act exempts trusts managed by an AMF from the scope of the Trustees Act, the AMF is bound by the full confidentiality obligations of the Civil Code. Accordingly, it may not disclose information about the settlor, the trust assets or the nature of the trust relationship to third parties, including public bodies.

The aim of the AMF Act was to create a unique trust instrument by blending the features of an AMF and a trust. The resulting hybrid trust improves upon the static structure of trusts and family foundations in other jurisdictions. Unlike traditional trusts, it enables not only passive but also active asset management. This distinctive hybrid structure, with its focus on achieving specific objectives within a single framework, stands out internationally and aims to be a leading wealth management solution.

58 AMF Act, Article 2 Section (4).
59 AMF Act, Article 2 Section (3)c.

Appendix I: Translation of the Czech Civil Code

Important notes

- There is no official or authorised translation of the current iteration of the Czech Civil Code.
- The translation below is of the part of the Code that relates to trusts.
- This translation draws on a 2013 translation of an earlier version of the code prepared by the Czech Ministry of Justice.[1] It is provided for guidance and information only. For authoritative wording please refer to the original Czech language version.

89/2012 Sb.
ACT
of 3 February 2012
the Civil Code
the Parliament has adopted the following Act of the Czech Republic:

Division 4
Trust

Subdivision 1
Definition of a trust and its creation

Section 1448

(1) A trust is created by setting aside part of the property owned by the founder in such a way that the owner entrusts the trustee with the assets for a specific purpose through a contract or disposition *mortis causa*, and the trustee undertakes to keep and administer those assets.

(2) The creation of a trust establishes separate and independent ownership of

1 The 2013 Ministry of Justice translation of the Czech Civil Code is available at: http://obcanskyzakonik.justice.cz/images/pdf/Civil-Code.pdf. The full text of the current iteration of the Civil Code is available in Czech at: www.zakonyprolidi.cz/cs/2012-89. An official English language version of the full text is not yet available.

the assets that have been set aside and the trustee is obliged to take charge of the assets and their administration.

(3) The rights arising from the right of ownership in the assets of the trust are exercised by the trustee in his or her own name and on behalf of the trust; however, the property in a trust is not owned by the trustee or the founder, or the person entitled to receive performance from the trust.

Section 1449

(1) A trust may have a publicly beneficial or private purpose.

(2) A trust established for a private purpose serves the benefit of a certain person or in his or her memory. Such a trust can be established for the purpose of investing to make a profit to be distributed among the founders, employees, partners or other persons.

(3) The primary purpose of a publicly beneficial trust may not be making a profit or operating an enterprise.

Section 1450

(1) A trust must have its own designation.

(2) The designation of a trust must express its purpose and contain the words '*svěřenský fond*' (trust).

Section 1451

(1) A trust is created when a trustee accepts the mandate to administer it; if there is more than one trustee, it is sufficient if at least one of them accepts the mandate.

(2) A trust comes into existence on the day it is entered in the Register of Trusts.

(3) However, if a trust has been established by a disposition *mortis causa*, it is created upon the death of the decedent. It is entered in the Register of Trusts after its inception.

Section 1452

(1) Every trust must have a statute. The statute of a trust is issued by its founder. Where a trust is established by a disposition *mortis causa*, Section 311 applies *mutatis mutandis*.

(2) The statute shall contain at least:

a) the designation of the trust;
b) identification of the assets that constitute the trust upon its creation;
c) definition of the purpose of the trust;
d) the conditions for the provision of performance from the trust;
e) information on the duration of the trust; in its absence, the trust is conclusively presumed to be established for an indefinite period;

f) if the trust is to be paid to a person as a beneficiary, the designation of that person or the manner in which the beneficiary is to be designated; and
g) the number of trustees and the manner in which they act.

(3) The statute requires the form of a public instrument.

Subdivision 2
Administration of a trust

Section 1453
(1) Any person with full legal capacity may be a trustee.
(2) A legal person may be a trustee, where provided by statute.

Section 1454
Under the conditions provided under Section 1453, the founder of a trust or a person who is to receive performance from the trust may also be a trustee. In this case, however, the trust must have an additional third-party trustee and the trustees must make juridical acts jointly.

Section 1455
(1) A trustee is appointed and removed by the founder. A founder may determine another method of appointment or removal of the trustee in the statute.
(2) On the application of a person with a legal interest therein, a trustee is appointed by a court if the person authorised to do so fails to appoint a trustee within a reasonable period, or if a trustee cannot be installed under Subsection (1).

Section 1456
A trustee is entitled to exercise full administration of the property in a trust. A trustee is registered in a public or other register as the owner of the property in a trust with the note '*svěřenský správce*' (trustee).

Subdivision 3
Beneficiary

Section 1457
(1) A founder has the right to appoint a beneficiary and determine the performance to be provided to him or her from the trust, unless the statute of the trust provides otherwise.
(2) If the founder fails to exercise his or her rights under Subsection (1), the trustee appoints the beneficiary and determines the performance to be provided to that beneficiary from the trust. In the case of a trust established

for private purposes, a trustee may exercise that right if the statute determines the group of persons from which the beneficiary may be appointed.

(3) The appointment or other designation of a beneficiary of trust established for a private purpose shall be effective on the date on which the beneficiary is entered in the Register of Trusts.

(4) A beneficiary may be granted the right to the fruits and revenues from the trust, or the right to property from the trust, or, where appropriate, a share of them.

Section 1458

(1) A person who is authorised to appoint a beneficiary or determine the performance to be provided to a beneficiary from the trust shall proceed in accordance with the statute and at his or her own discretion. He or she may change or cancel his or her decision under the conditions determined by the statute.

(2) No person is authorised to appoint a beneficiary or determine the performance to be provided from the trust to a beneficiary for his or her own profit.

Section 1459

A beneficiary's right to performance from a trust is created under the conditions determined in the statute.

Section 1460

(1) If a trust has been established for a private purpose, a beneficiary's right to performance shall arise no later than at the end of one hundred years from the establishment of the trust, even where the statute stipulates a later time. However, even after 100 years, a beneficiary may acquire the right to such performance if he or she is entitled under the statute to a share of the property no later than upon the extinction of the last right to the fruits or revenues, as well as if he or she was a contemporary of the founder or a child of the founder or of his or her contemporary, provided that, according to the statute, he or she is to succeed no later than upon the death or demise of the beneficiary who, given his or her order, precedes him or her, in order to be the following ultimate beneficiary to acquire the fruits or revenues; throughout his or her life, other persons may acquire fruits or revenues along with him or her.

(2) If a trust has been established for private purposes, a beneficiary's right to fruits or revenues is extinguished no later than after one hundred years from the creation of the trust; however, in the case of individuals, such a right may last until death.

Section 1461

(1) During the existence of a trust, a beneficiary has the right to request that in conformity with the statute, he or she be provided with the relevant performance.

(2) A beneficiary of a trust established for private purposes may waive his or her rights under Subsection (1) by means of a declaration made in the form of a public instrument.

Section 1462

In the case of a right to fruits or revenues and in the absence of any other beneficiary to whom such a right could pass, it passes to the beneficiaries who are entitled to the right to property from the trust.

Subdivision 4

Supervision over the administration of a trust

Section 1463

(1) Supervision over the administration of a trust is exercised by the founder and a person designated as the beneficiary, or by other persons if so determined by the statute.

(2) Where provided by law, the administration of a trust is supervised by another person or a group of persons, or a public body.

Section 1464

If a trust has been established for the benefit of a beneficiary who does not yet exist or cannot be determined on the date on which the trust is created, the founder shall appoint a person authorised to supervise the administration of the trust in the interests of that beneficiary. If this is not possible, or if the founder is inactive, a court shall appoint such a person on the application of the administrator or a person with an interest in it.

Section 1465

(1) The trustee shall, without undue delay, deliver to a person with a statutory right to supervise the administration of the trust a notification which shall state at least the designation, purpose and duration of the trust and the trustee's name and address. The notification is not necessary if the person authorised to supervise is already aware of these facts.

(2) At the request of a person with the right to supervise the administration of the trust, the trustee shall allow the documents of the trust to be checked and submit to that person the requested accounts, reports or other information.

Section 1466

(1) The founder, a beneficiary or any other person with a legal interest therein may apply to the court to order or prohibit the trustee from performing a certain act, or to remove the trustee or appoint a new trustee. These persons may also invoke the invalidity of a juridical act whereby a trustee damages the trust or a right of a beneficiary; however, if a third party has acquired a right in good faith, this must not lead to that third party's detriment.

(2) On the application of the person referred to in Subsection (1), a court shall authorise such a person to initiate or pursue proceedings in the interest of a trust instead of and in the name of a trustee if the trustee is inactive without sufficient cause.

Section 1467

If a trustee, founder, or beneficiary participates in acts intended to intentionally harm the rights of the founder's creditor or harm the trust, they are liable jointly and severally.

Subdivision 5

Changing a trust

Section 1468

A person who increases the property of a trust by a contract or disposition *mortis causa* is not its founder. Property so acquired is subject to administration under the statute and the law.

Section 1469

(1) On the application of a person with a legal interest therein, a court may decide that a trust be cancelled if it is impossible or difficult to achieve its purpose, especially as a result of circumstances which were unknown or unpredictable to the founder. Where a trust has been established for a publicly beneficial purpose, a court may decide to replace its original purpose with a similar one.

(2) If, in accordance with the original intention of the founder, the purpose of the trust can be achieved or better served by amending the statute of the trust, the court shall amend the statute.

Section 1470

Before making a decision under Section 1469, the court shall seek the opinion of the founder or the founder's legal successor, the trustee, the beneficiary and the person entitled to supervise the trust, unless they are applicants.

Subdivision 6
Termination of a trust

Section 1471
The administration of a trust shall end if the period for which a trust has been established expires, if it achieves the purpose for which it was established, or if the court so decides. If a trust has been established for private purposes, its administration shall also end if all the beneficiaries waive their right to receive performance from the trust.

Section 1472
Upon the extinction of the administration of a trust, the trustee shall surrender the property to the person entitled thereto. The beneficiary and, in the absence of a beneficiary, the founder of the trust are presumed to be entitled to the property; in the absence of both, the property passes into the ownership of the state.

Section 1473
(1) If the administration of a trust established for a publicly beneficial purpose is extinguished because it is impossible to fulfil that purpose, a court shall, on the application of the trustee, decide that the property will be transferred to another trust or into the ownership of a legal person aiming to achieve a purpose which is as close as possible to the original purpose of the trust. Before making the decision, the court shall obtain the opinion of the person entitled to supervise the administration of the trust.
(2) A decision under Subsection (1) may not be made if the statute of the trust provides for the manner in which property should be disposed of upon the extinction of the trust.

Section 1474
If, upon the extinction of administration, the trustee disposes of the property in accordance with the statue, or if the trustee surrenders the property under Section 1472 or transfers it under Section 1473, the trust ceases to exist. The trustee shall file a petition for the deletion of the trust from the register of trusts within 30 days of the termination of the trust.

Appendix II: Translation of 2019 Act on Asset Management Foundations

Act XIII of 2019 on Asset Management Foundations
(Unofficial translation of the text of the law in force on 14 February 2024)[1]

1. General provisions

Section 1

(1) This Act encompasses foundations established in accordance with its provisions or whose articles of incorporation were amended per its provisions, and which are registered by the court as asset management foundations.

(2) Unless otherwise specified in this law, the rules of Act V of 2013 on the Civil Code (hereinafter: Civil Code) applicable to foundations shall apply to asset management foundations.

2. Foundation conditions

Section 2

(1) An asset management foundation can be established to manage assets assigned by the founder, along with the derived income, for purposes stated in the founding deed and for the benefit of designated individuals.

(2) As an economic activity, the asset management foundation may manage assets assigned to its benefit or placed in trust for the purposes stated in paragraph (1).

(3) In the case of a fiduciary asset management legal relationship established for assets placed in trust asset management by the asset management foundation:

a) The asset management foundation shall be considered the exclusive beneficiary of the managed assets, with the obligation to manage them to achieve the goals in paragraph (1).

1 For references to the Civil Code, see the following website for an official translation by the Ministry of Justice: https://njt.hu/jogszabaly/en/2013-5-00-00.

b) Section 6:326(3) of the Civil Code does not apply; the fiduciary asset management legal relationship terminates with the termination of the asset management foundation.
c) This legal relationship does not fall under the Act XV of 2014 on trustees and the rules of their activities.

(4) The founder may include a unilateral legal declaration in the founding deed regarding the transfer of assets to trust management. In this case, the founding document – within the framework and under the conditions specified in the founding document – may alter from § 6:316 of the Civil Code

Section 3

(1) In order to establish an asset management foundation, assets equivalent to at least HUF 600 million must be assigned to the foundation (hereinafter: minimum capital).
(2) The founder of the asset management foundation is obliged to indicatemust specify the assets assigned to the foundation in the founding deed for each asset, providing details necessary for identification.
(3) Prior to applying for foundation registration, assets corresponding to the minimum capital must be made available to the foundation.
(4) If the exercise of the founder's rights belongs to the executive body of the foundation (hereinafter: the board of trustees) or the foundation's asset supervisor and the founder fails to transfer the assets exceeding the minimum capital, which has not yet been made available to the foundation within the set deadline, the foundation can demand fulfillment of this portion.
(5) If the founder reserves the rights and fails to fulfil the obligation according to paragraph (4) despite the board of trustees' written request, the board of trustees is entitled to exercise the founder's rights until compliance.
(6) The founder or successor, according to the articles of incorporation, may commit to making additional assets available to the asset management foundation – in addition to the asset assignment undertaken at the time of founding or joining and fulfilled in accordance with it – with the aim that with this asset allocation increase the assigned assets of the time establishment, or upon joining. Paragraphs (2) and (4) apply accordingly to this asset increase.

Section 4

(1) An asset management foundation can also be established for a purpose of public interest, including financing and supporting educational, higher education, research, health, charitable, social, family, child and youth protection, cultural, or sports activities, or the maintenance and operation of institutions providing such activities.
(2) An asset management foundation is considered of public interest if:

a) Founded for a purpose of public interest according to paragraph (1).
b) The scope of its beneficiaries is open in terms of individuals.
c) The founder requests classification as of public interest.

(3) Based on this law, a trust foundation registered with the court and indicating public interest status in accordance with paragraph (2) (hereinafter: public interest asset management foundation) is considered to have non-profit legal status if claimed. Non-profit legal status must also be indicated in the register upon the asset management foundation's request.

(4) Sections 3:379(4), 3:386, Sections 3:397(3) and (4), and Section 3:404(1) of the Civil Code apply only to the public interest asset management foundation.

3. Exercise of founder rights

Section 5

(1) The founder of an asset management foundation can appoint the foundation's board of trustees to exercise the founder's rights in the founding document. The founder of a non-public asset management foundation can also appoint a foundation supervisor according to § 7 instead of the board of trustees, or transfer these rights to the foundation. The founder may stipulate in the founding deed that the founding rights are transferred to the foundation in the event of his or her death, termination without legal successor, or the occurrence of a condition specified in the founding deed.

(2) The board of trustees or the foundation's supervisor exercises the rights of the founder in certain cases as specified in this law.

(3) If the board of trustees exercises the founding rights, absent a different provision in the founding deed, the board of trustees, along with the supervisory board, shall decide on the appointment of members and the chairman of the board of trustees and supervisory board, in case of vacancies, requiring a majority vote from the affected governing body members. Additional qualified majority provisions may be established in the articles of incorporation for decisions on this matter. If the foundation's rights are exercised by the foundation supervisor, unless otherwise provided in the founding deed, the foundation supervisor decides on the appointment of the foundation's board of trustees and supervisory board members, as well as the chairman, after seeking the opinion of the board of trustees and the supervisory board.

(4) The decision to recall members of the board of trustees and supervisory board, along with the chairman of the asset management foundation, can be made in the same manner as their appointment. The right to recall may be subject to conditions in the founding deed and may be limited.

4. Organisation of the asset management foundation

Section 6

(1) The public interest asset management foundation is managed by a board of trustees consisting of at least five natural persons.

(2) In the case of an asset management foundation, the appointment of a supervisory board and its operation, along with the appointment of a permanent auditor, is mandatory. The supervisory board consists of at least three natural persons, and the chairman is elected by the members from among themselves, unless the founding document specifies otherwise. The founding deed of a non-public asset management foundation may stipulate that the foundation does not have a supervisory board; in this case, the tasks and powers of the supervisory board are exercised by the foundation's asset supervisor.

(3) The founding document may establish qualification, educational, and other professional requirements for the chairman and members of the board of trustees and the supervisory board.

5. External control of asset management of the asset management foundation

Section 7

(1) If, in the case of an asset management foundation, the founder has appointed the board of trustees to exercise the founder's rights or has transferred these rights to the foundation, the founder must appoint a foundation asset supervisor in the founding deed. The foundation asset supervisor monitors the exercise of these rights and the asset management of the foundation independently of the foundation's control body, in line with the goals in the founding document. If the founder of a non-public asset management foundation has appointed the foundation asset supervisor instead of the board of trustees to exercise the founder's rights, the appointment of a supervisory board is mandatory.

(2) In the founding deed, the founder may also authorise the asset management foundation to appoint the foundation asset supervisor. In this case, the board of trustees and the supervisory board jointly decide on the appointment or commission of the foundation asset supervisor, with the approval of the registry court required for the appointment or commission. The person appointing the asset supervisor must submit the asset supervisor's acceptance statement, along with the requirements in paragraph (3), to the registry court.

(3) Only an auditing firm, auditor, law firm, lawyer, or another person with a clean criminal record and a specialised higher education qualification

specified in the founding deed may be appointed or entrusted as a foundation's asset supervisor. The founder, the member of the board of trustees and the supervisory board, the chairman, or other officials, employees, auditors, beneficiaries and their relatives of the foundation cannot be auditors of the assets of the foundation. The articles of incorporation may also define additional conflict of interest rules for holding this position.

(4) In the event of the death of the foundation's asset supervisor, his or her termination without a legal successor, his or her resignation from this position, or if he or she no longer has the necessary conditions to perform his or her duties, the provision according to paragraph (2) shall be applied to the appointment of the asset supervisor.

Section 8

(1) The task of the foundation's asset supervisor is to check whether the asset management of the asset management foundation complies with the goals set out in the founding deed, the founder's regulations on asset management and the investment regulations. The foundation's asset supervisor also checks the fulfillment of the statutory obligations of the board of trustees exercising the rights of the founders and the supervisory board.

(2) The foundation's asset supervisor has the right to express an opinion on matters falling within the scope of the founder's rights exercised by the board of trustees. The foundation's asset supervisor has the same rights as the supervisory board with regard to the right of access to and information on the foundation's documents.

(3) If the operation or procedure of the board of trustees exercising the founder's rights or the supervisory board does not comply with the provisions of the law or the founding deed, the foundation's asset supervisor shall call the relevant foundation's body to ensure proper operation. If the relevant body does not comply with the invitation, the foundation's asset supervisor can initiate a legality supervision procedure at the registry court.

(4) If the founding deed authorises it, the foundation's asset supervisor may, in the cases specified in the founding deed, ask the court to annul the decision made by the board of trustees or the supervisory board that violates the law, or conflicts with the founding deed or the investment regulations.

(5) If no decision is made on the subject of the board of trustees or supervisory board membership or the holding of a position within 90 days of its occurrence, the court of registry shall decide on this issue on the recommendation of the foundation's asset supervisor.

(6) The foundation's asset supervisor is entitled to remuneration. The remuneration of the foundation's asset supervisor must be paid to the foundation assets managed by the asset management foundation.

6. Articles of incorporation

Section 9

(1) The founding document of the asset management foundation must be included in a public document or a private document countersigned by a lawyer. Legal representation is mandatory in the court registration procedure.

(2) The basic goals and principles of the management and use of the foundation's assets must also be recorded in the founding deed. The founder may attach the investment regulations to the founding deed as part of it.

(3) The investment regulations must include the definition of the portfolio making up the foundation's assets, risk management, and the decision-making method applicable to investments.

(4) If the founder does not attach the investment regulations to the founding deed, then within six months from the date of registration, an investment regulation must be prepared based on the goals and principles according to subsection (2) and the content according to subsection (3), upon the proposal of the supervisory board and approval by the practitioner of founding rights. If the board of trustees exercises the founding rights, the board of trustees and the supervisory board jointly decide on the approval of the investment regulations, seeking the opinion of the foundation's asset supervisor.

(5) In the founding deed, the founder may provide differently from the provisions of § 3:387 of the Civil Code, in the case of an asset management foundation that is not considered to be of public interest.

(6) The board of trustees may only exercise the right to amend the articles of incorporation if the founder expressly authorised it in the articles of incorporation. However, the articles of incorporation may be amended even without this authorisation, if circumstances have changed or legal requirements make it necessary to achieve the goals. The founder can also stipulate in which matters the board of trustees may not amend the founding deed. If, due to changes in the law, an amendment in these matters becomes necessary, the approval of the foundation's asset supervisor is required for the amendment of the founding deed by the board of trustees.

(7) If the asset management foundation is of public interest, or if the founding rights are exercised by the board of trustees, the purpose of the foundation can only be changed under the conditions specified in the Civil Code.

(8) The amendment of the founding document does not affect the fulfillment of obligations already established and due for the benefit of the beneficiaries.

7. Limitation of asset management of the asset management foundation

Section 10

(1) In the founding deed, the founder may determine the amount of assets assigned to the foundation, below which the assets of the asset management foundation may not decrease, and it may not be less than the minimum capital. In the absence of a definition, the minimum capital must be considered as such.

(2) If the assets of the asset management foundation in the founding deed fall below the amount according to paragraph (1), the payment of the benefit due to the beneficiaries must be reduced proportionally, or it must be withheld until the foundation's assets reach the amount according to paragraph (1).

8. Termination of the asset management foundation

Section 11

(1) A non-public interest asset management foundation can be terminated at the request of the founder exercising his or her right of founding. In the case of a founder's request for termination, the registry court will determine the cause resulting in the foundation's termination in civil non-litigation proceedings. The termination of the foundation does not affect the fulfillment of obligations already established and due for the benefit of the beneficiaries.

(2) The asset management foundation is terminated even if its assets do not reach the minimum capital amount for three full years; this should be considered as the realisation of the purpose of the foundation has become impossible.

9. Final provisions

Section 12

This law enters into force on the 15th day after its promulgation.

(1) For references to the Civil Code, see the following website for an official translation by the Ministry of Justice: https://njt.hu/jogszabaly/en/2013-5-00-00.

About the authors

Michaela Dražková
Attorney at law, EMUN
michaela.drazkova@emun.cz

Michaela Dražková is an attorney at law specialising in capital market law and AML/CFT regulation. Michaela earned both her doctoral titles (JUDr, PhD) in law and legal science and theoretical legal sciences and her economic title (Ing) in economic policy and administration from Masaryk University in Brno.

Michaela is a member of the Czech Bar Association, the Ethics Committee of the Capital Market Association of the Czech Republic and a full STEP member. As the head lawyer at EMUN – a leading Czech multi-family office dedicated to efficient and comprehensive asset management of major clients and the first corporate trustee of trusts licensed by the Czech National Bank – she focuses on setting up succession and wealth transfer services in the area of structuring and administration of trusts and investment, especially private portfolio management and the establishment of qualified investor funds.

Daniela Gadasová
Partner, CEEtax
daniela.gadasova@ceetax.com

Daniela Gadasová is a partner at CEEtax in Prague, Czech Republic. She specialises in personal, estates and IP management for clients. Daniela has been involved in directorship and private affairs governance since 1995, managing the private and business affairs of celebrity athletes and entertainers. She directs various companies and foundations, and acts as a trustee.

Daniela formerly worked for the Czech Ministry of Culture, analysing the internal structures of cultural organisations – comprising governmental organisations as well as private foundations – all over Europe. She was also executive director of a private family philanthropic foundation, as well as the CEO of the first and only private copyright agency in the Czech Republic, representing and managing, amongst others, the business and private financial affairs of the country's president, Vaclav Havel.

Daniela is a member of STEP and of the Asociace pro podporu a rozvoj svěřenských fondů (APRSF).

Bohumil Havel
Associate professor, Charles University; Of counsel, PRK Partners
bohumil.havel@prkpartners.com

Bohumil Havel is an associate professor at the Faculty of Law of Charles University and a research fellow at the Institute of Law of the Czech Academy of Sciences. He specialises in legal entities, company law and insolvency law. He is also the author of the Czech Law on Business Corporations and the Czech Law on Preventive Restructuring.

He is an attorney at law who focuses on the administration of foreign property, including the establishment of companies, foundations and Czech trust-like institutions, their interconnections and the setting up of intergenerational transfers. He is also a member of STEP.

Bohumil has also collaborated and cooperates with the Czech Ministry of Justice in the drafting of a number of legal regulations (eg, the Civil Code) and is a member of the Legislative Council of the Government of the Czech Republic.

Štěpán Holub
Partner, Holubová advokáti s.r.o.
stepan.holub@holubova.cz

Štěpán Holub is a partner at Holubová advokáti s.r.o., specialising in real estate and multigenerational planning for international clients, with a focus on cross-border issues. He holds a law degree from Charles University, Prague, and has studied in Stockholm. His career includes roles as an attorney-partner since 2008 and a judge at the Supreme Administrative Court of the Czech Republic since 2019. A recognised speaker on trusts and estate planning, he has contributed to major conferences and publications, including the *STEP Handbook for Advisers*. Štěpán is a member of the Czech Bar Association, STEP and AIJA, and is proficient in Czech, English, German and Swedish. His achievements include extensive *pro bono* work and contributions to AIJA.

István Illés
Board member, APELSO Trust
istvan.illes@apelso.hu

István Illés is a founding partner of APELSO Trust Zrt, a licensed trust company belonging to the APELSO Wealth Management Group. István is a wealth and estate planning expert and a practising attorney at law in Budapest, Hungary. He also acquired an LLM degree in United States and global business law at Suffolk University (Boston, MA), as well as an MBA at Budapesti Műszaki és Gazdaságtudományi Egyetem.

In 2010, István prepared a study on trusts and analogous civil law instruments as part of a research programme financed by the Law Reform Committee of the New Hungarian Civil Code. Since then he, together with György Antall, has advised many high-profile Hungarian individuals on their family structures such as wills, trusts, family arrangements and holding companies.

More recently, the APELSO Group acquired a licensed alternative investment fund manager known as APELSO Capital Zrt. István played a major role in transforming the whole group into Hungary's first comprehensive wealth management firm.

Petr Jakubec
Attorney at law, ROSE Legal s.r.o., advokátní kancelář
p.jakubec@roseeurope.eu

Petr Jakubec serves as a senior counsel at ROSE Legal, specialising in various areas including commercial law, contracts, real estate, litigation, alternative dispute resolution, asset management and succession planning, including inheritance law. He earned his doctorate in law from Charles University in Prague in 2003 and has been practising as an attorney since 2006 after becoming a member of the Czech Bar Association.

As one of the co-founders and longstanding chairman of the non-profit Asociace pro podporu a rozvoj svěřenských fondů (the Czech Trust Association), Petr is actively involved in addressing the legal complexities of trust funds. He is a recognised trustee in the Czech Republic and a registered trust and estate practitioner (TEP). Since 2014, he has been providing advisory services for the establishment and management of trusts and private foundations, with a focus on asset planning and succession.

Additionally, he has been researching trusts since their introduction and he is also a frequent speaker and publisher. He is the author of multiple chapters in the book *Trusts, Opportunities and Risks* (*Svěřenské fondy, příležitosti a rizika*) published by C. H. Beck in 2018 in Prague.

Ivan Kovář
Partner, BDO Czech Republic
ivan.kovar@bdo.cz

Ivan Kovář works as a tax advisory partner at BDO. He graduated from the University of West Bohemia in Pilsen and has over 25 years of experience in tax consultancy. He has extensive knowledge in corporate income tax, tax structuring and tax optimisation. Since 2000 he has been a certified tax adviser with the Chamber of Tax Advisers of the Czech Republic. He specialises in assisting Czech-owned companies and entrepreneurs in distributing funds from their businesses.

Petr Laštovka
Partner, EMUN
petr.lastovka@emun.cz

Petr Laštovka is a founding partner and chairman of the board of EMUN – a leading Czech multi-family office dedicated to efficient and comprehensive asset management of major clients and the first corporate trustee of trust funds licensed by the Czech National Bank. Petr is a prominent personality in the world of finance and a graduate of the Faculty of Finance and Accounting at the University of Economics in Prague. He worked as an auditor and tax adviser at TPA consulting company and later took the position of division director focusing on investment banking. He is also a member of STEP. Within EMUN, Petr focuses mainly on asset structuring, creation of holdings and Czech and foreign trust and foundation structures.

In addition, Petr has extensive experience in trust fund administration. Since 2014, as an individual, he has been a trustee of dozens of trusts, which he administered until 2023, when their administration was transferred to EMUN investiční společnost, a.s. As a result, he can compare the rules and requirements for individual trustees with those for corporate trustees. Petr contributes significantly to the transfer of international practice in the creation and administration of trusts and foundations to the Czech Republic, the development of the field of asset management and the cultivation of this environment within the country.

Csaba Magyar
Managing partner, Crystal Worldwide Law Firm
csaba.magyar@crwwgroup.net

Csaba Magyar graduated in law and later attained Accredited Tax Consultant certification. He passed the bar examination before attaining accreditation as an insolvency practitioner and asset controller. He became a chartered international tax expert, later graduating as a trust and estate practitioner. He is a postgraduate specialist in investment funds, corporate finance and stock exchange, the co-founder of the Society of Hungarian Trust and Estate Practitioners and vice-chair of the Association of Hungarian Tax Experts.

Csaba holds seminars and courses on international taxation and trust law in a number of training institutes and universities for tax advisers and lawyers. During his tenure at Crystal Worldwide Law Firm, he has focused primarily on wealth planning, tax advice and business consulting. He combines expertise in asset protection strategies and international tax structuring, including handling complex transactions and managing cross-border investment issues.

Ákos Menyhei
Managing partner, Primus Wealth; Aliant-Menyhei-Molnár-B. Szabó Law Firm
amenyhei@aliantlaw.com
akos.menyhei@primus-wealth.com

Ákos Menyhei is managing partner of Primus Wealth and Aliant-Menyhei-Molnár-B. Szabó Law Firm in Budapest, as well as a member of STEP. Ákos has extensive international experience in providing tax and estate planning, as well as structuring and wealth management services to high-net-worth families and individuals around the globe. He is a co-author of *Limits to Tax Planning* (Linde Verlag, 2013), *The Trust* (HVG-ORAC 2014, 2018 and 2023), *Business Law in Hungary* (Patrocinium, 2016) and *The Foundation* (HVG-ORAC, 2021), and the editor of *Introduction of the Trust in Hungary and the International Practice* (HVG-ORAC, 2017). Since 2014 he has been a regular contributor to the Oxford Journals-published *Trusts & Trustees* periodical. His research interests include the implementation of the trust in civil law jurisdictions. He is an h.c. assistant professor in the trustee diploma programme of St Stephan University, Budapest.

David Neveselý
Partner, Havel & Partners
david.nevesely@havelpartners.cz

David Neveselý specialises in mergers, acquisitions, corporate law (with a special emphasis on local and cross-border mergers and transfers), financial law, collective investment law and tax-motivated transactions.

He shares responsibility for providing legal and tax advice to private clients, including the ultimate beneficial owners of successful local and foreign groups of companies belonging to the Czech Top 100 and top managers, and also artists and athletes.

David has advised clients on numerous acquisitions, divestitures and group restructurings on both the buy and the sell sides, mainly in the areas of private equity, construction, the automotive industry, banking and finance. Before joining Havel & Partners, he worked as a lawyer for nearly five years with a leading Czech consultancy providing comprehensive economic advisory services with a special focus on tax planning. David has been repeatedly listed in *Chambers* in the field of private wealth for the Czech Republic, often the only Czech individual cited. He is a member of the Czech Bar Association.

Paolo Panico
Chair, STEP Europe
paolo.panico@privatetrustees.net

Paolo Panico is a Scottish solicitor, a Registered European Lawyer in Cyprus, and a Romanian *avocat*. He was also an *avocat à la Cour* in Luxembourg until 2022 and a licensed legal adviser (*conseil juridique*) in Monaco until 2023. He is a director of trust companies in Luxembourg, Cyprus, and Wyoming, US.

Paolo is an academic supervisor for the Certificate in International Family Wealth at the International University of Monaco and teaches courses for the master's in wealth management at the University of Luxembourg and the LLM at the University of Liechtenstein. His publications include *International Trust Laws* (2nd edition, Oxford University Press, 2017) and, as an editor, *Trust Laws in Cyprus: An International Perspective* (Globe Law and Business, 2022).

He is the deputy chairman of STEP Worldwide and chairman of the STEP Europe Region, a member of the board of directors of the Associazione Il Trust in Italia, and an academician of The International Academy of Estate and Trust Law (TIAETL).

Vlastimil Pihera
Partner, Kocián Šolc Balaštík
vpihera@ksb.cz

Vlastimil Pihera is a partner at Kocián Šolc Balaštík, one of the oldest and most renowned law firms in the Czech Republic, and a research fellow at the Institute of State and Law of the Czech Academy of Sciences. He has more than 25 years of experience in the law of corporations, foundation and trust law and financial market regulation. He is the author of numerous publications in the Czech Republic and abroad.

Vlastimil is a member of the Appellation Commission of the Ministry of Industry and Trade of the Czech Republic, and the ethics committees of the Association for Capital Markets and the Czech Association of Financial Advisory and Intermediary Companies. He is recommended by the prestigious *Chambers & Partners Guide* and the *IFLR1000 Guide* as an expert on capital markets in the Czech Republic. Vlastimil has been a full STEP member since 2023.

Jiří Pokorný
Associate, Havel & Partners
jiri.pokorny@havelpartners.cz

Jiří Pokorný specialises primarily in advising private clients on the creation of family office structures and trusts and endowment funds, family and inheritance law, corporate law and public benefit entities.

In providing comprehensive legal and tax advice to private clients, who include the wealthiest entrepreneurs in the Czech and Slovak Republics, Jiří focuses mainly on the creation of family offices, that is, property management structures that ensure not only the continuity and transfer of personal (family) property, the elimination of fragmentation of family property (according to the so-called 'aristocratic standard'), provision for minors or incapacitated persons, protection from potential creditors and participation in companies and cooperatives, but also the fulfilment of charitable purposes and public benefit activities.

Jiří Pokorný joined Havel & Partners as a student in 2017, becoming a junior associate in

2019 and, after passing the Bar examination, an associate in 2022. Jiří is a member of the Czech Bar Association.

István Sándor
Attorney at law, Kelemen, Mészáros, Sándor and Partners
istvan.sandor@kelemen-lawfirm.hu

István Sándor is professor of law at the faculty of law of Eötvös Loránd University in Budapest. He is also a practising lawyer and graduated as a political scientist. In addition, he is a private professor at the faculty of law of Károli Gáspár University of the Reformed Church in Hungary. He earned a doctorate from the Hungarian Academy of Sciences (DSc) and is chair of STEP Hungary.

He has visited several universities as research fellow or visiting lecturer and has been a speaker at numerous international conferences. He specialises in commercial law, company law and trust law.

István has published several books and articles on company law, trust law, legal history and civil law.

In 2017, he was awarded the Knight's Cross of the Order of Merit of Hungary in the civilian division, and in 2021 he received the Academic Award of the Hungarian Academy of Sciences.

Sára Seszták
Partner, Seszták Ügyvédi Iroda
sara@sesztaklegal.hu

Sára Seszták is the head attorney at Seszták Ügyvédi Iroda. She graduated from the faculty of law and political sciences of Eötvös Loránd University in 2018. During her studies, she had the privilege of being a member of the István Bibó College for Advanced Studies. After graduation, she was awarded a scholarship to pursue further studies in the United States of America at the Benjamin N Cardozo School of Law, where she had the opportunity to study various areas of intellectual property law.

Sára has gained extensive experience in intellectual property law, corporate law, commercial law and trusts and foundations.

Helena Svárovská
Director, J&T Family Office
svarovska@jtfo.cz

Helena Svárovská has been with J&T since 2003, when she joined J&T BANKA in the private banking department, initially as part of the back office team, but gradually transitioning to focus on the highest segment of clients. Currently, she serves as the director of J&T Family Office, where she primarily deals with asset management and intergenerational wealth transfer. She is responsible for financial planning, personnel matters, and the company's strategic development.

Helena began her professional career during her studies when she joined the Czech Consolidation Agency. She graduated in economics from the University of Economics in Prague.

Gábor B Szabó
Attorney at law, Aliant-Menyhei-Molnár-B. Szabó Law Firm
gszabo@alianthungary.com

Gábor B Szabó is a partner at Aliant-Menyhei-Molnár-B. Szabó Law Firm in Budapest, Hungary. He is also a managing member of the board of trustees of Primus Asset Management Foundation, the first Hungarian multi-family office. He has specialised in several forms of private asset management, trusts, foundations, equity funds, corporations, hybrid structures and international tax planning for over 30 years.

He is one of the professional pioneers of the Hungarian trust and asset management foundation. He was actively involved in the lawmaking processes and among the first service providers in this sector. Gábor was a member of International Tax Planning Association (ITPA) for over 15 years and has been a member of STEP since 2012. He is a regular speaker at conferences, co-author of several industry books and the author of numerous professional articles.

James Turnbull
Independent family succession adviser, Uplift
james@uplift.cz

James Turnbull holds a law degree and is enrolled as a barrister and solicitor of the High Court of New Zealand. He is a board member of the Asociace pro podporu a rozvoj svěřenských fondů (the Czech Trust Association) and a full member of STEP. He founded Svěřenské fondy a trusty s.r.o., the Czech Republic's first professional trust administration company, in 2014, and now works as an independent succession planning adviser to high-net-worth families throughout the CEE region. He is also a member of the Advisory Board of PTT CZ s.r.o., a specialist provider of business trustee services.

James has played an important role in the development of the trust sector in the Czech Republic through seminars and publications. He is co-author of the leading Czech trust textbook, *Svěřenské fondy krok za krokem* (*Trust Funds Step by Step*), and is one of the lecturers on the APRSF Trustee Accreditation course.

About Globe Law and Business

Globe Law and Business was established in 2005. From the very beginning, we set out to create legal books that are sufficiently high level to be of real use to the experienced professional, yet still accessible and easy to navigate. Most of our authors are drawn from Magic Circle and other top commercial firms, both in the United Kingdom and internationally.

Our titles are carefully produced, with the utmost attention paid to editorial, design and production processes. We hope this results in high-quality publications that are easy to read and a pleasure to own.

In 2021, we were very pleased to announce the start of a new chapter for Globe Law and Business following the acquisition of law books under the imprint Ark Publishing. Our law firm management list is now significantly expanded with many well-known and loved Ark Publishing titles.

We are also pleased to announce the launch of our online content platform, Globe Law Online, which allows for easy access across firms. Details of all titles included can be found at www.globelawonline.com. Email glo@globelawandbusiness.com for further details and to arrange a free trial for you or your firm.

We'd very much like to hear from you with your thoughts and ideas for improving what we offer. Please do feel free to email me on sian@globelawandbusiness.com. Happy reading and thank you for your time.

Sian O'Neill
Managing director
Globe Law and Business
www.globelawandbusiness.com